{ Sister Thorn } *and Catholic Mysticism in Modern America*

{ Sister Thorn } and Catholic Mysticism in Modern America

PAULA M. KANE

The University of North Carolina Press
Chapel Hill

*This book was published with the support of the Richard D.
and Mary Jane Edwards Endowed Publication Fund of the
University of Pittsburgh.*

Designed by and set in Espinosa Nova by Rebecca Evans
Manufactured in the United States of America

The paper in this book meets the guidelines for permanence
and durability of the Committee on Production Guidelines
for Book Longevity of the Council on Library Resources.

The University of North Carolina Press has been a member
of the Green Press Initiative since 2003.

Library of Congress Cataloging-in-Publication Data
Kane, Paula M.
Sister Thorn and Catholic mysticism in modern America /
Paula M. Kane.
pages cm
Includes bibliographical references and index.
ISBN 978-1-4696-0760-3 (hardback)
1. Reilly, Margaret, 1884–1937. 2. Sisters of the Good
Shepherd—Biography. 3. Nuns—United States—Biography.
4. Stigmatization—United States—History—20th century.
5. Catholic Church—United States—History—20th century.
I. Title.
BX4705.R43155K36 2013
271'.97—dc23
[B]
2013015617

17 16 15 14 13   5 4 3 2 1

Contents

Illustrations

Preface

I first encountered Margaret Reilly, known in religious life as Sister Mary of the Crown of Thorns, by accident when I read a typescript by "Father Bertrand" about his visit with a stigmatized nun in 1922. Intrigued, I pursued the obvious question: was there really an American stigmatic in the twentieth century? The document was a florid and, as I later learned, mostly inaccurate account of a priest's visit to a woman who was exhibiting stigmata at a convent in Peekskill, New York. The tale piqued my interest in Catholic life in the early twentieth century, a time when bodily expressions of devotion had purportedly faded from "modern" Christianity in favor of rational formulations of faith. From sources on two continents, I have been able to piece together much of the life and cult of Margaret Reilly—Sister Thorn, "the seer of Peekskill." My detective work included some ethnography as well as history since I was able to reach several of Margaret's living relatives and to spend time in convents with members of her religious order, the Sisters of the Good Shepherd (RGS). The Internet has expanded research possibilities dramatically since the project began. Now, an inquiry about stigmata also brings up Catholic tour and pilgrimage sites, pornography for nun fetishists, rock bands and songs that include the word "stigmata," and medical offers like those at www.woundbegone.com promising "fast wound healing."

My determination to tell this story only increased when I saw a photograph of Sister Thorn seated in a wheelchair with her Mona Lisa smile. The result is a work of Catholic history, women's history, urban history, and national history. It would be disappointing to find this book shelved with Catholic hagiographies since it is as significant a part of *American* religious history as the lives of well-documented figures like Ann Hutchinson, Ann Lee, Dorothy Day, Mary Baker Eddy, Aimee Semple McPherson, Lucretia Mott, Harriet Beecher Stowe, and Ellen White.

A book is never a private undertaking, and I have acquired many intellectual and personal debts in the process of writing this one. First, I thank the New York Province of the Sisters of the Good Shepherd and their archivist when I began my investigation, Dominica Rinaldi, RGS. In the same community, Clare Nolan, a remarkable ethnographer and historian in her own right, had gathered much data about Sister Thorn in the 1970s through interviews and questionnaires; Clare took time during a challenging illness during my first visit to the convent archives to converse with me as we strolled through the streets of Queens. She had already asked the crucial questions of her sources and gathered much of the information for the RGS archives that made my project possible. At that time, nothing about Sister Thorn had been cataloged, so I was presented with piles of folders, bags of material, and brown cartons at the Jamaica-Queens house.

Sister Clare now works as the Good Shepherd nongovernmental organization (NGO) representative to the United Nations, fighting to end trafficking in children and women. She remains committed to a socially activist agenda inspired by her Christian faith. I remain deeply indebted to her, and I admire her example and that of members of the Good Shepherds who strive to improve the lives of women in the many circumstances in which they encounter them.

I should note that the Sister Thorn materials have since been closed by the RGS; consequently, my endnotes will not correlate to any subsequent cataloging system added to the RGS archives. Other convent archives essential to this project include the St. Paul, Minnesota, RGS Province, which provided valuable assistance through its archivist, Sister Margaret Hamilton; and the Good Shepherd Provincialate in Silver Spring, Maryland, where I thank Sister Mary Angela Donohoe. I benefited from using the archives of the Benedictine Sisters of Perpetual Adoration in St. Louis, Missouri, and thank its archivist, Sister Mary Jane Romero (with whom I shared the exciting diversion of a tornado watch). In San Francisco, I am grateful to Sister Michaela O'Connor at the Holy Family sisters archives.

Among male religious orders, I thank Rob Carbonneau, CP, at the Passionist historical archives in New Jersey. Brother Quentin Kathol, OSB, archivist at Clyde, Missouri, provided helpful materials and context. Brother David Klingeman, OSB, at the St. John's Abbey archives at St. John's University helped out on a related project as I delved into the study of "victim souls."

Numerous Catholic archdiocesan and diocesan archives were also instrumental to this project. The key archive for an investigation of Sister Thorn—the Archdiocese of New York, Yonkers—lists in its catalog many letters regarding Sister Thorn; some of these were made available to me in microfilm, and I was permitted to see a limited amount of the original correspondence. Among other ecclesiastical archives, I thank Jeffrey Burns at the archives of the Archdiocese of San Francisco; the archives of the Diocese of Cleveland; and the archives of the Diocese of Newark, which is housed in the archives and special collections of Seton Hall University.

My debts to other university collections include the rare books and special collections of the Catholic University of America in Washington, D.C.; the staff of the Marian Library at the University of Dayton; the archives of the University of Notre Dame, led by the ever-efficient Kevin Cawley; the Cushwa Center for the Study of American Catholicism at the University of Notre Dame for a travel grant enabling me to use their collections; and the Georgetown University archives, especially Tricia Pyne.

I thank Thomas McCoog, SJ, at the Jesuit Archives of Great Britain, London; the Wellcome Library in London; Tine van Osselaer, University of Leuven; and Gerrit Vanden Bosch of the Mechelen diocesan archives, Belgium.

I am indebted to assistance from the Library of Medicine, Philadelphia; the Johns Hopkins University Medical Library archives; Firestone Library, Princeton University, and its interlibrary loan staff; the New York Academy of Medicine Library; and the New York Public Library.

There were many individuals around the world who aided in my search for obscure Catholic or occult periodicals, biographical data on priests and nuns, and so on. I single out a few individuals who responded promptly and helpfully to my messages: Mark Hallinan, SJ, of St. Ignatius Church, New York City; Michael Hutchings, chronicler of Theresa Higginson; and Richard Copsey, O. Carm, Institutum Carmelitanum, Rome. Others sent information unprompted about visionaries or stigmatics, including Patrick Hayes; William Portier, then at Mount Saint Mary's College; and Thomas Tweed, then at the University of North Carolina at Chapel Hill.

Finally, I must thank the relatives of Margaret Reilly for their gracious assistance with family trees, memories, photographs, and stories. These include Susan Guditus Walter, Margaret's grand-niece, and Eleanor Harnett, Margaret's niece. Eleanor provided this wish for me in a letter dated March 7, 1997: "God bless you and guide you on this big task of writing a book about Aunt Margaret. Maybe if you pray to her she might be your guardian angel. You never know." Indeed.

Research for this book began in 1996–97 while I was on sabbatical leave from the University of Pittsburgh and had the good fortune to be the visiting scholar at the Center for the Study of American Religion (CSAR) at Princeton University. (The CSAR has since become the Center for the Study of Religion.) I extend my gratitude to the center's directors—Albert Raboteau, Leigh Schmidt, John Wilson, and Robert Wuthnow—for their help, conversation, and good will; and to the CSAR's gracious staff, notably Anita Kline for her able assistance. Thanks also to the graduate students who participated in the weekly religion seminar at Princeton; most of your books have preceded mine into print. Among that group, special thanks to Brad Verter for archival help in London during his own dissertation research and for loans from his personal library of the occult.

When I returned to Pitt, my academic life took a new turn when I was installed as Marous Chair of Catholic Studies, endowed by John and Lucine O'Brien Marous. John died in September 2012. I am indebted to the generosity of the Marous family and to my colleagues and friends who have supported this endeavor. Those who have made Pittsburgh a community worth living in include my department mates Fred Clothey and Alex Orbach (both now emeritus), Tony Edwards, and Linda Penkower. More recently, we have been joined by Adam Shear, Clark Chilson, and Rachel Kranson. At Pitt, I treasure the friendship of Susan Andrade, Jonathan Arac, Renate Blumenfeld-Kosinski, Jeanne Ferguson Carr, Nancy Glazener, Janelle Greenberg, Ann Harris, Dennis Looney, Marianne Novy, Marcus Rediker, and Bruce Venarde. At neighboring Carnegie-Mellon University, I am thankful for Wendy Goldman, Donna Harsch, Kate Lynch, and David Miller. All of you have made the Pittsburgh winters less bleak by sharing your own scholarship and fellowship. Hülya Kennedy Foster knows how dear her friendship is to me, and I am thankful for her attention to issues great and small and for my relationship with Ali and Hasan. Edward Horton appreciates, I hope, how much he has increased my love of Pittsburgh and the endearing qualities of its "yinzers."

Tremendous support throughout the process came from Elaine Maisner, my editor at the University of North Carolina Press. No one could ask for a better ally or friend. I thank also the helpful staff at UNC Press, especially Caitlin Bell-Butterfield, who handled illustrations and permissions, and copy editor Jay Mazzocchi.

I am fortunate to have had parents, both former professors, who supported this undertaking with their usual intellectual enthusiasm and prayers, and who kept my mailbox full of clippings about stigmata, mystics, and visionaries. My father, a philosopher and a student of Jacques Maritain, died before he could see "the book" in print. My Aunt Mary, a voracious historical researcher, and my siblings, Stephen, Brian, and Christine, have been an inspiration through their gifts of advice, meals, music, and visits. My sister-in-law Olivia and my four nieces remind me that much creative life exists outside academia. They are also the sources of my unparalleled collection of nun kitsch. For many of the years that it took to research and write this book, my confidant, critic, and fellow historian has been Robert Resch. With gratitude and love, this book is for him.

{ Sister Thorn } *and Catholic Mysticism in Modern America*

Introduction

A Notorious Case of Bleeding

In 1922 a priest stationed in Manhattan was becoming annoyed by the number of persons confiding to him in the confessional that they were having mystical manifestations. After encountering one particular individual, he advised the archbishop of New York to "cut the publicity or notoriety of a case which, in my mind, must be stamped 'non probatus.'"[1] The case referred to was that of a woman under his spiritual direction who was convinced that she had received the stigmata of Christ. This book examines her unlikely story—that of a Catholic woman from Manhattan who spent most of her adult life paralyzed and ill in a convent after claiming that she exhibited the bleeding wounds of the Passion and endured demonic torments because she accepted God's demand to suffer vicariously on behalf of others. After her death in 1937, this controversial sister was promoted by a group of American laypersons, bishops, priests, monks, nuns, and sisters as a candidate to become the first American saint. While many American readers will already know of Elizabeth Ann Bayley Seton, a convert from the Episcopal Church who received the title of the first American-born saint in 1975; or of Frances Cabrini, an Italian immigrant who was canonized in 1946; or of Bishop John Neumann, an immigrant from Bohemia who was canonized in 1977, few, if any, will have heard of Margaret Reilly, Sister Mary of the Crown of Thorns.

Sister Thorn's celebrity spanned less than two decades, from 1921 to 1937. Because efforts to launch canonical investigations into her sanctity stalled around the time of Vatican II in the 1960s, and because the generation of Catholics who knew her and prayed to her are themselves departed, her life has been nearly forgotten. I was fortunate to gain access to Reilly's uncataloged archives, held by her religious community, to meet several Good Shepherd archivists, and to contact some few remaining relatives and friends. My task in this book is twofold: first, I intend to represent the life and Catholic milieu of Margaret Reilly; and second, I will show that her experience, while unusual, reveals American Catholicism in a transitional moment between the urban immigrant church of the nineteenth century and the assimilated one of the mid-twentieth. It examines that underexplored period in a unique way. We are accustomed to studying American Catholics through the lenses of ethnicity, leadership, movements, and institutions, but we are still expanding our ways of understanding the faith as experienced by ordinary Catholics. The expansion of studies of "lived religion" in America has been a phenomenon of the last twenty years, and it has often been conducted through ethnographic work. My investigation of Sister Thorn could tap ethnography only slightly, given the death of most of her generational cohort, leaving me reliant upon traditional archival work that has its limits as well. Thus far, the study of religion-as-lived has taught us much about the complex devotional practices of Catholics, which has included veneration of the saints, the activity of prayer, and the use of holy objects. Through Sister Thorn, whose stigmata are the first such case reported in the United States and which unfolded in a convent setting, we are able to perceive how one subset of Catholic experience—mystical forms of religion—also contributed to the long-term structural forces at play in the assimilation of American Catholics.

In its mystical dimensions, of course, the tale of Margaret Reilly is not representative of all or even many American Catholic women of her generation. While thousands of Catholic women did enter religious life, more of them became wives and mothers. To categorize Reilly as a mystic further posits her on the margins of religious orthodoxy among her own community. The Catholic Church has often perceived mystics as threatening to church authority and dogma because of the highly individual nature of mysticism and its often prophetic criticisms of institutional religion. Yet Margaret's mystical claims are important because they transcended her own life to distill two important themes—pain and sacrifice—that resonated strongly with Catholics worldwide in the interwar period. After 1919, Europeans and Americans were contending with unbearable loss and grief. The sacrifice of an entire generation on the battlefields of Europe during the First World War unleashed extreme physical and emotional pain and in its wake created an obligation to honor the war dead for their heroism. In the final year of the war, an influenza pandemic led to the added deaths of millions around the world—including in the United States, where the misnamed "Spanish flu" probably originated.[2] On the religious front, the combination of the war and the deadly virus magnified the pressure among the survivors to justify existence, leading Catholics to learn to conceive of their faith as an active rather than passive force in which suffering played a central part. Sister Thorn managed to do likewise, leading others to interpret her vicarious suffering for them as a dynamic living out of faith that served a higher purpose rather than as a meaningless tragedy that must be endured.

After the First World War ended, the contrast between the social contexts of the devastated European nations and a booming New York City was widely observed. Unlike western Europe, the United States was enjoying expanding prosperity, which raised the social status of American Catholics as well. Although Catholics had never before enjoyed the security of being members of an established social cohort in the eyes of American Protestants, they now constituted a majority religion in the United States through sheer numbers. In addition, Catholics were improving their economic status by finding employment in the civil sector as public schoolteachers, policemen, and politicians. As they grew powerful enough in several metropolises to be able to dispense their own political patronage, Catholics became the targets of a renewed nativism in the 1920s. From the populist Right (the hostile activities of the Ku Klux Klan), from the elitist Right (the exclusion of Catholics from WASP strongholds in the economy, government, and higher education), and from causes that united both wings of the Right (attacks on the presidential campaign of Catholic Al Smith in 1928), Catholics were marginalized in discourses about the nation at the close of the decade.

The 1930s brought about an abrupt change in national priorities, however, as an economic depression affected all Western nations and leveled all socioeconomic sectors. The Catholic working class was hard hit. Widespread hardship and unrest in Europe led the pope to deliver "social encyclicals," building upon the precedent set in 1891 by *Rerum Novarum*, which addressed the economic realities of industrial capitalism and lent support (albeit limited) to working people and labor unions. Papal sentiments, for a time, dovetailed with American federal and state programs established during the Great Depression to create employment, health insurance, and social security. American Catholics took the pope's social encyclicals to heart, but the Depression produced radically different social solutions that exposed the divisions in the Catholic population regarding its relationship to success in a capitalist society. Extreme Catholic figures who emerged during the thirties included a demagogue, Charles Coughlin, a priest whose initial support for big government and labor transformed into vicious criticism; and Dorothy Day, a socialist convert who founded the Catholic Worker Movement to challenge capitalism and private property by advocating voluntary poverty embraced by small communities that lived by the charitable example of Jesus. The majority of Catholics, however, were not inclined to turn their backs on labor, private property, or capitalism as they lent their support to President Franklin Roosevelt's New Deal. While the dire financial adversity of the 1930s and the resulting social crises seemed to demand communal solutions framed in terms of social justice, the immensity of America's problems also made a stigmatized nun an unlikely prospect to represent the United States in sainthood at that moment, which may explain in part why Margaret Reilly's cause did not advance immediately when she died in 1937.

Thirty years later, the reforming spirit of Vatican II (and of Jesuit John Courtney Murray's "Declaration on Religious Freedom") brought different emphases to Catholic practice and political theory by replacing the dominant discourse of pain and suffering with a commitment to social justice and to outreach outside the formerly exclusivist Catholic Church, which seemed finally to recognize that American pluralism was not its mortal enemy. From the Vatican's perspective, however, the democratic nature and constitutionalism of the United States still represented a barrier to imagining an American-born saint who could be fully Catholic from an Old World perspective. As late as 1908, the Vatican had categorized the United States as "mission territory" and seemingly regarded American Catholics as at risk by virtue of the democratic nation that they inhabited. Already on two occasions, in 1899 and 1907, the papacy had demonstrated its disapproval of American polity by condemning the heresies of Americanism and Modernism. This happened in part because the pope feared for the survival of the Catholic Church in nations where it lacked state support, and in part because the church feared that immigrants would lose their faith once they were exposed to America's allegedly perilous culture of hedonism, pluralism, and secularism. Although the Americanist controversy mostly addressed theological rather than social issues and has been called a "phantom heresy" that resided in the pope's imagination, it did have the effect of lining up conservative and progressive American bishops along the fault line of the merits of assimilation. The eastern bishops of the densely populated cities composed the conservative, antiassimilationist camp, while the midwestern hierarchy generally urged the rapid and comfortable merging of Catholics into American society. True to form, the archbishop of New York involved in Margaret Reilly's case opposed the modernizing currents of the day by mounting attacks on a cornucopia of issues, including birth control, theater and cinema, new dances, and women's clothing and makeup. Eight years after the rejection of Americanism, the Modernism dispute, again dealing with mostly theological matters, led to papal condemnations that reprised much of the contents of the "Syllabus of Errors" of 1864 and produced an anti-Modernist oath that clergy were obliged to take, which remained in effect until 1967.

During these two conflicts with the Vatican, which mostly involved the Catholic hierarchy, ordinary Catholics were not overly invested in theological matters. They formed attachments to the church through devotional

practices and strove to prove their loyalty to the American nation by supporting its democratic institutions. They endeavored to be good Catholics
and patriotic citizens, but they were willing to make their own compromises
with faith. The church had won their allegiance by serving the practical
needs of millions of Europeans who immigrated to the United States between the 1840s and 1924 by building networks of hospitals, orphanages,
parishes, and schools. Yet at the same time, the church-sponsored organizations had the effect of assimilating and separating its members from
mainstream America. In Margaret Reilly's lifetime, the hierarchy presided
over an expanding physical and institutional infrastructure that framed a
Catholic subculture. Myriad lay institutions—from professional guilds and
athletic teams to insurance agencies and philanthropies—were formed as
parallels to those existing in "Protestant" or "secular" society. The process
of establishing a bounded Catholic existence began (in theory at least) in
1884, when the American bishops mandated a national parochial school system, to be completed within two years, that would assert the church's reach
over young children.[3] Three years later, the bishops founded the Catholic
University of America in Washington, D.C., and encouraged the growth of
Catholic colleges and universities to preserve Catholic students from exposure to damaging secular theories. These anxieties of contagion even crept
into Margaret Reilly's visionary messages from Jesus.

Not all threats to Catholic unity came from external sources. Ethnic differences continued to play a role in dividing the Catholic community from
within. Until Vatican II, the American hierarchy remained in the hands of
Irish American clergy—to the sharp frustration of other ethnicities from
southern and eastern Europe. The very attempt to make Margaret a saint de-
lighted Irish Americans, but proposing her as an *American* saint also implied
a nationalist outlook, which, if successful, would demonstrate to the Sacred
Congregation of Rites in Rome the maturing of the American church as well
as its transcendence over ethnic factionalism.[4]

Margaret's mysticism was not particularly typical of her Irish ethnicity,
but during her lifetime, mystical forms of faith became useful to the Catholic Church as a way to overcome internal divisions in order to focus efforts
on its battle against modernizers and positivists.[5] Enemies of the church
might regard mysticism as a vestige of primitive thought and cultures, but
since the nineteenth century, when the Vatican had begun to perceive the
power of Marian apparitions and miraculous healing cults as a way to retain the loyalty of the laity, it began to endorse them, creating a so-called
affective Ultramontanism. Margaret's local recognition as a mystic and her
progress toward sainthood were not spontaneously accepted and, in fact,

were hampered by the fact that her dramatic self-proclaimed manifestations (stigmata; inedia, the ability to live without food; bilocation; revelations; and visions) had few precedents in the United States as yet, making her reception enthusiastic but limited. To American Catholics who feared the loss of religious identity through assimilation in the United States, the stigmatized body of Sister Thorn was a reassuring proof of supernatural presence; but as a mark of Catholic difference, it could prove frustrating to the accommodationist desires of other Catholics. If the laity were a key contributor to Catholic vitality in the United States in the interwar years, how did a stigmatic help ordinary Catholics understand themselves as fully modern Americans?

For some, devotion to a stigmatized nun detached from public life hardly seemed the ideal way to fuse the American ideals of freedom of religion with immigrant hopes for progress and social mobility. The ongoing tension among Catholics between modern and antimodern ideals, between assimilation and separatism, was fully apparent in clerical and popular responses to Sister Thorn, who, if she were canonized, might reconcile these oppositions through her identity as a sacrificial victim. At the very least, the kind of Christian mysticism that she represented thrived on metaphors of engulfment, immolation, and annihilation, which expressed the cultural fears facing Catholics from the 1920s to the 1940s—an era when assimilation, with its uncertain outcomes, both attracted and repulsed them.

What of the specific qualities of stigmatization that were evoked by the existence of Sister Thorn? One recent account of unusual religious phenomena suggests that "perhaps no miraculous power is more equated with sanctity in the popular mind than stigmata, the spontaneously duplicated wounds of Christ's crucifixion upon the body of a Christian."[6] Sister Thorn's supporters believed without doubt that her stigmatization came from God, and yet Catholics often harbor mistaken notions about stigmata that exaggerate their value in the tradition. As one of the so-called secondary phenomena of mysticism, stigmata have never been considered by the Catholic Church as proof of sanctity or of the "heroic virtue" demanded of its saints. That means that no stigmatic is deemed holy by virtue of displaying the marks, nor are Catholics obliged to believe in them. But Christians nevertheless have revered them and continue to do so.

Stemming from medieval origins, the tradition of persons being supernaturally marked with the wounds of the Crucifixion of Christ continues to the present day. Roman Catholics regard the tradition of stigmata as having originated with Francis of Assisi in 1224 C.E., although earlier instances had been reported in England. Francis, stigmatized during a religious vision while meditating upon his crucifix, became the model of the holy person chosen for this special intimacy with the suffering savior because the stigmata were interpreted as proof that he was actually beholding Christ. The stigmata of Francis have been variously interpreted as a spiritual gift resulting from the intensity of his prayer; as a sign to other Christians about the need to focus upon the savior's Passion; and as a political move by the Franciscans to gain a competitive edge on their two major rivals—the Cistercians and the Dominicans. Despite the centrality of Francis to the origins of stigmatization, the phenomenon, since the late Middle Ages, primarily has been a feature of female mysticism. This fact makes the recent reports of stigmata for Padre Pio, Father James Bruse of Virginia, and Father Gerard Critch of Newfoundland quite anomalous.[7] Historian Caroline Bynum, the scholar most closely associated with discussion of the embodied nature of female spirituality in the Middle Ages, has claimed that the church accepted and even valued women's visionary experience, including its erotic discourse, as a way to fight the dualist heresy and denial of the body being promoted by the Cathar movement. Because women bled, produced new life, and nurtured children, it was understood that their bodies could profoundly imitate the Passion of Christ, even more so than the bodies of men. It remains to be seen how these claims survived in the twentieth century or what altered form they may have taken. Sister Thorn may be the pallid trace of a once-robust miraculism.

Since the thirteenth century, stigmata have often been accompanied by other spiritual gifts, including the ability to live without food (inedia or "holy anorexia") or without sleep, as well as bilocation, clairvoyance, exudations, hierognosis (discernment of the authenticity of holy relics), levitation, prophecy, and telekinesis.[8] While manifesting these charisms, stigmatics often entered trance states of deep concentration that left them temporarily oblivious to their surroundings. In the nineteenth and twentieth centuries, ecstatics often filled these moments with dramatic reenactments of scenes from Christ's Passion.

Although Francis initiated the stigmatic saint, Margaret Reilly was more likely to be compared by her peers to Louise Lateau of Belgium, who served as the prototype for the modern female visionary-stigmatic. In the 1870s, Lateau received extensive coverage in the secular and religious press for her consistent and long-enduring bleeding episodes, which confounded physicians' efforts to explain them. Among the many reports of Louise's ecstasies, these observations by Dr. Lefebvre give a flavor of their theatricality:

She for the most part remains seated, her body slightly bent forward towards the edge of her chair. She is as motionless as a statue. Her bleeding hands, hidden from sight in their covering, rest on her lap, while her eyes, full open, are raised upwards. Her whole attitude is that of one absorbed in contemplation of some distant object. Her posture and her expression, however, vary much, and sometimes the eyes soften, and the lips are parted with a beatific smile. Then again a look of pain harrows the countenance, and the tears run down her cheeks; or at times there is seen a terror-stricken gaze, accompanied by starts and stifled cries. She does not always sit: sometimes she rises and comes forward, standing on tiptoe, in an eager, expectant attitude, as if about to take flight. The hands are uplifted, clasped, or spread wide open in the position of the Orantes in the catacombs. The lips move, and the countenance has on it a halo of glorious beauty, as that of an angelic being. Add to this terrible spectacle of the brow crowned with its bleeding diadem, the crimson drops trickling down over the cheeks.[9]

The finale of Louise's trances entirely lacked the aesthetic appeal of the ethereal Victorian woman and, in fact, seemed to oddly prefigure the exaggerated gestures of silent cinema. During scenes that Lefebvre described as "appalling," Louise stood with her arms limp at her sides and her head on her chest—eyes closed, nose pinched, face deadly pale, hands icy, pulse imperceptible, with a "'death-rattle' heard in the throat."[10] Nonetheless, the media fascination with Louise Lateau's grotesque appeal, and the inability of scientists to prove her a fraud, clearly influenced the next-generation observers of Sister Thorn, who constantly referenced the Lateau case.

Sister Thorn's stigmata marked a turning point in American Catholic life in another way as well. She expanded the sparse roster of supernatural events reported among Catholics in the United States since its founding in 1776.[11] There are more examples of colonial anti-Catholic feeling and fear of popish superstition from Protestants than actual instances of pious Catholic excesses. Fear of the mysteriousness of Catholic rites is evident in John Adams's letter to his wife about an alarming altarpiece of the Crucifixion that he witnessed in 1774: "But how shall I describe the Picture of our Saviour in a Frame of Marble over the Altar at full Length upon the Cross in the Agonies and Blood dripping and streaming from his wounds."[12] His concern, however, seemed more a reflection of class taste, an aesthetic preference that spilled over into Protestant and Catholic opinion about miracles, than a comment on the lived religion of Catholicism in the colonies. As R. Bruce

Mullin has pointed out, among Protestants, miracles were the province of an elite, whereas among Catholics, miracles exercised a populist function.[13]

For the first decades of the young American republic, the few reported Catholic miracles involved diabolic expulsions and healing cures and, on occasion, even involved Protestants. In the 1790s, Father Demetrius Gallitzin performed an exorcism for a Lutheran family in Kentucky, earning the odd nickname of the "Wizard Clip" for the demons' habit of shredding any pieces of cloth in the household. In 1824 Anne Mattingly was cured of a tumor in Washington, D.C., by Austrian prince (and priest) Alexander Hohenlohe (in absentia), who was attributed with curing seventeen other persons in America, mostly nuns.[14] Other than these cases, one finds only occasional mentions of miraculous cures of sickness or injury from the application of holy water imported from the shrines of La Salette and Lourdes. In addition, travelogues by Americans on pilgrimage to European shrines appeared from time to time in Catholic journals. No doubt a systematic search of archives would turn up other instances; yet the total number of miracles reported in the United States seems slight in comparison to the enchanted landscape of Europe. The litany of supernatural activity in Catholic America remained quite brief, even into the twentieth century. To cite the record of just one publication: *Catholic World*, founded in 1865, published only three articles on stigmatics in its first forty years of existence. Two of these were about Louise Lateau of Belgium, and one concerned Anne Catherine Emmerich of Westphalia.

Despite the fears of eighteenth-century British Protestants of the tyranny of Rome, there is little evidence of a colonial Catholic population in thrall to their beads, Pater Nosters, and Ave Marias that had repelled the fevered imagination of John Adams. The following century readily took up the devotional forms of faith, but as a private "family matter" rather than a national one.[15] Regarding stigmatization in particular, the only incident prior to Margaret Reilly that I have located in the United States is that of Sally Collins in San Francisco. Sally, of uncertain origins, was the housemate of Lizzie Armour, the adopted daughter of Richard Tobin, a prominent Irish banker. Lizzie had founded a religious institute to help the local poor in 1872, in which Sally had only quasi-official status, to her frustration. In 1873 Sally received all five wounds of the Crucifixion during a carriage ride along the scenic coastline to Cliff House. The local pastor, Father J. J. Prendergast of St. Mary's Church, who was called as witness and consultant, himself surmised that this was the first case of stigmata in the nation. Sally's claim, however, did not stand. Although her marks appeared on Good Friday and were preceded by Christlike pains and agonies (or merely "intense pain in the temples," according to the *San Francisco Chronicle*), her own father dismissed the episode as humbug, noting: "My daughter is completely under the influence of Father Prendergast, and I suppose if anything has taken place it is the working of a very vivid imagination." The local press soon dismissed the story, comparing Sally Collins to a trickster nun in Lisbon during the reign of Philip II whose wounds were endorsed by the Inquisition but were later found to be made with red lead.[16] In the end, Sally was judged less harshly in the press than her housemate, Miss Armour, who was described as a "lump of clay" as "ugly looking . . . as ever dame Nature turned out into human form." No stigmatic reports turned up until fifty-five years later, when Sister Amalia of the Scourged Jesus was hailed in 1928 in Brazil as "first case of stigmatization in the Western Hemisphere," thereby beating out Sister Thorn as a rival claimant, at least in the newspapers.

In the decades immediately following Margaret Reilly's life, stigmata seemed to undergo a democratizing moment: a few scattered examples of Anglican and Lutheran stigmatics appeared beginning in the 1940s; and in the 1970s, the stigmatization of an African American Baptist girl in Oakland, California, suggested that the phenomenon of stigmata is not unique to Roman Catholics and that the mere act of intense concentration on the Crucifixion—as this girl had done after being exposed to a graphic published account of Jesus's death—can produce bleeding wounds. (Scientific investigations have failed to give definitive explanations as to why this does not happen to everyone, however.) Nevertheless, the fact remains that while there are a handful of instances of male and of non-Catholic stigmatizations, the vast majority of stigmatics have been Catholic women living in the modern era: of the total of 340 stigmatizations reported, two-thirds have occurred since 1500.

By bridging the Catholic past and present and the Old and New Worlds, Margaret Reilly offers a rare case study for American Catholicism in the twentieth century, even though she was a failed saint and possibly a false stigmatic. The fact that others endorsed her claims was a testament to their own "will to believe" in her supernatural communications. For modern scholars, Margaret confirms the claim that "the mystic's own body becomes the site of contested discourses about the body—and about culture."[17] For my purposes, an interdisciplinary approach has proved to be the most useful way to examine her life and the formation of her cult. The past forty years of critical theory have greatly enriched the study of religion. Anthropology, cultural studies, history, psychoanalysis, and sociology all offer valuable approaches and methods for grappling with the difficult religious issues of individual versus community experience, embodiment, feminine sexuality, spirituality, and belief. Together they supply tools to study the subjective experience of the stigmatic and the social effects of mystical phenomena that help us explore the connections between the individual and the social. Catholic Studies, specifically, can benefit from an approach that can account for both the subjective and objective features of religious experience.[18] While scholars of Catholicism continue to search for ways to unite phenomenological and "scientific" approaches with insider and outsider perspectives on religion, critical theorists have been addressing these problems convincingly for decades. My hope in this book is to encourage historians of religion to consider the utility of these theoretical insights for our discipline and to enter the conversation more fully with these allied disciplines.

To do so, my method is necessarily that of the *bricoleur* in studying religious phenomena through anthropological, psychoanalytical, and historical-sociological approaches to explore the gaps in Margaret Reilly's life that available sources do not cover. This hybrid approach to Reilly has also led me to delve into scientific and medical fields, including dermatology, hematology, and oncology, all of which contribute to an understanding of how Reilly was regarded and diagnosed by health professionals and how similar types of spontaneous bleeding are diagnosed today. For those who are skeptical about the use of psychological categories to interpret religion and dead persons, it is useful to remember that psychotherapy, along with other research methods, gives explanations for the omnipresent suffering that dominated the experience of stigmatics and for the self-punishing behaviors of this generation of Catholics.[19] In contrast to the claims of its critics, the psychoanalytic approach is not attempting to "shrink" the dead from a position of haughty omniscience, nor did it emerge in isolation from the other social sciences or from religion. Ex-Catholic Jacques Lacan, for instance, a powerful if unorthodox voice in interpreting the creation of subjectivity, was heavily influenced by structural anthropology and linguistics, as well as by his religious roots and his brother, a Benedictine monk.

I am indebted also to recent historians of Catholic Studies who explore the relationship of Catholics to modernity in the early decades of the twentieth century, as well as to those who challenge this very model. Several historians have helped shape the interpretation in this book. From *Jazz Age Catholicism*, a study of postwar Paris, I have borrowed Stephen Schloesser's characterization of the Catholic Church's self-declared relationship to modernity as "off-modern."[20] By this, he means that Catholicism was but one of numerous "postwar avant-gardisms" linked by their hostility to liberal rationalism. In Schloesser's interpretation, the Catholic Church hoped to synthesize its antirealism with the prevailing realism of the nineteenth century to create a new/old "mystic realism." Catholics tried to advance the argument that their tradition was actually modern, and that what so-called moderns purported to be new was really a reappropriation of Catholic precedents. Although Schloesser's work highlights French Catholicism at this cultural juncture, much of the intellectual climate that he surveys is relevant to the United States, given the influence of French spirituality and religious orders on American Catholics—including the Good Shepherd congregation of Sister Thorn—and the fact that her mystical experiences occurred precisely during the flourishing of the interwar avant-garde in the arts and literature.

Catholic responses to modernity in America were shaped by the transformation of immigrants into Americanized citizens. Following Robert Orsi, who has plumbed the meanings of the devotional practices of immigrant and postimmigrant Catholics in numerous works, I investigate the same "in-between generations" of Catholics in the 1920s and 1930s as persons "both in and out of the modern world" because they continue to believe in the presence of the supernatural. He describes Catholics' affirmation of sacred "presence" as antagonistic to the modern world in some degree because it includes "the incarnated supernatural and experiences of real presences." In my study, Margaret Reilly represented this countervision. Her stigmata, which confounded natural explanation, offered proof that God's truth was still revealing itself to humankind. Her church insisted that her wounds affirmed an eternal truth, a revisionist perspective to those who imagined modernity implicitly as "not Catholic."[21]

Our understanding of Catholic practices can extend to the very basic activities of daily life, notably work and its material consequences. For the kinds of Catholics who made up Sister Thorn's mid-Atlantic audience as well as her religious congregation, *The Catholic Counterculture* and *On the Irish Waterfront* by James T. Fisher suggest that the struggle about modernity was less agonized among the laity. Ordinary Catholics made their own moral compromises, he found, especially in politics and on the docks, when they needed to justify certain behaviors without feeling the judgmental gaze of the Vatican peering over their shoulders. As Orsi investigates the cross-generational uses of devotionalism, Fisher addresses Catholics' relationship to capitalism among this assimilating generation of Americans, which he marks as an unresolved point of tension. What remained constant instead was the paradox between Catholics' embrace of suffering and their desire for success.[22] These values intersected in the lives of stigmatics, for whom suffering was a form of success. This book tries to uncover the intersection of the internal and external worlds of Catholics.

Margaret Reilly's experience as a woman is a reminder that in addition to the modernization question, lived religion, and socioeconomic factors, gender constitutes a dimension of Catholic Studies that deserves fuller attention. Kathleen Cummings helpfully synthesizes existing historical work on Progressive-era women in lay and religious life in *New Women of the Old Faith*. Like Schloesser and Orsi, she explores how Catholics used the past to "translate what was happening to them in the increasingly complicated present."[23] In detailing Catholic women's opinions on suffrage, higher education, and work, she offers rich evidence of the ways these women used figures from the near and distant Catholic past in an effort to build an American Catholicism by remaining faithful to Catholic institutions when responding to modern problems. The supporters of Sister Thorn, I argue, were engaged in a similar effort.

Using relevant insights from a variety of disciplines and building upon recent historical scholarship, my goal is to arrive at a portrait of Margaret Reilly that shows how she was installed (or interpellated) into an already-existent system of social relations, and to discern how she resulted from a specific cultural moment in Catholic spirituality and convent life of the 1920s and 1930s that was a product of cultural exchange between Europe and America.[24] My book is intended as a provocation for Catholic historians, but also as an inspiration to a new generation of scholars, who may find in it suggestions for new trajectories of research that do not abandon the powerful tools provided by critical theory developed in the 1970s and 1980s.

Sources

When Margaret Reilly entered a convent community in 1921 and reported the wounds of the Crucifixion on her body, Catholics already possessed a wealth of historical and legendary information to draw upon to comprehend her mystical experience. But they also wondered in practical terms (as I have), what did Margaret think about them? Who saw the marks, and how? How long did they last? Unfortunately, Margaret left no firsthand account— no diary, no autobiography, no spiritual reflections. Instead of focusing on "what really happened," this book examines the reception and impact of Sister Thorn's claims upon the Catholic community. Of the evidence available, the closest eyewitness to Margaret's stigmata was her superior, Sister Mary of St. Raymond Nonnatus (Bridget Cahill, 1870–1939).

The lack of documentation for Margaret's self-understanding of the peculiar events affecting her, and of artifacts that might give evidence of her stigmatization, poses a challenge for attempts to recreate her life from her perspective. Unlike recent interpretations of Saint Gemma Galgani that were able to draw upon the saint's intimate spiritual diary and letters, or profiles of Early Modern mystics such as Blessed Marie of the Incarnation (Marie Guyard), who left copious correspondence about her life as an Ursuline in New France, we are able to "know" Sister Thorn only through the impressions of others, through family memories, through second- and thirdhand acquaintances, and from a handful of photographs.

Of the items written in Margaret Reilly's own hand, most are greeting cards to family and friends written for the major Christian holidays. She occasionally scratched several lines in pen to friends and relatives or appended a brief note to a letter written by her superior. These handwritten bits contain little personal information except as pertaining to events in convent life. In part, Margaret's reticence represented her obedience to the archbishop, who, once the stigmata were reported to him, forbade contact with visitors from outside the convent without his permission. She was otherwise constrained from writing by her limited formal education and by the norms of convent life, which discouraged egotism and time wasting. The absence of a diary or a narrative in Margaret's own voice, despite causing frustrations for the researcher, reflected conformity to convent discipline, in which the lack of personal records for sisters and nuns was evidence of their avoidance of the sin of "singularity." Historians have noted that, "similar to the private woman behind the public man, individual nuns were subsumed into the community. Special talents were to be concealed to avoid pride or any temptation to receive individual accolades for activities."[25] Diary keeping, therefore, was permitted only upon request of superiors, and there is no record that Mother Raymond asked Margaret to put her experiences on paper. Furthermore, Margaret was frequently too ill to write, which obliged her to dictate from her sickbed or wheelchair. The opportunity for her to have two female scribes recording her words was an unusual twist in Catholic tradition, in which so many religious women's vitae were compiled and edited solely by men; and yet the sisters' complicity in this work involved the usual elements of self-censorship (which nuns had honed to a fine art) and of cautious editing with an eye to future investigative proceedings.

Sister Thorn's life as I reconstruct it represents a distillation, therefore, of her recollections and experiences as recorded by mostly sympathetic listeners. Despite the lack of autobiographical materials, I have located several narratives about Margaret Reilly in typescript and manuscript form. Some accounts are neatly typed sheaves of paper with handwritten notes creeping across the margins, sometimes added by a second individual. Additional information survives in correspondence and convent chronicles that I have collected and pieced together from archives in Belgium, France, Great Britain, Ireland, and the United States.

The two most important documents about Margaret Reilly were written by a Good Shepherd sister and a Benedictine nun. The first was Margaret's superior, Mother Raymond, who wrote a chronicle of events for the headquarters of the Good Shepherd sisters in France.[26] The second narrative was composed by a Benedictine, Sister Mary Carmelita (Elizabeth Quinn, 1895–1988), based upon the notes of Mother Raymond and Margaret's personal dictation to her between the years 1926 and 1928. Sister Carmelita added details about Margaret that she gained from conversations with her and with the Good Shepherds on occasions when she was temporarily in residence at Peekskill.[27] Sister Carmelita divided her 116 pages into nine chapters. The typescript contains blank spaces where she intended to add or correct information. On several visits to Peekskill from Clyde, Missouri, Sister Carmelita was accompanied by her prioress, Sister Dolorosa Mergen, who kept the document in her possession at their Clyde convent. (To avoid the dangers of breaking cloister, nuns and sisters were obliged to travel in pairs.) Incorporated verbatim into Carmelita's account are six pages from Mother Raymond's narrative of events at Peekskill, covering the time from Margaret's arrival in 1921 to an unspecified ending date.[28] The final section of Carmelita's typescript is entitled "Communications of Our Lord to 'Margaret,'" transcribed at Peekskill by Brother Lukas Etlin, the confessor at Carmelita's convent, from his visit of November 17–30, 1923.[29] After beginning with the messages that Margaret had received from Jesus in 1922, the subsequent divine revelations appear roughly in chronological order from 1913 and move forward in time. Some of these messages are quite humdrum, such as Jesus's warning that sisters should be "clean and tidy" and that superiors needed to exercise better oversight to prevent the sisters from wearing worn-out shoes.[30] Others give personal advice, as in Jesus's encouragement to Margaret: "Thorn, you are right not to care what is said of you. You who belong to Him should not think of reputation. Let Him dispose of your life, your reputation and your honor as He pleases."[31] (At some point in her later life, Sister Carmelita reported that each year she eliminated some of her correspondence with Sister Thorn, thus leaving even fewer clues for the researcher.)

In the 1970s, to supplement the biographies of Mother Raymond and Sister Carmelita, Good Shepherd provincial superior Victoria Andreoli encouraged further research on Sister Crown of Thorns. Sister Clare Nolan undertook an investigation, which included interviews with Sister Carmelita, who died in 1988 after serving in St. Louis as archivist of the Clyde Benedictines from 1968 to 1979. I entered the picture in the 1990s, when I met with Provincial Superior Sheila Kelly; the RGS archivist, Sister Dominica Rinaldi; and Sister Clare. With the superior's approval of my project, Sister Clare made her notebooks available to me, placing a variety of disparate materials into a coherent form that mark the beginnings of a historical treatment of Sister Thorn. As far as I know, I am the only external scholar to see and use the Good Shepherd archives of materials pertaining to Sister Crown of Thorns. Access to these materials, unfortunately, became restricted in 2007 without further explanation, leaving me unable to return to them after a new archivist began the cataloging process. The RGS acquired an archivist from outside the congregation who did not offer explanations for the closure of the Reilly materials. Undoubtedly, given my limitations with the uncataloged RGS archives, there are items that I missed, items that I was not permitted to see, or items whose significance was not apparent at the time.

A second category of information about Margaret Reilly comes from clergy authors. Among the three men who wrote narratives that eventually were intended as contributions to Margaret's potential vita were Lukas Etlin, Thomas à Kempis Reilly, and Father Scanlan. Etlin, a monk who had emigrated from Switzerland to the Benedictine abbey at Clyde, Missouri, has himself been a candidate for beatification since 1960. As of 2010, Etlin's cause is inert, but his papers are closed to the researcher. Fortunately, I located some of his letters in other archives.

A Dominican priest contributed a bound typescript about Sister Thorn called "Spinations," derived from the Latin word for thorn. The author, Thomas à Kempis Reilly (1879–1957), no relation to Margaret, gave many retreats to enclosed nuns and sisters throughout a busy career that included teaching philosophy at Maryknoll, New York, and serving as chaplain of Rosary College in River Forest, Illinois. For his research, Father Reilly was privileged to receive Mother Raymond's personal copy of Carmelita Quinn's transcriptions of the events at Peekskill. He had requested to see this document while giving a spiritual retreat to the Benedictine sisters in Missouri. The superior, Mother Dolorosa Mergen, never indicated her approval directly, but she gave permission to another sister to give the copy of Margaret's life to the Dominican. He later shared his composition with them.

At the time of Margaret's arrival at Peekskill in 1921, Father Reilly was stationed at a Catholic school in nearby Ossining, New York. In 1936, months before Sister Thorn's death, he gave a retreat at the Peekskill convent, making him one of the last priests to see her. In a matter of four months (February to May 1940), from a hospital in St. Paul, Minnesota, Father Reilly composed a life of Margaret from Carmelita's text, but he added embellishments and reflections of his own to create a document of over 300 pages. The fact that he was later forbidden by his provincial to publish anything about Margaret suggests that his interpretations were too far-flung. The priest's idiosyncratic punctuation, drawings, mathematical equations, and arcane references are puzzling and continue to frustrate even Dominican archivists, yet they serve as a reminder that many "primitive" or magical elements survived in the religious faith of American Catholics of the twentieth century. Father Reilly's interest in asceticism and spiritual gifts is hinted at by his authorship of the 1912 *Catholic Encyclopedia* article on speaking in tongues, as well as his familiarity with the works of his well-known French Dominican contemporary, Reginald Garrigou-Lagrange (1877–1964), an expert on ascetic theology.[32]

Father Reilly's use of numerology is also intriguing. He insisted, for example, that numerical connections between Margaret's life and certain Bible passages provided a key to interpreting her life. Father Reilly believed that Jesus had given Margaret a list of thirty-seven numbers that referred to pages in "the English translation of Saint Bernard's 86 sermons on the opening chapters of the Canticle of Canticles." Mother Raymond had written the numbers on a strip of paper and had given them to the Dominican, after which he concluded that "the pages seemed to have been alighted on, not haphazardly, but in such sequence that a consecutive presentation of the contents would bear the character of continuity and charm."[33] Why would Jesus give Margaret a list of page numbers relating to a translation of Saint Bernard's work? Did these details lead the discerning reader to significant spiritual insights? What monastic audience was Father Reilly imagining for his calculations, and how would that audience respond? Through Father Reilly's eyes, Sister Thorn was transformed into "the seer of Peekskill," a prophetic voice for the clergy whose stigmata were less important than her visionary messages and their scriptural sources. "Spinations" tried to bridge the passage from lived mystical experience to the rational discourse about that experience as filtered by a male cleric.

A second Dominican, Father Walter G. Scanlan (1881–1950), produced "Thorn: A Story of Divine Providence." Scanlan had preached annual retreats at Peekskill in 1924 and 1925 and thus had crossed paths with Father Bertrand and Brother Lukas. A copy of this typescript survives at the Good Shepherd archives in New York as a black notebook of 206 pages. Scanlan's identity is concealed on the title page, which states only: "Narrated by Godfather, Entrusted to SAINT DOMINIC'S MERCY SEEKERS at Detroit for prudent use and edification within the Monastery walls. Not for outsiders."[34] Its style is florid and pious and incorporates passages of dialogue interspersed with interventions by Scanlan, who refers to himself as Father Scant. His account opens with a recollection of Joan of Arc, in whose "voices" from heaven he saw parallels to Sister Thorn's messages from Jesus. The many scriptural references and numerological connections make this, like "Spinations," an unconventional document not intended to circulate among the laity. It is unclear what esoteric knowledge was supposed to be gleaned from it, or how his cloistered audience received it. At the least, the presence of such a manuscript produced for monastics suggests the well-guarded intellectual barrier that existed between lay and ordained Catholics. Because the laity were neither invited nor expected to understand the deepest spiritual meanings of stigmata and mystical visions, their instruction had to be entrusted to insiders. No wonder that the personal narratives of mystics were not given to Catholic laymen and laywomen unless under guidance by a priest. As devised by Reilly and Scanlan, the "hidden transcripts" of Sister Thorn's life were far more heterodox than the blanched versions that would be provided for public consumption.

In addition to the narratives of Sisters Cahill and Quinn and the priestly accounts of Etlin, Reilly, and Scanlan, there exists correspondence between nuns, chaplains, retreat masters, family members, and friends that provides a fuller, if still fragmentary, portrait of Sister Thorn. Errors crept into personal remembrances, proving that they are not necessarily the most reliable sources. For instance, Mrs. Mary McInerney Crandles, the sister of Daniel McInerney, a priest from Brooklyn whose aunt was a Good Shepherd at Peekskill, recalled Sister Thorn. When asked to record her memories, Crandles wrote:

> Margaret Riley, a poor sickly, uneducated [sic], appeared at Mt St Florence a rainy day accompanied by her physician Dr. __ Ferguson? She asked to be taken in as a novice but informed Mt St Florence was for Professed Sisters and Novitiate in another area. A plaque of Sacred Heart witnessed by all present left the wall and implanted itself in another space. Mother William (?)[.]
>
> Margaret was given a room in which she remained for the rest of her life a period of _____.
>
> She was known in religion as Sister Mary Crown of Thorns. She revealed that Sisters in her convent doubted her. She suffered the stygmates [sic]. She suffered untold temptations from the devil who appeared in form of collie dog. Very witty. Happy. Was concerned I was underweight and gave me a doll on the condition I would eat better. As children we called her "Little Sister." She called Mother & Dad Aunt Nell and Uncle Dan.[35]

The correspondence about Margaret left by nuns and sisters shares some common features. The authors' ingrained habits of frugality are evident, as the convented women covered both sides of the paper for their handwritten messages and often turned the page sideways to scratch across the margins as well. Whether in a precise copperplate or a scrawl, the letters offer poignant testimony to the often difficult conditions of convent life, the constant anxiety of each house over finances, the sisters' frustrations with the church hierarchy, the omnipresence of illness and suffering within the congregation (especially those Good Shepherds returning from foreign missions in Costa Rica, Nicaragua, Peru, and South Africa), and the crawling pace of transatlantic mail to and from the motherhouse in France. The New York Province of the Good Shepherds also supplied most of the sisters for their foundations in the British West Indies, Columbia, and Trinidad.

The collection of Good Shepherd materials about Margaret Reilly as I encountered it was in an uncataloged state in the community's house in Jamaica-Queens, New York, and included letters, official and unofficial reports, photographs, some personal articles, and bags of religious artifacts. Among the latter objects were holy cards, religious greeting cards, religious medals, badges, scapulars, embroidered bookmarks, crucifixes, and rosaries that helped mark special events in a Catholic's life and observed the Christian calendar with its annual cycle from Christmas to Easter. All of these items were part of a thriving Catholic economy of gift exchange in the early twentieth century, especially for nuns and sisters who professed a vow of poverty and lacked personal income for buying gifts. Holy cards, for example, were inexpensive items that, like baseball cards, could be exchanged and valued for personal identification with the achievements of the "players." While such items do not disclose much about Margaret's spiritual state, they do locate her in the context of the rich devotional world of pre–Vatican II Catholicism and inside an extensive and intact Irish American community that never missed the chance to celebrate St. Patrick's Day and related festivals of Hibernian pride.

The final written sources that I have located concerning Margaret Reilly are correspondence of the more than thirty priests and physicians involved in her case. I have traced these letters to the archives of religious orders scattered throughout the United States and the United Kingdom. Living relatives (including Margaret Reilly's great-grandniece) and other acquaintances loaned me cards, letters, Irish ephemera, holy medals, and even poetry related to Sister Thorn. The Good Shepherd sisters of New York have graciously provided anecdotes and correspondence and have shown me their collection of personal items belonging to Thorn, as they call her. The

Jamaica-Queens convent, for example, left her white woolen shawl on my bed during my stay there, showed me several Sacred Heart badges that she embroidered, gave me a silver locket worn by the congregation, and allowed me to try on religious habits from the pre–Vatican II era. In the summer heat during my visit, the habits were cumbersome and itchy, which made me think about the collective relief that may have accompanied the abandonment of the garb in the 1960s, as well as about the sorrow of those sisters who lamented its departure and who counted on the deliberation and precision that must accompany each day's donning of the habit—the guimpe folded just so, the three pins holding the veil in place, the Rosary dangling neatly from the blue waist cord. I decided to investigate Sister Thorn because of the unsettling mix of the mundane and peculiar details I had just begun to learn about her. In 1900, for instance, why would a young girl in Manhattan begin to wear a hair shirt as a form of penance? Did a raised image of a crucifix actually appear on her chest and then manifest itself on the convent wall? Was Margaret the megalomaniac and deceiver that some priests had claimed? Or was "little sister" the "dearest, sweetest soul" that her cousin described, and the first, best hope for an American saint?

Chapter Outline

The seven chapters of this book correspond roughly to the chronology of Margaret Reilly's life from her birth in 1884 to her death in 1937. At the same time, each chapter also locates stigmatization in the twentieth century in a topical framework as part of a larger concern of the Catholic Church to defend the reality of the supernatural in all of its forms. In other words, this book is not a portrait of a singular prodigy. Instead, it argues that the Catholic Church used mystics like Margaret Reilly to proclaim its return to the center of Western culture after World War I and to revive belief in God as the sole answer to the crises of modernity. Since the early nineteenth century, mysticism had been used to attack positivism and secularism in Europe, and now the same strategy was attempted in the United States, with mixed success.

Chapter 1 opens with Margaret Reilly's recognition that she had been chosen by Jesus for special purposes. After receiving a supernatural mark on her skin in 1917, she eventually entered the convent in 1921, although not by the usual path. The chapter describes her upbringing in Manhattan and puts the Reilly family into the contexts of Irish American history in New York City and of Irish Catholicism. The Reillys seemingly enjoyed a degree of economic success while at the same time bearing witness to the pain and suffering of the Crucifixion at the heart of their faith by observing severely ascetic habits at home. Certain elements of Margaret's life, including parochial school and encounters with influential nuns and confessors, helped fashion her penitential piety and prepare her for a convent vocation. A few days after arriving at a convent for a spiritual retreat, she began to display stigmata on her body.

Chapter 2 takes up Margaret's convent milieu in Peekskill with the Good Shepherd sisters, a congregation founded in nineteenth-century France to aid delinquent girls and women. The sisters had mixed reactions to Margaret's desire to enter the community and to her alleged stigmatization. Despite claiming to possess unique spiritual gifts, which could have been a boon to the congregation in terms of attracting new members and bequests, Margaret did not win its unanimous support. The presence of delinquent girls and women at the convent, reminders of the good/bad girl dichotomy in Catholic piety, threw Margaret's reputation into relief as well. Having subdued their own wills, the sisters' mission was to reform the characters of the drug addicts, incorrigibles, shoplifters, and unmarried mothers under their supervision. Yet it was rumored of Margaret's own past that her life may not have been so far removed from the fallen "Magdalens." The undercurrent of transgression lingered on to threaten her admission to the congregation.

Chapter 3 discusses how Margaret Reilly, now accepted into the Good Shepherds as Sister Crown of Thorns, energized a cadre of lay and clerical Catholics who believed that her mystical gifts furnished definitive proof for the existence of the miraculous. Although recent stigmatics, notably Louise Lateau, had been judged by "scientific" standards, the inconclusive results of Lateau's examinations led each side to claim victory. Forty years later, Margaret's circle of supporters busied itself defending religious faith in light of theological and scientific debates about mysticism that had been reinvigorated in Europe after World War I and alongside a wider cultural interest in mysticism that infused avant-garde artistic movements like surrealism. The First World War also affected the debate between revelation and reason because it heightened postwar connections between the members of religious orders in western Europe and their counterparts in the United States, who aided in rebuilding the church's physical and moral infrastructure. Among these priests and monks were some who eagerly supported Sister Thorn, finding in her messages from Jesus an inspiration for religious vocations and a vehicle to promote a transnational Catholicism in answer to the wartime sacrifice of a "lost generation."

Margaret's doubters and critics are discussed in chapter 4, which highlights her relationship with several physicians as an instance of the conflict between reason and revelation. As the first known stigmatic in the United States, Sister Thorn garnered quite a bit of attention. Her medical examiners included one of the most prominent and bookish laymen in the United States, Dr. James J. Walsh, and one of the most scholarly and widely published Jesuits of Great Britain, Herbert Thurston. Sister Thorn was also the patient of Thomas Gallen, with whom she fell in love, and of Thomas F. McParlan, the private physician of the archbishop of New York, who remained so convinced that she was a genuine mystic that he found himself unable to offer her treatment for fear of disobeying God's will. The medical men who examined Sister Thorn and wrote about her worked within the intellectual models of their generation, often content to dismiss female mysticism as hysteria while not abandoning belief in the reality of mystical experience. They seemed resistant to emerging models of human behavior, including psychoanalysis, which disturbed traditional Catholics by its undue emphasis upon sexuality and its rejection of supernaturalism. As scientists, Margaret's physicians could not resort to supernatural explanations for her stigmata, yet as the Catholic Church itself began to embrace the scientific study of mysticism by the 1930s, some opportunities opened up for less-antagonistic conversation on the borders between religion and science.

As a stigmatic who embodied Christ's Passion in the most literal way, Sister Thorn proved to be an able promoter of devotional Catholicism, particularly of the cult of the Sacred Heart. Chapter 5 examines the workings of devotional piety that characterized Sister Thorn's era through the role she created for herself in hand embroidering religious badges that she sent to her friends and petitioners. Crucifixes, holy cards, medals, relics, statues, and, most especially, her badge signaling devotion to the Sacred Heart of Jesus offer ample evidence of the importance of objects to Catholics of this era as sources of connection and healing. In response to the Marian-centered practices of the previous century, the church, under the direction of Pope Pius X, was calling for a renewed emphasis upon the Real Presence of Christ in the Eucharist, which Sister Thorn's identification with the Sacred Heart cult helped to foster. Sister Thorn's cloistered status limited the amount of contact she could have with the public; hence, her sewing and distribution of holy badges affirmed traditional norms of domesticity while at the same time serving the church's concerns for stronger identification among the faithful with the body and blood of Christ. That Eucharistic concentration had its limits, however, as evidenced by the perspective of a Benedictine monk who became one of Sister Thorn's closest advocates. Finally, Sister Thorn's involvement in a gift economy of handmade artifacts also marked the convent as representing a deliberate, although only partial, contrast to a capitalist economy and furnished one more instance of the church's ambivalence toward the contemporary world.

While Sister Thorn promoted the Sacred Heart cult, her followers attempted to promote her. Chapter 6 considers how Sister Thorn became a potential saint for a Catholic community that was attempting to elevate her on an international scale by associating her with a network of extraordinary individuals. The chapter shifts focus from Margaret's *experience* to her *audience* and examines how popular cults grew by establishing a bond between an individual and other spiritual virtuosi. Margaret's advocates linked her in oral and print culture to numerous charismatic figures, including an Irish girl who led the pope to lower the Communion age for children and several contemporary stigmatics. The group of Catholics that was associated with Sister Thorn demonstrates that far from being unique, she reflected a generational pattern within the cult of sacrifice and suffering that affected women especially but did not exclude men or children. It became less likely that Margaret Reilly would become Saint Margaret when the Catholic Church's standards for sainthood changed shortly after her death, shifting its rules to downplay mystical marvels in favor of honoring uniquely virtuous lives. Yet the tradition of stigmatics persists even today in localized cults, although the experience and the methods of diffusion have been altered by electronic media. The final stigmatic profiled in the chapter, therefore, is an Italian woman who died in 2009 whose cult serves as an instance of new technologies creating an international audience in contrast to the personal and face-to-face connections made by Sister Thorn's adherents.

Although Sister Thorn failed to achieve official recognition from the Catholic Church through canonization, the final chapter examines her death and seeks to comprehend her as part of what can be called a "Catholic International," an agenda pursued by the Vatican to establish a renovated Catholic faith that transcended nationalism in the twentieth century. In some ways, this program continued nineteenth-century Ultramontanism, but it was tempered by the sobering losses of the Great War. In the 1920s, when a Catholic Modernism emerged, notably in postwar France, it arguably served as "an attempt to restore meaning and self-identity to a traumatized culture" through "recasting of traditional Catholic tropes as the ultimate expression of postwar modernity."[36] In this regard, Sister Thorn's controversial mystical experiences represented an American variation on the cultural wars that had been waged in Europe in the closing decades of the nineteenth century, when the church had sought to revive itself through a papalist agenda as a robust institution. Again, after 1919, the church delivered an "off-modern" response to the First World War. While the concerns of American Catholics were not exactly parallel to those of Catholics in European nations, where a defiant church positioned itself in tension with anticlerical, positivist, and liberal movements, Americans were nonetheless being drafted into the Catholic International on behalf of its goals, and the religious orders were frequently the medium of those aims. In the postwar era, when the church lifted its rhetoric to a cosmic level, describing a world torn between the forces of Good and Evil, Sister Thorn's torments were implicated in this contest between divine and satanic forces. Even though Sister Thorn was an unusual figure in an American context, she was quickly linked to contemporaries in Europe whose parallels to her own life were so close as to suggest a shared piety that affirmed the emerging establishment of a global church.

The desire among Catholics for suffering spiritual prodigies like Margaret Reilly already existed because of the powerful symbolic value of such persons, even in ostensibly pragmatic, materialistic America. Reilly's "mysticism," however, was not the same as that of medieval and Early Modern Europeans who experienced stigmata and visions. Indeed, some of her "revelations" were shallow and mundane. Still, many of her acquaintances tried to locate her in that historic lineage of mystics, as though Catholicism and mysticism were always and everywhere the same. While the territories of New France and New Spain offer up rich evidence of mystical behaviors and experience in the colonial era, American Catholic historiography has rarely addressed its mystical facets—especially the interwar era's profound investment in mystical redemptive suffering. In this regard, Sister Thorn's milieu reflected an amalgam of influences from her Irish ancestry and from the French, German, and Swiss spiritualities of the various clergy and sisters who involved themselves with her. Thus there is much to gain from investigating an American mystical prodigy and comparing her with European prototypes and contemporaries. And by observing how Americans took some, but not all, of their cues from continental Catholicism in promoting Sister Thorn, we can see what was emerging as distinctive to New World religion as well.

{1} Now You Are My Thorn, but Soon You Shall Be My Lily of Delight

The Transformation of Margaret Reilly

A soul is of more value than a world.

—Rose-Virginie Pelletier (Saint Euphrasia),
founder of the Sisters of the Good Shepherd

Pain and grief, oh, do not spare me,
Let my soul and body smart,
Happy will I be to suffer
To console Thy anguished Heart.

—Stanza of "To the Lily of His Heart," a poem
written by Sister Mary Carmelita Quinn and sent to
Sister Mary Crown of Thorns in January 1924

Margaret Reilly received a nudge toward sainthood on an ordinary day in 1917 while cooking dinner. Although the kitchen seems an unlikely place for a mystical encounter, Margaret, while stooping over the oven to prepare a fish supper with her mother, felt a sharp pain over her heart and saw a three-dimensional crucifix emerging in blood. Her mother quickly put her to bed and immediately telephoned their pastor.[1] This event was not Margaret's first divine communication. Four years earlier, in November 1913, a two-inch-long red cross had appeared on her breast. On that day, she recalled, "It pleased our dear Lord to send me a very severe illness for which He prepared me in a most extraordinary way. In my illness, I beheld our dear L. nailed to the Cross and covered with Wounds. . . . 'Thorn,' He called me; 'upon thy breast I place a Cross.' My eyes raised above. He smiled and spoke: 'Take thou this Cross because 'tis Thorn I love.' Then a sharp pain . . . when suddenly my eyes closed to all around me. My very soul became entirely rapt and absorbed in the contemplation of the Most Holy Trinity."[2]

Margaret's divine rapture soon inspired others to offer their own interpretations of the events of 1917. One asserted that the arrival of the crucifix

MARGARET REILLY'S
MANHATTAN
C. 1920

Dr. McParlan's home
16 East 96th Street

St. Francis de Sales Parish and school
15 East 96th Street

Reilly family home
172 East 94th Street

Dr. Gallen's home
319 East 96th Street

Good Shepherd Convent
East 90th Street and East River

St. Ignatius Parish
East 84th Street and Park Avenue

Blessed Sacrament Parish
West 71st Street

St. John the Evangelist Parish
55th Street and 1st Avenue

Dr. James J. Walsh home
344 West 72nd Street

HUDSON RIVER

EAST RIVER

BROADWAY
COLUMBUS AVE
RIVERSIDE DRIVE
BROADWAY
W 90TH ST
W 80TH ST
W 60TH ST
W 50TH ST

5TH AVE
MADISON AVE
PARK AVE
LEXINGTON AVE
3RD AVE
2ND AVE
1ST AVE

CENTRAL PARK

E 90TH ST
E 80TH ST
E 70TH ST
E 60TH ST
E 50TH ST

EAST RIVER DRIVE

BROADWAY
5TH AVE
MADISON AVE
PARK AVE
LEXINGTON AVE
3RD AVE
2ND AVE
1ST AVE

Key sites in Margaret Reilly's Manhattan. (Digital drawing, Alec Sarkas, University of Pittsburgh; property of author) on Margaret's skin was the Lord's resolution of a dispute between Margaret and her confessor.[3] Apparently, Margaret had taken up the penitential practice of wearing a hair shirt, usually on Friday afternoons from twelve until three o'clock. After about eight months, Jesus told her to advise her confessor that she should stop wearing the shirt. The priest thought that Margaret should continue the practice, but he also came to understand that God would send a sign to both of them in the form of a cross on her chest.[4]

Whatever its origin, the crucifix over Margaret Reilly's heart in 1917 remained visible until December 8. In a friend's recollection, the mark resembled a "raised, sunburned area," pale pink, and not more than two inches long.[5] The three-dimensional corpus even changed color. According to one chronicler, "Sometimes it was red, sometimes purple, sometimes livid. Jesus revealed to Little Thorn the meaning of the changing of colors; it meant sufferings of His Church in various ways."[6]

Margaret's crucifix reappeared in a different venue four years later while she was making a spiritual retreat at Mount St. Florence, the convent of the Good Shepherd sisters in Peekskill, New York. There, in October 1921, the image again appeared on Margaret's chest and then transferred itself miraculously to the wall of her temporary residence. It was observed by Dr. Thomas McParlan, the physician who had accompanied Margaret to the convent, as well as by Mother Raymond Cahill, the convent superior, and several of the Good Shepherd sisters. Mother Cahill surrounded the transferred image with a picture frame, containing and protecting the vivid red stain on the stark white wall.

This chapter describes the unusual mystical events of Margaret Reilly's life and seeks to understand them in the context of Irish American history in New York and of American Catholicism of the early twentieth century. Most of the chapter is necessarily taken up with establishing a sequence of events and biographical details from archival sources. Later chapters will revisit significant episodes and continue through the end of her life. Using the accounts of Margaret's experiences compiled by several contemporaries, this chapter sketches the events of her stigmatization, then returns to follow Margaret's family life from childhood to young adulthood, her convent appearance in 1921, her experiences in the convent until she made her final vows in 1928, and her encounters with priests and sisters who interpreted her divine and diabolical experiences.

When the crucifix returned to Margaret's chest in 1921 after the preludes of 1913 and 1917, she had just arrived at Mount St. Florence, located in an idyllic and secluded setting on the heights of the Hudson River, to perform a Catholic activity known as a spiritual retreat. On a late September after-

Dr. Thomas F. McParlan (1870–1928), the archbishop's private physician and Sister Thorn's unwavering advocate. (Photo of prayer card by author)

noon, Margaret had taken the train north from Manhattan to Peekskill to undertake this silent exercise. Accompanied on the journey by McParlan, her family doctor—who had recommended the retreat, and this convent in particular, because of his friendship with the superior—Margaret had been granted a special favor. Ordinarily, a convent that housed any cloistered nuns did not accept outsiders, especially as overnight guests. McParlan, however, had close ties to the congregation and to the Catholic hierarchy, serving as the personal physician to the prior and present archbishops of New York, John Farley (1902–18) and Patrick Hayes (1919–38). With McParlan's approval, Margaret was installed in a makeshift room inside the parlor or in a cell inside the cloister.

Margaret's first three days at Peekskill were quiet and uneventful. Then, on the fourth morning, Margaret took a stroll to view a statue of the Sacred Heart of Jesus on the convent grounds. As she returned to her room to lie down, she had a vision of Jesus standing at the foot of the bed. He said, "I give you my cross upon your breast, because I love you much: and you are to suffer for My very own."[7] Jesus explained that "my very own" referred to priests and nuns. The same image from her chest was miraculously duplicated on the wall of her room at Mount St. Florence. About three inches in length, it was seen there by the Mother Raymond, who was further surprised to find that Margaret's left side and feet were now bleeding. Mother Raymond reported to one of Margaret's cousins, who was also a nun: "She has shown me her beautiful Cross and you may feel certain that she was most welcome." Even before Margaret's arrival at Peekskill, Mother Raymond

claimed to have witnessed (although she does not specify where) the perfectly formed cross and corpus with its feet resting on Margaret's heart, "at
time diffused with blood."[8] For the next thirty-three days—each day, as the
superior believed, symbolizing a year of Jesus's life—Margaret remained
bedridden at the convent in acute pain and bleeding profusely from four
wound sites in her hands and feet. Jesus told Margaret that the foot wounds
were the beginning of her complete stigmatization.[9] Puncture wounds appeared around her forehead as well, as though from a wreath of thorns. In
a vision, Jesus told her that she would now be named "Thorn."[10] "Now you
are my Thorn," he proclaimed, "but soon you shall be my Lily of Delight."[11]

In a breach of convent procedure, Mother Raymond herself cared for
Margaret, changing linens and bandages as they were saturated with blood.
Sister Mary of St. Luthgarde, the infirmarian, assisted Mother Raymond.[12]
The superior's activity recalled her novice days at the Brooklyn Good Shepherd convent, where her tasks involved doing the hospital laundry, washing
bandages, and even disposing of the remains of body parts left on the linens
and bandages from surgical procedures. Mother Raymond's niece recalled
that her aunt had intensely disliked this chore.

Mother Raymond was known as "a magnetic personality" with "wide
experience" who was trusted by the many persons who came seeking her
advice.[13] Born Bridget Cahill in Worcester, Massachusetts, she was the eldest
daughter of parents born in Ireland. Her father was a skilled shoe designer
who worked in the region's several small shoe factories. As a child, Bridget
contracted undulant fever, a chronic bacterial infection often caused by
unpasteurized cow milk or contact with other infected livestock. The family moved for a few years to the nearby town of Spencer, Massachusetts, as
recommended by the doctor. Bridget and her two sisters then attended all
twelve years of school at Ascension Academy in Worcester, directed by the
Sisters of Notre Dame de Namur, while the Cahill sons attended St. John's
School. At the time of her first Communion at age fourteen, Bridget beheld
a vision of the Christ child that spanned several nights. It ended when her
father entered the vision. Her pastor-confessor told her that she should be
at peace and that the vision would not return again. This story, passed down
in Cahill family lore, perhaps explains Mother Raymond's unqualified acceptance of Sister Thorn's mystical experiences.[14] Bridget was a clever and
creative young woman who even made money publishing poems under the
names of known authors, a common practice.[15] After high school, Bridget
asked the local department store to pack her trousseau and ship it to the
Brooklyn Good Shepherd convent. Her father, a lapsed Catholic for most of
his life, disavowed her and never visited her in the convent after her entrance

in 1900. Some ten years later, he resumed Mass attendance in Massachusetts, but it is unclear if he ever reconciled with his daughter.

As a young superior, Cahill was perplexed about how to deal with the disturbing circumstance of having a stigmatization within her religious community. No doubt she prayed for guidance and help from her chosen namesake, Saint Raymond Nonnatus, the patron saint of the falsely accused, as her own community began to challenge her support for Margaret. She began to keep a detailed daily journal of the appearance of Margaret's wounds.[16] Not until thirteen years later did Mother Raymond admit to any uncertainty about Margaret Reilly; a year after that, during a private chat with Mother Raymond at Mount St. Florence in 1935, the newly arrived Sister Martha Marie Crowley expressed doubts about reports of the "strange and threatening manifestations" that were occurring in Margaret's room. "I was not ready to believe in the mystical or occult," Crowley recalled. During that conversation, Mother Raymond also confided in Crowley about "her own doubts in her early associations with 'Little Sister' (as she was known in the community), her anxiety and her prayers to know the Will of God."[17]

Following Jesus's directive, Mother Raymond moved Margaret into the anteroom adjoining her own bedroom. This fateful decision meant that when Margaret later applied to enter the Good Shepherd order, she had avoided the deprivation of the regular postulants, who began their communal life in the small cells on the ground floor in the least heated part of the convent building. Within two months of her arrival at Peekskill, the bleeding of Margaret's stigmata had intensified in gruesome ways, and she continued to feel unbearable pain at the wound sites from Wednesday through Friday each week. On November 11, her face was marked as though by whips. Margaret said "she could feel the separate lashes as they were given on her face, also when they were given on her whole body. These lashes were sometimes inflicted by our Lord Himself, or by St. Michael or by her Guardian Angel. Margaret could even see this instrument: the discipline contained 48 strips of fine steel with thorn-like projections. There was also a piece of lead 2½ inches long attached to the center ring."[18] Mother Raymond reported that among Margaret's wounds, the scourge marks were "more painful than the wounds of the hands and feet and side. The pain in the chest is as if an army of people were kneeling on the chest."[19]

The cross impressed on the skin over Margaret's heart that began this chain of events disappeared entirely from her body around December 15, 1921, but her mystical communications did not end.[20] Throughout the following years, Margaret continued to receive spiritual gifts often associated with stigmatics: a crown of thorns around her head and a mystical marriage to Christ, followed by the replacement of her visible wounds by invisible stigmata. She reported a burning heat in her third finger of the left hand where Jesus placed a wedding ring, which was perceptible only to her.[21]

After three months at Mount St. Florence, Margaret left the convent at least once, although this trip is not mentioned in the convent's records. In December 1921 she visited her cousin Sister Rita (Mary Connolly) at the Ursuline convent of Brown County, Ohio, about forty-eight miles from Cincinnati.[22] Since Margaret had lost both parents in the preceding three years, her Connolly cousins were now her closest relatives. Her bleeding wounds ceased during that trip. That fact did not stop Sister Rita from quickly conveying her cousin's secret to others: barely two months later, the Holy Cross priest who was the provincial for Indiana requested from Archbishop Hayes an audience with "this favored child of grace," whose stigmata he had learned of from the "Ursulines of Brown County."[23]

While visiting her cousin in Brown County, Ohio, Margaret had the good fortune of receiving her postulant's veil from a distinguished Good Shepherd leader: Mother Mary of St. Francis Xavier (Catherine Margaret Hickey), the Visitor of the American congregations, who had come to the United States from Ireland to fill that position in 1920.[24] The Visitor's task was to call on each religious community about once a year in order to report to the Generalate (the order's headquarters, in this case in Angers, France) and to advise the sisters. At the moment that Margaret was visiting the Ursulines, Mother Hickey happened to be at the Good Shepherd house in Columbus, Ohio, where she summoned Margaret and presented her with her veil. Margaret was then immediately called via telegram to return to Peekskill for the visit of Archbishop Hayes, where she received a second postulant's veil from Mother Raymond. As if on cue, demons arrived at this crucial moment in Margaret's spiritual journey. "Since her reception of that garb," Mother Raymond reported of Margaret, "it has been a series of persecutions from Satan, *as if he would discourage her or those with her.*"[25]

The Good Shepherd Visitor, Mother Hickey (1861–1960), no stranger to supernatural events, divided her ninety-nine years equally between Ireland and America. As a young novice, her health was so poor that the convent's admission requirements had been waived to admit her. After that, the superior general sent Hickey to Lourdes for a cure; she returned there four times, a convinced believer in the healing power of the Virgin Mary. After meeting Margaret and providing her with her veil, she confided to Brother Lukas Etlin of Missouri: "It is good for our Congregation to give us such a chosen soul."[26]

Margaret, as related above, had gone to Ohio to visit Sister Rita. Marga-

Mother Mary of St. Francis Hickey (1861–1960), the Visitor for the Good Shepherd congregation. From Ireland, she visited Good Shepherd convents in the United States and met Margaret Reilly while Reilly was still a novice. (Photo taken in 1951; courtesy of the Sisters of the Good Shepherd, Minneapolis)

ret's other Connolly cousin, Catherine (1874–1925), also lived in Ohio as a Dominican nun and schoolteacher in St. Mary of the Springs. As Sister Sebastian, Catherine had already received some photographs or drawings of the mark on her cousin's skin from Mother Raymond, who concluded her letter with the entreaty: "Trusting, dear Sister, this will somewhat satisfy your interest, asking a little prayer, and begging to accept the enclosed pictures which are a true copy of the Cross and position on her breast."[27] The next summer, Sister Sebastian traveled to Peekskill to observe things firsthand, visiting Margaret on August 25, 1922, accompanied by Margaret's brother Tom. Like all of Margaret's relatives, Sister Sebastian had been born in Ireland. She and Tom saw her cousin in the company of Mother Raymond and talked for about twenty minutes. After dinner, the visitors talked with Margaret for "quite a while" but were not allowed to see her room and its alleged miraculous cross under orders from the congregation's appointed confessor, Father John F. Brady. Sister Sebastian registered her own disappointment: "Was I crestfallen? I showed it from head to toes." But then an opportunity emerged: Sebastian reported happily that Mother Raymond was able to take a break from attending to a plumbing leak in the convent to show them Margaret's room, which she had been given permission to do. Sister Sebastian found the space "small and very plain. I first looked at the miraculous Crucifix. It is much like the one on the picture, and about that size. I could see the Face of our Lord, and the lettering is also very plain.

We used the magnifying glass. From where I stood I kissed the feet, but would have to stand on something to reach the Face. The wall looks as if it had been well scrubbed, and I noticed a little holy picture pasted below, as was spoken of in the paper written at Brown County." Sister Sebastian also learned that during her first months at Peekskill, Margaret had been sending out blessed religious articles in response to requests from the public. Now that the archbishop of New York had forbidden this practice, "thousands of small packages from all over had to be sent back unblessed."[28]

Another visitor on that day, Sister Justina, saw Margaret alone; the three guests then conversed with her together. Justina asked Margaret if Jesus had visited her while Sebastian and Tom were with her, and she replied that he had.[29] Sister Sebastian explained that the crucifix was not apparent on her cousin's chest at the moment, but that she experienced the pain of invisible stigmata there and in her hands, feet, and side. Sister Sebastian's impression of Margaret was of "the dearest, sweetest soul, and heavenly in appearance, but as simple and as natural as a child."[30]

Except for one detail, Margaret Reilly's appearance was nothing unusual. Described as standing about five foot four and slender (but formerly rotund, in Raymond's account), Margaret was favored with "extraordinary" blue eyes that were usually remarked upon by those who knew her. Later photographs of her show an attractive round-faced woman with pale skin and a healthy appearance, even though by then she was confined to a wheelchair. Shortly after Margaret's miraculous episodes began, numerous outsiders had the chance to meet her. One priest described her manner as pleasant although nervous when answering questions, gazing with her eyes wide open in an expression of astonishment. She clutched her crucifix across her heart while in conversation with him. Others did not find Margaret so guileless: the convent was already dividing into camps divided by opinions about "Thorn."

One sister traveling from another congregation recorded that "the sight of Margaret's wounds aroused deep sympathy among the Sisters,"[31] although she was not so fortunate as to behold them. Visiting from Missouri, Sister Mary Carmelita Quinn added that seeing the raised corpus on the wall change from red to purple was "the only visible manifestation I beheld during the weeks I spent at Peekskill."[32] Invoking the life of Catherine of Siena, Carmelita testified that Margaret had prayed to have the stigmata disappear, leaving only the internal pain. Mother Raymond, for her part, carefully transcribed Margaret's interpretation of the wounds: they corresponded to particular intentions for whom she suffered willingly as God's victim to relieve or remove others' sin and pain. According to Margaret, "He tells me that the pain is in atonement for nuns of higher education who look for worldly advantages and forget their main duty of loving God and keeping their holy rules."[33] Margaret's "revelations" were perfectly attuned to a spirituality of victimhood that prevailed in some sectors of the church, while her rejection of worldliness fit the Vatican's recent enactment of stricter rules of cloister for women's congregations. In sum, Margaret's messages were closely calibrated to affirm recent conversations between the superior and religious officials about the need to limit external influences on the sisters. Not ignoring the fact that the presence of nuns in higher education was a significant issue for the church in the 1920s, it is also significant that from her privileged quarters in the superior's room and her post as the operator of the convent switchboard, Margaret had access to a wealth of private details that could inform her divine messages.

Margaret's life as a novice was atypical in other ways. First, she had never resided in the novitiate at 90th Street in Manhattan because in 1923, by order of the provincial, it was transferred to Peekskill, where it remained until 1972. In official histories of the Good Shepherd order, no hint of conflict surrounding the change is recorded. Instead, as one account stated, "In 1923 it was decided to move the entire plant to Mount St. Florence; the Novitiate went first. 'Moving day' began in 1923 and did not end until 1928."[34] In that year, the final remnant still living at 90th Street moved to Peekskill, having acquired twenty-eight acres of land from the existing religious community. The Manhattan convent had already expressed its frustration with the asphalt factory situated across the street from their house, which belched out massive quantities of "smoke and germ-laden dust."[35] Some sisters believed that the dampness of the East River location was a problem as well. But convent records are mute about the fact that the Good Shepherds had already arranged to sell the 90th Street complex of buildings and land to an apartment builder because their complex was slated to be razed in 1927 by the city of New York.

The sisters who accepted Margaret Reilly as a mystic ignored urban redevelopment and instead cited her as the providential cause behind the move to Peekskill. During the summer of 1922, the provincial of New York asked if Peekskill could admit some of the novices from Manhattan to place them in healthier surroundings since the newcomers had been fainting from the heat and leaving chapel early due to illness. The Sisters of the Good Shepherd had already purchased "Paraclete Point" in the Bronx to establish a novitiate that would be more suitable than the house at 90th Street. Mother Raymond, mindful of the limited space in her own convent and not imagining a full-scale transfer, suggested that the novices move to Peekskill in sets of ten. When the first busload arrived, "Thorn commenced to weep," crying aloud that "at last the holy will of God is being fulfilled." According to Sister Raymond, this was a surprising outburst "because the Superiors at the time had no intentions of transferring the novitiate to Peekskill."[36]

From France, the mother general of the Good Shepherds requested an investigation into the New York novitiate, and after several commissioned Visitors submitted their reports and Archbishop Hayes granted his approval, the novitiate was reestablished at Peekskill in 1923. By August 28, 1922, all of the Good Shepherd novices were settled there. The transfer process finally was completed in 1928, when a new building, Villa Loretto, was constructed at Peekskill to house the expanded numbers of novices. The 1930 federal census indicates that more than 100 "inmates" also resided there, referring to the delinquents in the care of the sisters. Girls younger than eighteen continued to be placed in the original house at Mount St. Florence.

The relocation of the novitiate to Peekskill involved Margaret in another way. On the very day that the provincial was to accompany Margaret from Peekskill to Manhattan to begin her novitiate, Margaret lost the use of her legs and never walked again. As Mother Raymond recorded, Margaret had returned to her cell after Mass in the morning and sat down. She became unable to walk, and her limbs grew stiff. She was carried to her bed. In Mother Raymond's telling, God had forewarned Margaret that she was to remain there because "the novitiate would come to Peekskill to her."[37]

Margaret's immobility added another challenge to the convent routine in addition to the special care required by her stigmata. Benedict Bradley, a Benedictine monk in New Jersey who visited Peekskill in November and December 1922, verified that Margaret was mostly bedridden. When she left her bed for chapel and meals, she moved about by crawling on her hands and knees.[38] Her spiritual director forbade her from doing even this after she reported that Satan had thrown her down the stairs repeatedly and filled her tunic with pins to prevent her from navigating the stairs on her knees.[39] Thus the sisters were now required to lift Margaret out of her wheelchair and carry her up and down stairs. Paralysis also prevented Margaret from performing the usual convent chores undertaken by every sister. Consequently, when she was permitted to remain at Peekskill, she was assigned to work the telephone switchboard located in Mother Raymond's office. (The 1930 U.S. census lists her occupation at the convent as "clerk" in "chg. of telephone.") The Good Shepherd sisters left no record of complaints about the difficulties involved in caring for Sister Thorn, such as moving her to bathroom and bathing facilities, carrying meals to her room, washing extra linens and bandages, and helping her dress. Yet Margaret required close and

Sister Mary Crown of Thorns at the Peekskill convent, ca. 1932. She is seated in her wheelchair, which is concealed by her habit, and is wearing the customary garb of the Good Shepherd congregation, with its silver locket and crucifix. (Courtesy of the Sisters of the Good Shepherd, Jamaica, N.Y.)

constant attention if what McParlan reported seeing during his visit was true: "Our Little Sister Thorn is in very sad condition. Her entire right side of chest, arm and down to hand [is] badly swollen and now she cannot even use a fork or plug in the telephone as she used to do."[40]

Margaret's increasing dependency placed burdens on her community, but it did not lack antecedents in hagiography. Teresa of Avila became paralyzed in her legs after recovering from a bout of a seemingly fatal illness in 1539. The medieval saint Lydwine of Schiedam, canonized in 1890, was paralyzed by an ice-skating accident. The Good Shepherd congregation had its own model of worthy suffering in Sister Divine Heart of Germany, who suffered from myelitis and had to be carried to chapel to pray, all the while being prepared through her suffering to carry out her "secret commission" from Christ.

Margaret's continued presence at Peekskill catalyzed two power struggles within the Good Shepherd leadership—one between Mother Raymond and Sister St. Germaine Dooley, a Peekskill member, and the other between

Mother Raymond and Sister Mary of the Good Shepherd Tellers, the current provincial of New York.[41] Sister St. Germaine was already responsible for "much of the restlessness" among the sisters regarding Margaret Reilly. She claimed that Margaret had been admitted to the congregation by an uncanonical procedure and that the sisters had bowed to pressure from secular advocates. In Mother Raymond's version of the story, Margaret was remaining at Peekskill rather than moving to the novitiate in Manhattan because "the visitations [of Satan to the impressionable novices] would cause some to leave through fear." Further complicating matters, it seems that jealousy had flared between Mother Raymond and provincial Good Shepherd Tellers about who would care for Margaret. In Mother Raymond's opinion, "He [Jesus] has blessed me by leaving her in my care, much as our Mother Provincial would wish to take her with herself."[42] The other power struggle, between Mother Raymond and Sister St. Germaine, involved a list of five grievances made by a handful of the Peekskill Good Shepherd sisters:

1. Mother Raymond's strictness and her support for Margaret Reilly
2. Resentment of the novitiate transfer from Manhattan (despite the fact that the move was warranted)
3. Resentment against Margaret, whom they regarded as "a deceiver and an unworthy candidate for the community"
4. Disagreement with the purchase of a Bronx property as the future site of the 90th Street convent
5. Concern of the "outdoor" sisters about the color of their mantles

To resolve the matter, a priest was sent to confer with the sisters. All of them promised to stop gossiping and leave matters to their superiors. Sister St. Germaine had a sudden change of heart, admitting that her complaint to the archbishop about Margaret Reilly was without tangible proof and had derived from "a series of misunderstandings, unlimited gossip, wild rumors and anonymous letters." For her part, Mother Raymond delivered a spiritual interpretation of the events: "By seemingly miraculous intervention," she wrote, "Our Lord accomplished his designs in effecting the removal of the novitiate to Peekskill."[43] McParlan, already Margaret's partisan, likewise credited supernatural forces: "Margaret has been paralyzed from knees down since January. It is simply the work of our dear Lord for a special purpose."[44]

Hints of the lack of convent unanimity concerning Margaret Reilly's mystical experiences and reported stigmata surfaced in the letters of various sisters. Her major doubters included Sister Mary of St. Clotilda; Sister Mary of the Ascension, who found Margaret "too loquacious"; Sister Mary of St. Charles; and Sister Mary of St. David. Sister Mary of St. Paschal, the *pharmacienne*, reported that she was "not at all satisfied."[45] Likewise, Sister Mary Martin(a) was "not contented." But neighborhood friends remained staunch defenders of Margaret. Sister Tarcisius, one of the sisters who had known Margaret from childhood, said that she and "Little Sister" were very close friends. Their fathers even "went to Mass every morning [at St. Ignatius] and always sat in the same pew."[46] Surely this was proof that Margaret was trustworthy.

Skepticism also surfaced among Sister Thorn's detractors outside the convent, including priests who had close connections to the Good Shepherd communities. A New York Jesuit, James McGivney, already known to the sisters, expressed his lack of confidence in Margaret. He had given retreats at the 90th Street house and was present during the height of the controversy surrounding her, including debates on her admission into the congregation. Speaking against Margaret, McGivney summarized some of his concerns in a "strictly confidential" letter to Herbert Thurston, a Jesuit in London known for his scholarly interest in mystical phenomena. "She is a notoriety seeker," McGivney wrote emphatically. "She apparently gave false claims about former employees (great ladies), and sent telegrams herself in their names vouching for her."[47] His comment referred to Margaret's claim that she was a friend of Lady Margaret Armstrong, an American married to a British diplomat who was active in Catholic philanthropy.[48] According to Father McGivney, this was just one more bit of evidence of Margaret's deceptive practices. She had once falsely presented herself to the parish sodality as the artist who had painted a banner of the Virgin Mary, an item that in fact she had bought and then passed off as her own work. While this episode seems relatively minor, it contributed to Margaret's dossier of grandiose behavior. More evidence of Margaret's devious actions surfaced during and after a failed romance in her life. According to Father McGivney, Margaret was extremely jealous of the nurse who had married Margaret's surgeon, Dr. Thomas Gallen. McGivney claimed further that in her resentment, Margaret had sent a series of threatening anonymous letters to Gallen. "This is only a small part of her megalomania," said McGivney. At that time, he remembered, Margaret had gone around sporting a ring that she falsely claimed was a gift from Dr. Gallen.[49] In the convent, Father McGivney reckoned, Margaret had fooled the superior with her fake stigmata and thus had secured a wide latitude for activities for which other sisters would have been reprimanded. As for the crucifix on her breast and the wall, the Jesuit suggested that a commercial stamp could have produced it. Somewhat cryptically, he added to Father Thurston: "She

One of the buildings at Mount St. Florence, the Good Shepherd convent in Peekskill, New York. (Photo supplied by Sisters of the Good Shepherd, Jamaica, N.Y.)

is capable of spending money to get herself known." McGivney bluntly dismissed McParlan's endorsement of Margaret: "His testimony is worthless."[50]

McGivney also had a low opinion of the way that the Good Shepherd sisters had handled the crisis within their community. As he saw it, "those on top seem to have no tops." "My theory," McGivney told Father Thurston, "is that Mother Theresa [i.e., Mother Raymond] after removal from office saw a *Deus ex machina* in Kate [Margaret]. This saint given to her was her defense, and proof that all against her were wrong. To my mind this explains very much." He also blamed the Good Shepherd Visitor from Ireland who had thrown her support behind "this girl" Margaret "instead of standing by her own Sisters." Sister Thorn has made the superiors a "laughing stock" and has "done much harm to their fine community," McGivney concluded.[51] McParlan was also critical of the religious leadership's treatment of Sister Thorn, but with a different twist: he regarded the male authorities as ineffectual, blaming Archbishop Hayes for caving in to pressure from Thorn's enemies in New York, who had taken their complaints about Hayes's protection of her to the pope.[52]

Even with these foes, Margaret Reilly was becoming a local celebrity. The public began to comment on her bodily manifestations, based on what they learned from priests and sisters who had seen or heard of her. Father Bertrand Barry (1866–1930), a Passionist priest, wrote a "slushy sloppy" letter that started the notoriety by providing much erroneous information about

Sister Thorn. Soon, Archbishop Hayes began to be deluged with requests to see the "good young lady with the Crucifix in her body" from numerous clergy in his archdiocese and elsewhere.[53] One priest in Wisconsin heard a rumor that Hayes himself possessed thorns broken from Margaret's crown: "The whole affair is so beautifully spiritual," he wrote, "that I would like to have your assurance that it is really so."[54]

An obvious risk of keeping a singularly favored sister in the convent was the heating up of any jealousies, tensions, and conflicts already simmering in the community, and Peekskill was no exception. Additionally, organized attempts to favor Sister Thorn moved slowly because of the untimely death of her key protectors. Although Lukas Etlin could not imagine any criticism of "little Sister," his premature death in 1927 silenced the voice of a strong ally. Father Bertrand, whose fanciful report about Margaret stirred up so much trouble, died in 1930. The deaths of Thomas McParlan in 1928 and of Mother Raymond Cahill in 1939 were additional blows. After Cahill, who had served as the Good Shepherd provincial between 1929 and 1939, the succeeding provincial, Sister Mary of the Presentation Hannigan, entirely opposed Sister Thorn. Holding her position from 1939 to 1955, Hannigan worked to suppress Thorn's cult by purging the Good Shepherd community of Thorn's followers, dispersing them to other convents and erasing mention of Thorn in the order's records. The Good Shepherd leadership was also aware of the cache of anonymous letters that had been forwarded to Archbishop Hayes in the 1920s that did not portray Margaret Reilly in a saintly light, and they were not anxious to expose these to the public or to the *promotor fidei*, the "devil's advocate" in the event of an authorized canonization investigation.

Family Matters

Before Margaret looked for spiritual refuge at Peekskill, her sense of self had been developed in a rigorously devout Irish family whose parents raised their children to fear the judgment of God. Whereas Margaret's family left evidence of their moral principles, they provided few clues about their outlook on America. If a Catholic "myth" of success involved the acceptance of suffering as inevitable, then the Reillys were tested on both the religious and economic fronts. In their premigration lives, the parents had known the privation that was embedded in Irish cultural and economic experience. In Ireland, the family unit had been conditioned by land and food scarcity, British colonization, the threat of downward mobility, and monasticism. Religion, especially since the Great Famine (1845–52), emphasized the Christian value of suffering. By capitalizing on that crisis, the Catholic

Church in Ireland had experienced a revival, inspiring Catholics as a source of identity, norms, and nationalism. The Catholic faith helped define and mobilize the Irish against the despised English colonizers, but it was no guarantor of economic success. In New York City, Irish Americans observed that they had escaped the yoke of the English only to find it again in the militant political Anglo-Saxonism of the United States. Their suspicion of the status quo in America put pressures upon families like the Reillys to survive by repeating the forms of localism that they had known in Ireland as established in new connections to New York's neighborhoods, parishes, and Catholic organizations and schools.

Ethnic identity remained a significant predictor of upward mobility within the city's Catholic immigrant populations. An Irish American family had opportunities to climb the social ladder, as Patrick Reilly demonstrated. After the Civil War, Roman Catholics comprised nearly 75 percent of the industrial working class and were concentrated in the nation's cities. The rise of a "Hibernarchy" in the United States between the 1850s and the 1920s guaranteed Irish Catholics pride of place in the priesthood, the episcopacy, and many women's religious orders but also in the nation's civic institutions—city governments, political parties, the police, and public schools. The years 1900 to 1920 were crucial to the process of Irish American integration, which led them to seek respectability above all else. Several programs created in the prewar decades demonstrated how Catholics tempered their separatist tendencies with a nationalist one, including temperance programs that appealed to the upwardly mobile second generation; the creation of a "fourth degree" by the Knights of Columbus to reward Catholics who displayed "conspicuous deeds of patriotism"; and the Holy Name Society for men, which flourished in virtually every parish and sought to stamp out swearing and blaspheming.[55]

Given its investment in the local, the practical, the patriotic, and the profitable, Irish America was hardly the place one expected to find curiosities like stigmatics. Nor did Irish Catholicism lend itself to the physical expressiveness that characterized these bleeding prodigies. Since the Great Famine, Irish piety had been marked by Jansenist severity and denial of the body, closer to its Calvinist rivals than to the Baroque flamboyance and embodied spirituality associated with Catholicism in Spain, Italy, and Austria. In supporting the stigmata and visions of Sister Thorn, twentieth-century Catholics found a way to continue the battles of the so-called Long Reformation.[56] Where Protestants denied the efficacy of the saints and limited the presence of the body in religion, Sister Thorn would be their rebuttal. Her wounds, and the rituals surrounding her, including the Sacred Heart cult, were the gestures of American Catholics within and against a Protestant landscape barren of these practices.

The Reilly children, rather than their parents, faced the dilemma that vexed the Catholic community in the 1930s: "If the spirit of suffering was intrinsic to Catholicism, then what was the true nature of Catholic success?"[57] Thirty years ago, William Halsey addressed the issue of Catholics' relationship to capitalism in the United States. He theorized that the Catholic generation of 1920 to 1940 was inoculated from the complexity of ethical questions stemming from their rising incomes because of the black-and-white answers provided by the church's neo-Thomist theology, which permitted Catholics to retain a naïve perspective on their compromises with success as their fortunes improved after World War I. Halsey found that the various pieces of the Catholic subculture, especially education, boosted the Irish to bourgeois gentility, while the formidable edifice of neo-Thomism prevented self-doubt about getting ahead by insulating Catholics from turning a critical glance on themselves and upon Protestant individualism and capitalism.

Evidence suggests that the Reilly family lay somewhere on the spectrum between immigration and adaptation, between innocence and assimilation. Margaret's parents were both born in Ireland, while their extended kin included nuns in Ireland and Irish-born nuns living in America. Their cultural milieu continued to be Irish, and they prospered enough to move to better housing in northern Manhattan, but their economic progress was unstable due to the variations in the building trade that was Mr. Reilly's livelihood. The financial comfort that they achieved could not be taken for granted by the next generation; Mr. Reilly's construction and contracting career advanced to a certain point and then suffered from the consequences of an unforeseeable setback.

In New York, the family's routine cleaved to the rhythms of the religious calendar in food and prayer practices, which inspired them to perform a wealth of devotional rituals on a daily or weekly basis. If the Reilly family did not express any apparent signs of conforming to an "Anglo" American identity, it was because certain structural conditions permitted them to live as though already part of the dominant group in the United States, nurtured by what Halsey termed "American Catholic innocence."[58] In brief, as for many Irish Catholics, the Reillys' faith became a refuge and a blinder. The family was surrounded by a network of Irish Catholics at home, in the parish, at school, and at work and used those ethnic contacts to advance in the United States. They remained close to relatives in Ireland, but their American relations included a cousin who was integrated enough to manage the New York sports team that represented "the national pastime."

Mr. and Mrs. Reilly could not have predicted that their daughter would receive the stigmata, but as was typical of many Irish families, they gave two of their seven children to the church. Such close connections between parish and family had been widely observed in Irish Catholicism, a pattern that the Reillys continued in the United States. Before her marriage, Margaret's mother, Mary McLoughlin, had herself considered becoming a Presentation nun in Ireland.[59] Mary achieved that goal vicariously through her son Thomas, who became a priest, and her daughter Margaret, who hoped to become a sister. Her two nieces were already nuns in Ohio.

At the time of her marriage to Patrick Reilly, Mary McLoughlin bought a large picture of the Annunciation. When she became pregnant, she knelt before it daily "with her hands folded in prayer."[60] She bore five girls and two boys, all of whom reached adulthood.[61] Margaret was the youngest child, born on July 25, 1884. Her brother John died prematurely, as did her favorite sister, Annabelle Carmelita, who died at age twenty-six.[62] On July 29 Margaret's parents baptized her at their parish, the Church of St. John the Evangelist at 55th Street and 1st Avenue in New York City. Her godfather was her mother's nephew, recently arrived from Ireland. He was unfamiliar with his role in the christening, and when the family arrived at the church, to Mrs. Reilly's surprise, he laid the infant in front of the altar to the Virgin Mary instead of standing at the baptismal font with Margaret in his arms.[63]

Numerous stories of Margaret's childhood reveal religious influences that contributed later to her profound sense of unworthiness as well as her sense of chosenness. Even as a child, she used toys to express her early and intense devotion to Jesus. Margaret preferred her crucifix to a doll and treated the former as such, taking it for walks in her doll buggy, wrapping it to keep Jesus warm, and hugging it to her at night.[64] When her daughter required discipline, Mrs. Reilly threatened to take away the crucifix as punishment. Margaret was a delicate child, a loner who did not make many friends while she was "in the world."[65] She even described her mother as her "only friend." To assuage her loneliness, Margaret spoke often to her guardian angel and played games by herself as instructed by Jesus.[66] Early on, Margaret discovered penitential practices, such as putting cinders and rocks in her shoes as a form of self-mortification—learned from the Sisters of Charity who staffed her parochial school.[67] When Mrs. Reilly noticed piles of grit on Margaret's bedroom floor, Margaret informed her that "Sister said we would become saints if we hurt ourselves."[68] She drew upon this advice for the rest of her life. The devotional culture of Catholicism could exact a heavy toll on those who learned from childhood to structure the self around the notion that love was inextricably linked to the renunciation of will, to guilt, and to pain.

The Reilly family moved from midtown to 172 East 94th Street in the developing Upper East Side, somewhat north of the elegant Beaux Arts and neo-Renaissance mansions already lining Fifth and Park Avenues and just before that area became home to the city's most expensive real estate.[69] (The family of Jimmy Cagney also moved to Yorkville on East 96th Street at this time.) The Irish often chose to move within the boundaries of Manhattan because they could get more for their money once they left the lower part of the island. The Reillys' move northward preceded by a good twenty years the larger-scale Irish migrations to the Bronx, Queens, and Brooklyn that occurred when a building boom allowed Irish families to achieve a better life and own a bigger house in the boroughs without a parallel rise in income. As one study has found, "Between the wars, Irish wages were often sufficient to enable a family to raise their standard of living simply by moving."[70] Not only were the New York Irish moving; they also were moving away. Although not perceived as such during Margaret's lifetime, the Irish presence in New York City was already beginning to decline, and Manhattan was no longer the Irish stronghold it had been since the colonial era. In 1910 about 88 percent of the city's Irish immigrants lived in Manhattan and Brooklyn; fifty years later, more than 50 percent were living in the Bronx and Queens.[71]

When a real estate corporation compiled a list of factors that prompted New York City Irish families to move within Manhattan, it concluded that women played a significant role in the choice, seeking, among other priorities, proximity to churches and schools.[72] The Reillys' new parish, St. Francis de Sales, was indeed nearby—only two blocks from their home at 96th Street between Park and Lexington Avenues. Margaret neatly inscribed her home address in the sodality manual she received there. Lay participation in Catholic organizations was strong at St. Francis and included the Children of Mary, populated with girls like Margaret; the Holy Name Society for men, with 250 members; and the Junior Holy Name Society with 100 members. The membership of St. Aloysius and Angels' sodalities totaled 500. The parish also hosted a Sacred Heart League, a Rosary Society, the Society for the Propagation of the Faith, religious education classes for children, the St. Vincent de Paul Society for charitable work, and the Debt Paying Association. Sunday school was taught by the Sisters of Mercy, assisted by nearly 100 lay teachers.[73]

Although the Reillys lived close to St. Francis, they also joined St. Ignatius Loyola parish ten blocks away at East 84th Street and Park Avenue.[74] St.

Ignatius was founded in 1851 and entrusted to the Jesuits in 1866. The grand Italian Renaissance structure—designed by William Schickel, a parishioner and German emigrant, in partnership with Isaac E. Ditmars—was begun in 1895 and dedicated in 1898 by Archbishop Michael Corrigan.[75] For over a century, St. Ignatius Church has served as the parish of prominent Manhattan Catholics, including Jacqueline Kennedy Onassis, whose funeral was conducted there in 1994.

When Margaret's parents grew older, it was more convenient for them to attend weekday masses at St. Francis, although they kept their pew at St. Ignatius. Pew rentals were a creation of the nineteenth century to provide financial support for parishes. They were common but not universal; they endured among American Catholic urban parishes until about 1920, when parish debt declined and weekly collections from the congregation often began to surpass the amounts raised by pew rentals. Only wealthier families could afford rentals, anyway, and some Catholics regarded the practice as undemocratic. (In this matter, at least, they found that it was best to adopt American principles.) The Reillys' connections to multiple parishes gave Margaret many opportunities for service to the church. As a member of the Guard of Honor at Blessed Sacrament Church (the family's third parish affiliation), she watched over the consecrated Host as it was displayed on the altar for individual prayer and adoration. While her appointed hour was on Thursday from 2:00 to 3:00 P.M., Margaret often remained two additional hours until the ritual of benediction had been completed.[76]

The Reilly parents defined the traditionalism of the family. When they moved uptown, Patrick and Mary raised their seven children in a devout, even severe, Christian environment. One account of Margaret's childhood noted that "Mrs. Reilly was insistent upon banishing all levity from her home."[77] "No loud voices in the house" was her instruction to her children. Her husband supported and even set the devotional tone of family life. Not only did Mr. Reilly lead daily prayers, but each day he also embraced the crucifix in the entrance hallway before going to work, inspiring his children to kiss the feet of Christ each time they left the house.[78] Patrick attended Mass each morning as well and often returned to church on his way home from work to pray the Stations of the Cross. His spiritual leadership embodied the ideal of "patriarchal domesticity" for his children's religious education and bridged the space between home and society by subsuming everything under the leadership of Christ.[79]

Mr. Reilly's career endured a severe setback in 1911 when a pedestrian was killed accidentally by a dynamite explosion at a construction site at 72nd Street and Columbus Avenue, where he and his son had been hired by the city to lay drainage pipes. Margaret recalled that her father was nearly ruined by the consequences.[80] Churchgoing and hardworking, he was the polar opposite of the legendary brawling, drunken Irishman, and yet even he ended up facing homicide charges and near financial failure from a workplace mishap. Patrick died clutching a crucifix on Good Friday in 1917, having been privileged to witness the raised red corpus that had appeared on his daughter's skin just a few months before.[81]

At the entrance to the Reilly home, a crucifix and a font of holy water hung by the front door, and the family recited the Rosary together each evening. In addition, Margaret and her mother prayed the Rosary daily before noon at the oratory devised by Margaret in a bedroom that was made available after her sisters had married.[82] These at-home rituals drew laypeople closer to the routines of monastic life, in which the monks or nuns observed the hours of the day by reciting certain prayers. The domestication of such rituals by families can also be understood as part of a process to build a "Catholic International" that began in the nineteenth century when the church attempted to merge traditional religious structures and identities with modern technologies and a global outlook focused upon leadership emanating from the Vatican. One goal of the Catholic International was to strengthen sectarian politics in Europe and to restore Catholic control that had been lost since the French Revolution and during the Kulturkampf, but its progress in the United States faced challenges from a different social milieu in which Catholics began as the interlopers and underdogs.[83] The tensions implicit in the attempts to establish European Catholic culture in America surfaced in the events surrounding Margaret's stigmatization, but its origin was the intense ritualization of family life that created a symbiotic bond to the Catholic Church.

Margaret's parochial-school education reinforced her family's pious practices and connections to parish life. Education of Catholic children had become a lightning rod in New York since Catholics had challenged Protestant control of American society on the issue of the public schools. Since the mid-nineteenth century, Protestant leaders had regarded America's common schools as tools of nonsectarian assimilation. New York City became a testing ground for this assumption when the archbishop of New York, John Hughes, assailed the so-called public schools as bastions of Protestantism.[84] By defending their freedoms as citizens, Catholic parents argued for their prerogative in school choice. The church moved in a different direction, however. Following the Baltimore Plenary Council's decree of 1884, the year of Margaret's birth, Catholic parents were encouraged to avoid public schools altogether by sending their children only to parochial institutions.[85]

Blessed Sacrament Church, West 71st Street, Manhattan. One of
Margaret's favored churches, Blessed Sacrament is where her confessor,
Monsignor Matthew Taylor, served as pastor. (Wurts Bros., *West 71st
Street, Blessed Sacrament Church, ca. 1919*; from the collections of the
Museum of the City of New York)

Margaret's school, St. Francis de Sales, was not one of the city's select
Catholic institutions for girls, such as the Manhattanville Sacred Heart
School, which educated Catholic daughters of the most affluent families.[86]
Rose Fitzgerald Kennedy (1890–1995), for example, was enrolled in the
Manhattanville class of 1910. In 1905 the Manhattanville school, originally
located at 17th Street in Manhattan, had moved to Maplehurst, an eleven-
acre estate in the Bronx. Catholic orders of women were purchasing and
occupying a series of former estates of Protestant elites that stretched from
Maplehurst in the Bronx, up the Hudson River past Mount St. Florence in
Peekskill, and on to Mount St. Vincent in Riverdale, the residence of the

Sisters of Charity. By 1914, Manhattanville was the largest Sacred Heart institution in the United States, with 95 nuns, 168 boarders, and a parish school with 530 students. But the Good Shepherd convent at Peekskill was not far behind, boasting a total of nearly 400 students in 1910.[87] What distinguished the Good Shepherd sisters from the Sacred Heart sisters was an invisible veil of class distinctions, vestiges of European social formations. Even though in 1914 nearly one-third of the members of the Sacred Heart congregation were coadjutrix sisters—namely, the second-class portion of the congregation who performed manual labor for the community—the mystique of the elite Sacred Heart "Madame" (and the ungrammatical "Madames") who comprised the upper level of choir sisters has prevailed nearly to the present day.[88] The Good Shepherd sisters, by contrast, were a slightly newer French congregation that attracted a cross-class distribution, even while their membership in New York was a fairly homogeneous group dominated by Irish and Irish American women.

Margaret was not destined for Manhattanville or the Sacred Heart Madames, and her educational progress at her parochial school was poor. As Mother Raymond explained, young Margaret was so drawn to Jesus that she could not concentrate upon anything else. In recounting Margaret's relationship with the Lord, Sister Carmelita used the metaphor of her seduction by her Divine Lover.[89] Years later, Margaret's inability to sleep more than two hours a night in the convent was also ascribed to the "vehemence of His love."[90] According to Margaret's chroniclers, God's grace worked upon her even in her childhood to detach her from the demands of the world, and thus she stopped attending school after seventh grade. As if to punctuate this fact, a youthful demeanor remained one of Margaret's defining features. Even when she was nearly forty years old, physicians and priests continued to refer to Margaret as an innocent, nearly illiterate girl.

At school, the Reilly children received religious preparation for the three sacraments of confession, Communion, and confirmation. These sacraments were administered at different ages and in different order than has been customary for Catholics since Vatican II. In the 1910s, children generally made their first confession at about age seven, followed by Communion at eleven or twelve and confirmation during adolescence. Following this custom, Margaret made her first confession in 1891 at age seven.[91] Five years later at her confirmation, Margaret chose the name of Dolores for Mary, Mother of Sorrows.[92]

The children were encouraged to join in allied practices, including prayers to the Blessed Sacrament and Sacred Heart of Jesus.[93] The latter devotion had grown popular in the nineteenth century with a goal of restoring the "social reign of Christ" through the family. As a family event led by the father, the "enthronement" movement led millions of Catholics to place an image of the Sacred Heart in their homes and, ideally, to install a statue of Christ as the King of the family. Family behavior would reflect Christ's influence by avoiding swearing and un-Christian books and pictures, and by promising to attend Mass, respect the Sabbath, fast on Fridays and during Lent, and hold family prayer sessions that included prayerful defenses of the pope and the institution of the papacy itself. That Margaret's parents received Holy Communion daily was an unusual thing when "probably only three or four persons in the parish" did so.[94] After making her own First Communion, Margaret also secured special permission to become a daily communicant.[95] This represented some hardship, obliging her to walk ten blocks before breakfast to attend Mass and then return home for a quick meal before walking to school.

Margaret also developed a fondness for the Stations of the Cross. (She sometimes prayed the stations three times in one day, until a sister told her to stop.) The Reillys also pursued a stricter regime of abstinence from meat than the church required. They avoided meat three days each week rather than only on Fridays. For this sacrifice, they knew that they were receiving extra indulgences and were helping the souls in Purgatory reach heaven more quickly. Although it seems that the Reilly family could afford meat for supper, they chose to deny themselves for purely penitential reasons. Margaret's abstemious eating habits as an adult may have continued a lifelong pattern of denial fostered at home.

Through their daily rituals and education, the Reilly children—whose Irish-born parents were members of the Great Famine generation, with its convented aunts and extended family on both sides of the Atlantic—exemplified the continued success of the Irish embrace of the Devotional Revolution. When this process began in Ireland as a response to the social disintegration caused by the chaos of the Great Famine, it bound Irish Catholics more closely to the universal center of the church in Rome and to the local life of the parish, which tried to discourage any household practices that contained vestiges of paganism.[96] In Ireland, devotions to the Sacred Hearts of Jesus and Mary were commended to Catholic families by the postfamine cohorts of newly minted, Roman-educated Irish priests. In further hopes of increasing Catholic fervor and replacing the boisterous family wakes and pilgrimages to holy wells, lakes, and mountains, the church emphasized the cult of the saints to such a degree that the annual calendar was virtually filled up with saints' feast days. The observance of feast and fast days was a constant reminder of Catholic difference in America, of practices and relationships not shared by the Protestant and secular enemies of the church.

This rekindled Irish faith transferred itself to the United States. Carmelita Quinn, one of Margaret's biographers, recalled that even on the plains of Nebraska, her own grandfather, an illiterate Irish immigrant, walked a half mile daily to get the morning newspaper, seeking news of the pope's health. "Pope Leo XIII was dying," she marveled, "and here on another hemisphere was an Irish emigrant, with a Rosary in one hand, the daily newspaper in the other, proving loyalty to the Holy See by concern for the health of the Vicar of Christ!"[97] Margaret herself received a constant flow of Irish-themed holy cards and delivered one divinely inspired poem, "Ireland, Hope!," which summed up the intimacy between the Irish and the church:

> The Faith of St. Patrick,
> Thy glory and fame,
> To root out forever
> Was tyranny's aim.
> But each ruddy life-drop
> That sprinkled thy sod
> Served only to bind thee
> More closely to God.[98]

Benefiting from the unprecedented emergence of mass-production techniques for printed religious materials and manufactures, Irish Americans supplemented printed texts in their homes with religious items—inexpensive color lithographs of Jesus, Mary, and the saints, as well as objects such as small altars, holy-water fonts, and statues. Calendars, religious certificates, charity boxes, samplers, statues, and wall brackets filled out the domestic decor.[99] Especially popular in Catholic homes were images of the Sacred Heart, noted above, which were granted special indulgences by the pope in 1915.[100] Each of these items would assume significant roles in Margaret's life.

Around the date of her first confession in 1896, Margaret was introduced to Monsignor Matthew Taylor, who became her confessor until his death in 1914. For eighteen years, Taylor, a sought-after spiritual director in New York, exercised a powerful influence over Margaret. Mother Raymond wrote approvingly that the young girl "saw in Msgr. Taylor the representative of God, and she submitted entirely to his directions."[101] Margaret's selection of Taylor marked a spiritual turning point that developed the trait of obedience, which was one of the hallmarks of the ideal nun. Under Taylor's direction, she was made to remain standing during an appointment with him, although she had arrived already exhausted. He added further tests, such as sending Margaret to buy him two potatoes (an embarrassing task because stores were reluctant to sell such a small quantity); asking her to refrain from ever looking in a mirror; and requiring her to walk in the rain without an umbrella or boots on her feet.[102] At Taylor's request, she performed the painful daily penance of kneeling on her hands for fifteen minutes, and she began wearing a hair shirt on Fridays. Taylor's direction reflects the pastoral formation of priests of his generation, emphasizing unquestioning obedience to authority. This kind of self-abasement was understood by Catholics as a means to increase spiritual humility, not as arbitrary punishment. Taylor's demands prepared Margaret for the convent life she later sought, a life centered around constant self-denial and perfect conformity to rules that insisted that human suffering served some higher spiritual purpose.[103]

Margaret's siblings were not entirely impressed. They found their sister to be annoyingly pious and complained that they were being deprived of new clothes by their parents just because Margaret had declared that she was satisfied with hers. Margaret's brother and sisters concluded glumly that "she will die in church."[104] Following Father Taylor's death in 1914, when Margaret was obliged to find another priest at Blessed Sacrament to hear her confession, she would shift from a crowded confessional to an emptier one. "This she did from a motive of charity," wrote Sister Carmelita a decade later.[105] Carmelita's judgment is but one instance of a dossier of sanctity being constructed retrospectively for Margaret. Two further examples of this tactic appear in Carmelita's claim that "Our Lord often used Margaret as His instrument in reclaiming souls." Carmelita's "proofs" of this were the occasions when Margaret engaged strangers on the streetcar and "her persuasive language frequently was the means of bringing the erring person back to God," and Margaret's impromptu street baptism of a Jewish girl who later married a Catholic.[106] No detail was too insignificant, and each one was chosen to highlight Margaret's saintliness.

Despite her virtuous habits, Margaret was delayed in receiving her postulant's veil at Peekskill. Ordinarily, the Good Shepherd order invested a postulant with her habit and veil after the first six months, but Margaret's probation lasted two years. Even eight days prior to her vows ceremony in 1923, she was still being dogged by opponents in the community who tried to expel her. Among their several tactics, Mother Raymond noted, was negative gossip. After "Margaret had once undergone an operation for appendicitis," wrote the superior, "her enemies endeavored to prove that this operation was performed at a private hospital for another cause." It was rumored that Margaret was having an abortion, and the fact that her doctor was a gynecologist hardly helped. Father Brady, however, claimed that he examined the medical records and "found the true nature of the operation."[107] There is no evidence that Margaret entered the hospital to have anything other than an appendectomy (or ulcer surgery, as was stated elsewhere), but the rumors remained as part of the record, tied to speculation about her failed romance with her surgeon.

On December 8, 1923, the Feast of the Immaculate Conception, Sister Mary of the Crown of Thorns was finally able to make her preliminary vows as a Good Shepherd. McParlan remembered that on that date two years earlier, at the request of Archbishop Hayes, he had arrived with his wife to perform the task of examining the miraculous cross on Margaret's wall. When Margaret had been transferred from her original cell at Peekskill to Mother Raymond's room, the crucifix "flew" from Margaret's breast to the wall "when the investigation of the chemist was to take place." McParlan rubbed chemicals on the mark to remove it but declared: "The more I rubbed, the redder it became." When it was time for him to try the same test on the crucifix on Margaret's skin, however, as the linen patch covering her heart was removed, "to their astonishment" the cross had completely disappeared, with no trace of a scar or wound. On the day she made her vows two years later, Margaret enjoyed a vision of the Virgin Mary, who remained with her during her ceremony. Margaret's state of prayer apparently was so deep that "she seemed insensible to all around her, and those who witnessed the ceremony could discern that she was being supernaturally favored."[108] The cross on Margaret's skin reappeared three times in the next week and then disappeared entirely around December 15.

Another episode involving this mark has all but disappeared from Sister Thorn's redacted history, although that likely reflects its uncertain origin. Margaret's confessor, Monsignor Taylor, took a picture of Margaret's chest marking and sent the negative of his photograph to France. The French publishing house responded that they already had the same picture or plate, advising Taylor to save money by not insisting upon using his new picture to make prints. This information seemed "queer" to Father John McGinn (who was also involved in the case).[109] Taylor's reaction is unknown, but he must have wondered if Margaret had used an existing holy card as a template for her chest marking, like a decal. Did she also paste this image on the Peekskill convent wall in an attempt to convince others that it was a miraculous reproduction of the crucifix above her heart? Margaret had already been caught in several lies to enhance her reputation—passing off the art of another painter as her own at a parish fair, claiming that financier Bernard Baruch was a personal confidant, providing fake letters from previ-

ous employers, falsely claiming to be engaged, and "boasting how some of
the wealthiest men in the country would visit her and tell love."[110] By surrounding herself with an aura of divine favor, Margaret could easily draw
upon the legends of the saints she had learned in church and school, including Margaret Mary Alacoque, who burned or carved the name of Jesus into
her own breast, and Anne Catherine Emmerich, whose mark on her chest
copied the unique crucifix on her parish altar.

Suffering is implicated in the religious name that Margaret Reilly chose
in 1923: Sister Mary of the Crown of Thorns. Eight years earlier, on the first
day that her breast was imprinted, Jesus had named her "Thorn" to signify
that she would one day wear the "cap of thorns" of mystical suffering, and
through her suffering with him, bring sinners back to God. Jesus revealed
that this was a special privilege: no one else enjoyed this "intimate union
with Jesus to whom our Lord has given this name." Jesus repeated his message on several occasions, as on January 18, 1917: "Already I have named you
'Thorn,' but in a few years you will be the 'Lily of my heart.'"[111] From Jesus,
Margaret even received supernatural knowledge of the condition of various
sinners who had rejected the Lord's appeals to them because they resented
her exposure of their faults. "As a result," noted Sister Carmelita, "they
spread calumnious reports about Thorn which brought upon her a bitter
persecution." Nonetheless, she would bravely endure further suffering to
atone for their sins.[112]

Margaret offered up her agonies on behalf of priests and sisters. Her
acceptance of vicarious suffering illustrates the impact of the flourishing
cult of spiritual victimhood among Roman Catholics, in which a divinely
chosen victim is able to obtain spiritual graces for others by transferring
their suffering onto herself. The more she abandoned herself to the Passion
of Christ, the more souls she could ransom. Accordingly, Sister Carmelita's
narrative highlighted numerous cases of Sister Thorn suffering for others,
extending well beyond her commission from Jesus to suffer for priests and
nuns. Sister Thorn was able to rescue "Mae," for instance, from a sinful
relationship with a freemason. Acting on behalf of Sister Thorn, Mother
Raymond telephoned the girl at her boardinghouse in New York City to
warn her not to meet her date that evening. While Mother Raymond was
speaking on the phone, demons threw Thorn from her bed and against the
wooden folding door in her room, where she struck her head. "In all such
attacks," Sister Carmelita Quinn reported with satisfaction, "the Litany of
the B.V.M. disarmed the demons."[113]

Given the gossip generated by those who witnessed the miraculous marking on Margaret's chest and wall, her difficulties did not end once her pos-

tulancy began. Instead, the naysayers continued their offensive, prompting Mother Raymond to take a tally of all the sisters under her leadership two months after Margaret's vows ceremony. A six-page document, dated February 9, 1924, summarizes the community opinion about Margaret's stigmatization. The tally included every sister at Peekskill and even the five women living at the fledgling RGS community in the Bronx on Atlantic and Hopkinson Avenues.[114] No doubt, Raymond was seeking to put an end to the wild rumors about Sister Thorn. After all, some sisters were "completely satisfied" or "satisfied" with the claims made about Margaret and did not protest her entrance into the congregation. One member, Martha Marie Crowley, remained such an ardent supporter of Thorn that after Thorn's death, the superior who succeeded Mother Raymond transferred Crowley to the Hartford, Connecticut, house as part of a plan to eliminate such sentiments among the New York Good Shepherds.[115]

The convent chronicle for Peekskill declared that "many" sisters saw the "Five Wounds" in September 1921. Mother Raymond even recalled inserting three fingers in the deep wounds that appeared on Margaret's chest and thighs. A convent visitor, Father Bertrand Barry, reported looking at the wounds in 1922, although his account has proved to be untrustworthy. Except for Dr. McParlan, physicians who examined Margaret found nothing wrong with her, however, not even signs of recent cuts or of healing scars on her skin. Even the evidence offered by Margaret's bloodied clothing was suspect. Although Mother Raymond had saved Margaret's blood-spotted shirt to present to her own superior, she recalled that, "when I went to the drawer to get it to show to Mother Provincial, all the blood stains were cut out; not one was left!"[116]

The list of twenty-four choir sisters appears on the first page of Raymond's report with the superior's comments. Among them, only two sisters stated that they had witnessed Margaret's stigmata: Sister Mary of St. Martina, the teacher of the Commercial Class, "saw open wounds on Reilly"; and Sister Mary of St. Agneta, the seventh-grade teacher, told Raymond that she "saw stigmata." Three sisters—Luthgarde, Anastasia, and St. Nicholas— were described as "enthusiastic" about Margaret. Still others were satisfied, or satisfied *and* enthusiastic. This camp included Sisters Leonilla, Tarcisius, Romaine, Martina, Angeline, Agneta, and Alexis. They were teachers of grades four through seven, and one was the roberian (who oversaw that religious garb was worn properly) and second mistress of novices. Sister Mary of the Immaculate Heart, the school principal and also the eighth-grade teacher, said she "believes strongly in" Margaret. Sister Holy Angels, a sacristan who performed machine work at the convent, called her a chosen soul. Sister St. Austin, however, was "*not* congenial with mother" concerning the matter.

On the third page, Mother Raymond listed the lay sisters (separated even on paper from the higher-ranking choir sisters). Hand-written comments appeared after the names of twenty-eight of the twenty-nine lay sisters. All were listed as "perfectly satisfied," except for three sisters. Two of these were not satisfied: the children's kitchen worker and the altar-breads maker; and Sister M. of St. Paschal, in charge of the pharmacy, was "not at all satisfied." Her doubt is significant because she would have seen whatever medications and bandages were administered to Margaret, as well as consulted with Raymond about how to treat the bleeding wounds.

On the fourth page of Mother Raymond's tally was a list of thirteen names who may be the *tourière* sisters.[117] It is less clear what happened with this group's poll. Maybe Mother Raymond ran out of energy, or maybe she did not intend for these votes to count. There are only notations for two sisters—one declaring to be "fine" and the other "not" followed by an illegible word (consulted? contented?). Three other sisters have the word "Habit" written after their name. This may refer to the recent complaints about the congregation's rule of providing a different veil for the outside sisters; or perhaps, like Margaret, these three sisters had recently received their habits and successfully entered the postulant stage.[118]

Before Margaret completed her vows, her path to the convent had been vexed by family, economic, and health problems. The recent death of her parents may have left her without enough income for the obligatory dowry to the convent. Even though some American congregations had decided to waive this European tradition, it was still customary for a sister's family to provide at least a $100 to $500 donation to the religious order. The Good Shepherds were neither Margaret's first choice of a religious congregation nor her first attempt to enter religious life. Seeking a rural, secluded convent after the death of her mother in 1920, Margaret had applied to enter the Ursulines of Brown County, Ohio, where her cousin was a member.[119] She had been refused for health reasons—specifically, the stomach ailment that made it impossible for her to observe the order's demanding fasting practices. Hoping to treat these problems, Margaret had an ulcer operation in February 1921, clutching a crucifix in her hand during surgery. She awoke from the anesthesia proclaiming "at the top of her voice": "Sweet Jesus, I love thee!"[120]

Margaret applied again to the Ursulines of Ohio soon after being rejected. William Ennis, SJ (1862–1925), of New York City, who had ministered to Margaret's mother during her blindness and final illness in 1920 and had arranged to help Margaret conceal the mark on her breast during her surgery, wrote a commendation for her. When Margaret's attempts to join the Ursulines faltered, Ennis put her in touch with the Good Shepherds. In the midst of an admirable career in teaching, administration, and mission work, Ennis had served at St. Ignatius parish from 1900 to 1903 and again from 1918 until his death in 1925. There, he presided over public novenas, especially to his favorite devotion, the Sacred Heart. Judging from the popularity of the *League of the Sacred Heart* newspaper in New York, Ennis was preaching to a Catholic population already touched by the Sacred Heart's intensity. Proof of his popularity with the parishioners at St. Ignatius was the fact that his confessional was always besieged by penitents on Saturday evenings. During Margaret's recovery from her first ulcer operation, Ennis met Sister Mary of the Good Shepherd Tellers, the New York provincial, while he was conducting a retreat at their convent in Albany.[121] He advised Margaret to meet with Tellers at the New York house on 90th Street as soon as possible.[122] Despite his initial enthusiasm for Margaret and his kindness toward her family, Ennis later repudiated her. His rejection must have been a hard blow for Margaret.[123]

At Peekskill, Margaret continued to face attacks, this time from invisible sources. As soon as she began bleeding from her feet and hands, Mother Raymond not only nursed her but also began to make entries in a notebook to document the surprising course of events. On September 14, the Feast of the Holy Cross, five sites across Margaret's body bled profusely. Over a period of three to five hours, "sheets, linens and all were profusely saturated with blood. The wounds in the hands, feet and side were plainly visible."[124] Just as spectacular, however, were the repeated assaults on Margaret's body by demons. An entire section of Raymond's chronicle was devoted exclusively to these malignant attacks that began in the final month of 1921 and persisted through the decade.[125] They became sporadic in 1926, when Margaret suffered a severe illness in the summer that became very extreme in August. "Satan often visited then," Raymond jotted down.[126] Later, Sister Carmelita used Raymond's notes to compose her own piece about Margaret titled "Assaults of the Evil Spirit."[127]

Mother Raymond and Sister Carmelita chronicled the work of demonic forces in such a way that reveals a matter-of-fact acceptance of their existence. On December 9, 1921, the day after her first veil reception at Peekskill, Margaret faced her first attack. "As she was eating her supper," wrote Carmelita, "her plate was broken, coffee spilt on the bed and she was pulled and dragged around for sometime."[128] "Sometime previous to that," she said, "M. had complained of noises in her room at night, but it was attributed to other causes." Throughout December, most of the unusual activity continued to involve ordinary household objects: the turpentine bottle left in Margaret's cell by Dr. McParlan was broken, flower vases were overturned, liquids were spilled, china was cracked, a holy-water font was broken, embroidery was burned, dress buttons were removed, and the glass on a picture of the Infant Jesus was shattered. "For some days," Raymond also recalled, "the whole house smelt of sulfur."[129] On the night of December 9, Margaret asked Raymond to stay with her and not let the "evil one" tempt her "with some evil suggestions he was making."[130] Satan often assumed the appearance of Jesus in an attempt to fool Margaret.[131] Several days later, a demon shattered a jelly dish against the radiator in Margaret's room.[132] These demons were apparently being kept at bay by divine decree: Mother Raymond reported that Thorn had said "that no matter what Satan tried to do to her, he always did it with some sort of an instrument. Never have his fiendish claws been permitted to touch her body."[133]

Given these descriptions, many of the forms of mischief that involved breaking, throwing, and spilling things could have been performed by Margaret herself, even from her wheelchair. For example, on December 11 her postulant's veil was burned or cut before supper. A replacement veil was then destroyed during the convent's evening recreation time.[134] There were moments even in communal life when a sister could be entirely alone and unobserved, and these provided opportunities for Margaret to vandalize. The slashing of Margaret's veil in chapel—and, later, the destruction of seven other veils and the slitting of her postulant's black gown at the abdomen area—were likewise easily accomplished by her, especially if the veils were the flimsy temporary items known as sham veils used prior to first vows. To some, the symmetrical slices in the fabric suggested the use of scissors rather than random tearing by a demon's claws.

The last time that shredded cloth had been featured in demonic activity in the United States was in the so-called Cliptown affair in early nineteenth-century Kentucky, where a Lutheran household was plagued by malicious events after denying the request of a dying Irish Catholic guest to secure a priest to administer the last rites.[135] At Peekskill, the tormentors seemed to rely on broken glass; stolen items; and destruction of clothing, food, and furniture. Perhaps some psychological significance was attached to the prevalence of spilled liquids such as coffee, turpentine, ink, and water, or perhaps they were simply at hand.

One result of the assaults on Margaret's body was her deformed feet. The devil was blamed for crippling her by twisting back her toes and ankles.[136] A more disturbing incidence of diabolical activity, however, occurred early in 1922, when Mother Raymond reported that a crucifix and a medal were torn off her own neck and pushed up Margaret's vagina. Raymond had to remove the crucifix and "to work over the abdomen to extricate the medal."[137] One can imagine the apprehension of the superior when called upon to dislodge the two articles from Margaret's body and her discomfort about reporting the incident. Sister Raymond's notes stated merely that Margaret had fears of impurity and was troubled by the evil spirit. Almost seamlessly, these events were interpreted by the nuns as Satan's attacks on Margaret's sexual purity, a familiar trope in countless hagiographies and in monastic life generally. Faced with the devil, for instance, Lukardis of Oberweimar was able to safeguard her innocence, so that even when she stood upside down, her dress did not fall away immodestly from her body.[138] Margaret endured taunts from the demons, who showed her "awful pictures" and "impure sights" that she declared were "far more painful to her than the beatings."[139] In a later vision, the Virgin Mary comforted Sister Thorn and told her that spirits would no longer assault her.

Even if they disagreed on the particulars of demonic activity, the Good Shepherd sisters believed that the manifestations of evil at Peekskill were an unavoidable part of the quest for sanctity. Otherwise, how can we understand Mother Raymond's notation that "this morning the demons ran around the room for about 15 minutes while the life of St. Colette was being read"?[140] As for the devils who conjured Margaret's impure thoughts, while they might seem to be throwbacks to earlier centuries, they actually were not unexpected visitors at the convent. Not unlike the Calvinist Puritans of seventeenth-century New England who discerned that they were bedeviled during the witch craze because they were the purest remnant of Christianity, monasteries and convents (and even holy lay individuals) were regarded by Roman Catholics as special targets of the devil and his legions. Wherever holiness was most concentrated, it seems, it was most tested.

Such attacks occurred commonly during transitional phases of training for religious life or preparing for the sacraments.[141] Demonic injuries to Margaret, for example, clustered around her postulancy in the spring and summer of 1922; most were attempts to thwart her reception of the Eucharist. Mother Raymond left many notes stating: "One attack at Holy Communion as usual." On another occasion, "Margaret sustained an awful attack after holy Communion near the confessional. Satan threw her down, tore off her postulant's cuffs, threw her shawl over the head of Sr. Mary of St. Luthgarde, seemingly to blind them so they could not protect Margaret; pulled feet to break them; slapped her face so it could be heard; jerked her and dragged her, then left her."

Thorn's experience, though outlandishly Gothic in an American context, had historical antecedents and was common enough in convents and among mystical women throughout the Catholic world. Two such contemporaries included Sister Josefa Menendez and Gemma Galgani. Menendez (1890–1923), a Spanish stigmatic and visionary, entered a Sacred Heart convent in Poitiers, France. There, she endured a hazardous postulancy much like Sister Thorn: "Persecution by the devil was particularly severe before her first vows, which she took on July 16, 1922."[142] On one occasion, the devil tortured Josefa by forcing her along a dark, narrow hallway full of stinking smoke and voices uttering obscenities and then driving her into a niche to endure six hours of agony there.[143] As with Margaret, "All the demon's efforts, during a long period of nine months, were concentrated on the destruction of Josefa's vocation." Like the observers of Sister Thorn, the editor cast Sister Josefa's life in terms of a "cosmic battle" between the "simple little Spanish nun and the supernatural powers."[144] An Italian laywoman, Gemma Galgani, who had died in 1903 and was beatified in Margaret's lifetime, likewise suffered *terribili assalti* from demons. Her hagiography was widely read by Margaret's generation. Satan's attacks on Margaret, Josefa, and Gemma are consistent with many more anecdotes reported by Father Herbert Thurston in his publications on mystical phenomena and hagiography. In the lives of the saints, these episodes represent virtue overcoming temptation, and they and perform the equally important function of reminding humans of the reality of Satan and his power and of the real consequences of evildoing. Through these tales of persecution, Roman Catholics were able to personify the abstract concept of evil in order to better fight it with prayers and virtuous strategies of resistance.

The humiliation of Margaret, Josefa, and Gemma at the hands of the Evil One also recalls centuries of Christian theological and popular traditions relating to a "heroics of virginity." Attacks on the chastity of persons preparing for lives of celibacy as members of religious orders is a long-standing theme in Christian hagiography. From medieval times, romance genres linked women's loss of virginity to their degradation and contrasted it with entrance into the convent.[145] For a nubile woman, diabolical attacks were tests of her virginity before her wedding, whereas for religious aspirants, they were trials of fidelity in their marriage to Christ.[146] For male saints, such as Anthony and Augustine, who wrote at length about the ferocity of their sexual temptations, a large degree of misogyny and fear of women also inspired their writing, much of which made its way into Catholic lore addressing the weakness of women.

Finally, the fact that the unusual episodes afflicting Margaret were recorded dutifully by Mother Raymond suggests the superior's anticipation of a future moment when Margaret might be investigated by the church. Because of her awareness of such precedents in Christian hagiography, Raymond was careful to document other preternatural events in Margaret's convent life by compiling lists of credible witnesses. Convinced of the conflict between good and evil taking place within Sister Thorn's body, her companions described themselves as privileged witnesses to the eternal battle in Christianity between God and Satan. In retrospect, however, some of Margaret's mishaps sound like poltergeist pranks that could have been self-inflicted, while others were clear imitations (or repetitions) of events in the lives of women saints who endured harassment, rape, or martyrdom.[147] When Margaret suffered from a mattress thrown on top of her and blows to her face and legs, it reprised an event in Anne Catherine Emmerich's hagiography—the first English translation of which had appeared by 1885 and was quite familiar to Father Lukas Etlin. Additional demonic activity at Peekskill included window smashing and the unsettling noise of Margaret's face being slapped without any visible cause.[148] At times, Margaret was thrown bodily from her chair; once, she was strangled in bed by the handkerchief around her neck, on which was hung a crucifix.[149]

The devil at Peekskill was a shape-shifter, taking on the forms of a black cat, a rat, a seal, slime, and handsome and ugly men. Similar black cat episodes appeared in the life of Gemma Galgani, which Margaret possibly learned of in a letter from Etlin, or possibly Etlin inserted the event into Margaret's biography by inadvertently merging the lives of the two women. Father Bertrand Barry offered a second cat anecdote. He stated that a Franciscan told him of two fellow friars who visited the Peekskill convent in late January 1922 in hopes of meeting Margaret. When they arrived, they saw three cats in the doorway "seeming to try to bar the way; facetiously they made remarks on the incident, when one of the cats showed a determination which they declared to be diabolical, to oppose their entrance." The friars also perceived a "stench that was not ordinary" and learned later that "the devil had taken the form of a cat when tormenting Margaret on several occasions." Although the Franciscans were denied permission to meet Margaret, they did visit her cell and see the "remarkable Crucifixion picture mysteriously placed on the wall."[150] In the same letter, Father Bertrand reported that a Franciscan told him that the devil broke a window pane in Margaret's room; tore up a book (*The Life of St. Colette*) that she was reading; and threw her down a hill after snatching her from the supporting hands of sisters who were assisting her in getting some fresh air outside in the convent grounds.[151]

Extraordinary things continued to happen at Mount St. Florence. In March 1922 Margaret was tossed around in the bathroom, and two persons heard her being slapped in the face.[152] Yet the Lord made it apparent to her that she was not alone in fighting the devil. Margaret said that Jesus returned to her at 6:45 P.M. that very evening, urging her to have courage in her vocation and reprising his promise of her transformation and redemption: "On the day you receive the habit, you shall be the lily of My Heart, the flower that will never die."[153] During the summer of 1922, the superior temporarily left Margaret in the care of Sister Luthgarde, the convent nurse; when she returned, she found Margaret on the floor next to the telephone switchboard. The switchboard had been overturned on Margaret's head, leaving a lump over her eye and knocking plaster out of the wall. Raymond was so embarrassed when the electrician commented on the extensive damage that when another incident smashed windowpanes and bookcase glass, she was reluctant to contact a repairman for fear that outsiders would think that the convent was a "roughhouse."[154] Yet another violent episode occurred during Mass. On November 21, 1923, while the sisters were listening to the doxology (the final portion of the Eucharistic prayer), Margaret was thrown from her wheelchair to the floor and her head was jammed under the radiator. For all of its weirdness, diabolical activity had usefulness beyond the convent walls in redeeming sinners: even as Margaret struggled with a demon who knocked her down and twisted her leg around a chair, St. Colette reassured her in a vision that "a certain soul has been saved through your struggles."[155]

In 1926 Dr. McParlan reported to Lukas Etlin that Margaret continued to receive inhuman abuse even during a spell of grave illness:

Now in regard to our little friend in Peekskill. She is very sick again and suffering intensely. The weakness is so great that she has hiccoughs at times and get[s] very exhausted and heart action almost imperceptible but then comes to and is her own happy smiling self. Her eyes are very blood shot for want of rest and when we think she only takes one hour a day, you can imagine how little rest she is getting from suffering. "The beast" that "prince of Idiots" the Devil is constantly beating and abusing and tempting her. One can hear the blows and see the marks on her face and see her thrown in her weak suffering condition from her bed.[156]

In 1928 Margaret took her final vows to become Sister Thorn. The conflicts that characterized the five years between her vows ceremonies only increased the impression of her supporters that she had been chosen to manifest the work of God to transform her from thorn into lily. Father Brady provided his impressions of her ceremony in a letter to Archbishop Hayes:

Yesterday I went to Peekskill and in your name rec'd the perpetual
vows of S. M. Crown of T. Her ceremony was private, no one being
present but members of the community. She was radiant with joy—
I never saw such spiritual gladness. During the ceremony many, including the Provincial wept greatly. Sister was very calm & read her vows
very distinctly and with remarkable emphasis. She asked me to thank
your Eminence for the long years of fatherly care and benevolence
you have bestowed upon her. She looked the picture of perfect health,
though during the retreat she was thrown around very frequently. She
feels she is safe at last and forever. Her prayers will never be wanting
in Your Eminence's behalf. Poor Dr. Tom [McParlan, who died a few
months earlier] must have rejoiced in heaven.[157]

During the ceremony, as was customary, Sister Crown of Thorns prostrated
herself under a pall to ritually enact her death to the world, to selfishness,
and to sin. She donned the white serge habit of the order, a white Rosary, a
wedding ring, and a wreath of lilies.

In Margaret Reilly we have an unusually intimate source of documentation about an Irish Catholic girl in turn-of-the-century New York. Manhattan in 1921 presented a layering of past, present, and future, a place where
women bearing stigmata, demons wielding knives and scissors, and crucifixes jumping from bodies to buildings shared the city with avant-garde art,
motion-picture theaters, political confrontations, speakeasies, steel-framed
skyscrapers, and subways. Key aspects of Sister Thorn's upbringing—intense
piety shaped by family, school, and spiritual direction; mystical experiences;
and determination to enter religious life—were shared by innumerable stigmatics of the modern era. Not all of these women ultimately became nuns
or sisters, however. "Are we then to conclude," asked Herbert Thurston,
"that those who are favored with the visible marks of our Lord's passion are
not, for the most part, nuns living in the retirement of the cloister?" His
response is elusive: "The question is not altogether easy to answer."[158] Yet
even if Margaret's stories of stigmata, diabolism, bilocation, and Eucharistic
miracles are pure invention, they signify a genuine bond between Margaret
and a convent community who desired to interpret and label these events
as recognized themes in the narratives of saints and mystics. "It is hardly
an exaggeration to say," Kenneth Woodward points out, "that the saints
are their stories. In this view, making saints is a process whereby a life is
transformed into a text."

As the next chapters will demonstrate, within one generation, the life of
Margaret Reilly—schoolgirl, stenographer, sufferer, stigmatic, and Catholic

sister—was rapidly distilled into a text that affirmed Christ's presence in salvation history in America. The less palatable and credible details of her stigmatization were erased from a vita that was already being imagined for consumption by a Christian audience beyond the cloister and made accessible through modern media. The edited account of the life of Sister Thorn would touch modern Catholics by restoring them to the central drama of their faith—namely, the bloody death of Christ, which offered the promise of eternal life through the sacraments. Even as a figure of folk piety, a modern stigmatic was put to use in performing several functions at once: reminding the faithful of God's power to transform unlovely thorns into lilies; affirming the sacramental power of Communion; repudiating modern materialism; and recalling vestigial connections to religion's ancient "bygone culture of blood."[159]

{2} The Monastery Is a Hospital of Spiritual Sick

The Lure of Convent Life

The monastery is an academy of strict correction where each one should allow herself to be treated, planed and polished so that all the angles being effaced, she may be joined, united and fastened to the will of Jesus.

—Words from Jesus to Margaret Reilly, in Sister Mary Carmelita Quinn, "Sister Mary Crown of Thorns," 88

The particular object of our congregation is charity— charity which urges us to walk in the footsteps of the Divine Shepherd going in search of the poor sheep that have strayed from the fold.

—Saint Mary Euphrasia, quoted in James Conniff, *The Good Shepherd Story* (1957), 83

Margaret Guditus, Margaret Reilly's grandniece, recalled her visits to her aunt at Peekskill in a poem titled "Mount St. Florence."

> Nuns with veils and habits flying
> while they led me through the hen house
> and we gathered eggs
> or sat on the lawn to brush the dogs
> or brought flowers to the small graveyard.
>
> In the late afternoon
> I would play their great piano
> for my invalid aunt who would listen
> from the landing above
> then later surreptitiously,
> we would share dinner together.

Dear blessed aunt
how your stigmatisms
have etched a place in my life.[1]

The poet, who died on Long Island in 1996, captured a sense of freedom and girlish playfulness that is not commonly associated with convent life of her great aunt's era. One wonders how the two women managed to eat secret dinners in Sister Margaret's room, or if they dined on fruit from the convent's orchards and eggs still warm from the henhouse. Did the niece ever witness her great aunt's stigmata, or had the bleeding episodes long ceased, surviving only in family and convent legends?

Margaret Reilly's very presence as an Irish American woman in a Roman Catholic convent of French origin in Dutch New Amsterdam suggests the richly layered ethnic, political, and religious history of the Hudson River valley of New York. Nearly three centuries before the convent interludes of Peggy Guditus, Peekskill appears on the map as the first European settlement on the Hudson River as Dutch settlements expanded northward from New Amsterdam, the colony at the mouth of the river. Peekskill (Peek's Creek) was named after settler Jan Peek, who had sailed upriver from his home in New Amsterdam and traded with Native Americans around 1650. In the mid-eighteenth century, when the land was primarily in the hands of tenant farmers, control of the region shifted from the Dutch to the English. During the American Revolution, a youthful General George Washington and his Continental army established Peekskill as the regional command center for the Hudson valley following his inspection tour there in November 1776. Legend has it that he took shelter under an oak tree overlooking the river while searching for British troops. This tree, later called the "Whipping Oak" after being used for the "severe correction" of colonial army deserters, stood on the tract acquired by the Good Shepherds a century later.[2]

The Hudson River played a less-significant economic role in the twentieth century than it had when it served the fur-trading merchants of the Dutch and British colony. For more than a century, the river functioned as a busy commercial waterway, lined with numerous tanning, milling, and shipping industries and harboring steamboat passenger and freight services, some of which survived into the 1900s. The Hudson River Railroad came to Peekskill Village in 1849 and by 1850 was connecting New York City and Albany. During the Civil War, the village served as a station on the Underground Railroad. Peekskill did not become a city until 1940.

Until the mid-twentieth century, Upstate New York's dominant social forces were white and Protestant, and its divisions reflected religious rather than racial or political affiliation. In the mid-1800s, the scenic views and the quiet village on the Hudson palisades had convinced the nation's premier evangelical preacher, Henry Ward Beecher, to build his summer home there. After the Civil War, however, Peekskill became home to several communities of Catholic women religious, including the Franciscan Missionary sisters (who still run the Assumption School) and the Good Shepherd sisters, who acquired the Craig estate and named it Mount St. Florence. Their complex included the convent, an orphan home, a school, a house for delinquent girls and women, and several additional buildings added over time. A century later, in the 1970s, the Good Shepherds noticed regretfully that "one house after the other is closing: Mt. Florence is now used by the Provincial and her Council. The Magdalens (now called 'Sisters of the Cross') also live there, but there are no girls at all. Villa Loretto is closed, no one is there—Hartford, closed and waiting to be sold—Springfield closed, one building used for a convent for the older Sisters—Morristown takes no more girls."[3] After serving the needs of New Yorkers for over a century, the Good Shepherd complex at Peekskill was vacated and closed in the 1980s. Both the Beecher estate and the Good Shepherd property were transformed into rental apartments, condominiums, and townhouses, while some of the convent buildings and the apple orchard were preserved.[4]

This chapter charts the history of the Good Shepherd congregation from its origins in France in 1835 to its New York foundations in Manhattan and Peekskill and its ministry during Margaret Reilly's lifetime as a transnational women's congregation that served a multiracial and multiethnic population. It evaluates the convent milieu that sheltered and produced Sister Crown of Thorns and describes her habituation to Peekskill, a process that instilled in her the virtue of unquestioning obedience to rules. As a nontraditional postulant, Margaret was still expected to embody the ideals of the sisters and their exemplary commitment to troubled girls and women. But the rumors and gossip about her hinted that she would bring shame upon the congregation's members with a past that was similar to the delinquents whom they supervised. Margaret's mystical gifts, handicapped body, demonic encounters, and alleged misdeeds made her the target of envy, suspicion, and criticism, which did not square well with the congregation's virtuous endeavors. The Good Shepherd sisters' work as schoolteachers, and their central ministry to "fallen" women, served the public, but it—as well as the divisive presence of Margaret Reilly—brought the sisters into conflict with anti-Catholics, journalists, and state-run agencies and charities seeking to change and secularize the charitable work and methods represented by the Good Shepherds.

The founding of the Religious of the Good Shepherd (RGS) in France in 1835 was part of a "silent revolution" in the Catholic Church following the French Revolution. In response to the closing of monasteries and convents by the revolutionaries, French Catholics founded more than 400 new women's congregations in the century between 1789 and the passage of the restrictive Laic Laws of 1880.[5] The official title of the RGS—the Convent of Our Lady of Charity of the Good Shepherd—reflected the order's emergence from an existing order in Tours known as Our Lady of Charity of the Refuge. Rose-Virginie Pelletier, daughter of a bourgeois family, had originally entered that order as Sister Euphrasia. Stymied in her efforts to expand the order's mission by opening a convent in Angers, she petitioned to start her own community, which ultimately became the Good Shepherds.[6] The RGS brought its silent revolution across the Atlantic, establishing convents in the United States in Louisville in 1843, in Montreal in 1844, and in Philadelphia in 1850.

The Good Shepherds made their first foundation in New York City with four sisters in 1857.[7] The wide-ranging Eastern Province of the congregation would come to include Brooklyn, New York City, Peekskill, and Troy. The Peekskill house was founded in 1890 with twelve sisters; in 1938 there were forty-two sisters attending to the 168 delinquents who were the wards of the congregation.[8] The first Good Shepherds in New York City lived in a house rented by laywomen at 191 14th Street. Sheltering twenty-five children plus the sisters and novices, the house became overcrowded within just two years, so in 1860 the sisters moved to a new location on the East River at 90th Street. At that point in Manhattan's urban development, this northerly location offered "a wooded, blossom-bowered retreat" that was perfect for the isolation and rehabilitation of delinquent women.[9] About one-third of the cost of the new mansion (which totaled about $16,000) had been paid for by Dr. H. J. Anderson of Jersey City, New Jersey.[10] Judging from histories of neighboring Good Shepherd communities in Boston and Newark published in 1907 and 1925, respectively, the congregation could not have survived in the United States without the steady influx of bequests from laypersons and gifts from the wills of priests or financial aid from entire congregations. In Newark, for example, local priests donated a horse and cart for the uncloistered sisters to use while shopping for food.[11] Between 1860 and 1864, the New York Good Shepherd house added several more buildings to contain its various departments, and this configuration endured until 1928,

The Good Shepherd House in Manhattan, 1890. Within two decades of its construction at the northern edge of Manhattan's settled areas, the impressive Good Shepherd convent at 90th Street and East End Avenue was surrounded by new commercial buildings, including an asphalt plant whose dust and fumes annoyed the sisters. (*House of Good Shepherd, ca. 1890*; from the collections of the Museum of the City of New York)

when most of the 90th Street community's buildings were leveled by the city for its project of clearing the land in Yorkville from 89th Street to 90th Street.[12] By 1934, the site was transformed into a playground, now included within the boundaries of Carl Schurz Park. Nearby stood Gracie Mansion, which became the official residence of the mayor of New York City in 1942, subsuming a property built in 1799 by Archibald Gracie, a Scottish shipper.[13] Nearby on the waterfront was the colorfully named Hell Gate, where the Harlem River met the East River in a rush of roaring water. During the Gilded Age, the sisters developed the practice of keeping their observatory and convent well lit at night in hopes of deterring suicide attempts into that surging river.[14]

The mission of the Good Shepherd sisters was to reform "fallen" women. As summarized by a priest: "The object of the order is the rescue of girls from the danger of immorality, and the reform of those who have gone astray."[15] For nineteenth-century Irish Catholics, who comprised most of the membership and inmates of the RGS, the loss of female virtue was, along with alcohol, one of the greatest enemies of the faith. It was no wonder that the arrival of the Good Shepherd sisters was greeted with little enthusiasm by Reverend John Hughes, who became the first Catholic archbishop of New York City, serving from 1842 to 1864. Hughes did not doubt the good-will of the sisters, but his sense of morality prevented him from believing that a woman who had lost her virtue could regain her most prized pos-session. "To the Irish," wrote one sister, "the white path of honor seems so natural and easy for a woman that they can find no excuse for her who leaves it. . . . This natural and supernatural horror of the desolating vice was strong in the Irish-American Archbishop."[16] Another version of Bishop Hughes's reaction to the sisters recalls that he simultaneously denied the existence of prostitution among Catholics and regarded the problem as too immense for the Good Shepherds to address.[17]

Fortunately, from their earliest history in Manhattan, the Good Shep-herds had received sponsorship and financial support from local non-Catholics. Flora Foster (1807–82), for example, the matron of the Tombs Prison when the sisters arrived in 1857, was a stern Irish-born Episcopa-lian. She helped convince Bishop Hughes to support the opening of a Good Shepherd convent in Manhattan by pointing out that Irish girls and women who went to prison often came out more hardened than reformed. When several leading Catholic women of New York City, including Mrs. Sophia Ripley, a convert and the wife of the founder of Brook Farm; Mrs. Blatch-ford; Mrs. Foote and her sister, Miss Scott; and Miss O'Reilly visited the Tombs in an attempt to inspire the Catholic girls to reform, they realized that there were few or no employment prospects for former prisoners. Due to the influx of Irish immigrants fleeing the Great Famine, thousands of ill and destitute women had ended up in port cities like New York. Even Irish workingwomen often had to resort to small-scale theft to survive, as Wil-liam Sanger documented. In his report on prostitution in the city that was published in 1859, Sanger found that Irish women made up 35 percent of the 2,000 prostitutes he had interviewed at the Penitentiary Hospital. In the following year, Irish women constituted nearly 70 percent of the inmates at the penitentiary, of whom 80 percent had been convicted of petty larceny.[18] These struggling Irish women occupied the same turf as the Bowery gangs and the Irish crooks and politicians who likewise drew support from and preyed upon the immigrants.[19] In the voluminous and rapacious culture of New York City, the Irish were well represented in both the higher ranks of government and the lower ranks of criminality.

Mother Mary of Saint Magdalen Clover, the RGS provincial of New York from 1874 to 1879, sought a better environment for troubled girls and "friendless women," so she began to develop the Peekskill property, with its fabled oak tree. On a site forty-five miles north of Manhattan and composed of eighty-four picturesque acres overlooking the Hudson River, the Good Shepherds planned to build a residence (typically referred to as a "monastery") for the delinquents in their care. Beginning in 1897, when the residence was completed, the sisters in Peekskill cared for disadvantaged and troubled girls and women, whose numbers included non-Catholics as well. A special division of the convent was set aside for a group of women known as the Magdalens—reformed delinquents who wished to stay within the conventual community and observe certain religious vows but who would never be permitted to join the Good Shepherd congregation. Some of them were offered membership in the "third order" of Carmel.[20] This tertiary status within the Catholic Church's structure of religious organizations rewarded the Magdalens' triumph over sin and at the same time recognized its enduring stain.

When difficulties arose during the construction of the residence for the Magdalens, the Peekskill property was temporarily occupied by some of the sisters from the Manhattan convent at 90th Street, who grew and tended the produce for the farm.[21] Its fruit and shade trees also provided healthful remedies for the "delicate" sisters from the city.[22] This pattern continued until 1890, when the international superior of the Good Shepherds decided to appoint Mother Mary of the Presentation as the first superior for Peekskill. Until the appointment of Mother Raymond in 1919, the leadership had changed numerous times.[23] Under Mother Immaculata O'Grady, for example, Mount St. Florence became a fine school dedicated to "destitute and indigent girls."[24] Immaculata also transferred the Saint Joseph's class from Manhattan to Mount St. Florence in order to alleviate overcrowding in the city and also because of Saint Joseph's lack of playground space. The sisters' main focus was on the delinquents, not on the orphans and students. In addition to the three customary vows of religious life—poverty, chastity, and obedience—each Good Shepherd sister added a fourth vow of zeal, obliging her to work for the salvation of troubled girls and women.[25] Despite early opposition from Archbishop Hughes,[26] within fifty years of the Good Shepherds' arrival in New York, their work was praised as exemplary in a survey conducted in 1919 and 1920 that was sponsored by Archbishop Patrick Hayes in his effort to reorganize the charities of the archdiocese into a coherent unit.[27] In the secular terminology of early twentieth-century reformism, the RGS directed "correctional institutions." The sisters refused this label, insisting otherwise that "the House of the Good Shepherd is not a prison, reformatory or penitentiary. It is a Home, where the Sisters are addressed by the sweet title of Mother, and the penitents are called children. It is a home where these 'unfortunate ones' are well cared for."[28] The sisters often substituted the term "retreat" for the reformatory vocabulary, glossing over the criminal sentences that lay behind the arrival of many of the women. Some children who arrived at the Good Shepherd communities came of their own accord, while others were delivered by friends or came as wards of the courts. By the mid-twentieth century, however, the RGS specialized less in children and adult women and focused their ministry exclusively upon troubled adolescent girls.

The sisters modeled themselves on Jesus the Good Shepherd, who gathered in the "lost sheep" and displayed kindness to social outcasts, even toward rejected figures like the Samaritan woman at the well, the adulterous woman saved from stoning, and Mary Magdalen herself. By instruction and example, the Good Shepherds hoped to lead the "unfortunates" to remorse, penitence, and restored virtue.[29] After all, even Mary Magdalen had achieved sainthood through repentance. Identification with the Good Shepherd's compassion inspired the sisters, as did their devotion to the Sacred Heart of Jesus, whose power to "repair the wreck caused by sin in a soul" was said to be overwhelming and irresistible to those who were truly contrite.[30]

Armed with their faith in the restorative power of the Good Shepherd, the sisters divided their energies between the so-called senior and junior classes. In the former group were women who arrived at the Good Shepherd communities voluntarily, perhaps brought by friends or committed by the courts. The city of New York paid the sisters a weekly allowance for each girl and additional daily fees for education and vocational training. The women who were referred were alcoholics, drug addicts, felons, prostitutes, truants, unmarried mothers, vagrants, or victims of abuse. In a 1936 study of St. Germaine Home, within the study group, 28 percent of the girls were pregnant while 22 percent had venereal disease.[31] The RGS reported with pride that under their influence, many of these penitents became daily communicants.[32] However, it was also the case that some convicted women opted to serve their jail sentences instead of accepting an even longer term of commitment at the Good Shepherd house.[33]

The junior class at Good Shepherd homes was composed of wayward children who, the sisters believed, could be reformed by living in better surroundings. In their promotion of a pastoral retreat away from the city, the RGS tapped traditions of rural virtue and, at the same time, implicitly seemed to accept the notion of Progressive reformers that environment affected behavior. Removing at-risk children from the temptations of city life could not help but to transform them. During the 1920s, the Good Shepherds began to move away from the old strategy of merely secluding "sinners" from society and began to engage the emerging trend in rehabilitation: the casework method, which offered guidance, counseling, and social services.[34] By the time of Margaret Reilly's death in 1937, the convent had again updated its image by advertising its "modern methods" in child training at Villa Loretto, by which the sisters hoped to break down old patterns of moral delinquency and equip a Christian soul to rejoin society as a regenerate and productive member. "A fully equipped modern clinic" was installed at the Villa, and each girl received an examination from a physician, a psychiatrist, and a psychologist before being assigned to a grade.[35]

The orderly environment at the Good Shepherd communities was not typical of all Catholic religious orders who dealt with the public. The Franciscan projects nearby in Rye, New York, and in New Jersey, for instance, were singled out in the auxiliary bishop's report to Archbishop Hayes for their deplorable conditions. In 1922 Bishop Dunn complained that among the Franciscans, "there seems to be a lack of a strictly religious spirit. Many excellent sisters, it is true, are to be found in all the Houses of the community, but it would appear that they did not have the advantages of a proper religious training in the novitiate."[36] One house had a novice mistress who was too "timid" to leave an impression on the characters of the postulants and novices; the house where boys were placed was called "sub-normal." "There is," Dunn confided, "a 'happy-go-lucky' sort of atmosphere about the house. There is a general disposition to visit Manhattan, and little consideration is given that important work over which they have charge; so much so, that it is often neglected." At St. Mary's Hospital in Orange, New Jersey, "conditions [were] utterly bad," Dunn judged, because the superior failed to control her sisters. Bishop Dunn also disapproved of the lack of a segregated convent building there, which obliged the sisters to pass "through the corridors of the hospital proper." The result was that "a strong secular spirit pervades the place, due in a great measure, to their intimate contact with the patients, and due also, I might say, to a lack of religious observance." Whatever flaws might be found among the Good Shepherds at Peekskill, they were not guilty of lacking firm discipline and strict methods for correcting insiders and outsiders and for keeping the two groups decidedly separate.

Margaret Reilly did not encounter a large religious community at Peekskill in 1922. According to the *Official Catholic Directory*, there were twenty-six sisters then residing in Saint Germaine's Home, led by Mother Raymond Cahill. By contrast, the 90th Street convent housed 49 sisters (including the New York Provincial), 28 novices, 14 lay sisters, 13 outside sisters, and 17 postulants, for a total of 149. When Mother Raymond became the superior at Peekskill in 1919, she had already served as directress of the girls at the Providence Good Shepherd community and as superior of the Brooklyn house for a decade. One lasting impact of her tenure at Peekskill was the purchase of more land, so that by 1934 the grounds extended to 125 acres.[37] The Good Shepherds developed the property along aesthetic and practical lines, taking advantage of the physical beauty already provided. The entrance to the grounds featured a stone bridge over a stream, landscaped areas and fruit trees, and an artificial lake near the house. A separate building at the entrance housed the chaplain; a conservatory taught children to grow and tend the flowers used in the chapel; farm pastures and an apple orchard nurtured produce for consumption and for sale; a printery manufactured bulk orders of holiday and greeting cards; classrooms with sewing machines allowed the older girls to learn sewing and dressmaking; and large kitchens provided daily meals for the more than 300 children in residence and also taught home-making skills. The daily routine at Peekskill unfolded in a tranquil setting much like that exquisitely imagined by Ron Hansen in *Mariette in Ecstasy* (1992), his novel of an order of Belgian "Sisters of the Crucifixion." This fictive religious community—"Tallow candles in red glass jars shudder on a high altar. White hallway and dark mahogany joists. Wide plank floors walked soft and smooth as soap"[38]—had relocated to Upstate New York in 1901 to escape harsh anti-Catholic repressions in Europe. In the novel, the daily chores of the sisters are always juxtaposed with details from the natural world, signifying the organic connection between labor and nature in monastic life. In 1906 the routine is disrupted by the arrival of a novice who begins to have ecstatic experiences that culminate in stigmata on Christmas Eve. The sentiments of religious fervor, doubt, jealousy, and confusion that she stirs up are precisely those raised by the presence of Margaret Reilly at Peekskill.

The Good Shepherd community on the East River was thus nearly six times the size of the newer Peekskill house, although its environment was far less idyllic. Even before 1910, the Good Shepherd sisters found their Manhattan home "being enveloped by the heart of the City. The many departments of the House were overcrowded." To provide hygienic, spacious surroundings for their young charges, the nuns hoped to abandon 90th Street "for more commodious quarters for the children." As the sisters suffered intensely from the summer heat, it must have been hard for them to watch fellow New Yorkers, notably the "Dead End kids," swimming in the East River from the embankment and promenade near their convent buildings. The "furnace-like" city house not only affected the health of novices but also made some sisters reconsider their vocations. To add further aggravation, the convent was bombarded by constant dust and dirt, produced by the "cement" factory across the street.[39] This structure was actually the

Municipal Asphalt Plant, which endured until the 1990s, when it was converted into an athletic facility renamed, poetically, Asphalt Green.

The decade between 1922 and 1932 brought the greatest changes to the Peekskill convent since its founding, apparent in the increases in the size of its community and inmate population and a demographic shift to a mostly American-born membership for the religious congregation. American strategies for addressing criminality among women also began to change as well, as a shift in attitudes now saw a sexually promiscuous girl or woman as a threat rather than a victim. This new outlook would affect the methods of the RGS as well.

The 1920 federal census data listed a total of twenty-seven sisters in residence at the Peekskill Good Shepherd house, of whom eleven were born in Ireland; in 1930 the census listed thirty-four sisters there, of whom only four were born in Ireland, plus the congregation's Visitor (Mother Hickey from Ireland) and her companion. Only twenty-one inmates were listed at Villa Loretto in 1920, rising to seventy-one in 1930. The composition of the inmate group reflected considerable diversity: thirty-eight women were born in New York, but seven were Italian-born; the remainder came from Austria, Brazil, England, Hungary, Poland, and Syria.

The 1920 census data from the house of the Good Shepherd at 90th Street listed more than 270 "prisoners" of the community, most of them grouped by their "occupation" as machine operators, domestics, or laundresses (as categorized in the industrial curriculum advised by the state). This large group of nearly 300 girls and women was transferred to Peekskill between 1923 and 1928. At the end of the 1920 census's tally of residents at 90th Street are thirty-six girls designated as the "colored class," ages eleven to nineteen, with different patterns of origin than the rest of the community. Most of these African American girls reported parents from Florida, North Carolina, Virginia, or the Caribbean. Velmar Dabney, for example, was born in the West Indies to parents from North Carolina; Annabel Chestnut was born in New York to parents from South Carolina; Eleanore Scott was born in Texas, her mother's home, and her father was from Puerto Rico. The presence of a multiethnic and multiracial group of delinquent or abandoned girls as wards of the RGS suggests a convent environment that was far more diverse than the prevalence of Irish American names among the sisters indicates at first glance. Although they were obliged to work with these diverse populations every day, the Good Shepherds, as Suellen Hoy described in her story of the congregation's work in Chicago, did not participate in public life nor "openly challenge the status quo."[40]

Prior to 1969, when the Good Shepherd rule was revised to reflect the reorientation of religious life after Vatican II, the sisters had three ranks of membership: choir sisters, lay sisters, and outside (*tourière*) sisters. Each section of the Good Shepherd congregation was kept apart from the others, converging only when attending chapel. The Good Shepherd sisters were rather late among women's religious orders to eliminate the elitist tier system. The Sisters of Saint Joseph of Carondelet, for example, had abandoned the distinction between choir and lay sisters in 1908. The choir sisters—so named for their traditional role in singing in Latin during liturgical functions—had the highest educational level, meaning they could read and, hence, had the highest religious functions to perform by reciting the Divine Office daily. At the time of the founding of the RGS, they were the only literate segment of the sisterhood.[41] The choir sisters were entirely cloistered and took their final vows after three years.

As the RGS imposed discipline on the three groups in their care, they subjected themselves to stern regulations as well. Disciplining the bodies of religious women through dress and rules that restricted movement to the cloister was part of creating an ideal Christian space set apart from the world. Religious communities nonetheless took on the contingent colorations of their ethnic and cultural origins, allowing the RGS to retain its Francophilic and hierarchical character—following its foundress, who was raised as a privileged daughter of a lawyer in the Vendée within the class distinctions of the *Ancien Régime*. During Margaret Reilly's lifetime, the American RGS houses still reflected their French origins in myriad ways, from the classist structure of the congregation to the names of the offices held by individual sisters in each house, such as *économe, lingère, pharmacienne, robiere,* and *surveillante*. The lay and outside sisters were under the supervision of the *éconôme*, or treasurer. The lay sisters performed the necessary kitchen and household chores for the community but had no voice in governance. To distinguish themselves, they wore sturdier habits of a slightly different design and fabric than the choir sisters. Only the *tourière* sisters had regular contact with the outside world, and in this role, they received visitors and donations and purchased food and provisions for the community.[42] Because of the greater temptations of the world to which they were exposed, outdoor sisters made annual vows each year for five years before being able to take perpetual vows. The lay sister rank was suppressed in 1945, and the *tourière* category was dropped in 1948. These terms were abandoned altogether in about 1956 as the RGS constitutions were revised.[43] The preservation of the French vocabulary for over a century of RGS life in the United States, however, suggests the hybridity of American convent cultures prior to Vatican II, as well as the push-and-pull factors that encouraged the sisters to understand themselves as rooted in Europe while serving American society through modern (yet staunchly Christian) rehabilitative techniques for girls and women.

The temperature extremes and industrial soot that aggravated the novitiate at 90th Street in Manhattan was balanced by the social respect that the sisters received as "brides of Christ" who sacrificed themselves for others. In Margaret's lifetime, Catholic religious orders were entering four decades of sustained growth that peaked at mid-twentieth century, as illustrated by the alluring advertisements for congregations that flourished at that time throughout the Catholic press, usually highlighting a bridal motif that was not present in earlier decades.[44] At the turn of the century, the opposite theme for nuns—denial of marriage—had prevailed in American popular culture. Despite a steady increase in vocations, convents were often discussed by the Catholic press as institutions "in crisis," and Catholics were always enjoined to support them financially.

In the 1920s, expanding social opportunities for the daughters of immigrants would seem to pose an enormous challenge to the success of Catholic gender ideals for religious life in America; but by the 1950s, the emergence of a Catholic middle class that had embraced postwar ideals of domesticity meant that even religious life could promote itself as a parallel path to married life. In the fifties, in an effort to recruit more novices, religious orders of women became more media savvy and began to publish vocation books. These books (which might be no more than short pamphlets) lasted until just after Vatican II and were circulated via the parochial schools with the goal of making "the convent appear as an attractive alternative to the limited career options offered young women in the postwar, pre-feminist era."[45] In a 1957 history of the Good Shepherd order, appearing a decade before the end of the national vocational growth spurt, the author caught the spirit of the vocation books, gushing that the sisters were searching for "girls who like giddy hats and dreamy formals, but who also have enough poetry in their souls to see a special kind of beauty in a 'new look' of flowing religious habit, trim oxfords, chaste white wimple and scapular."[46] The ideal Good Shepherd candidate was fashionable, humorous, spunky, and well-balanced, "with the kind of high-spiritedness that is likely to take two stairs at a time—when no one is looking"—which sounds much like the perky heroines of American popular fiction, such as Nancy Drew of the mystery novel series that originated in 1930, except that the convent girl's passion was "following the example of Christ in all things" instead of "sleuthing." The timeless qual-

Late nineteenth-century images of nuns in popular culture that represented them as missing out on marriage—such as the song titled "No Wedding Bells for Her" (1898)— later gave way to their self-representation as enjoying equivalent social functions in convent life, as seen in the above image of Good Shepherd novices in their bridal gowns. (Sheet music courtesy of the New York Public Library; photo of sisters in bridal gowns from James C. G. Conniff, *The Good Shepherd Story* [Peekskill, N.Y.: Graymoor Press, 1957])

ity of the vocation books rendered them virtually the same, with no details that would locate them in a particular year or time or even to a specific congregation, since they all promised "a bigger, bolder, and more exciting life than their schoolmates who had gone the usual route of marriage and motherhood."[47]

In Margaret Reilly's era, convent manuals, vocation books, and retreat sermons did not attract women to religious life by the postwar pitch of advertising it as more adventuresome than marriage. Instead, as a popular work of 1919 declared, the convent "presents to women the sublimest way of following Christ . . . It is almost an assurance of eternal salvation to enter the convent. Living as the rules ordain gives virtually a guarantee of salvation."[48] Mother Raymond and other leaders of women's congregations understood that obedience was a double-edged tool for women. Abundant evidence of Catholic sisters' deference to church officials appears in the obsequious tone of the formal correspondence between mother superiors and ecclesiastics in this era, but nuns and sisters became skilled at parlaying their submission into gaining influence with the powerful.[49] Mother Raymond relied on the Christian topos of elevation of the lowly as a model of social reversal that the Good Shepherds could hope for and that had long been used by Christian women to make their situations tolerable. Although nuns and sisters were reliant on priests to provide a sympathetic ear for their concerns, absolution of their sins, and affirmation of their vocation, women still derived a measure of autonomy inside a system that demanded female subordination.[50] Women's ultimate dependence upon clerical authority, however, was a constant reminder of their secondary status and lack of autonomy within the Catholic Church.

The obedience required of Margaret Reilly when she began her convent existence was even more stringent because of momentous revisions to the code of canon law in the Catholic Church in 1917, which had greatly increased the strictness of cloister. Cloister rules were strengthened yet again in 1950 in Pius XII's bull *Sponsa Christi*.[51] Jo Ann McNamara aptly refers to the intervening decades as an "ice age" for women's status and rights in the church. In short, women's congregational life prior to Vatican II was overly stern and rigorous.[52]

From the church's viewpoint, increasing the regulation of women religious was necessary to reverse dangerous tendencies toward worldliness. The revised Code of 1917 was the first major alteration to canon law since the changes enacted by the Council of Trent in the sixteenth century and the revisions made in its wake. At that time, the Tridentine reforms had increased the regulations governing women's communities as a way to sequester them fully from the world, but also to moderate what were deemed "false" expressions of faith—the excessive physical mortification and visions, ecstasies, and physical penances that were attempted by convented women and mystics in the Early Modern era. Although the decrees of Trent had tightened enclosure, historians have pointed out that dozens of new women's uncloistered foundations emerged in the seventeenth century, especially in France.[53] A "French connection" to congregations who later migrated to North America was established early on by these Counter-Reformation sisterhoods, whose choice to take simple vows enabled them to work in charity, nursing, and teaching despite the prevailing sexism of civil and ecclesiastical society. Even though the Vatican tried to suppress "all organizations of activist women" following the Council of Trent, these communities endured.[54] A second wave of them, which included the Good Shepherds, began to appear in the 1830s. When the RGS migrated to the United States as a semicloistered order, they joined a growing set of women's religious communities that preferred active over contemplative vocations.

When the Roman Catholic Church regulated convent life more severely in 1917, it did so in opposition to changing gender norms in society that were permitting women greater roles in the public sphere and more choices in determining their lives. In late nineteenth-century New York, these shifts in gender roles for women had resulted from three factors: a rise in wages for young unmarried women that produced greater freedom, their use of income to help their families, and the rise of cheap popular entertainments that "combined to spur young women's experimentation with new forms of sexual barter."[55] In cities like New York, perhaps 55 percent of single white women worked for pay in 1900, which "gave young women self-confidence, relatively free access to the streets, and a degree of anonymity few had enjoyed in the nineteenth century." But 86 percent of these working women who lived with their families turned over their paychecks.[56] We do not know if Margaret Reilly gave a portion or her entire salary to her parents to boost the family income. Nor do we know if she exercised her street freedom to socialize widely while working as a stenographer or office cleaner, or if she learned about new courtship rituals, which included premarital sex, from the working-class women who were the pioneers of this new gender economy. In Thomas Hine's account of the rise of the American teenager, the 1920s were uniquely characterized by a youth culture "defined by the newly recognized sexuality of girls who used to be 'good.'"[57] In this sense, Margaret Reilly came of age in late Victorian culture but entered the convent when young persons experienced, for the first time in American history, a culture in which young people arranged their own lives and often rejected their parents' standards of morality and propriety. Nonetheless, despite the so-called freedoms of the Jazz Age, the numbers of Catholic women who joined convents at this time continued to rise, and it is this paradox of liberation and constraint that Margaret Reilly embodied.

The 1917 cloister revisions that determined Margaret's convent experience stood squarely against the expansion of socioeconomic opportunities and agency for women by exacting more submission and segregation from them. Nonetheless, three aspects of cloistered religious life may have permitted women greater freedom in a convent than outside one. First, the conviction that monastic life participated in universal and eternal truths by acting as a microcosm of a grand system gave each individual a sense of valued significance. From an anthropological perspective, the convent "was partly autonomous within a larger hierarchy, the diocese, the order, the church." As Mary Douglas explains: "If there is something that a hierarchy is good at providing for its members, it is meaningfulness. It deploys all the symbolic capital it can collect in order to create and maintain a high level of meaning. It has developed the art of self-justification to a high degree. Each legitimation rests on the others; the symbols refer back and forth to the same structure of metaphors, resonating to one another as in an echo chamber."[58]

A second lure of the convent was an effect of that "echo chamber," which convinced sisters that its intertwined rituals led to the salvation of their souls. The ritual activities of convent life centered upon making vows and learning to keep them. A nun's veiling ceremony began her novitiate, followed by the taking of her preliminary vows. At the reception of final vows, the ritual takes the form of a Catholic wedding ceremony because nuns and sisters become "brides of Christ," following the metaphorical description of Christ in the New Testament as the bridegroom of the church. At this ceremony, nuns and sisters don wedding gowns, rings, veils, and flowers and present "dowries" to their congregations. For her vows ceremony, Margaret Reilly, too, wore a wedding gown. The archbishop sprinkled her new veil and wedding ring with holy water and incensed them during the Mass, following the usual rite.[59]

The dowries given by the family of the novice helped fund and sustain each religious congregation. Despite the oft-repeated notion that Catholicism is a communal system, individual contractual relations were essential to the convent regime. By the terms of the contract of their religious vows, nuns abandon private property except for their personal articles of clothing and hygiene and their prayer books, while each sister's dowry becomes the property of the community. Some orders had demanding dowry requirements; others, like the Good Shepherds, were flexible, following the example set by its foundress, who even overlooked the dowry requirement for some of the novices whose families could not afford them.

Finally, the obedience of each sister in the hierarchy of the convent shaped the orderliness of communal life based upon an unvarying annual routine that liberated her to serve others. Each Good Shepherd house observed the rhythms of the Catholic liturgical calendar in its passage from the season of Advent, culminating in Christmas (the birth of Christ), to Lent, the penitential season in preparation for Easter (the death and resurrection of Christ). The celebration of Catholic feast days and those of specific importance to Good Shepherd history punctuated the calendar at Peekskill and defined sacred from ordinary time. A Good Shepherd sister quoted Canon Sheehan of Ireland, a Catholic favorite, on the topic of feast days: "We are going to eternity as fast as Time can bear us. The feasts of Our Lady fly by like lights upon a railroad. Let us watch them well, making them landmarks of grace upon our great journey to eternity."[60] Among the other "landmarks of grace" that the RGS observed annually were the Immaculate Heart of Mary (February 8); Good Shepherd Sunday (the second Sunday after Easter); the feast of Saint Mary Euphrasia Pelletier, the foundress (April 24); the canonization of Saint John Eudes, patron, on May 31, 1925, whose feast day was August 19 (now August 18); the feast of the Sacred Heart in June; Saint Euphrasia's birthday, July 31;[61] the canonization of Margaret Mary Alacoque (October 16 but later October 17); and the Feast of the Presentation (November 21), which was the traditional day for all Catholics making religious vows.[62]

Not only was time controlled and marked by sacred events, but so was every facet of the life of a sister. The use of time, space, the body, and objects were closely regulated, as were eating, sleeping, and tending to the sick and dying. The superior watched over each sister's appearance, behavior, cell, and even the contents of their closets and communications. Each day in the convent was divided into periods of silence devoted to prayer or simply to the discipline of not speaking, punctuated by periods of intense labor, teaching, chores, meals (often held in silence), singing, and conversation.

The positive side of this unvarying routine was that its predictability was meant to inspire greater devotion to life in Christ even through the most humbling chore, while a frequent critique of this custom was that it stifled women's energies and intelligence, as evidenced by the convent life of the often frustrated Thérèse Martin at Nevers.[63] Historian Bonnie Smith, who has provided a comprehensive portrait of nineteenth-century Catholic women in her study of northern France, showed how the convent continued to propagate a traditional domestic model for women's lives long after society had been transformed around them. She concluded: "Girls in the convents learned to substitute love of God and obedience for knowledge—either carnal or intellectual—by directing their energies toward worship of His authority."[64] The repression of creativity in everyday life—and its constant sublimation into the acts of prayer, domestic chores, farming, sewing, and teaching according to a communal schedule—could be exasperating as well as uplifting. The convent offered few outlets for young women's intellectual energies other than religious pursuits and hard physical labor. Even menial assignments like flower arranging, tending plants, baking communion wafers and setting type for the printing press must have been welcome respite from the monotony.

The requirement of virginal purity for nuns and sisters, symbolized by the lily in Christian iconography (as in Jesus's attribution of Sister Thorn as his "lily of delight"), necessitated their isolation from ordinary society. Because convents of the early twentieth century were haunted by fears of the encroachment of worldly temptations, they stepped up emphasis on the vow of obedience nearly at the expense of other religious vows. Placing a premium on keeping the rules often led to an exaggerated sense of their importance and permanence. In the last half century, many modern women, who began to regard themselves as autonomous subjects, came to see things differently. From their viewpoint, women's religious life before Vatican II meant that "silence, the disciplines of deference and obedience, the public confession of faults and repentance all seem infantilizing and boring."[65] Nonetheless, the constantly rising vocations in the golden era of American sisterhoods between the 1920s and the 1960s suggest that sublimation of the self appealed to Catholic girls who found glory in humbling themselves in total abandonment to the will of God by following rules that appeared to be eternal.

A modest appearance signaled sisters' departure from the world and distinguished them from the delinquents. *The Tablet* of Brooklyn commented in 1922 that the nun's garb "imparts a certain dignity—the similarity of appearance prevents criticism, jibes and emulation."[66] The habit and veil that identified convented women worldwide was also a leveler of individuality. Like any uniform, habits were meant to erase differences among the nuns and sisters and to prevent competition about appearance and status.[67] Inside the convent, the habit expressed renunciation of the world and the abandonment of family obligations and material possessions in order to truly find God. Outside the cloister, the habit's long concealing shape, lack of decoration, and sober colors erased sexuality while at the same time identifying the wearer as a person set apart from the world and its traps.

The designs for nuns' habits in the modern era generally adopted one of two looks from European precedents: a modified widow's weeds or the plain garments of the peasantry. Ironically, the details such as bonnets, cuffs, fringe, silver buttons, veils, and lace edging that were necessary to make each order's official habit distinctive often ended up creating high-maintenance garments. French religious orders had used even minor details of their habits to mark class distinctions. Wearing a veil versus a bonnet, for example, could indicate the failure of one sister to provide a dowry to the order. A superior could assign a certain value to a white veil or a black veil. Among congregations that wore black habits, special white habits were usually donned if the sisters performed hospital or nursing work.

When Mother Euphrasia founded the Good Shepherds, she proposed a white ankle-length gown made of durable serge cloth, a silver locket, and a blue waist cord with tassels. The wimple was a cloth veil that covered the natural shape of the head and fell to midback. The Vatican, however, did not approve this design until it was distinguished more fully from the community that Euphrasia had originally entered. By Margaret Reilly's lifetime, the RGS habit had been modified again. In all religious orders, the novice adopted different garb following the completion of a spiritual retreat and a ceremony in which she had donned a wedding gown and asked to be received into the order. The novice's attire consisted of a robe, guimpe (wimple), bandeau (headband), sham veil (later replaced by a real veil), a floral crown, and a rosary. Waist cords were added to the newcomer's attire in the Good Shepherds a short time before the taking of first vows, along with a silver heart locket on a chain. The motto of their congregation, "Live Jesus and Mary," was inscribed there. One side of the locket bore an image of Jesus as the Good Shepherd. On the other side, the Virgin Mary held the infant Jesus and was surrounded by lily fronds.

The serge cloth layers that made up the RGS habit were heavy to wear and burdensome in high temperatures. As the sisters knew, no concessions could be made to revise their attire without a lengthy legal process to change the constitution governing the order. Undue attention to the habit sometimes caused the women to focus on inessential details: one RGS archivist recalled the occasion of a "dramatic" change in the number of pins used to fasten the sleeves at the wrist; some of the older nuns chose to retain the former number, associating them with a special spiritual blessing. When Archbishop Hayes was obliged to settle disputes at Peekskill, even he noted that one cause of "resentment and discontent" among the convent's *tourière* sisters was "the color of the mantle."[68]

The concern to protect the integrity of the convent regime from external secular interference could be seen in every detail of RGS life. When Jesus appeared to Margaret Reilly, for example, warning that "America will be the grave of the religious life," Mother Raymond superimposed her particular interpretation that religious life was ailing because the sisters were now obliged to attend normal schools. She was referring to a church-state conflict that arose in the United States when the Catholic Church balked at the obligation for its religious personnel to receive state accreditation at institutions such as teachers colleges, as required by new laws in the 1920s.[69] New York was one of the leading states in raising standards of teacher training. In support of the church's position, the RGS therefore resisted state regulation. By opposing outside efforts to standardize teacher training in America, nuns and sisters believed that they were demonstrating religious obedience, and they found themselves, as with the obligations of stricter cloister, moving in opposition to educational and social trends in the United States.

The campaign to accredit all schoolteachers reflected two parallel trends in America: the Progressive political movement's thrust to standardize social programs and an anti-Catholicism that was reaching a new peak in the twenties, as even the Ku Klux Klan and Masons agitated to require all American students to attend public schools. Inadvertently, as John McGreevy noted, "another notably undemocratic institution, the school, became the site of the most sustained debate over Catholic influence in American culture."[70] In this contest, American Catholics were striving to overcome the prevailing prejudice that only public education fostered and safeguarded democratic habits, while parochial schools were hotbeds of tyrannical mind control and superstition. It was common for leading educators such as James Bryant Conant, the president of Harvard University, to tout public schools as "the common denominator of all religious faiths."[71] His predecessors and successors at Ivy League universities often voiced their contempt for Roman Catholicism with impunity. The simmering debate on Catholic schooling and public education would be reprised again in the Cold War era, stoked by the anti-Catholic diatribes of Paul Blanshard; but in the twenties, America's nuns and sisters abided by the church's rationale that less, rather than more, state oversight of teacher training was needed.[72] It was the same logic of defending the autonomy of the church that led sisters to seek ways to undermine their compliance with the National Industrial Recovery Act of 1933 when it interfered with their wage and hour structures for the inmates of the Good Shepherd houses. The sisters did not try to flout the law but interpreted their work in rehabilitation of young women as unrelated to the world of business, and therefore they saw their laundries and other small-scale employments as exempt from the law.[73]

Although one of Jesus's revelations to Sister Thorn inspired Mother Raymond to oppose teacher accreditation, he generally avoided overtly political matters and offered ordinary and even generic advice to the sisters. "Speak little and gently, little and well, little and frankly, little and amiably," he advised. And he heartened the sisters with these words: "Thorn, I am never discouraged in finding defects, provided there be good will; where this exists, there is material for work." Still, one constant theme of the Savior was to warn the sisters about the rise in selfish or "worldly" behaviors at Peekskill: "Sisters going out alone. Postulants going out. Too much worldly spirit in Convent."[74] Jesus deputized Sister Thorn "to bring back your illustrious Order to its ancient rigor." "You will face constant opposition," he warned. "By penance and prayer you will draw My blessing upon the Church and your Community."

In her imputed role as reformer of her congregation, Margaret seems to have been trying to position herself as a Catherine of Siena or a Colette of Corbie. A delicate balance was at play. If Margaret became too influential, she ran the risk of undermining her superior and violating the rule of obedience, becoming too confident of Jesus's special assurance that he had given her "the spirit of wisdom" and filled her with understanding.[75] As an invalid and an older postulant, Margaret might lose her status as an object of pity to become a target of resentment. Armed with her divine communications, she hoped to become an engine of renewal who gained the deference of the sisterhood through her special revelations from the Lord. In Weberian terms, her charisma was a fragile thing and needed to constantly defend its legitimacy against institutional forms that worked against self-assertion.

At the heart of the novice's life was attention to convent rules, and one of the central features of Margaret's observed behavior was judgment about her obedience to these rules. For the first year, in order to preserve cloister, Margaret could not leave the convent grounds. During her novitiate, she was also immersed in learning the history of the congregation and its rule. Not surprisingly, most of the mischievous attacks on Margaret occurred during this threshold period. At Peekskill, as at all Catholic convents, the governing of the congregation and its daily routine, etiquette, offices, and vows were determined by the order's historic rule—second only to scripture. Canonical language in the Catholic Church distinguishes between the four historic rules—originating with Saints Augustine, Basil, Benedict, and Francis of Assisi—which have defined Catholic monastic life, and the specifics of each order's constitution, which revised the chosen rule to suit the particular congregation. Sisterhoods reflected both the cultural milieu in which the congregation had formed and the need to adapt to local social conditions.

In the United States, where women religious tended to be of French or Irish origins, their congregations continued to be flavored by those ethnic roots, even in the postimmigrant decades.

The Religious of the Good Shepherd used a modified version of the Augustinian Rule combined with the constitutions of Saint Francis de Sales, both of which had been further tailored by Saint John Eudes in the seventeenth century and again in the nineteenth century by RGS foundress Rose-Virginie Pelletier.[78] From the contributions of Eudes and Pelletier, therefore, the RGS foundation story credits a male and a female founder, although they were separated by more than a century. The Good Shepherd order is a cloistered one, meaning that sisters could not leave the convent except in "extreme cases of necessity."[77] Inside the community, however, the RGS sisters had adopted a modified rule of cloister in order to permit them to pursue their ministry to girls and laywomen in the fields of education, psychology, and social work.

The spirituality of the community was Salesian, reflecting the social engagement and down-to-earth approach to godliness of Francis de Sales, a seventeenth-century French bishop who was canonized in 1925.[78] The Jesuits and their spirituality also became significant to the Good Shepherds, in part through their shared dedication to the cult of the Sacred Heart of Jesus. The Sacred Heart was one among many Catholic devotions that undertook to comfort the persecuted, and hence it was often supported by women victimized by their own powerlessness in society. When the Jesuit order rose to become major champions of the Sacred Heart (as well as the major opponent of Gallicanism and Jansenism in France because of their fierce loyalty to the pope and their defense of his universal power), it is not surprising that Jesuits often served Good Shepherd convents as confessors, chaplains, and retreat masters. Much of the mysticism that flourished in seventeenth-century France had been nourished by a Jesuit version of it. Two centuries later, the Jesuit connection to Margaret Reilly's case remained vital: at least seven of the more than twenty priests involved in her spiritual formation were members of the Society of Jesus.[79]

The Good Shepherds embraced a mixture of spiritual influences from Augustine, Eudes, de Sales, Pelletier, the Jesuits, and others. But did the Old World context of the Good Shepherd order—namely, its French bourgeois and antirepublican heritage—translate to the United States? While many women heeded the call to convent life in the new congregations of postrevolutionary France because it involved a unique chance for public service in a limited sphere, their hierarchical structures seemed antidemocratic in Jazz Age New York, where the opportunities for women were increasing in urban life and numerous public agencies offered the chance to perform the same rehabilitative work as the sisterhood.

As nearly textbook illustrations of anthropologist Victor Turner's concept of liminality as the stage between separation and reintegration from a group, Margaret's trials in the course of her passage to her final vows were read by her superior as tests of her commitment to God's will. After freely roaming through Manhattan and earning her own income for at least a decade, Margaret may have found Peekskill and its cloister safe and admirable, but also limiting. At nearly forty years old, she was no ingénue being ambushed by convent discipline. After a specified period of time, she, like each novice, was examined by a lawyer from the archdiocesan chancery office to ascertain that she was not being coerced into entering religious life. Her initial vows ceremony was uncharacteristically private: only Reilly family members were present, along with Archbishop Hayes, Dr. Thomas McParlan, and Father Brady (whose emotional letter about it appeared in chapter 1). The ritual was held in the convent's large community room before an altar erected for the occasion that was crowned by a statue of the Immaculate Conception taken from "Murillo's famous painting," which by now served as a shared mark of taste among Catholics and Protestants.[80] Lukas Etlin sent his priestly stole to Margaret as a gift for the occasion, while the archbishop offered his "special blessing."

Ordinarily, Sister Thorn could expect to make final vows between three to five years later, with a possible extension period of three or more months. The fact that her interim period lasted more than five years—from 1923 to 1928—attests to the existence of dissension within the Good Shepherd community about her candidacy. Archbishop Hayes himself noted that Margaret was one of five major causes of disagreement among the RGS, a novice "whom the mal-contents [sic] regarded as a deceiver and an unworthy candidate for the community."[81]

One strategy that helped Catholic religious orders to sustain membership and attract new members was the promotion of religious heroines. These edifying women became familiar figures in convent culture through the repetition of anecdotes and the communal reading of their biographies, which often highlighted their triumph over affliction. In Margaret's lifetime, the Good Shepherds elevated Mother Euphrasia Pelletier in this way, and the sisters were now also building legends around a more recent leader, Mother Mary of the Divine Heart Droste zü Wischering (1863–99), a German who entered the RGS in 1888 and served as the superior of a convent in Oporto, Portugal.[82] Appearing in a vision to Thorn, Mother Euphrasia coined a memorable phrase when she described "THE MONASTERY [AS] A

HOSPITAL OF SPIRITUAL SICK." She elaborated: "All who desire to be cured and to this end submit themselves to the knife, to the lancet, to be burned, to be bled, and so to all kinds of bitter remedies. O my dear daughters, firmly resolve that you will submit to all this, and pay no attention to what self-love may urge to the contrary; but sweetly, amiably and lovingly, take the blessed resolution to die, or to be cured."[83] Euphrasia was well acquainted with the culture of pain: after enduring a bronchial infection in Angers in the 1860s, she concealed from others a growth on her side that became infected and that was variously described as a malignant tumor or an infected ulcer, which led to her protracted and painful death.[84] Evidently, no one offered her sedatives for temporary relief, so she joined the ranks of the many nuns, sisters, and invalids of the nineteenth-century who embraced physical suffering for spiritual goals. Immolating herself so that others could live (a detail much impressed upon Sister Thorn's generation), Euphrasia Pelletier died in 1868 and was buried inside the chapel at the Good Shepherd motherhouse in Angers. She was beatified in 1933 and canonized in 1940.[85]

In her comparison between the convent and the hospital, Euphrasia implied a spirituality that emphasized the general sickness of the human condition due to original sin and the need for "bitter remedies" to make things right. The choice was clear: sickness and death versus submission and salvation. Sisterhoods already made extensive claims for convent life as the entrée to eternal life. By picturing the convent as a home for the "spiritual sick," the Good Shepherd superior supplied further justification for young women to submit utterly to communal rules, adding another piece to the interlocking code of the convent's place in the grand system. The same kind of all-or-nothing model also was applied to the delinquent girls and women in RGS homes. The sisters had more in common with their wards than they may have recognized.

The ancestors of Mother Divine Heart's illustrious family included several bishops of Cologne and Münster, while several living family members were married into the Hapsburg royalty. Heroic legends about her began with her father, a count. When he went on pilgrimage to Rome, Pope Leo XIII greeted him with the words: "Happy are you to be the father of a Saint."

While convent lore praised Mother Divine Heart's refusal of her privileged social status, it was her life of heroic suffering for others that was meant to inspire the Good Shepherds. Her 1906 biography told how she was admired as a living saint because of her virtue and her endurance of persecution and humiliation by the Portuguese.[86] She was called the second Margaret Marie Alacoque by her confessor because of her intense preoccupation with the Sacred Heart and her physical suffering. She adopted the phrase "More suffering, more love," as her motto. For the three years prior to her death, Mother Divine Heart endured a painful inflammation of the spinal cord that, her biographer insisted, "almost literally nailed [her] to the cross on her bed of suffering." To confirm Mother Divine Heart's importance for the universal church, the RGS credited her with urging Pope Leo XIII to consecrate the world to the Sacred Heart of Jesus, which he did on the day of her death in June 1899. The Good Shepherds were convinced that she alone had led the pope to elevate a local devotion into a universal feast. Mother Divine Heart's transformation from unpopular superior to heroic sister happened quickly with the aid of print media and contained the requisite ingredients for veneration and imitation, including the uses of illness to support sanctity, the spiritualization of pain, and her role in legitimating the Sacred Heart devotion. These elements anticipated the contents of legends constructed about Margaret Reilly in the same congregation twenty years later.

At Peekskill, the sisters struggled with the moral and ethnic or racial divide between themselves and their inmates. Their primary tool for preserving the innocents from polluting influences was spatial segregation. Thus when the Good Shepherds built a series of residences at Peekskill, each one was dedicated to a different set of charges as defined by their moral purity. The newest residence, Villa Loretto, housed adolescent girls; Mount St. Florence, about a twenty-minute walk away, housed the younger girls; and Saint Ann's Home housed the orphans.[87] For residents of Villa Loretto who chose to leave Peekskill and return to Manhattan, the sisters also supervised a building of furnished rooms and apartments on 17th Street.[88] For some years, Villa Loretto also served as Public School No. 617 of the New York City school system, assisting children who needed special attention.

In 1904 almost 400 children from grades one through eight were transferred from Manhattan to the orphanage at Peekskill. Between 1928 and 1975, St. Ann's Home served an astonishing total of nearly 9,000 girls, mostly orphans, and these children were *not* the major ministry of the RGS.[89] Over those forty-seven years, the sisters took in an average of 191 homeless and orphaned girls per year. As the institutional history states, "The desire of the Sisters was to separate them wholly from the more sophisticated children," but as a concession to the cold winters, the red brick home was linked to the convent by a covered walkway.[90] The St. Ann's Home for Girls received glowing reports from the state school examiner after his 1907 visit. He rated the facility as Class 1, "showing practically no defects."[91] The facility, which could house 500 children, had spacious views of the Hudson River from the western windows, while "the varied and beautiful landscape, which meets

The summer store at St. Ann's Home for Destitute Children, Peekskill. At their monthly store, the children at St. Ann's Home spent the money they had made from the sales of various crocheted articles. The presence of American flags suggests a date of July 4 or perhaps Flag Day in June. The Good Shepherd sisters looked upon the store as a means to teach the relationship between work and reward and "the use and value of money as a medium of exchange." The RGS ended this work in 1913 to concentrate exclusively on delinquent girls and women. (From *St. Ann's Home for Girls, Mount Florence, Peekskill, New York, in Charge of the Religious of the Good Shepherd* [1907])

the eye at every turn, is regarded as having the happiest effect, moral and aesthetic, upon the plastic mind of the child."[92]

The girls in the care of the sisters were taught traditional forms of manual work, including hemming, crocheting, and fine needlework, as well as food preparation, farming, floriculture, and laundry. The one avenue of industrial production was the printery. The Good Shepherd convent gained revenue by its sale of handmade and printed religious cards, forging an ongoing commercial connection to the outside world that supported the religious community, supplemented by purchases and donations made by visitors attending special events at Peekskill. The timing of the Good Shepherds was fortuitous: the American Catholic publishing industry, including printeries at convents, expanded during the 1920s. The Good Shepherds were encouraged by the success of the press that was founded in 1901 at Clyde, Missouri, to generate pamphlets promoting frequent Holy Communion among Catholics. In a few decades, the Clyde Benedictines had secured a national consumer market, while in Peekskill, the community was also learning to make a reliable income from their production and sale of holiday cards.[93] According to one historian of the congregation, "The original designs are made by the children, supervised by a Sister, and when the die is made, the work is printed by the children in their own printing plant."[94] The printing department also set type, bound books and pamphlets, and produced the cards designed by the art section. For the community itself, the Peekskillers printed a monthly magazine, *Voice of the Good Shepherd*, which contained stories and verses about community life.

Public opinion is fickle, however, and in the late 1920s, the reputation of the industrious Good Shepherds was tested when they were charged with inhuman treatment of the girls who had been remanded to them by the criminal courts. A union leader with the Amalgamated Clothing Workers (ACW) wrote to Governor Franklin Roosevelt of New York, accusing the sisters of putting their "prisoners" in straitjackets and of providing bad food and unsanitary conditions.[95] The attending physician at Peekskill quickly denied the charges and turned the tables, instead portraying the sisters as victims of the unruly girls. In his judgment, the sisters were "handicapped by not being able to employ more stringent methods to enforce discipline." Mother Raymond herself learned of the complaint for the first time from the newspaper story and immediately invited the governor to make a personal inspection of the St. Germaine Home.[96]

The slander against the Good Shepherd sisters was motivated by fear of unfair economic competition. George Gooze, the accuser and the manager of the Shirt, Boys' Waist and Collar Workers, an affiliate of the ACW, claimed that the convent forced young captive women to perform excessive hours of work. Ruthless, exploitative, unfair: he piled up charges against the sisters. When the superior pointed out that the laundry was the only place where the inmates worked—and at that, for "only a few hours a day"—the story subsided. The accusations, however, tapped a rich vein of anticonvent feeling that dated back to nativist attacks on Roman Catholics in the 1830s. In New England, especially, mob assaults on convents and innuendos about nefarious secret goings-on created mistrust of the nuns and sisters of the young United States, despite their obvious and public charitable contributions to American society.[97] As at Peekskill, in Charlestown, Massachusetts, economic envy of the sisters' success was a root cause of the rioting. The Good Shepherds, given the very nature of their vocation to help the marginalized, were likely targets of accusations during the outburst of nativist feeling in the 1920s, which led to such events in New York as Ku Klux Klan marches throughout the decade and savage attacks in 1928 on the presidential candidacy of Al Smith, the state's first Catholic governor. In nearby Quebec, Canada, during the same decade, Catholic institutions fell prey to a series of arsons. In January 1923 the *New York Times* reported that the Good Shepherd convent there became the eleventh to be burned, a tragedy that surely increased the anxiety of the New York sisters.[98] As with the New England convent riots ninety years earlier, the financial motives underlying the attacks on the New York convent were disguised under charges of the sisters' cruelty and perversion.

Of the three groups present at many Good Shepherd institutions—the boarding children who attended the school; the destitute and mostly orphaned children who lived in a separate home (following a request from the state, this work was ended in 1913 to focus exclusively on the delinquents);[99] and the Magdalens, or delinquent women—it was only the last who were completely secluded from everyone else. After a year's probationary period with the Good Shepherds, the delinquents were consecrated to Saint Mary Magdalen, given a new religious name, and permitted to don a semireligious black dress.[100] They could not take religious vows, however, due to their sins.[101] If a consecrated Magdalen was still living in the community after four years, she was permitted to have a "more impressive ceremonial" that conferred on her a silver cross and a black veil. Each Magdalen shared in the house's labors and recreations but was free to leave if and when she wanted. The group earned a living through needlework and observed some monastic rules by praying and meditating together daily.

Although the Magdalens could not become RGS sisters, they constituted an accepted third order within the Catholic Church, described as "an austere, contemplative community. They follow the rule of the third Order of Mount Carmel, and prayer, penance and manual labor and just enough recreation to prevent them from becoming discouraged or morose, fill their days."[102] They had their own choir, distinct from the sisters and the children. When they became Magdalens, they "cut themselves off from all association with the penitents, even the consecrated." The 1930 federal census lists thirteen Magdalen sisters at Peekskill, isolating them even in the census document on a separate page from the inmates, schoolchildren, and vowed sisters. The presence of girls and women who had criminal records provided an undercurrent of danger and transgression at the convent and fueled its metaphors of contagion. The contrast between the kind of women represented by the streetwalkers and the celibate sisters could not have been more pronounced. On the other hand, as Sister Thorn vividly demonstrated, the American Catholic convent preserved (or perhaps was acknowledging for the first time) an equally treacherous underground culture of the demonic;

of sexual violation; of belief in spirit possession, numerology, and prophecy; and of the physical forms of mysticism. These dimensions of Christianity were activated by the report of Margaret's stigmatization at Peekskill, but they were not necessarily distinct from the threatening subcultures represented by the offenders.[103]

To put the Magdalens into local perspective, one need only compare them with the Bedford Hills Reformatory for Women, run by the state of New York and established in 1901.[104] Its director, Katharine Bement Davis, had compiled a report for George Kneeland's *Commercialized Prostitution in New York City*. Only 16 percent of prostitutes, Davis found, came from middle-class families. Most came from working-class backgrounds or the poor; many *children* of immigrants, including the Irish, European Jews, Austro-Hungarians, and native-born African Americans, were likely to enter lives of prostitution.[105] Davis speculated that immigrants' children learned about prostitution from American-born, working-class peers and then imitated them—a finding that, if valid, would have wide import for the Catholic population and give ammunition to Catholic conservatives who opposed assimilation into such a defiantly godless American society. A comparison of the federal census data for the Good Shepherd community at Peekskill in 1920 and 1930 reveals that many of the delinquents were the offspring of foreign-born parents—the very group most likely to fall into self-destructive habits.

In addition to working with grown women, the Good Shepherds also rehabilitated juvenile offenders. "*Rehabilitation* means to clothe anew," noted a historian of the congregation.[106] The sisters began with the assumption that criminal acts resulted from a flaw in character, which could be remolded in their institution. The sisters' understanding of their charges reflected a general cultural uncertainty about when maturity began: was an adolescent, a category of human development that was just emerging in the early twentieth century, a child or an adult? This ambivalence endures today in the American justice system regarding whether young offenders should be tried as adults or children.

The American juvenile court system dates from the early 1900s, with all states but two installing one by 1919. In New York City, as in other major cities, the sisters faced the daunting statistic that between 50 and 64 percent of the defendants brought before the court were Catholics.[107] Soon they would have to accommodate the state's assignment of Catholic children to a Catholic probation officer (a volunteer position that became salaried over time), adding to the culture of expertise in social work and challenging the sisters whose method depended on moral training rather than "social treatment."[108]

The sisters were proud to report that they regarded the "inmates" as sinners, not as social experiments. In their preoccupation with saving wayward girls, however, Catholics and Progressives shared the same concern. Despite the fact that boys outnumbered girls two or three to one in all juvenile institutions, society became obsessed with the "girl problem."[109]

Among the women rehabilitated by the RGS, a typical anecdote in the casebooks involved Bertha, identified as a non-Catholic of nearly forty who worked in the medical profession (possibly as a nurse) and who had become a morphine addict.[110] After two years in treatment with the RGS, she was restored, though not without a few setbacks along the way (she stole a purse in the convent and was discovered with drugs that had been sneaked in by a visitor.) Bertha began to show interest in Catholicism, although the Good Shepherds were quick to point out that they did not proselytize. Their claim is a bit disingenuous, since all delinquents were obliged to attend prayer and chapel together no matter what their religion, and there were also protests from non-Catholics at the convent who resented being sent there.[111] While the Magdalens were not forced to attend classes in Catholic doctrine, they were contained within an entirely Catholic environment, in which the constant presence of sisters, religious images, and rituals surely had some impact on their future religious choices. The sacrament of confession was constantly offered to them, and it is not surprising that many of the delinquents took the option to unburden themselves.

Six years after her sojourn with the RGS, Bertha was drug-free and partially reinstated in her former job. Why did her treatment succeed? The RGS credited "Divine help" rather than institutional strategy, "which is to analyze the individual in order to find the 'why' back of her anti-social, or delinquent action."[112] The Good Shepherds did not completely ignore factors such as the environment, heredity, and physical condition of a girl that might contribute to her delinquency.[113] But even while using whatever psychological and educational diagnostic tools were available to them, the sisters regarded delinquency as a personal, willful choice that could be corrected fully only through the aid of Jesus, the Good Shepherd and ultimate healer.

The New York court system showed its confidence in the work of the Catholic sisters by remanding many women charged with crimes to the Good Shepherds. In June 1923, for example, the twenty-one-year-old mother of an abandoned infant was charged with shoplifting from Bloomingdale's. Unlike the three other shoplifters arraigned with her, who were sent to the workhouse, Mrs. Nettie Robilotto was sentenced to the care of the sisters.[114] Not everyone accepted being committed, however, and occasional reports of girls escaping the 90th Street RGS facility appeared in the press. In 1890, for instance, three enterprising girls hoisted a plank against a wall, scaled it, and were met by friends with a boat on the East River at 89th Street. In 1919 an escapee died after crawling out on the window ledge and sliding down knotted sheets, only to lose her grip and fall.[115] Newspapers were one of the few media venues that revealed the presence of conflicts within the Good Shepherd houses by reporting on the aggressive or transgressive behaviors of the wayward girls. Their rebellious voices intrude into the sisters' narrative of the redemption of fallen women only at infrequent moments like this, a marked contrast with the published histories of the Good Shepherds that highlight only the successes of their rehabilitative efforts.

The sisters' guidance in providing moral training for children came from the copious instructions of Mother Euphrasia. Her compilation, *Practical Rules for the Direction of the Classes*, still steered the Good Shepherds in the twentieth century.[116] Among her words of advice were reminders that the ultimate goal was the soul's salvation: "We should never lose sight of the end of our vocation as Religious of the Good Shepherd; we should in all things aim at forming our children with a view to their eternal salvation, and not shrink from the trouble of having them taught all that can help them in after-life."[117] Did that prove to be useful advice for seventeen-year-old Alvira, a girl of Spanish descent who was not a Catholic? She had been sent to the Good Shepherds after stabbing and killing a woman in the butcher shop where she was employed. Facing life imprisonment, she was set to work doing needlework, in which she came to excel. As a consequence of listening to the sermons and weekly instructions, the sisters said, Alvira soon converted to Catholicism. However, her health failed, and she died not long after. The RGS author commented gravely: "Sometimes it requires death itself to seal the conversion."[118] Judged by Mother Euphrasia's standards for rehabilitation, Alvira's death was a positive outcome because her immortal soul had been redeemed.

By the 1940s, the RGS had largely abandoned its work with adult female offenders, who were sent instead to a state-run prison. From then on, the sisters concentrated their energies upon molding the moral fiber of adolescents, usually fourteen to eighteen years old, and in educating the indigent children sent to them. For information about their clients, the RGS now relied on data supplied by state institutions through the social worker, the probation officer, or the placement agency. Yet the sisterhood continued to defend its autonomy from and superiority to state-run efforts by arguing that modern techniques could not properly build character. Only the training and strengthening of the will in the RGS manner, tailored for each individual, would enable the penitent to change her life—with God's help.[119]

In their ambition to build children's character and rehabilitate adults, the Good Shepherd sisters expressed some condescension toward "fallen" women, notably in their constant reference to them as children and the requirement that the inmates address the sisters as "Mother." Still, RGS programs were among the few available in American cities to help women who were otherwise forsaken by preparing them for employment, albeit as laundresses, seamstresses, and machine operators. The sisters enforced strict rules upon their clients. The reformed women were not allowed to speak about their previous lives to anyone, especially to each other. Girls in the care of the RGS could ask advice from the sisters "as from a mother" but could not discuss their pasts, even with them. The delinquents were thus sealed from their sexual and criminal histories by the sisters' refusal to acknowledge them. The sisters took this rule from Saint John Eudes, who cited Saint Paul's injunction that Christ had freed humans from death to give them a newness of spirit.[120] The RGS interpreted "newness" here as a form of willed amnesia intended to preserve the sexual innocence that divided the pure from the depraved.

How successful was the RGS in its main task of reforming "troubled" and "friendless" girls and women? The city of New York itself certainly offered a daunting laboratory. It had the largest Catholic population in the nation in 1918, including many lawbreakers, and its decentralized Catholic charities were just entering the process of being consolidated, in part as a response to the Strong Commission's investigations of the State Board of Charities in 1915 and 1916.[121] In the 1920s, RGS sisters continued the reform projects that they had begun before the Civil War, but now they were obliged to conform to regulations enforced by state and city health and welfare agencies and to compete with a host of new secular experts—social workers, psychiatrists, psychoanalysts, and public-health reformers—mostly clustered in the nation's cities. The sisters' efforts to rescue "abnormal" women were also challenged by the emergent notion of psychiatry, as the latter was shifting its focus from insanity to normality in the early twentieth century in order to address the existing cultures of the asylum and prison.[122]

The sisters kept their concerns and their approach to remolding the characters of their charges rooted in the nineteenth-century traditions of their religious order rather than realigning their ministries to the modern categories of the adolescent, the criminal, and the mental patient. The RGS dealt with women who were marginalized by society, but they were not necessarily compassionate toward those who had lost their chastity—although by embracing them as their life's work, the Good Shepherds present a marked contrast to the Sisters of Mercy, who chose only to assist "good" women with job training and placement.[123] The new class of specialists that had arisen during the Progressive era to treat social problems defended their work from a scientific basis, whereas the Catholic sisterhoods tried to resolve problems through the partial embrace of new ideas combined with their traditional faith in prayer, care, and training in practical vocations. They continued to understand their work as helping to substitute a new self for the old sinful one, to encourage "the formation of strong, noble characters by training to replace the weaknesses and disorders that formerly held sway."[124] Yet instead of simply passing moral judgment, the sisters at least tried to see any previous wrongdoings from the point of view of the girls and women they treated.

Because Catholic social-service providers were not accustomed to diagnosing social deviance as a consequence of social structures, they were unprepared to wholeheartedly endorse and shape state-run programs to alleviate poverty, contain perversity, and fight the social and economic causes of desperation. In the end, Catholic sisterhoods and charitable agencies derived their practices from the starting point of individual sinfulness and their moral notions of what defined a "good girl," even at the very moment when the ideal of celibacy in Catholic religious life and abstinence in marital life was itself being judged as perverse by the new cultures and lexicons of psychiatry and psychoanalysis, which often exaggerated the opposite pole by defining women as "hypersexual."[125] If the monastery was indeed a "hospital of the spiritual sick" as Mother Raymond imagined, then who exactly was being treated? Deviant or normal women?

Because the RGS considered immoral behavior as a problem of will rather than reason, the sisters, even when they claimed to adopt "modern" educational strategies, judged these secular models to be flawed: "It is no exaggeration to say that the modern world has a false notion of education and of character formation. True education and true character formation are based on the Ten Commandments and the principles stressed in the Sermon on the Mount of Truth, Himself. For this reason neither our latest literatures nor current pedagogical theories, nor the tenets of modern social economy, are competent to aid a generation that does not comprehend this fundamental truth."[126] Given this understanding of moral formation, the Good Shepherds' attempts to remedy the Magdalens' characters by creating moral strength contained a dose of disdain toward secular strategies of the self.

Between the 1840s and 1920s, the spiritual formation of Catholic sisters in the United States became regimented and standardized, and numerous accommodations were made between European motherhouses and their American communities to address the New World environment. Carol Coburn and Martha Smith identify four traits that made American Catholic women's religious communities unique: ethnic and class diversity; lifelong education and work; perpetual vows; and a distinctive environment and tradition that assured their existence and growth "well into the twentieth century."[127] Other than the Irish homogeneity of their New York congregations, the RGS displayed these elements. The efforts by the Catholic Church to strengthen cloister after 1917, however, went against the program of apostolic ministry and spirit of modified enclosure that defined the Good Shepherds. The RGS was a relative newcomer among religious communities for women, and its charitable work with women and children helped sisters maintain public goodwill in France, although they were not permitted to receive state funds due to the suppression of religious orders during the Revolution and in the uncertain political climate of the next decades.[128] The seesaw between imperial and republican France continued throughout the nineteenth century, such that the revolutionary goal of complete separation of church and state in France was not achieved until 1905 in the closing years of the Third Republic. Many Catholic congregations who had a transnational presence by this time were affected by the politico-religious conflicts in France, including the Sacred Heart order, which was forced to send several thousand French sisters to American convents at that point. As for the Good Shepherds, whose modern form dates from the 1830s, they were in the paradoxical position of having been tolerated but not supported by nationalist elements in France, whereas in the United States, they served nation-building goals by their supervision and teaching at public schools in New York, their care for orphans, and their court-related assistance to at-risk girls and women in teaching them industrial skills to survive in a society that valued independence and self-sufficiency. Such job training, while initially understood by the RGS as the means of character reform, became seen as a "cure" for prostitution and other forms of urban vice in the early twentieth century.

This chapter has described how the Good Shepherds labored to create a harmonious environment for themselves, orphans, schoolchildren, delinquents, and Magdalens alike. The presence of Sister Thorn, with her mystical claims, added a new, unpredictable factor. The superior's treatment of Margaret Reilly was closely watched by others, since it implicated women's governance of women, a factor scrutinized by the male hierarchy because of its new determination to enforce stricter rules for cloister. Not long after Margaret's arrival, Peekskill's leader, Mother Raymond, became the target of protests from several members of the 90th Street Good Shepherd house. Archbishop Hayes, however, was "far from favorably impressed" with the malcontents' leader at 90th Street, Sister St. Germaine, whose complaints led him to visit the sisters, conduct interviews, and hold a long meeting with the community to address grievances. The Good Shepherd provincial also wrote to Hayes and provided a very critical assessment of St. Germaine. Hayes, however, was soon gratified by St. Germaine's "change of attitude."[129]

The disgruntled sisters had contended that Mother Raymond was a severe administrator, even though, they admitted, she did not exempt herself from the rules. (The sisters made much of the story that she did not break cloister even to attend her own father's funeral. Although Raymond was not bound by the rules on this occasion, she refused to take any privilege she would not permit to her convent.) As superior, however, Mother Raymond did not prove to be at her best in the crises facing the Good Shepherds due to Sister Thorn, nor was the advice that she received from male chaplains and confessors consistent or uniformly helpful. If Sister St. Germaine showed a malicious side in spreading gossip about Margaret Reilly, then Mother Raymond acted too harshly in overseeing all matters except those pertaining to Sister Thorn. This indulgence led Raymond's successor as Peekskill superior to pursue the extreme strategy of trying to altogether erase Sister Thorn from the congregation's memory. Margaret's role, as a middle-aged novice confined to a wheelchair, supplied a story of divine intervention and stigmatization that gave her a unique chance to secure special status inside the congregation and to influence the world beyond the convent as a conduit of supernatural power. To achieve some influence, she would need allies, which Mother Raymond supplied.

The Peekskill RGS convent of the twenties and thirties shows evidence of a transitional quality in the sisters' approach to many dimensions of life, from the personal to the communal. Their uncertainty mirrors the position of the children of Catholic immigrants facing an unknown future and recognizing that many of the choices facing them demanded pragmatic action that did not necessarily match the church's moral teachings.[130] Some of those points of compromise appeared in the events of convent life. First, the Good Shepherds' decision to admit Margaret Reilly to the congregation was then undercut by her extra-lengthy probationary period. Second, although the sisters sponsored and staffed a public school at the convent, they disparaged the state's mandate for their accreditation as schoolteachers. Third, while the RGS chose to focus on transforming young women, they also infantilized them through forms of discipline intended to repress their adult, and often criminal, pasts. Finally, the RGS's treatment and training of adult women delivered a mixed message: the sisters taught job skills to troubled women to help them gain employment and a measure of autonomy, yet they preserved Catholic traditional ideals of womanhood through a domestic curriculum of cooking, laundry, and sewing and by constant reminders to the Magdalens that they could never overcome the loss of their virginity. For those unmarried Magdalens who had children, the church's answer was to oppose birth control, a position that perversely became more rigid during the decade of the Great Depression, when even married couples could ill afford children.[131] The "rehabilitation" of penitents exposed the unspoken conflicts between sexuality and maternity in the strategies of the Good Shepherds and the double standard that judged women more harshly for expressing their sexuality. For prostitutes and unwed mothers, the option to become a Magdalen—membership in a tertiary religious order—presented another halfway solution that required them to keep vows yet fell short of recognizing them as an authentic religious community. The only other option for these vulnerable women—leaving the care of the RGS—meant a return to all of the world's temptations. The sisters themselves were living in new territory, as well: as daughters of immigrants who grew up in the same neighborhoods that supplied their inmates, they applied formulas that were not always attuned to the real-life situations of their wards but that they believed reflected the divine commandments of their Good Shepherd.

{3} Mad about Bleeding Nuns

Sister Thorn's Champions

If I lived in the 1820s I'd be mad about bleeding nuns.
—André Breton, 1923

Sister said we would become saints if we hurt ourselves.
—Margaret Reilly to Sister Mary Carmelita Quinn, quoted in
Quinn, "Sister Mary Crown of Thorns," 5

New Yorkers did not first learn of the bleeding nun at Peekskill through the press; nor through the Catholic networks in Manhattan at Blessed Sacrament, St. Francis de Sales, or St. Ignatius; nor from the gossip of the Good Shepherd sisters. Instead, Margaret Reilly was introduced to New Yorkers through "a sloppy slushy letter written by a Passionist."[1] After visiting Margaret in 1922, Father Bertrand Barry composed a sort of "spiritual chain letter" that he sent to numerous friends. It became an embarrassment to the Good Shepherds because it contained many errors and drew unwanted attention to the religious order, but its odd details excited the public and drew fervent crowds to the convent.[2]

Father Bertrand's involvement began in Peekskill on a chilly November evening in 1921 while he was visiting Father J. E. B. Daly, a diocesan priest who was the convent chaplain at Mount St. Francis for the Franciscan Missionaries of the Sacred Heart. The two men sat on the hard formal sofas of the convent parlor, used only for clergy and favored visitors, who were served there by the sisters as though royal guests. Father Daly could not resist telling his guest about the "remarkable case at the Good Shepherd convent" nearby that had attracted the attention of the archbishop and numerous priests and physicians. Father Bertrand was especially intrigued since he was scheduled to offer a spiritual retreat to the Good Shepherds in preparation for the annual renewal of their vows. Soon, he would meet the source of the unusual attention.

After arriving at Mount St. Florence, Father Bertrand felt somewhat deflated that a day and a half passed without any mention from the sisters or the superior of "this favored child dwelling in their midst." Bertrand was determined not to reveal his curiosity about Margaret, but he finally did catch a glimpse of her at Mass on Sunday morning, again as she left the chapel, and a third time on the grounds of the convent. Finally, Mother Raymond arranged for him to meet Margaret after breakfast the next day. Bertrand "tried to appear indifferent and wanted to leave it all in God's hands," but when the superior ushered him into Margaret's cell, he felt himself "face to face with a chosen soul, an ardent lover of Jesus Crucified and, with God's grace, perhaps a saint." On the wall, he saw the crucifix in blood, which he examined with a magnifying glass. His next privilege was to see "the crucifix she has had over her heart ten years." As he gazed "most intently and earnestly," he found "an identical crucifix with that on the wall" that prompted him to ask to touch it. "Reverently I touched the congealed blood that gives the figure to the body of my Savior." "How can I tell my feelings?" he wondered. "Again the thought of my first Mass and the real presence of Jesus before me on the Altar was recalled by my soul."

Margaret then told Father Bertrand how she had received the stigmata "seven times, when her hands and feet were pierced and her side opened." Each time, the pain was so severe that without God's consoling words, she could not have borne it. She gave him a brief sketch of her life, including a description of her friendship with Monsignor Taylor; her recent employment in the office of "Bernard Barnell [sic], the New York banker"; and her delayed vocation. Bertrand inquired about any satanic interference, and Margaret promptly supplied the details. When he asked if she suffered in any ways other than the stigmata, she showed him through the material of her black stockings her "open wounds and glistening blood covering every part of her frail limbs." The scourge marks were "more than I had been prepared to see," the priest confided. After about an hour, Mother Raymond returned, ushering Bertrand into the dining room, where they discussed these events. There, the superior revealed that Margaret's wounds were sometimes deep enough for her to "lay her finger in the furrow." The marks bled so profusely that "she had bundles of clothes soaked in blood before she was able to stop the copious flow." Although Margaret was already thirty-seven years old, Bertrand judged her to be "a child" of about twenty-seven. From Mother Raymond he heard about Margaret's relationship with Monsignor Taylor, the arrival of the crucifix on the wall at Peekskill, the visits of Dr. Thomas McParlan, and the testing of her blood. Despite the many peculiar details that were reported to him, he found Margaret's manner natural and ordinary, "most agreeable in her manners and vivacious in her speech."

Margaret's stigmata were accompanied by other signs and wonders, Father Bertrand learned. For instance, when Margaret had left Peekskill briefly for a visit to the Philadelphia Good Shepherd convent, a sister who passed by Margaret's guest room at night "beheld a light so brilliant . . . that it was impossible for her to gaze upon it," although it had no discernible source. The provincial of the Philadelphia Good Shepherds told Bertrand that Mother Raymond had received a crucifix on the wall of her cell similar to the one in Margaret's room, although Raymond had made no mention of it. Margaret also assured Bertrand that God had even foretold his visit to her and expressed pleasure with the priest "because of his work and the souls he has brought to Me."

Soon after he left Peekskill, Father Bertrand learned that Archbishop Patrick Hayes had forbidden any visitors to Margaret and had silenced the community from speaking about her. By March 1922, Bertrand concluded in his report, "nothing more can be added, than Thorn is leading a more and more mystical life, and that by love and suffering she is becoming more and more extraordinary." He was convinced that "the patience of this willing victim can only be understood by those whose privilege it has been to come near to her in her Novitiate life. Never has she been free from suffering as she has never been restored to what might be even regarded as fair health."[3] He added: "The few privileged friends who have been permitted to meet her tell of a cheerful and patient spirit resigned to the Savior's will and a grand example of charity—the real love of God and one's neighbor—can be found evidenced in so a [sic] frail human being." Bertrand's faith in the sickly Margaret was only deepened when he learned of her miraculous cure of the illness of a sister's family member in Dunkirk, New York, near Lake Erie.[4] His "chain letter" concludes with this "marvelous" event.

Father Bertrand's report was thick with details and personal musings, but it also was rife with errors. Despite, or because of, his former experience as a newspaper writer, he invented or embellished many items (including Margaret's "employment" with Bernard Baruch), and he bungled the names of Father Daly and Dr. McParlan and got Margaret's age wrong. From a theological perspective, the most striking part of his account is the connection he drew between perceiving the mark on Margaret's chest and the Real Presence of Christ in the Eucharist. Three times, Bertrand remarked that seeing and touching the raised bloody crucifix put him in mind of offering his first Mass and the power of consecration, taking "my God and my All" into his own hands. While he clearly was hungering for spiritual intensity, he also focused on the sacerdotal (priestly) privilege that he possessed as something that distinguished him from lay Catholics. A modern reader is also struck by the eroticism of his encounter with a sister he had never met before. To display her wounds and the crucifix on her chest, Margaret had to open her collar and undergarment and also lift her skirts to bare the thigh. For Father Bertrand to scrutinize her as he did (with a magnifying glass) and to touch her "frail limbs" seems highly unusual, even more so if "good, practical" Mother Raymond was indeed absent from the room, as he reported. In 1922 Bertrand suffered a stroke, but it is unknown whether it occurred before or after his visit to Peekskill, and thus it is unclear whether he was seeking healing for himself or fulfilling a quest to witness a "privileged soul" before his death.

After Bertrand sent his letter to numerous recipients, two other accounts of Margaret Reilly surfaced. The first, "Spinations," was produced by Father Thomas à Kempis Reilly, a Dominican priest whose elaborate ramblings and numerological equations expose an occult dimension to Catholicism. Fixating on Margaret's statement that Jesus himself gave her a list of thirty-seven pages from the English two-volume translation of St. Bernard's eighty-six sermons on the Song of Songs, he labored to draw connections between the nuptial imagery in these "choice texts" by Bernard and the spiritual wisdom to be found there. Another Dominican, Walter Scanlan, provided his own twist to the story by compiling his diary entries as "Thorn: A Story of Divine Providence." Finally, the correspondence between the more than twenty priests and physicians involved with Sister Thorn fills in some of the gaps in her mystical experiences and also acts as a corrective to Father Bertrand's account.

Margaret Reilly's religious community, the Good Shepherds, was a semi-cloistered order that combined active and contemplative pursuits and believed in the certainty that contemplation and deep prayer could initiate mystical experiences. Consequently, they had no desire to deny Margaret's experiences, but they feared the publicity she was receiving and the apparent defiance of the vow of obedience. The RGS had only been active in New York for about sixty years and had endured a difficult start, as the sisters found it hard to convince the bishop of the propriety of their mission to delinquent girls and women. In postrevolutionary France, where the Good Shepherds began, it became the task of such congregations to adopt a social (rather than cloistered) mission that would ingratiate them with the secular state; hence, most of these new sisterhoods took up teaching, nursing, or the care of children—in short, a practical, nonmystical vocation that would offer valuable assistance to society and not affront secularists who held political control.

At the onset of her reported stigmata, therefore, Margaret was an anomalous figure, a novice who possibly shared the background and experiences of the delinquent girls and women housed in the convent but who also was useful to the Catholic Church as proof that any pious Catholic could receive mystical gifts, although these were not regarded as the primary goals of monastic life. Nonetheless, Margaret's experiences fit the assumptions of an audience who held similar beliefs about mysticism, even if it represented an archaic form of piety to some Catholics. This chapter asks how Margaret Reilly's fame spread beyond the convent and how a nascent cult emerged with the help of her lay and clerical allies, who believed that her mystical gifts furnished proof for the existence of the miraculous, which they connected to a two-fold divine plan to protect religious vocations from decline and to defend America from evil forces at large. Sanctity is a social construction, and as earlier chapters have indicated, Margaret was shaped from childhood by piety that taught salvation through suffering, an outlook encouraged by her spiritual directors, Monsignor Matthew Taylor and Father Brady. Once she entered convent life, several priests, sisters, physicians, and even a British historian began to record and interpret her life. These accounts chose to highlight certain elements: first, demonic powers working to prevent Margaret from achieving her vocation; second, the importance of secret wisdom that Jesus delivered to Margaret; and third, Margaret's mission to preserve religious vocations in America. In a decade when newspaper reporting took on an unprecedented national significance, the press further contributed to her notoriety by garbling many of these strange details and feeding them to an audience already hungry for thrills.

A first factor contributing to Sister Thorn's wide circle of supporters was her spiritual training from sisters and priests who were well-known and respected in the New York Catholic community. From childhood, her parochial schoolteachers had shared stories of the lives of the saints and their penances to inspire holiness in the students. Margaret recalled how "Sister said we would become saints if we hurt ourselves." In her young adulthood, Margaret developed significant relationships with two spiritual directors, Monsignor Taylor and Father Brady. As discussed earlier, Taylor took special interest in Margaret, serving as her confessor for eighteen years at Blessed Sacrament parish from about 1896, when she was twelve, until his death in 1914. Father Brady succeeded him, having already been appointed by Archbishop Hayes as ecclesiastical superior of all the Good Shepherd sisters in New York. Following Margaret's unexpected relocation to Peekskill in 1921, Mother Raymond requested that Brady be permitted to travel there from St. Francis de Sales to continue as Margaret's confessor.[5] Sister Carmelita described Brady as a staunch friend and a priest who neglected himself on behalf of the poor. However, she suspected that it was Brady rather than Taylor who had imposed penitential tests upon Margaret, such as having her walk in the rain with an unopened umbrella and walk with an open umbrella on a sunny day.

A second factor contributing to the spread of sister Thorn's reputation was the work of several bedside scribes. Her primary biographer, Mother Raymond, served multiple roles as her central eyewitness, religious superior, nurse, and roommate.[6] Every day, Mother Raymond made notations on Margaret's stigmata and other events in a bound notebook, soliciting opinions from community members about the wounds and extraordinary episodes affecting "little sister." As witness and audience, Mother Raymond mediated information to others about her postulant. Beyond merely looking, however, the superior had already begun redacting the events theologically, making interpretations with the assistance of the convent chaplain, who supplied works of mystical theology by the continental theologians for her to read.[7]

The practical Salesian spirituality that had directed the Good Shepherds at their founding was now, with the events affecting Sister Thorn, blending with other European spiritual currents, namely, an emphasis upon suffering and mystical experience. When Sister Thorn's stigmata appeared, Mother Raymond took up reading *The Mystery of Jesus* by Savinien Louismet (1858–1926), the Benedictine author of numerous books on mysticism.[8] Born in Belgium, Louismet visited the United States in 1891, assisting at the dedication of several churches in Oklahoma Territory that were staffed by Belgian Benedictines. In 1915 and 1916, the core of *The Mystical Life* had appeared in serial installments in the *American Catholic Quarterly Review*, a serious-minded journal directed at convents and monasteries.[9] Louismet's interest lay in helping clergy develop their interior spiritual lives but also in bringing methods of affective contemplation to a wider Catholic audience, thereby diffusing monastic ideals into the everyday world. Through her reading of Louismet, Mother Raymond could gauge whether Thorn's symptoms fit the genuine mysticism described by the author.

In his preface, Louismet established his parameters: "The Mysticism I speak of in the following pages is Catholic Mysticism. Not any sort of Catholic or would-be-Catholic Mysticism: but Catholic Traditional Mysticism," which he further defined as "purely and simply the mysticism of our holy Mother the Church, who is the Bride of Christ and the teacher and infallible oracle of truth."[10] His description reflects the confidence of nineteenth-century Ultramontanism, as he defends mysticism as a traditional part of the infallible church.[11]

Nonetheless, in an era of theological disputes that tended to get mired in the minutiae of debates about "acquired" versus "infused" contemplation, Louismet presented mysticism as something available to ordinary Christians. He does not limit the mystic to an overly dogmatic or intellectual domain. Moreover, his inclusive sense of it reveals the interlocked features of the church's symbolic capital: Louismet's mysticism resided not only in the scriptures but also in "the Mysticism of the Missal, of the Ritual, of the Pontifical, of the Ceremonial of Bishops, of the Breviary, of the Martyrology, of the Catechismus Concilii Tridentini, as well as of the Penny Catechism."[12] Although Louismet was just one voice in a discussion about the nature of mysticism within the early twentieth-century church, he reflected the spiritual concerns of many Catholics, triggered in the 1890s by fin de siècle anxieties and again during and after the Great War by the horrors of warfare and the sacrifice of an entire generation.[13] The survivors looked to religion to renew their belief that supernatural help was universally available and not confined to spiritual elites. It is not surprising that mysticism, the direct path to divine power, was one facet of Christian tradition that was rediscovered in a time of crisis. In Margaret's generation, its rediscovery led to countless Catholic dissertations and journal articles in the United States that mirrored this transnational debate about the legacy of the Enlightenment, and which argued that rationalism was a dead-end trap that swallowed up the inner life sought by mystics.

In her role as scribe, Mother Raymond was soon assisted in compiling Margaret Reilly's life by two visitors from a Benedictine community in Missouri. Her motives for believing in Margaret may have been partially selfish: as the superior of the Brooklyn convent, Raymond had been "inclined to do extra things herself," resulting in a troubled environment there, for which she had been rebuked by the superior general in Angers. When Mother Raymond was subsequently named superior at Peekskill, she found in Margaret Reilly a deus ex machina "and proof that all against her [Mother Raymond] were wrong." A Jesuit concluded: "To my mind this explains very much."[14]

Even though Mother Raymond was understandably fearful about what was going on at Mount St. Florence in Peekskill, much of the activity surrounding Margaret caused verbal and physical violence but was not life threatening. The fight against the devil became a major theme in her diaries during these first months. In Catholic mystical theology, even such mundane events as alteration in the taste of food or food revulsion were perceived as signs of the Evil One. Visiting Peekskill from Missouri, Sister Carmelita Quinn recorded an episode on February 17, 1922: "Breakfast and dinner were spoiled, it meant that Margaret Reilly thought the food had a bad taste and smell. Often, Margaret envisioned little black bugs on the food and bread that repelled her from eating." Margaret's observers recalled how Anne Catherine Emmerich, the Westphalian stigmatic, was tormented even by the smell of cooking and once burst into convulsive coughing "because her sister had approached her impregnated with the smell of warm bread just taken from the oven."[15] This same sister was determined to compel Anne to eat, force-feeding her sauerkraut on one occasion and beer on another.[16] Italian stigmatic Maria Domenica Lazzari was so revulsed by food that "a small fragment of sugar caused vomiting so violent that she almost choked, and the smell of a piece of toast produced such discomfort that she fainted away."[17]

The attempt to place Margaret in a lineage of devilish meddling with the eating habits of stigmatics belongs to a tradition of demonology developed in medieval Catholicism that associated demons with orality and the tongue with lust.[18] Spoiled food and food snatched from Margaret's lips were a familiar manifestation of evil forces at work, but this was, quite literally, only the tip of the tongue. In the Middle Ages, demons had multiple mouths—on their breasts, genitals, and buttocks—which represented a popular fear of manifold utterances. The notion of demonic "evil mouths" uttering profane words and blaspheming contrasted with its sacred opposite in Catholic tradition: the incorporation of the Body of Christ through the mouth in Communion. As one of many such binary pairings in Christian theology, it framed the contrast between good (the desire to consume the Host) and evil (the fear of being consumed by Satan).[19]

Sister Thorn's physical torment by devils was not without purpose: through suffering, she embraced her mission of vicarious atonement, as she told others.[20] Pain in her left foot indicated prayers for Archbishop Hayes and the pope; pain in her right foot meant prayers for priests; her left hand was dedicated to laypeople praying to her; and her right hand was to atone for nuns seeking higher education who forgot their duty by seeking worldly advantages. Finally, Margaret's heart symbolized the Good Shepherds and "another convent dear to Jesus." Sister Thorn claimed that the scourge marks on her thighs and the crown of thorns on her forehead were offered for priests who were offending Jesus. She endured these torments to fulfill God's special mission for her to obtain grace for others, especially for priests and religious.[21] Sister Thorn's attempt to create a narrative out of the wounds themselves is a significant feature of the connection between mysticism and the body. As Benedict Anderson has famously noted of nationalism, it must be narrated in order to be brought into existence.[22] So, too, the experience of Catholic saints. As curious as it might seem that Sister Thorn's devotees spent their time divining the meaning of the changing colors of the corpus on her chest and wall and distinguishing the spiritual intentions of her hands and feet, their determination speaks to the desire to affirm the bond between suffering and sanctity in her life.

Within two years of observing the strange phenomena affecting Margaret at Mount St. Florence, Mother Raymond enlisted the help of a cloistered nun well-known for her piety and good sense to interview the postulant and to offer her impressions. Margaret's second observer was Sister Carmelita (Elizabeth Quinn, 1895–1988), a Benedictine at the Conception Convent of Perpetual Adoration in Clyde, Missouri. That community had been founded by Swiss women who came to the United States with the monks from Engelberg Abbey. These monks established Conception Abbey nearby and served the German and Irish immigrants in Missouri. Sister Carmelita's upbringing could not have been more different from those of the urban eastern Good Shepherd sisters. Raised in the "Sullivan settlement" in rural Nebraska and the eldest of five children, Elizabeth Quinn lost her mother at a young age and was sent by her father to an academy staffed by the Sisters of Perpetual Adoration. Up to that point, the Quinn family had attended monthly Mass, presided over by a Franciscan who served their "mission" homestead. Elizabeth entered the Clyde, Missouri, Benedictine foundation in 1912 at age seventeen against her father's wishes, professed in 1914, and took her final vows in 1921. Her official biography charts her achievements but fails to mention the health crises that dogged her life, which were even more numerous than Sister Thorn's ailments. Quinn suffered diphtheria as a child and was nearly killed by the injections to cure it. A period of jaundice followed, then rectal surgery and abdominal surgery, an ovariectomy at age twenty-one, intestinal surgery, pneumonia from the Spanish influenza epidemic in 1919, smallpox in 1920, and a series of pulmonary hemorrhages beginning in 1921, which she constantly aggravated through physical labor. Emergency surgery for an infected molar, recurring pulmonary lesions, and colon surgery conclude the tally at the midpoint of her life. When she encountered Margaret Reilly, Quinn had entered a relative period of vocational calm and good health. At that point, she was coediting *Tabernacle and Purgatory* and serving as secretary to Lukas Etlin, and in 1927 she became novice mistress for her community.

During the 1920s, Sister Carmelita visited Peekskill three times for several weeks at a time. During each stay, she took dictation from Margaret, then transcribed her shorthand notes and typed them when she returned to Clyde, integrating them with the entries from Raymond's notebook. Fifty years later, in 1978, she was contacted by the Good Shepherds seeking further information about Sister Thorn for a potential beatification dossier.[23] During the next five years, Sister Carmelita earnestly answered questions posed by the Good Shepherds about her memories of Sister Thorn. Despite never seeing Margaret's stigmata, Sister Carmelita believed in them, stating: "It is most remarkable that no wound, even those of the hands and feet which penetrated through and through, have left a scar. The skin reveals not the slightest sign of a wound."[24] Carmelita's own mystical experiences had included inner visions, guardian angels, and, in 1919, the acceptance of her secret role as a victim soul on behalf of priests.

Margaret's third scribe-editor was Brother Lukas Etlin, Sister Carmelita's chaplain and colleague at Conception Convent in Missouri. His interest in mysticism dated even from his adolescence, when Anne Catherine Emmerich's mystical revelations became his favorite book. When an anonymous translation of Brentano's *The Passion of Our Lord Jesus Christ according to the Revelations of Ann Catherine Emmerich* (1833) was published by the printery at Clyde in 1914, it was probably Etlin's work. In his descriptions of Sister Thorn's experiences, Etlin seems to have freely interpolated details from Brentano's life of Emmerich.

Born in Sarnen, Switzerland, in 1864, Etlin attended the Benedictine *Realschule* there, then the college of the Benedictine abbey at Engelberg. In 1886 he came to the United States as candidate for monastic life at Conception Abbey in northwest Missouri and acquired the religious name of St. Luke because of his artistic talent.[25] Shortly after his ordination in 1891, Etlin was appointed chaplain to the Benedictine sisters at Clyde, where he served until his death thirty-five years later. At Conception Abbey, Etlin also used the liturgical arts to promote his traditionalist theology. Founded in 1891 by Swiss monks to serve the largely German local Catholic population, the congregation had chosen to decorate its abbey and chapel in the hieratic Byzantine style. After tornado damage to the chapel in 1893, Brother Lukas, who was assigned to oversee the design of the new mosaics, frescoes, and murals, chose to execute them in the similarly severe frontal "Beuron" style. Beuron Monastery, founded in 1863 in southwest Germany, had recently provided three monks to Conception Abbey, two of whom had studied art.[26]

Etlin's interest in directing the spiritual lives of nuns and sisters led him in 1905 to initiate a monthly magazine of Eucharistic devotion called *Tabernacle and Purgatory*. Its title recalled the concern of Catholics at that time for souls languishing in Purgatory. The publication received assistance from

Brother Lukas Etlin, Swiss Benedictine from Conception Abbey in Missouri. The mystically inclined Etlin was one of Sister Thorn's chroniclers and strongest advocates. (Prayer card from the author's collection)

the sisters at Clyde, especially from collaborating editor Sister Carmelita.[27] The magazine soon had 40,000 subscribers to its English edition and 14,000 for the German version. In its pages, the magazine occasionally mentioned the Good Shepherd sisters or addressed mystical phenomena related to the Eucharist. A 1912 issue discussed "Little Nellie of Holy God," a ward of the Good Shepherd sisters in Ireland who was celebrated as the child who influenced the pope to lower the age of first Communion. In the 1930s and 1940s, the magazine featured articles on the stigmata of Therese Neumann. The journal changed dramatically in 1965, when it abandoned its singular emphasis on Eucharistic devotion and was renamed *Spirit and Life* to reflect the innovations of Vatican II.[28]

Brother Lukas's personality was deeply austere. He practiced ordinary forms of daily self-denial such as fasting, then increased his penances by denying himself water during the exhausting summer harvest at Clyde and by keeping himself awake at prayer through much of the night. In Lukas's cell at Clyde, the life-sized painting of Mary was often stained with drops of his blood. "These," his biographer reports, "were the result of some thorn branches which he had tied together and therewith scourged himself. The Sister who had been given charge of his room kept the secret during his lifetime and frequently cleansed the picture and the floor from the drops of blood."[29] Lukas also kept a whip made of leather straps and wore a wooden heart under his robe with nails facing his bare chest.[30] The Benedictines were obliged to send him back to Switzerland several times to recover his health, which was compromised by his "labors and penances."[31]

After World War I, in conjunction with Cardinal Michael Faulhaber of Munich, Etlin directed the "Caritas" project that raised funds on behalf of seminaries, convents, and orphanages in thirty-two nations, especially those damaged and destroyed by the war. From 1920 until his death seven years later, Etlin collected and distributed more than $2 million to a list of nations that expanded from Austria and Germany to include China and Russia. For his role in fund-raising, especially in providing postwar aid to the former Axis powers, Etlin was hailed as "a second St. Vincent de Paul"[32] and received papal recognition. But by sympathizing with the vanquished "Huns," Etlin, although Swiss, also placed himself in a delicate political position in the United States. Americans were resentful of German aggression, a situation not improved by Cardinal Faulhaber, who blessed Germany's "avenging" of the assassination at Sarajevo in 1915 as "the prototype of a just war."[33] Etlin's role in postwar philanthropy that aided Germany was at once Christian and arguably anti-American. The European church, on the other hand, benefited enormously from Etlin's work because Caritas funds were used to provide scholarships to train some 2,800 new priests at a crucial moment when war casualties had decimated the priesthood and the cost of sending a son to seminary after the war was prohibitive for most families.[34] The Benedictine sisters, Etlin's unheralded partners, proudly noted that "His Eminence Cardinal Stepinac, and His Eminence Joseph Cardinal Wendel of Munich, were both educated on scholarships from Clyde!"[35]

Lukas embodied the devotional mindset of those pre–Vatican II priests who were preoccupied with penitence and sacrifice. Rather than expressing a theology of inclusiveness that welcomed the participation of all Catholics in the sacrament of the Eucharist, he described it in private and possessive terms, as in his sermon on the theme that "Jesus is all mine." Although frequent Communion, which his monastic community advocated, has become the norm for Catholics since Vatican II, during his life, Lukas was "sometimes criticized for what was considered an undue emphasis on the adoration of the Blessed Eucharist."[36] That is, he tended to worship the Eucharist as a sacred object in order to elevate the unique powers of priests to transform ordinary bread through consecration, rather than emphasizing the sacrament's effects on Christian living and accessibility to all Christians. The splendor and mystery of the Latin Mass enacted this hierarchical relationship by placing the laity, whom Lukas did not regard as equal to the clergy, into the position of observers rather than participants.

The spirituality evolving in Etlin's community at Clyde was already moving in the direction of change, however, as it began to share in the movement originating at St. John's Abbey in Collegeville, Minnesota, whose Benedictines were spearheading a drive for liturgical reform among Catholics. Their emphasis upon including the laity in the central sacrament of the church flourished alongside an older spirituality that emphasized the Eucharist (and the priest) as a sacrificial offering. At St. John's Abbey, that latter position was represented by the spirituality of Joseph Kreuter, a Benedictine who, like Etlin, championed the cult of vicarious suffering, embodied by the "victim soul."[37] These opposing tendencies within one religious congregation marked a crossroads in religious life between nineteenth-century devotionalism as a private means to spiritual fulfillment and a twentieth-century Eucharistic theology directed at the transformation of society. Both are hinted at in the responses to Sister Thorn by laypersons and religious.

From his spiritual formation in Switzerland and Missouri, Etlin embodied a stern asceticism, sacrificial piety, and the Benedictine charism of *ora et labora* (work and pray). He took up devotion to the Sacred Heart after contact with Father Mateo Crawley Boevey (1875–1960), the founder of its apostolate in 1908 who created its ritual of "enthroning" the image of the heart in the home to inoculate the family against worldly evils. As Etlin became the spiritual core of the Peekskill circle, he united the sisters, the monks and friars, the laity, and the local priests surrounding Margaret through the Sacred Heart cult as well as through their participation in physical penances, Eucharistic adoration, and Passion mysticism. For Etlin, a stigmatic offered a unique opportunity to stand in the presence of one chosen by their Savior to represent his suffering most intimately, and he tried to be there as frequently as possible.

Lukas visited Peekskill for the first time and met Margaret on November 13, 1923. During his two-week stay, he produced a typed booklet, "Communications of Our Lord to 'Margaret.'" After transcribing her remarks, he typed them on standard-sized paper and then cut it down to nearly pamphlet size (about eight by eight inches). Even years before Margaret came to Peekskill, Lukas learned, Jesus had promised her: "Already I have named you 'Thorn,' but in a few years you will be the Lily of My Heart."

On Etlin's second visit during November 1924, he saw Margaret every day. Although his retreat obligation for the Good Shepherd sisters lasted only three days, he remained at Peekskill for three weeks. He came again for prolonged stays in 1925, 1926, and 1927. Etlin's absences from Clyde to visit Peekskill caused conflict with the Benedictines, who reproached him for spending more time with Sister Thorn than with his own order. The monks were already annoyed that in Missouri, Etlin resided at the convent in Clyde rather than at his own monastery some two miles away. He died there unexpectedly in a car accident in December 1927, leaving behind a package of Holy Land rosaries addressed to Margaret.[38] Etlin's piety inspired Catholics to launch a campaign in 1960 in the Diocese of Kansas City–St. Joseph to beatify him, which is still open, although inert. Mother Raymond, among others, contributed a sketch of Etlin's life, as did several Benedictine priests, including the German archabbot.

It was the greatest hope of Sister Thorn's promoters that she would become a saint, but the arduous process barely reached its initial stage by the time of Etlin's death. Pared down to the eyewitnesses who spent considerable time with Margaret, her vita was being constructed from the material that she dictated from her sickbed to two sisters and a monk, and also from their personal observations. Mother Raymond Cahill, fourteen years Margaret's elder, began to record events immediately as they started in 1921, supplemented by Sister Carmelita Quinn's several visits in 1927 and 1928. Because of the strictness of cloister rules, Carmelita's trips to Peekskill were kept secret and therefore not noted in the annals of her house. Information about her activities survives from her letters sent to Clyde as a form of obedience during their eastern journeys. The notebooks and typescripts of Mother Raymond and Sister Carmelita provided the groundwork for Etlin's contributions, which also included information gained during his frequent visits to Peekskill from 1923 until his death.

The documents being written by Mother Raymond, Sister Carmelita, and Brother Lukas remained in private hands and only circulated among a very few Benedictine and Good Shepherd insiders. The Good Shepherd community was disturbed, naturally, by the impact of Father Bertrand's chain letter as it filtered from his recipients to a wider audience, but news of Margaret Reilly would not have spread widely among the general public without the work of secular journalism. The newspaper press turned Margaret Reilly into a media sensation as soon as it learned of her ten months after her strange experiences had begun. On Saturday, July 8, 1922, readers of the *New York World* were met by the headlines:

Girl with Vivid Cross on Body Puzzles Both Clergy and Laity

At Indefinite Periods Blood Gathers about Mark
and She Suffers Intensely—

Many Hold That Case Is Surely Supernatural[39]

The 1920s represented a turning point in relations between the public and private realms as American newspapers became investigators of private lives, even those of Catholic sisters. Intrusiveness by the press became socially accepted in part through sheer aggression, as the reporter began to use the

"stakeout" and the "ambush" to get his "scoop," no matter the cost. The competition between rival local newspapers also ignited a demand to be the first
to cover a story. However, as reporters lined up outside the Peekskill convent, they were stymied by their lack of access to the cloistered community.
One "newspaper man" tracked down Father Bertrand by phone, seeking an
interview and suggesting a joint visit to Peekskill. Bertrand eluded him by a
white lie: when the reporter referred to Margaret's convent as Mount Hope
rather than Mount St. Florence, Bertrand answered that he "did not know
of any such place." Other investigators were stonewalled as well. Instead of
interviewing a knowledgeable source or even an individual sister, they had
to rely upon hearsay and invention. One reporter had boldly tried to make
a personal connection with Margaret by telephoning the convent directly
on July 5 (prompting Jesus to tell Margaret to be courageous), but neither
she nor the other sisters could foresee how their refusal to talk would lead
to many untruths in the journalist's story.[40] Lacking factual information, the
press produced a fictional stew for readers that merged a bit of stigmatic lore
with the popular taste for sensationalism.

The *World* described "Mary Reilly" as a girl just past twenty (she was
thirty-eight) who was making a quiet retreat at St. Germaine Villa, Peekskill,
conducted by the Good Shepherds. The article stated that a cross made of
blood appeared on her side. Until recently, she had lived with her parents or
other relatives in East 76th Street and was a stenographer in a business house
in the city. Already, the *World*'s account was riddled with errors, including
Margaret's name, age, and family address and the location of the cruciform
mark. The reporter included a suggestion from archdiocesan sources that her
skin marks resembled those of two nineteenth-century women, Catherine
Emmerich and Maria Mörl; Mörl, like Margaret, had lived at home with her
parents.[41] The *World* also claimed that in the last week of the previous April,
"Mary" had gone voluntarily to the convent at 90th Street, informing the
sister who answered the door that she had been sent there. The *World* stated
that Archbishop Hayes was informed of Margaret's case within forty-eight
hours, and that two months later, she was transferred to St. Germaine Villa
in Peekskill. These initial news accounts differed from the nuns' version of
events in numerous details.

The *World* claimed further that Archbishop Hayes had issued an order
forbidding any discussion by those who had seen Margaret. While this was
not entirely accurate, it was standard chancery procedure to protect itself
and the sisters from publicity that it could not control. "Nuns Forbidden
to Talk," the headline shouted. According to Dr. McParlan, however, the
archbishop had it in mind to protect Margaret as the situation unfolded.

Girl With Vivid Cross on Body Puzzles Both Clergy and Laity

At Indefinite Periods Blood Gathers About Mark and She Suffers Intensely—Many Hold That Case Is Surely Supernatural.

In the quiet retreat of St. Germaine Villa, Peekskill, N. Y., conducted by the Sisters of Charity of the Good Shepherd, is a girl just past twenty years who is the subject of rigid investigation and much discussion by the Catholic clergy and laity of all this section of the country.

The cause is a mysterious—supposedly supernatural—manifestation on the girl's side. The World is informed that it is the form of a cross. Blood is said to gather about this mark at indefinite periods and she suffers intensely.

The World is told that the girl is Mary Reilly and that before going to the villa she lived with her parents or other relatives in East 79th Street and was a stenographer in a business house in this city.

Girl Goes to Nuns.

Just at evening in the last week of last April the girl appeared at the door of the House of the Good Shepherd, 90th Street and East River. She told the sister who answered her ring that she had been sent there. She was admitted and had been there not more than forty-eight hours when Archbishop Hayes was informed of her case. Two months later she was transferred to St. Germaine Villa.

During all this time the girl has been under the observation of many priests—some from the leading monasteries of the country—and by physicians. A chemist is said to have been called in too.

The World received information of the girl from many sources, but when investigation was started it was found that Archbishop Hayes cannot understand this business, unless it be a fiendish attempt to keep her from going through with her vocation. Bring me any one who has seen her who can state positively that she has manifested anything resembling the things you talk about."

In answer to a question whether there was a pathological answer to the statement concerning the girl, he said:

"There are forms of nervousness that cause peculiar effects."

Dr. McParlan refused to answer questions as to other physicians having examined his patient. He denied knowledge of spiritual leaders having visited her.

Archbishop Reticent.

Archbishop Hayes is on retreat at Dunwoodie Seminary. A reporter who sought to interview Auxiliary Bishop John J. Dunn was told by the Bishop's secretary, Father Duggan:

"Bishop Dunn requests me to say that he knows about the matter to which you refer."

Further information from the Bishop was refused.

Another reporter went to St. Germaine Villa. The sister who answered at the door said:

"We are not permitted to talk about the matter. Anyway, I will have to ask the Mother to see you."

The sisters were in retreat, conducted by Father Murphy of the Jesuits. However, Sister Mary of St. Raymond, the Mother Superior, left the chapel and met the reporter.

When asked if it were true that Mary Reilly was in the convent, the sister answered:

"I will neither confirm nor deny that. The Archbishop has forbidden

A portion of the *New York World* article, July 8, 1922. Together with Father Bertrand's letter, this report stirred local interest in the supernatural happenings reported in Peekskill.

Archbishop Patrick Hayes of New York, leader of the largest archdiocese in the nation. Hayes oversaw the investigation of Sister Thorn, which began some three years before he was named a cardinal. (Bettman Archive/Corbis Images)

After Margaret took her final vows, McParlan wrote to Lukas Etlin, "His Eminence intends to lift the strict seclusion he has thrown around her and leave her free for whatever Mission Our dear Lord intends. His Eminence often told me he is holding in this strict manner in order that her enemies cannot appeal to Rome to put her out of the order. I tell you this in confidence that they are so bold the one wrote a complaint to the Holy Father against the Cardinal for protecting Thorn so there is no telling how far they would go in their bitter hatred of her."[42]

During the week that Margaret was stigmatized, Archbishop Hayes was himself making a spiritual retreat thirty miles away at Dunwoodie Seminary in Yonkers. Journalists customarily received official statements from the archbishop through Auxiliary Bishop Dunn, but in this instance, Father Joseph Nelson (1883–1963) served as the archbishop's liaison to Sister Thorn. Nelson, a professor at Dunwoodie, was a valuable source of information on Reilly because of his "special friendship" with Lukas Etlin, and also because he was the spiritual director of Sister Tarcisius at Peekskill, a childhood friend of Margaret.[43] The press soon reported that Archbishop Hayes sent experts (including his physician, McParlan, as recounted previously) to Peekskill to remove the wall "painting," which was described as about a six-inch-square picture of Christ bearing the cross and looking down at

Margaret. Other news stories depicted it as nothing more than a small crucifix. All accounts agreed that efforts to remove the image from the wall proved to be futile, even when scraped.[44]

Lacking interviews from chancery spokesmen, the press contributed to the growing folklore about Sister Thorn throughout New York, New Jersey, and Pennsylvania, such as the persistent rumor that a pink, three-dimensional cross continued to reappear on Margaret's cell wall even after being plastered over and that Margaret had healed the sick by laying her hands on them.[45] According to one sister, at the foot of Thorn's bed within the superior's room at Mount St. Florence, the crucifix embedded in the wall even changed colors.[46] Unfortunately, there is no trace of the single piece of evidence that reproduced a likeness of the wall crucifix: the images from Mother Raymond that she reported sending to Margaret's cousin, Sister Sebastian Connolly.

Margaret had benefited from the attention of dedicated sisters and spiritual direction from well-connected clergy, though her admission to religious life was certainly not guaranteed as she neared the age of forty. The special connection between sisters and confessors had its origins in medieval and Early Modern Christianity that led, over time, to different strategies that defined that relationship.[47] Among the modern mystical theologians, one camp of opinion urged confessors to exercise restraint. "In other words," wrote British neurologist Sir Francis Walshe, "we get the stigmatics we make, and there is reason to believe that we should see many more were their activities not 'nipped in the bud' by wise directors or pastors."[48] The *Catholic Encyclopedia* warned spiritual directors to be on guard against the testing of the soul by Satan but reassured them that "rules for the discernment of spirits are set down to enable directors to determine their source and to apply proper means of relief."[49] Another camp, which included English clergyman Herbert Thurston (1856–1939), blamed those very directors for encouraging the excesses of their female clients. Thurston wrote:

> I cannot disguise my conviction that, in the case of many suggestible characters, harm is done by ill-advised priestly direction. The director, having filled his mind with mystical theology and with the marvels recorded in the *Lives of the Saints*, is apt to welcome with enthusiasm the not too common experience of a soul that is *exaltée*, but fervent and courageous. He is spiritually uplifted by the thought that this is a most precious treasure confided by God to his care. If he were equally well-versed in the literature of what we may, for brevity's sake, call hysteria, all would be well. But that is a rare combination.[50]

If Thurston is correct that priests were too easily swayed by their penitents, then he was still somewhat unique in proposing that clergy needed to
understand the etiology of hysteria. In his typically wry fashion, Thurston
suggested: "Just as I should like to hear of a stigmatica who had no bad family history, and had always herself been a thoroughly healthy subject, free
from neuroses of any kind . . . one looks, but looks in vain, for the name of
one who was free from strange previous inhibitions in the matter of diet
and whom the neuropath specialist would have pronounced to be perfectly
sound and normal. No competent physician could possibly have said this of
Louise Lateau or Teresa Higginson, or Domenica Lazzari, or Anne Catherine Emmerich, or St. Lidwina of Schiedam."[51] If he considered Margaret
Reilly to be on that list, then Thurston, the priest-intellectual, was equating
mystical behavior with the irrational feminine, a well-worn path found in
the testimony of overeager confessors since the Middle Ages and now vali-
dated by the scientific diagnosis of hysteria.

As a spiritual director, Lukas Etlin fell into Thurston's category of fervent
but overly enthusiastic. Letters from Lukas provide insights into his own relationship with Margaret, but they are challenging to read due to his cross-outs,
misspellings, drawings, and comments and revisions scattered in the margins
and throughout the page. On one occasion, he offered these "sentiments" to
Margaret in a letter marked with drawings of hearts and arrows that connected devotion to Mary's immaculate heart and the Sacred Heart of Jesus:

> The main reason for my coming to Peekskill was to obtain a union
> of the heart of Carmelita with the dove of the Sacred Heart with the
> Thorn, the lily of the Sacred Heart and that I myself to[o] would share
> in this union.
>
> It is my intention in every holy Mass as long as Margaret the
> Spouse of the Cross is with us[,] to have her & Carmelita with me on
> the Corporal. Most ardently shall I pray till both Spouses have attained
> to highest Sanctity. You carry his Stygmata your heart is consumed by
> love. Carmelita must have the arrow, it must go throu and throu her
> heart. Do[?] violence to God to obtain it.
>
> As to the poor little brother, o now you must pray. Here is the arrow
> (drawing of my heart). Now lily of the Heart of Jesus, you must take
> my hand in your right hand and Carmelita my left hand and then you
> pray for poor little brother along on the way to Calvary. . . . Through
> all eternity we shall be very closely linked and shall live very near to
> one another, privided [sic] the lily of the Sacred Heart . . . forces Jesus
> on my behalf.[52]

What emerges from Etlin's letter is his desire for a spiritual household with Carmelita and Margaret, where he is "little brother," drawing himself into a sibling relationship with his "little sister." As the letter somewhat incoherently suggests, Lukas imagines his divine union occurring with the aid of his "sisters," although Sister Thorn's dealings with her various confessors (Taylor, Brady, Benedict Bradley, and Etlin) displayed a blend of spiritual and erotic feelings implicit within such relationships, even while they invoked the discourse of the "sexless couple" or of sibling types that were normative for the confessor and mystic in Christian history.[53]

Among stigmatization cults, the spiritual family was a commonplace metaphor. Yet it was still a patriarchal family. Thus in the history of modern stigmatizations, a priest always assumed a leadership role: Father Naber of Bavaria served as interpreter, pilgrim's guide, and publicist for Therese Neumann, as Curé Niels had done for Louise Lateau in Belgium, Father Germano for Gemma Galgani in Italy, Father Schmöger for Catherine Emmerich in Germany, Canon Snow for Teresa Higginson in Great Britain, and Father Mariano Pinho for Alexandrina da Costa in Portugal. Benedictine monk Benedict Bradley publicized Sister Miriam Theresa Demjanovich in New Jersey, and Father Finet presided at Marthe Robin's home in France, where Father Vinard also mediated the cult of Josefa Menendez at her convent. Adrienne von Speyr had a long (and rather unorthodox) association with a prominent German theologian, Hans Urs von Balthasar, who was not only her spiritual director and biographer but also (with his wife) her housemate. While spiritual families can take surprising and unorthodox forms, Margaret's spiritual direction nonetheless reflected a traditional model of paternal authority that molded her to fit the demands of the Lord.

The intimacy built up over time between confessor and sister, based on shared intellectual and spiritual experiences—the constant traffic in pamphlets on lives of the saints, handpicked readings in Christian mysticism, exercises in contemplation, and emphasis at convent retreats upon spiritual victimhood—contributed to an environment ripe for producing what sociologist Max Weber termed spiritual "virtuosi." Further, the confessor-penitent dyad encouraged mystical culture to flourish in the convent as a spiritual underground that represented a welcome (if stealthy) form of emotional intensity different from the suppression of all "special" relationships between individuals in monastic communities. The idea of nuns and monks merging their love and pain in Christ and sharing union through his sacrifice on the cross became an accepted expression of this spiritual goal, as well as the vent for many human emotions, including friendly, sexual, and excessively pious ones. Margaret's advisers preferred to emphasize, rather, the tradition of sibling friendship between male and female saints, such as between Francis and Clare and Francis de Sales and Jeanne de Chantal. Hence, Lukas, Carmelita, and Margaret became brother and sisters in their quest for union with Christ.

Margaret's confidential relationship to her confessors involved the presence of secrets and also a spiritual emphasis on mystical union. As noted by Georg Simmel a century ago, secrecy is important for its power to create boundaries by constituting social groups and for its power to produce certain effects.[54] Catholic secrets are essential to the Marian cultists of Fatima and Lourdes, for example, and in stigmatic cults, they had the effect of magnifying the legends of women like Sister Thorn and giving weight to her elect status. Her cousin Sister Sebastian, for instance, reported eagerly to her fellow Dominican Sister Inez that Margaret had a secret for her from Jesus, but that she was prevented from revealing it yet.[55]

Without an audience who wants to be informed, secrets would cease to matter. Unlike commodities in a market economy, spiritual secrets have no monetary value and are removed from the world of things and commercial transactions. But as a type of exchange in the convent economy, secrets functioned to create boundaries between insiders and outsiders and to make new hierarchies that destabilized existing ones. Secrets also offered psychic gratification to convent women who, deprived of virtually all other forms of enjoyment, could lay claim to a rich history in Catholic tradition of private locutions from Jesus and Mary and of secret insights into the church's doctrinal mysteries. In the Middle Ages, secrets were used by holy women such as Mechtilde of Magdeburg to legitimate her mystic status against the church's masculine authority. Her special connection to "the flowing light of the Godhead," often expressed in erotic language, was experienced "in secret" (with the exception of her confessor). Whether or not Margaret Reilly was a genuine mystic, she also fits within this topos of (feminine) spiritual secrets posing a challenge to (masculine) theology. Sister Thorn's secrets were analogous to the uses of the "secret" wisdom claimed by the church in its so-called mysteries of the faith (the Trinity; transubstantiation; the Resurrection of Christ). In the modern era, the church used secrets and mysteries to reject modern scientific knowledge, thereby ensuring its own power. Numerous reports of Sister Thorn's secret knowledge of souls, clairvoyance, and spiritual communications among her circle suggest that secrets continued to play that role in the early twentieth century.

In Margaret's already-unusual existence as a religious postulant, she used secrecy to obtain a degree of power. As her spiritual parents, confessors assigned her penances to develop the virtue of humility, but because she was obliged to tell them everything, they learned about her divine secrets. Thus the same confessors also became Margaret's clients, reversing the usual patron-client relationship. As this shift occurred, Sister Thorn gained leverage to operate outside of the usual constraints on cloistered women because she claimed to be hearing directly from the Lord. The privilege of experiencing a sweet fragrance after she visited the convent chapel was denied to some nuns who "came from unworthy motives," for example.[56]

Most of the spiritual "revelations" given to Margaret, however, seem fairly trivial. She ratted on a prioress who owned too many religious habits and a friend who had broken something in the convent without admitting it. Her supernatural information extended beyond the convent setting to Lady Armstrong, who told Archbishop Hayes that Sister Thorn had been able to name the very street in Dublin where Armstrong's mother had died, though Margaret had only been nine years old at the time.[57] Still, Armstrong marveled at the contrast between Sister Thorn's "simple piety" and the fact that "she seems to know all things."[58] Within the Good Shepherd leadership, the congregation's Visitor, Mother Hickey, was amazed that Margaret knew why Hickey had been called to France for a meeting with the superior general in 1924 (a tidbit whose very concreteness sounds like information that was overheard by Margaret, perhaps at the Peekskill telephone switchboard where she assisted).[59] Although Margaret used her secret information to build intimacy with individuals in positions of power, her strategy could easily backfire. In the convent, as in any closed community, secrets could become a source of conflict that undermined communality. When the Lord revealed to Sister Thorn that one of the New York prioresses was a drug addict, for instance, Margaret gained an enemy for life by reporting this news.

Church authorities did not sanction reports of private revelations and soon ordered Sister Thorn to remain silent about her experiences. Further, nearly all requests from outsiders to visit her were rejected by the archbishop as his way of mounting a strong barrier between her alleged revelations and the church's regulation of objectified knowledge. Not all of the religious leaders were in agreement about how to handle reports of visions and secrets, however. Mystically inclined priests found their own rebelliousness echoed by Sister Thorn, who sidestepped the church's hierarchy by professing to have direct communications from the Lord. Lukas Etlin, to the frustration of his abbot, was one such nonconformist who sought out the mystic virtuoso, but even a distinguished superior of a men's congregation contacted Margaret to seek her aid on a "particular matter" in his community. Charles O'Donnell at Notre Dame, Indiana, begged Mother Raymond to ask Sister Thorn to "offer up some part of her sufferings for our spiritual warfare" because he believed in a connection between a matter in South Bend and "the young woman who has the stigmata."[60] In a second letter, sent to Margaret Reilly's pastor in New York City, Father O'Donnell described his clerical vocation as engaged in warfare against "a wicked and adulterous generation" and nervously admitted to having undergone a mystical experience at several recent funerals that he could not explain through natural means. Margaret's special wisdom, he supposed, would solve his dilemmas. Some of the monks and priests who visited (or tried to visit) Margaret believed that she possessed oracular or clairvoyant powers that could help them. Like the anxious clients of fortune-tellers, they beseeched her for details of their orders' construction projects, financial stability, and so forth. As the Lord's mouthpiece, Margaret gave them advice, justifying her newfound authority by claiming that "Oh, but Jesus says when a priest is concerned, this is work for me."[61] Whether assuming the role of prophet, apostle, or even *alter Christus* (another Christ), Sister Thorn had found a way to transcend gender limits, as some medieval women had done.

Finally, Sister Thorn's relationship to secrets and secrecy sheds light on a transition under way among her generation of American clergy and sisters in their role as spiritual leaders for North America. They, along with the laity, were still in the process of fashioning a distinctive "American" Catholic identity. No longer obliged to pursue theological education in Europe because of the foundation of the Catholic University of America in 1889, some of the priests who knew Margaret were seminary trained in the United States or Canada. Yet when they participated in vernacular religion in times of real or fantasized distress, they seemed little different from their "folk" counterparts in Europe. One of Sister Thorn's biographers even described the many freedoms of the United States as a disguise for a vast satanic conspiracy at work in the nation: "America's FREE-FOR-ALLISM protects these agencies, these foreign minorities that constitute Lucifer's FIFTH COLUMN FROM HELL, provided only they PLAY THE GAME of America's sociability and be not too open in boasting of their respective ambitions. No doubt about it. Thorn SAW the truth."[62] From his perspective, the undiluted faith of American Catholics was being endangered by greed for success and by "mixed marriages," which "fling the doors wide open to any, if not all, of their remorseless depredations." A coordinated patriotic defense of the United States expressed by American-born priests was still rather tentative, indeterminate, or even lacking altogether, while foreign-born priests often kept close ties to their countries of origin, even after World War I—as Lukas Etlin had done, at some peril to his own reputation.

Benedict Bradley was a familiar presence at the Peekskill convent. His letters to Lukas Etlin provide valuable information about Margaret, including his conviction that she had been divinely sent as a warning and inspiration for "all religious and priests."[63] Stationed at St. Mary's Abbey in Morristown, New Jersey, Bradley arranged Etlin's retreat assignment at Peekskill precisely so that Etlin could meet "the little mystic." The two men had met through their work as retreat directors for nuns and sisters. Bradley, who assisted at least five women's congregations, had already led several retreats for the sisters at Etlin's convent in Missouri. Mother Raymond esteemed him because he had the gift of discernment of supernatural communications. One of Bradley's biographers, however, remembered him as a man whose "judgment was often guided more by imagination than by reason," and who "evidently gave little consideration to the ideas and wishes of his co-workers," a criticism that was also made of Etlin.[64] Nevertheless, Father Bradley was an instrumental publicist in the Thorn case. By his own account, he gladly spread stories about her to the numerous convents where he offered retreats. In the letters that he wrote to Etlin, Bradley even underlined key passages, lest Lukas miss the obvious comparisons between Thorn's experiences and the yearnings of other Christian mystics. On December 8, 1922, he wrote to Lukas: "She told me she *longs for the night*, for during the silent hours there is nothing to disturb her loving intercourse with the Master. *He is present to her visibly, begs her to be familiar with Him, allows her to embrace and kiss Him and call Him her Lover!*"[65] Here, Margaret invokes the familiar metaphor of sweetness and erotic submission so familiar to the mystical generation that preceded her, which in turn had precedents in the "bridal mysticism" of the Middle Ages.

Benedictines as well as Jesuits had a strong influence on the Good Shepherd sisters as spiritual guides and educators. Bradley and others desired better education within sisterhoods. As a popular convent retreat master, Bradley used one of Etlin's published pamphlets for instruction at Peekskill in 1922, noting that "the nuns everywhere are suffering from want of direction. It's a pitiable thing. I have volunteered to give weekly conferences in Newark to three different Communities and I find all the nuns so greedy."[66] Margaret's avowed gift of divine knowledge stood out in marked contrast to the shortcomings in the instruction of most religious women. When Etlin was scheduled to offer a retreat at Peekskill, Bradley advised him not to prepare any remarks in advance since Sister Thorn, "by her prayers, obtains all the inspirations you need. . . . So don't write out anything."[67] And although Bradley described Margaret as "an ignorant and innocent girl, almost illiterate!,"[68] she was still able to give him detailed descriptions of her interior life "since the material is provided by the Lord."

As a frequent visitor to Peekskill, Bradley supplied details about Margaret's daily circumstances. Bradley felt privileged to hear her confession and her tales of torment by devils. On the other hand, he never witnessed her stigmata, seeing only the two crosses on the convent walls. He observed that, "at present, and for some months past she is a cripple—miraculously so—and doctors can find nothing wrong. They wheel her to the chapel; otherwise she must crawl on hands and knees, even up and down stairs. HE [*sic*] has humbled her to the very dust. But she enjoys it. She lives in the cell of the Mother and sleeps in another cell adjoining with her bed near the Mother's. The reason for this is to protect her in the physical violence offered by the wicked spirit."[69] Once, when Bradley witnessed a diabolic attack that threw Margaret from her chair, he was able to dispel the demon by making the sign of the cross. With his next letter to Lukas, he enclosed two cloth badges with images of the Sacred Heart of Jesus embroidered around the edges by Sister Thorn. The gifts were left over from a box of badges that she had given to him for the sisters in his three communities of Benedictines.[70] Dr. McParlan had told him that a deaf patient was cured recently by applying one such badge to her ear for the nine days of a novena to the Sacred Heart.[71]

A final admirer of Sister Thorn was Herbert Thurston, a London province Jesuit priest, historian, author, and lecturer who shared the exact lifespan (and much of the curiosity) of Sigmund Freud.[72] As a scholar of Catholicism, liturgy, mystical and occult phenomena, and parapsychology, Thurston occupied himself with "prominently historical and psychic questions" whose breadth continues to impress and influence scholars today.[73] Before achieving that renown, Thurston had endured the rather fragmented training that produced a Jesuit priest in Victorian England, when it was still a punishable offence to be one. As late as 1902, Thurston and several other young Jesuits were cited for this offense against the Emancipation Act, which imposed banishment from the United Kingdom for life.[74] As one of the last English Jesuits trained in the nineteenth-century fashion, Thurston and boys of his age were kept together throughout their schooling, which forced them into exile to circulate through the roster of the Jesuit institutions founded on the Continent since the time when Elizabeth I had outlawed Catholic education in England.[75]

Thurston became a Jesuit novice in 1874 at the age of eighteen. Following the pattern set by the Reformation, he began his education in France at the St. Malo Seminary, moved on to St. Omer, and then continued at Liège for courses in philosophy. Novices like him slept in cubicles and rose at 5:00 or 5:30 A.M. for prayers and a day of work. The young men then finished their course of training at Stonyhurst in Lancashire, England. The embargo on Catholics enrolling at the "dangerous" universities of Oxford and Cambridge was not lifted by Cardinal Vaughan until 1895. In addition to Stonyhurst, therefore, Thurston attended Mount St. Mary's, Derbyshire; Manresa House, Roehampton; and the University of London.

Thurston published numerous books and pamphlets and more than 700 articles.[76] To a general Christian audience, he is probably most familiar as the editor of the revised edition of *Butler's Lives of the Saints*.[77] When he took up that enormous project, Thurston interrupted his manuscript on poltergeists, which remained unfinished. His biographer surmised that it was "through his interest in queer psychic phenomena that he came to investigate the psychical phenomena of the mystics."[78] After Thurston's death, his Jesuit editor compiled selected articles into several books that reflected Thurston's career interest in "borderland cases in the psychology of mysticism."[79]

Thurston's Jesuit community at Farm Street in London's posh Mayfair neighborhood remembered him spending six days a week in the nearby British Museum Library or the London Library. Thurston had devoured the forty or so folio volumes of the *Acta Sanctorum* and had collected biographies of many 17th- and 18th-century mystics during his visits to the Continent, especially from the huge Bollandist library at Brussels.[80] Given the sad state of Catholic historical writing at the time of his birth, Thurston provided valuable uplift in method, quality, and quantity in a publishing career that spanned six decades from the death of Pius IX to the accession of Pius XII.[81]

Unlike many solitary, bookish persons, Thurston was recalled fondly at Farm Street as genial and affable at all times and also an avid cricket fan. Precise and orderly, Thurston inhabited the same room for forty-five years. He displayed an ascetic dimension by walking eighteen miles—while fasting—to offer Mass at Beaumont, a Jesuit college in Windsor at which he had taught in the 1880s. He also generously gave time to numerous religious organizations. For members of the Catholic Medical Guild who attended his occasional talks, "the picture of Father Thurston sitting beside the Chairman and reading his lecture from a bewildering assortment of odd pieces of paper, some typewritten, some printed and some in handwriting will be a happy recollection."[82] Thurston was also a member of the Society for Psychical Research (SPR), whose broad-minded membership included William James, Sir Oliver Lodge, Andrew Lang, Mrs. Eleanor Sidgwick, and Marguerite Radclyffe-Hall. The society met periodically to sip tea and, in this case, to listen to Thurston read from his longhand lectures about his curious investigations into stigmatica, liquefying vials of blood, luminous crosses, levitating saints, incorrupt corpses, and poltergeists.

During his lifetime, Thurston attracted correspondents who included his

Father Herbert Thurston, British Jesuit scholar of mystical phenomena. Thurston wrote about mystics and stigmatics, including Margaret Reilly, disguising her identity as "Kate Ryan." (Courtesy of Thomas McCoog, archivist of the Jesuit Archives, London, UK)

Stonyhurst schoolmate, Arthur Conan Doyle, who debated him on the topic of spiritualism, and Agostino Gemelli, an Italian Franciscan physician and professor of theology who investigated several stigmatics for the Vatican.[83] Thurston was also contacted by admiring Jesuits worldwide, by persons interested in psychic research, by nuns, and by individuals seeking private spiritual advice or help. Louise Guiney, for example, a Boston Catholic expatriate in England, sent several poignant letters asking his help in finding someone to adopt their ward, Loulie.[84] "Nesta of the Forest," a clairvoyant medium from Bournemouth, expressed her concern to him about the lack of empathy between spiritualists and Catholics, who would seem to be natural allies.[85] World War I veteran Geoffrey Woodward sent personal letters, detailing his terrifying dreams and asking Thurston's advice about the need to give up his customary bedtime pint of beer.[86]

Thurston had made a stir by pronouncing the Shroud of Turin a fraud in 1903, and by the time he became aware of Margaret Reilly twenty years later, he had already studied four recent claimants of stigmatization: Teresa Higginson, Bertha Mrazek, Nellie Brown, and Padre Pio.[87] Unlike these four, Margaret received Thurston's lukewarm support. He doubted the authenticity of Higginson, a histrionic schoolteacher whose reenactments of the Passion and stigmata had unfolded in Lancashire, England, and Edinburgh, Scotland, in the 1870s. "In spite of Teresa's mortified life and protestations of unworthiness," Thurston concluded, "there is a latent element of self-absorption which seems to me to point more in the direction of hysteria than of true sanctity."[88] Higginson was indeed fond of notoriety, and her dramatic self-inflicted injuries included burning herself with a crimping iron, throwing herself into a pit at a lumberyard, pouring burning cinders down her dress, and wrenching out her toenails.

Although Higginson would be hard to top in the extremes of her masochism, Thurston went on to expose Bertha Mrazek ("Georges Marasco") as a colorful fake. In her flamboyant life, Mrazek/Marasco had been a cross-dresser, single mother, caricaturist, poet, lion tamer, circus contortionist ("femme serpent"), and secret agent who was accused of spying for the Germans against her native Belgium during World War I, despite her friendship with the heroic English nurse-martyr Edith Cavell (1865–1915). Cavell, whose execution by Germany helped prod President Woodrow Wilson to enter the war, had run a spy network against the Germans even from within a Red Cross hospital that had been occupied by them.[89] During their nursing years, Cavell had advised Mrazek to change her name to something more "civilized." Choosing a masculine identity in order to advance her poetry career, the newly christened "Georges Marasco" went about Belgium dressed accordingly, "looking something like a boy scout."[90] She was called an hysteric, a split personality, and, according to the Belgian press, a madwoman. Her stigmata reportedly appeared after she had experienced a miraculous cure at the prominent Belgian shrine of Notre Dame de Hal in 1921. There, she kept a circle of followers busy writing down her "endless revelations which were to be communicated to the Pope." In three photographs, sent to Thurston by one of his Belgian acquaintances who was a partisan of Mrazek, she obligingly lifts her shirt to reveal a gouge on her torso.[91]

Although doctors condemned Mrazek's ravings and mythomania, Thurston was sympathetic to her situation and nonjudgmental about her theatrical behavior. He was also relieved that, although she was probably undernourished due to postwar food shortages, she did not attempt to profit by her stigmatization. Thurston also speculated that Mrazek/Marasco suffered from multiple personality syndrome. From the evidence available, he concluded that she "was an hysterical subject whose abnormalities had taken on a religious coloring."[92] Dr. Francis Walshe, a fellow Briton, believed that Thurston was too kind to Mrazek, suggesting that Thurston's "great lack" was "that of any personal experience of hysterics and their hysterical illnesses."[93] Nevertheless, Thurston had weighed Marasco's claims to be a victim soul and found them wanting:

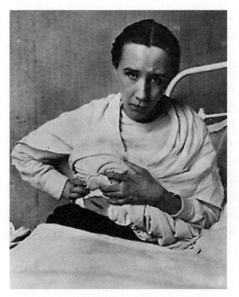

Fraudulent stigmatic Bertha Mrazek/ Georges Marasco of Belgium displays her torso wound. The *News of the World* exhibited the photo on November 16, 1924, with the headline: "Priestess in Prison: Girl Lion-Tamer Who Became a Spy—Amazing Masquerade and Miracle Cure." The image was reprinted by Father Thurston in his article about Marasco in *The Month* in 1925, where he declared himself "satisfied that the photographs have not been faked, that the wounds are real and that they cannot have been self-inflicted." As a circus employee of Van Been Frères, Marasco courageously worked with the lion Brutus, who had recently killed a male tamer.

One special sanction of Georges' mission was the fact that "she had received the gift of substitution"—so it was phrased to me—that is to say she was permitted to take upon herself the maladies and sufferings of others. She made expiation by suffering in their place and they were restored to health or relieved of their anxieties. No one who is familiar with Father Schmöger's *Life of Anne Catherine Emmerich* can fail to recall how large a part this same idea played in the prolonged infirmities of the nun of Dülmen. Indeed this feature meets us constantly in the biographies of mystics who have lived in the repute of sanctity. I must confess, however, that surprising as these details might seem they did not greatly impress me.[94]

Father Thurston's third stigmatic investigation was for Nellie Brown, a girl who lived in Leeds whose first wound had appeared around 1916.[95] As with his study of poltergeists, Thurston seems to have decided to abandon the case since he never published anything about Nellie. Among his papers is a thick folder containing several blood-spotted photographs, a stained handkerchief, and Nellie's spiritual meanderings written in lined notebooks at the request of her confessor.[96] Regarding Padre Pio, who claimed that he was stigmatized in 1918, Thurston did not debate the genuineness of the wounds but commented only that it was appropriate for the Vatican to pronounce that no proof of their supernatural origins was available.[97]

By 1923 Thurston had learned of Margaret Reilly from physician James J. Walsh of New York, with whom he had been corresponding about the Peekskill curiosity. Because Walsh had warned him that the case could not yet be publicly discussed at that time, Thurston waited two years to publish a study of Margaret Reilly, whom he concealed as "Kate Ryan," for an article in the British Catholic journal *The Month*.[98] At that time, Thurston was rumored to be one of four Vatican consultors for the Reilly case.[99] When Walsh visited him in London in September 1925, seven months after Thurston's article had appeared, the American confided happily that their conversations confirmed that "he and Thurston were skeptics together about a great many things."

Father Thurston had also gathered information about Margaret Reilly from several Jesuit informants: Edward P. Anderson of Cincinnati and Chicago; William Ennis of St. Ignatius parish in New York City, and James McGivney of the Maryland–New York Jesuit Province. In 1925 McGivney wrote to him and to Archbishop Hayes about Margaret Reilly and enclosed a series of anonymous letters sent to Dr. Thomas Gallen in New York City accusing him of a variety of improprieties. Thurston also gained news of Margaret from Lady Margaret Armstrong, who frequently traveled between London and New York with her husband.

In his 1925 article for *The Month*, Father Thurston got some of the facts wrong, but he did not mistake the historical parallels between "Kate's" wounds and those female stigmatics familiar to him from the Bollandist collection. One similarity that he noted lay in the sudden disappearance of any traces of the stigmatic wounds from the skin. Thurston heard that on her thirty-fourth day in the convent, when Margaret was to return to Manhattan and be examined by Dr. McParlan, her skin became clear and healthy. He had remarked without prejudice on the same "convenient coincidence" about Bertha Mrazek's wounds, but he was troubled by the inconsistencies between accounts of Margaret's experiences provided by Sister Rita, Mother Raymond, and a priest.[100] Following her stigmatization, "Kate" soon experienced the usual accompanying mystical symptoms: luminosity, perfume, miraculous communion, and conflicts with the devil.[101] Thurston was obviously intrigued by unverified details, such as the claim that Mother Raymond could pass her fingers and a cloth through Margaret's wounds, and that her scourge markings contained real thorns, three of which were extracted and later presented to the bishop.[102]

Despite its amazing breadth, Thurston's scholarship in mystical phenomena was not entirely neutral. His junior colleague Father C. C. Martindale (1879–1963), a distinguished social reformer in Great Britain, remained "puzzled to the end" by Thurston's acceptance of "'spooky' marvels" when the Jesuit was otherwise critical of similar events purported to be miracles.[103] Martindale found his friend less "systematic" about them than his investigations of the levitation of Saint Joseph of Cupertino and the San Gennaro blood prodigies in Naples. Further gaps in Thurston's work were its lack of attention to Marian apparitions and a critical examination of devotion to the Sacred Heart of Jesus, a practice closely associated with his own religious order.[104] Martindale argued that the Belgian Jesuit, Hippolyte Delehaye (1859–1941), author of *Legends of the Saints* (1907), had been a more rigorous judge of these prodigies than Thurston.

For his part, Thurston was "reluctant to agree to" Martindale's suggestion that "God gives to a generation, or a certain society" (like Italy or Peru), "the *sort* of saint and miracle that they *like*"—a comment that opens the door to social-constructionist explanations at odds with Thurston's implied position that historical research affirmed the universal character of sanctity. Thurston's scholarship embodied the tension between topic and method among Catholics who examined mysticism and the lives of the saints using a historical approach; piling up lists of similar cases and details still failed to explain if and why the phenomenon occurred. The upsurge in supernatural events reported during Margaret Reilly's lifetime worked against Thurston's rationalist principles, but he conceded that a mystical revival was understandably related to the traumatic effects of the Great War, as he witnessed firsthand in Britain in the craze for contacting the dead through spiritualism, séances, and Ouija boards. All of these occult practices, originating in the so-called Victorian crisis of faith, sought material evidence of the unseen world, especially after 1914, when so many more inhabitants were dispatched there.

Families whose loved ones did not return from the gruesome battles of the western front did not always find comfort in the "sacred union" of faith and patriotism. Some mourners turned to spirit mediums and other occult techniques that promised to reunite the living and the dead. Thurston understood that the two major foes of spiritualism were the Church of England and the Catholic Church. As early as 1864, in the "Syllabus of Errors," Pope Pius IX had authorized the church to expend its energies defending itself against the false movements, philosophies, and worldviews associated with modernity. While positivism and materialism posed the strongest threats, false forms of religion like spiritualism, séances, and faith-healing were also dangerous. In Catholic dogma, the living prayed for the dead, not vice versa, and it was sinful to believe that one could communicate with a disembodied soul or that the bodies of the dead hovered around the living.

As one Catholic psychoanalyst suggested: "Imperfect logic and the inveterate human hankering for consoling fictions . . . give birth to spiritualism and theosophy."[105]

The hunger for the supernatural was prolonged in the United Kingdom after World War I by the Irish Civil War that followed, alerting Christians that they could not relent in their cosmic battle against evil. Thurston was certainly sympathetic to those concerns, having seen the war's impact upon the Continent and among his countrymen and -women, and especially upon his Stonyhurst schoolmate Arthur Conan Doyle, whose "conversion" to spiritualism in 1916 after the war deaths of his son, brother, and brother-in-law shocked many. Thurston's fellow member in the SPR, Sir Oliver Lodge, a prominent physicist, famously tried to communicate with his dead son, Raymond, a war casualty in 1915. In Conan Doyle's view, it was not spiritualism but Catholicism that was the problem, enslaving the minds of its members: "To the orthodox Roman Catholic, there is nothing good outside his own dogmatic fence."[106] That inflexibility was evident in the Catholic Church's condemnation of spiritualism: "The practices of spiritualists are then forbidden by God, and they are a virtual invitation to evil spirits to intervene in the lives of men. Spiritualists have dealings with evil spirits who are the enemies of God. . . . In other words, the beliefs and practices of spiritualists are a kind of false religion, they are rightly called superstitious beliefs and practices."[107] Thurston repeated these points in his own full-length attack on spiritualism (and Doyle) that was published in 1928, which he followed up in a second book and a pamphlet for the Catholic Truth Society.[108] The vigorous campaigns of the Catholic and Anglican Churches against spiritualism before and after the Great War are instances of organized religions treading the thin line between defending their own belief in bleeding prodigies, mystical visions, and satanic spirits while condemning spirit mediums and other rival practices.[109]

The attempts of the generation of the twenties to respond to the suffering caused by the Great War by pursuing alternative religions spawned alarm among Catholics about the inviolable claims of individual experience. Could anyone converse with the dead? Did personality continue on after death? How was contacting the dead any different from belief in the communion of saints? In this matter, the Catholic Church stopped well short of endorsing the democratization of revelation and of alternative spiritualities. Many priests, as expressed above, attacked spiritualism to reassert the primacy of the male priesthood and its sacramental powers against the largely female-dominated culture of mediumship, and in this sense, they were defending clericalism and patriarchalism. Thurston's view of Sister Thorn's stigmatization did not directly engage these debates about the limits of personal religious experience but revealed him to be her qualified supporter: such marvels as stigmata could exist, he decided, but so did hysteria. Taking refuge in a historical approach to such phenomena, Thurston noted the many similarities between Margaret Reilly and stigmatized women of the seventeenth and eighteenth centuries. Nonetheless, he suspected Margaret of "hysterical neurosis" since her behavior—seeking out sympathetic priests and nuns to witness her wounds—contradicted the modesty of a genuine saint, who would avoid publicity and egotism. He also concluded that despite the Great War's revelation that "hysteria is not, as was once supposed, an exclusively feminine disorder, ... women were and are much more subject to hysterical fits than men."[110]

The Catholic Church's attacks on new "false religions" like spiritualism, and on new physical and psychical conditions like hysteria, touched the larger concern among theologians and scholars about the very nature of mysticism. As modern Christians tried to locate and define an "essential" mysticism that would not be confused with false forms or led astray by signs and wonders like stigmata, ecstasies, and visions, a burst of publications in Europe on mysticism and the mystical following the First World War signaled a widespread revival of interest in the topic. They included Thurston's research on the hagiography of mystics in the Bollandist collections; Delehaye's legends of the saints; *The Mystical Wave* (1920) by Jules Sagaret; *The Mystical Invasion* and *The Mystical Conquest*, the first two volumes of Abbé Bremond's eleven-volume literary history of France; and even the postwar plans to restore Europe's ruined abbeys, churches, and monasteries lest the heritage of mystical contemplation vanish forever.[111] Nostalgia for an idealized notion of mystical experience was a powerful component of this quest to define authentic mysticism, but so was the desire to make this legacy seem modern. The solution to this dilemma was the "off-modern" strategy pursued by Catholics, whereby the church presented itself as antimodernist and ultramodernist at once—that is, as a force moderating between the extremes of positivism and irrationalism.[112] Catholicism took advantage of the "call to order" that followed the war that allowed it to proffer Christianity, an artifact of the premodern, as a source of postwar renewal.

Many have written of the legacy of the Great War in modern memory, but it remains hard even today for Americans to appreciate its impact since none of the fighting occurred on American soil. The war demanded remembrance of the sacrifice of the dead, which the Catholic Church compared to the Passion of Christ. The connection between commemoration of the dead and of the Crucifixion was manifested in the masses and funerals led by chaplains, through preaching, and in the campaigns to resurrect the destroyed churches, abbeys, and convents. Some of that traditionalist sensibility and the desire to rebuild the body of Christ returned to Catholics in the United States with the chaplains and veterans of the Great War.

In a short time, Europeans and Americans came to commemorate the war losses through a combination of civic and religious rituals. In Great Britain as in the United States, the dead were oddly invisible, since there were few corpses or cemeteries, even though 10 percent of Englishmen under forty-five had been killed.[113] Beginning on the armistice of November 11, 1919, Britons adopted silence as a public rite to honor the sacrifice of an entire generation on foreign soil. Following a two-minute period of silence observed across the country, Remembrance Day was accompanied in London by ceremonies held at the Cenotaph in Whitehall, which was the national monument erected for the war dead. The mourning rites of the state church, however, apparently failed to soothe the anguish of British citizens, many of whom took refuge in spiritualism to the chagrin of Anglican leaders.

Across the channel on the western front in Flanders and France, where most of the fallen lay in unidentifiable mounds and mass graves, it was likewise impossible for families to hold a proper funeral and burial. Thus the dead were memorialized in state-managed cemeteries containing rows of graves or ossuaries, which housed the mixed remains of unknown Belgian, French, and German soldiers. These military cemeteries immediately saw an unprecedented volume of visitors. In 1920, for example, 100,000 persons visited the cemetery in Ypres in just three months, an average of more than 1,100 persons per day.[114] In that same year, the French government finally permitted families to reclaim the bodies of their relatives and ship them home at government expense, which proved to be an additional bureaucratic and emotional challenge.[115] Repatriation of remains was a controversial issue for the United States, France, Belgium, Germany, and Great Britain. The latter decided to forbid the practice for any citizens of the British commonwealth.

The United States suffered few casualties in World War I in comparison with the British commonwealth forces and the nations of Europe.[116] Nevertheless, in Margaret Reilly's Manhattan, the priests who served as military chaplains on the western front were the instruments who brought the war home to American congregations and made its existence real, steeped in the language of the heroism of the dead. Archbishop Hayes of New York, who had been named as the first chaplain to the Military Vicariate in 1907, now held the title of first ordinary for the American armed services. A locally

Church at "SIVRY"

1,2,3 Ruined Churches at Bapaume, Albert and Nantillois
1 Bapaume
2
Albert
3 Nantillois
4 Shell hole trap for taxis' — Paris

Distressing images of European Catholic churches in ruins following World War I inspired many charitable campaigns by American and European Catholics to rebuild them. Lukas Etlin directed one such campaign, known as Caritas. These postcards (1917), brought to the United States by returning veterans, also contain added pencil drawings of a rosary, architectural details, and a priest celebrating Mass. (Courtesy of the New York Public Library) beloved figure was Father Francis Patrick Duffy, the nation's most highly decorated chaplain of the armed forces. Duffy, a veteran of the Spanish-American War, served with the 42nd "Rainbow" Division during World War I, for which he received several medals.[117] Duffy's memoirs of his experiences on the western front, published in 1919, quickly became a best seller. He recalled that the French were moved by the fact that he wore the French tricolor with a Sacred Heart badge on his tunic, "pinned there by the great Cardinal of New York."[118] (He did not mention that the symbol was divisive for the French army, which did not welcome a revival of religion in the trenches.) In 1920 Duffy returned from France to serve as pastor at the new Holy Cross parish in Manhattan's theater district. Duffy united various constituencies of Irish Americans, Catholics, priests, and soldiers, asking them to continue their sacrifices on behalf of the nation in peacetime.

Sister Thorn's stigmatization followed immediately upon the return of American soldiers from Europe and the attempts of church and nation to honor their sacrifice and properly mourn the losses of the Great War without giving in to nihilism or apocalypticism. Her experiences now harmonized with a religious climate sympathetic to mysticism, which also served the church's interest in checking its rivals, from spiritualism to psychoanalysis. Their interest in holy women who communicated with Jesus, Mary, and the saints spoke to Catholics' need for consolation and reassurance after a devastating war, as well as their desire to avoid religious frauds and fads. It also fit the rhythms of the internationalization of an Ultramontane Catholicism that benefited from the canonization of several popular figures in the decade after the war, including Thérèse of Lisieux (a favorite of many Allied soldiers, who read her autobiography while stationed in France or Belgium) and Joan of Arc (patroness of France), and by the continuing diffusion of popular devotions, especially to the Immaculate Heart of Mary and the Sacred Heart of Jesus.[119] (The latter was taken up especially by Sister Thorn, as chapter 5 will explore.)

Because of World War I, American Catholic soldiers had encountered the rich sacred landscape of Europe and discovered precedents for their own barely developed culture of visionaries and prodigies. Since the founding of the United States, Catholics had few home-grown mystics to call their own, and local miracles mostly involved physical healing. The cure of Ann Mattingly in 1824 in Washington, D.C., stands out in the historical record, and even that case gained attention in the Catholic press mostly because the healer was a Bavarian aristocratic priest, Reverend Prince Alexander Hohenlohe (1794–1849). Mattingly, the sister of the mayor of Washington, was cured of a breast tumor by the healer in absentia, who arranged to offer Mass in Germany simultaneously to one being offered at midnight at her parish in Georgetown. Following Mattingly's reception of Communion, her tumor and ulcerated back were immediately healed. Prince Hohenlohe's slide into obscurity by 1870 may indicate the lack of support in a democratic nation for the model of the aristocratic gentleman as wonder-worker and concern among American Catholic leaders not to stir up nativist resentment among their fellow citizens by drawing undue attention to the supernatural.[120]

A century after the Mattingly miracle, the stigmata of Sister Thorn were still a novelty among Americans, but she was made less unusual when placed in the company of European stigmatics, visionaries, and victim souls.[121] Throughout the nineteenth-century, debates between French Catholics (who had produced many such figures) and the secular French (who had taken the lead in dismissing such women as hysterics) had established the gender politics of modern mysticism. The creation and diagnosis of hysteria became a means for controlling and subduing women that also lent sup- port to an anticlerical, antisupernatural politics in Europe, as evinced in the aftermath of the apparitions of the Virgin at Lourdes.[122] As Paolo Apolito has pointed out, events like Marian apparitions "all served to stoke the flames of a church polemic against the 'errors of modernity': liberalism, positivism, atheism, and so on."[123] Similarly, when a Marian visionary who imitated Lourdes was reported in a German village during the Kulturkampf, the medical community used the occasion to denounce Catholic piety as a form of superstition and ignorance that were inimical to Germany's progress.[124]

A diagnosis of hysteria could handily exclude both women and Catholics from political and social power in the secular state. But the well-defined rivalry between European Catholics and three factions—Protestants, po- litical liberals, and positivists—did not translate neatly to Margaret Reilly's context in the United States. In at least three ways, the position of American Catholics differed from their European counterparts. First, since the Catho- lic Church had never been the established religion of the United States, it could not trade on former authority or use nostalgia to drive a popular campaign to restore a lost golden age. American Protestants, after all, had been able to contain Catholic power since the colonial era by successfully equating Romanism with tyranny and their own brand of Christianity with democracy.[125] Second, during Margaret Reilly's lifetime, the defining fea- ture of the American Catholic Church was its immigrant and devotional character, which encouraged the faithful to embrace the Catholic Revival in order to build connections to the old traditions of Europe and to aug- ment their own lack of sacred sites, shrines, and pilgrimage customs. This stage of Catholic separatism in the United States was soon to be augmented after World War I by an increased self-confidence. Third, unlike Belgium, France, Germany, and Italy, where disestablishment of religion had targeted the Catholic Church to diminish its force, in the 1920s American Catholics were enjoying a rising degree of economic and social power and were starting to flex this new-found power through increasingly public expressions of faith. In the 1880s, Catholics had begun a process of sacralizing the American landscape through a boom in church and school building, but they also had devised new sites of popular devotion. Pilgrimages to these newly designated shrines in the United States "mushroomed between the 1920s and the Second World War."[126] For a brief time, Peekskill became one of these pilgrimage sites.

With Sister Thorn's religious advocates and the distinction of being studied by Herbert Thurston, was it likely that she would become a saint? Narratives of mystics and would-be saints do not appear ex nihilo, although it sometimes appears so because few Christians understand, examine, or dispute the conditions that go into the making of such documents. As Margaret Reilly became Sister Thorn, her congregation already began to think about establishing the preliminaries for her potential candidacy for sainthood. Typically, the Good Shepherd motherhouse in Angers, France, would initiate a request to the local superior at the Peekskill convent to submit a report on events. Mother Raymond had done so, thereby providing the raw material for future redactors of Sister Thorn's vita.

Although it had also been common since the Middle Ages for women to be commanded by their spiritual directors to dictate or compose their spiritual autobiographies, there is no evidence to suggest that any director solicited Margaret's life in her own words.[127] It would not have been unusual for Margaret's confessor, Monsignor Brady, to make such a request. Yet Margaret produced nothing like the spiritual autobiography that had made Therese Martin into a household saint during Margaret's lifetime.

In building a vita for Margaret without her own testimony, her Catholic contemporaries used the strategy of suggesting the affinities between her, the prospective saint, and well-known saints. This approach, for instance, led Therese Neumann's inedia to be compared to that of Catherine of Siena, Saint Maria Maddalena de' Pazzi, and Blessed Columba de Rieti.[128] Devotees of Teresa Higginson in Great Britain credited her founding of a cult of devotion to the sacred head of Jesus as an extension of the Sacred Heart devotion established by Saint Margaret Marie Alacoque and as connected to the Holy Face of Jesus devotion from Thérèse of Lisieux. In the case of Josefa Menendez in France, she saw in a vision the words of Margaret Marie Alacoque in a book commissioning her to serve Jesus as a victim soul. Josefa's editor obligingly concluded: "It would seem that . . . it was Our Lord's intention to associate humble little Sister Josefa with the saint."[129] Margaret Reilly's hair shirt, the ashes in her shoes, her mystical marriage to Christ, and the demonic attacks on her body and virtue reprised episodes in the lives of Rita of Cascia, Anne Catherine Emmerich, Catherine of Siena, and Gemma Galgani, as Margaret's supporters noted without cynicism. The appearance of similar anecdotes in the lives of Margaret's stigmatized contemporaries (including Alexandrina da Costa, Rose Marie Ferron, Josefa Menendez, Therese Neumann, and Marthe Robin) suggests that other confessors shared the same narrative strategies and drew upon the same reserve of hagiographies for strengthening their candidates among a Catholic audience.

As her advocates worked to establish the extraordinary suffering and sanctity of Sister Thorn, the process confirms how saints are made through narrative. First, the lives of stigmatics and mystics must be rendered acceptable to church authorities, who are uniformly male. This meant that feminine mystical experiences were judged by theologians and priests whose discourses of power have often worked against marginal and oppressed groups in the Catholic Church, including women religious. At the time of Margaret's death, given the spate of recent visionaries and stigmatics in Europe, her spiritual revelations and experiences may not have been remarkable enough to merit sustained attention (perhaps occupying what J.-K. Huysmans described as the "zone of tepid piety" of most Christians), or they may have been dismissed as examples of hysteria, or perhaps they were deemed unsuitable to represent the ethos of an intensifying American Catholic Church. At the time of Margaret's death, Frances Cabrini's canonization seemed to signal that an active do-gooder from Italy had a better chance than a medieval throwback.

The redaction of the lives of potential saints is an inevitable part of the hagiographic process. In the narratives produced about Sister Thorn by her champions, the subjectivity of the authors shaped their interpretations of events in her life, yet in each vita, Catholicism itself had to be established as the feature that trumped all other identities (gender, race, class, region, nationality). Therefore, in a remarkably short time, Margaret Reilly's life was distanced from the strange events and controversies associated with her past and with her first years in the convent. The collaborative process that was already beginning to edit the eyewitness accounts was anxious for a narrative that would fit Catholic norms of spiritual autobiography. Accounts by Fathers Bertrand, Reilly, and Scanlan were either limited to monastic readers or edited to turn Sister Thorn into an acceptable "type." Any arcane or unorthodox details of her life would soon disappear from accounts intended for the public. A particular instance of strategic editing is the omission of details that undercut the picture of Margaret's entry into the Good Shepherd convent as a singular, successful event. Sister Mary Carmelita Quinn's narration, for example, fails to mention the fact that Margaret had already failed to gain admission to the Ursulines, and that she had visited the Good Shepherds at their 90th Street house in Manhattan before going to Peekskill. Omitting such facts enhances the dramatic impact of Margaret's sudden appearance at the Peekskill convent as the fulfillment of God's command. In Quinn's version, Margaret achieved her goal of religious life immediately, despite her extended postulancy among the Good Shepherds and several brief departures from Peekskill.

In retrospect, attempts to create a uniform written account of Sister Thorn's extraordinary holiness, the usual vehicle for standardizing a saint's vita, were fragmentary and inconclusive. Since Thorn generated no diary, the narratives of her life composed by others continued to reflect their authors' idiosyncrasies. Even individual testimonies collected about Sister Thorn varied greatly. Some called her genuine, sweet, and patient, even during her spells of illness; while other members of her convent community found her backbiting, gossiping, grandiose, meddling, and insincere. Still other acquaintances changed their opinions of Thorn over time. Sister St. Margaret Mary Roche, for instance, reported in 1944:

> In my early religious life I firmly believed that Sister Mary of the Crown of Thorns was a chosen soul. At that period my contact with her consisted of occasional visits at rare intervals. Later when my work necessitated spending long periods with her, I was surprised to note her spirit of criticism and uncharitable remarks. . . . She was untruthful and revealed serious matters of conscience that had been entrusted to her by the sisters, friends in the world, priests and other ecclesiastics. She meddled with community affairs even tho she was not a consellor [sic] nor held any office in the community. The affairs of the house and even of the province were discussed at her bedside, so that it was not surprising that she knew the private affairs of the sisters. These things have caused grave doubts in my mind which I cannot reconcile with either holiness or sanctity. I write this in the spirit of obedience at the request of my Superior, with no malice or animosity in my heart for the Sister concerned.[130]

On the other hand, stigmatics and their followers have embraced marginality as part of their spiritual capital. Some forms of popular religion succeed by avoiding appropriation by the religious elite, as in the case of

Padre Pio of Italy and countless cult figures in the history of Roman Catholicism who relied on their demotic credentials and audiences. Margaret Reilly's would-be hagiographers, too, associated her with other humble saintly women. At various points in his writing, Lukas Etlin merged her experiences freely with those of the pitiable Anne Emmerich, whose *Passion of Our Lord* had caused him to "weep bitterly."[131] A Salvatorian priest called Margaret a second Gemma Galgani.[132] Still other details of Margaret's hagiography-in-progress recall the biographies of recent stigmatics Palma Matarelli or Louise Lateau, which were reaching American readers for the first time. Other writers were quick to compare Sister Thorn with her stigmatized contemporaries—Marie-Julie Jahenny, Therese Neumann, Sister Amalia, Sister Rumolda, and Helen Polezar. The fact that these women lived in vastly different parts of the world (France, Bavaria, Brazil, Flanders, and Ohio, respectively), mattered little because the impetus behind such comparisons was the church's desire to internationalize itself among a generation brutalized by a world war and besieged by religious doubt. It redoubled its efforts to extend the Ultramontanist spirit of the mid-1800s through a new emphasis upon the Eucharist, all the while lending support for cults of the Sacred Heart, the Virgin, and the saints and finding ways to merge them with Passion mysticism.[133]

A stigmatic cult in the United States could have proved to be the perfect devotion for interwar Catholic piety because it combined passive and active forms: meaningful suffering and fighting evil. However, the growing internationalism desired by the Vatican did not eliminate nationalist or ethnic sentiment in America. Because cults are always constituted by local circumstances before being affirmed by the church as universal, it was not surprising that within one decade of her death, Margaret was being eagerly promoted by Irish Americans, who touted her as the foremost candidate for the title of first American saint. But perhaps shifts in American piety were replacing the need to commemorate the past that had inspired the immigrant church with the desire of its grandchildren to engage the contemporary world as American citizens. Within a few decades of Sister Thorn's death, in the renewed church anticipated by Vatican II, the saints would be fighters for social justice who gained their inspiration from Christ the liberator, not Jesus the Man of Sorrows, while activist women in lay and religious life would challenge older models of passive suffering and endurance. There was less need for devotions based on tears, blood, and apocalypticism and more emphasis upon building the divine kingdom on earth.

Sister Thorn's champions were unsurprised by her extraordinary physical suffering, however, and defended the notion that pain and suffering *are* the core of Christianity. Even controversialists like Oscar Wilde had contended that "the worship of pain has far more often dominated the world. Medievalism, with its saints and martyrs, its love of self-torture, its wild passion for wounding itself, its gnashing with knives, and its whipping with rods—Medievalism is real Christianity and the medieval Christ is the real Christ."[134] Wilde's identification of "real" Christianity with self-torture resonated with the victim spirituality that dominated the Catholic Church in the interwar decades, but it was out of step with the emotional climate of the United States, whose optimism and pragmatism disdained the tortured virtuoso. Even if Sister Thorn proved herself worthy of the spiritual heroics associated with medieval saints, would she have been canonized in the modern era? Even as her cause was gathering support in the 1940s, scholars were pointing to the "passing of the saint" as a sign of the disjunction between hieratic and democratic societies.[135] Medieval Catholics found the legends of miracles and extreme suffering appealing in a culture where their social status was immutable, whereas in a democratic nation, the cult of Sister Crown of Thorns conflicted with nearly all cultural trends influencing Americans.

Ultimately, Margaret Reilly was not canonized, nor did she gain recognition for being the first of anything. Tellingly, hardworking Mother Frances Cabrini (1850–1917) of Italy became America's first immigrant saint in 1946; her hagiography notably lacked any traces of mystical experience but did furnish the necessary two miracles. Cabrini was followed in 1975 by Mother Elizabeth Ann Seton, an Episcopal convert who became the first American-born saint.[136] (North Americans tended to ignore the fact that Rose of Lima had been named the first saint of the Americas in 1671.) The canonizations of Cabrini and Seton bookend an era during which Sister Thorn's advocates tried and failed to secure that honor for her by downplaying her more Gothic attributes in order to compile a dossier of sanctity composed of evidence of healing miracles, testimonies about her extraordinary holiness and virtue, and, most especially—following post-1917 canonical standards—her total obedience to the church hierarchy and clergy.

We Are Skeptics Together about a
Great Many Things
Catholics and the Scientific Study of Stigmata

I fully believe in the prevalence of a great deal of subtle
and often seemingly purposeless fraud.
—Herbert Thurston, *Surprising Mystics* (1955), 204

There has never been and never will be a social order that
does not demand of a female child some conformity to
some gender ideal of femininity.
—Louise J. Kaplan, *Female Perversions: The Temptations of
Emma Bovary* (1991), 50

Mysticism vs. Positivism

To understand Margaret's diagnosis and treatment at the hands of medical
experts, this chapter examines the scientific community's impact on the
American understanding of stigmatization in the early twentieth century.
First, it analyzes and contrasts the involvements of the three physicians central to Margaret Reilly's experience: Thomas Gallen, Thomas McParlan, and
James J. Walsh. Margaret fell in love with Gallen, involving her in a romantic
triangle that reveals the emerging challenges to rigid gender attitudes and
roles in Manhattan for a Catholic woman possessing more life options than
she would have in prior decades. Although Margaret loved Gallen, he married someone else, soon becoming the target of anonymous letters that were
probably instigated by Margaret around the time she entered the convent.
Gallen's response is unknown, but the actions and opinions of McParlan
and Walsh shed light on the Catholic reception of scientific investigation
of stigmata and, indeed, on the church's willingness to accept new scientific methods, including the premises and methods of psychoanalysis and
psychology. Catholic medical opinions at that time ranged from a lingering
fascination with the fin de siècle interest in hysteria to an emerging critique
of psychoanalysis and psychology as threats to religion.

Because the terms of both debates in America often followed and relied upon the further-advanced discussion taking place in Europe, this chapter's second emphasis traces the connections between Margaret's Catholic examiners in the United States and their engagement with Catholic commentary on the Continent's leading medical and psychological interpreters of stigmata (primarily, "Napoleon of the Neuroses" Jean-Martin Charcot and his student, Sigmund Freud). I do not intend to "prove" medical or psychological causes for Margaret's mystical experiences but rather to locate the reception of such models, first in their Catholic milieu and then in the larger social and political contexts of her lifetime (which included the effects of World War I), the concept of hysteria, and the emergence of psychoanalysis. Third, after examining Catholic engagement with these seminal figures who tried to explain mystical phenomena as rooted in physiology or the psyche, this chapter considers the developments in thinking about stigmatization among contemporary scholars who include stigmata in their study of religious pain. These reflections include revisions to Freudianism offered in the last three decades by post-Freudians and by feminist approaches to the psychology of women.

Much has been made of the conflict between science and religion in the modern era, the battle lines of which had been drawn during the Scientific Revolution in seventeenth-century Europe. During the late 1800s, the contours of the debate between supernaturalists and naturalists were further defined. Nineteenth-century medical practitioners now looked to science to debunk mystical phenomena such as religious apparitions, miraculous healings, and stigmata.[1] Neurologists demonstrated how religious passion posed a threat to reason by parading their (mostly) female patients before their students, calling the patients delusional in their claims to have seen the Virgin Mary or the saints, spoken with Jesus, and even received his wounds.

Neurologists were soon joined (and also challenged) by new experts— "alienists," psychoanalysts, and psychiatrists—who began to study religious behaviors, usually employing the category of "hysteria" to dismiss them as inherently neurotic or as the Other to women's erotic impulses, as seen in the fictional Madame Bovary. The experiences of several female patients of these neurologists became so familiar to fin de siècle audiences that they were known by their first names: Augustine, Geneviève, Madeleine. Sister Thorn would never achieve that degree of notoriety in America, yet in the early twentieth century, she too became part of the attempt to both revive and contain modern mysticism. The substitution of "scientific" explanations for formerly religious categories of diabolic possession or mystical revelations is a central part of the intellectual history of the nineteenth century. The case of Sister Thorn follows that debate up to the mid-twentieth century and raises questions about cultural difference regarding the exceptional (or unexceptional) status of American Catholicism.

Positivism, especially the anticlerical version of Charcot in France, inspired a Catholic backlash against science, which undoubtedly delayed fruitful interactions between psychology and Catholicism in the following century. On the other hand, positivism did have an impact upon theology, as seen in Catholics' determination to distinguish a genuine mysticism from mere curiosities and in the attempts by theologians and intellectuals to depict and classify elements of mysticism as though they operated by scientific stages and laws. Hence, the definers of mysticism of the early twentieth century fell into at least two camps: those determined to preserve its sui generis status and those concerned to enlist science to identify "essential" mysticism and its functions, albeit for the apologetic reason of preventing counterfeit forms of the interior life from gaining a foothold in Catholic practice. Empiricism's influence can be seen even in the entry for "Mysticism" in the *Catholic Encyclopedia*, which declared: "Mystical theology is the *science* which treats of acts and experiences or states of the soul which cannot be produced by human effort or industry even with the ordinary aid of Divine grace."[2]

Margaret Reilly's examiners were indebted to this nineteenth-century legacy of scientific investigation of supernatural events, notably, the studies of Louise Lateau (1850–83) of Belgium, who became the prototype of the modern stigmatic given over to testing and investigation. By 1870, two years after Lateau's stigmata appeared, already more than 100 people had offered opinions on the case, usually after visiting her home during her Friday ecstasies. Undergoing rigorous observation and a set of religious and physical tests, Lateau embodied the contest between mystical theology and positivist science that preoccupied students of mystical events in the closing decades of the nineteenth century. To satisfy the churchmen, Lateau pledged that she could distinguish true from false relics that had been brought to her in a box from Brussels Cathedral; for the scientists, she agreed to experiments with bright lights, chemicals, a penknife, pins, and electric shock. It was even a church official, Monsignor Ponceau, the vicar-general of her Diocese of Tournai, who proposed a trial that consisted of encasing Lateau's arm in a glass tube to discover if her stigmata would appear on Friday as always. Cosponsored by the bishop and the Belgian Royal Academy of Medicine, this momentous test began on December 16, 1868, when a kid glove was sealed on each of Lateau's hands and not opened until Friday. When the

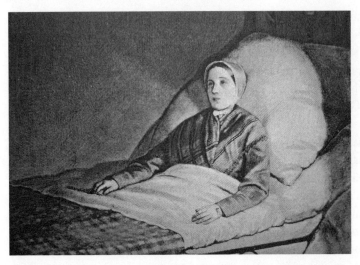

Louise Lateau (1850–1883) of Belgium, the most celebrated and examined stigmatic of the nineteenth century in the bedridden pose that seemingly imagined all stig- matics as invalids. (Frontispiece from A. J. Riko, *Louise Lateau en andere mystieken met afbeeldingen en volledigen lijst der gestigmatiseerden van 1186 tot op onze dagen* [Amsterdam: C. L. Van Langenhuysen, 1891])

glove was removed, it was discovered that Lateau's wounds were bleeding as usual. Thus the vaunted contest between science and faith ended with no decisive victor. The scientists could not explain what they had witnessed, while Catholics continued to use Lateau's wounds to rebuke enemies of the church and nonbelievers.[3]

While Margaret Reilly did not attain the celebrity of Louise Lateau, it is nonetheless surprising that the archbishop of New York, on the advice of Dr. Walsh, did not pursue a similar controlled observation by neutral outsiders not connected to the Catholic Church. Fifty years after Lateau, and in a differ- ent political climate, the American church seemed oddly tentative about what science might prove. The partial and uneven quality of the role of medical expertise in analyzing Margaret's stigmata reveals the church's own uncer- tainty about how to proceed: although it procured the testimony of physi- cians, it confined their contributions to private discussions between bishops and clergy and prevented public access to and contributions on the matter.

A Failed Romance

Margaret Reilly's contact with the New York medical community began in 1912 with a stomach ache that led to ulcer surgery some years later. Dr.

Thomas Gallen operated on her in 1917 and possibly again in 1921.[4] These operations failed to resolve her pain, however, prompting her to seek a doctor's advice again. When Dr. James Walsh visited the Peekskill convent in the summer of 1922, therefore, he also examined Margaret for stomach trouble, giving her a dose of calomel and a prescription for a stomach tonic. He was convinced that her problems were not ulcers. Margaret simply did not eat enough, he said, producing nutritional deficiencies that were the cause of her stomach pain and constipation. For this condition, physicians at the time typically prescribed calomel, or "mercurous chloride," as a diuretic and a purgative.[5] When Margaret reminded Walsh that she had been examined by him ten years before at the request of her confessor, Walsh had no recollection of it.[6] It was a second physician, Thomas McParlan, who informed him that in the years following her first appointment with Walsh, Margaret had undergone surgery to remove stomach ulcers, although none had been found. Her distress, as hysterics were commonly told, was all in her head. Soon, both McParlan and Walsh would play key roles in the investigation of Margaret's stigmatization.

The first doctor who treated Margaret, however, ended up being less significant for his medical role than for his role in Margaret's fantasy life. The New York Good Shepherd archives contains references to the "Gallen letters," items that complicate Margaret Reilly's biography and saintly image. Some two dozen unsigned letters were sent to Thomas J. Gallen, who had performed Margaret's stomach ulcer operation. The existence of the correspondence was first remarked upon by Father James McGivney, a Jesuit provincial living at Fordham University in the Bronx.[7] In McGivney's understanding, the letters began to arrive after Gallen's marriage to a nurse: "Now it happened that Miss Murphy [Mahoney] and the Doctor were keeping company. Miss Murphy is now Mrs. Thomas Gallen. The Doctor was kind to Margaret and Margaret thought the Doctor was in love with her. When she found out that he was keeping company with the nurse, her jealousy became very violent and it is said that she wrote Doctor Gallen 25 letters with no name attached."[8] Over time, McGivney learned much more about the love triangle and became fed up with the entire situation. As he explained confidentially to Father Herbert Thurston: "I could almost write a book yet on the insanity."[9] Gallen and his wife, Mary, received letters at their home, both by mail and by hand delivery from child messengers. The two letters that I located at the Jesuit archives in London came in ordinary postmarked, typed white envelopes that were mailed from Manhattan's postal station "K."[10]

Margaret Reilly was named as the source of the anonymous letters because they arrived immediately after Mother Mary of St. Francis Xavier

McGinty (1845–1921), the superior of the 90th Street Good Shepherd convent, had received a similar hostile message. Her anonymous note demanded that Mother St. Francis, who had just voted to refuse Margaret entrance into the religious community, "*repent* and *mighty soon* of your scandalous talk in regard to the saint that He has given this Convent. . . . You should be ashamed to wear the habit of Good Shepherd Nun, for you are unworthy of such an honor, much less worthy to be a Superior. Be decent and resign." It also stated: "Margaret Reilly is a stranger to me, but I tell you I have no habit, just a poor wretch in the world, but from the first I heard of her, I knew absolutely it was *God alone* who was working in Margaret Reilly."[11] The indignant author demanded that Mother Francis get rid of her "damn pride" by going to confession, threatening that "the good God will wreck His vengeance upon you before long." Apparently, Mother St. Francis had told others that Margaret was a "fakir," a charge that enraged the author, who threatened to expose McGinty's "hellish work" to the Good Shepherd provincial and to the archbishop. The postscript concluded spitefully: "Note envelope, I did not put *Rev.*, you are not entitled to it."[12]

This communication to McGinty caught Father McGivney's eye because it contained a biblical reference that reminded him of Margaret's egoism. The letter writer had cited Jesus's words about his temptation by the devil: "Could I not ask my Father, if I so wished, and He would send me legions of Angels, but the Scriptures must be fulfilled." Judging its tone and content, Father McGivney surmised that McGinty's letter, and those sent to the Gallens, were Margaret's work, but he reassured Archbishop Patrick Hayes that "none of the [Good Shepherd] Sisters have read them although all know something about [what] they call the Gallen letters."[13] McGivney had received the letters from a sister who had gotten them from a friend of Gallen, with the caveat that none of the sisters would be permitted access. On behalf of the Good Shepherds, McGivney advised the archbishop that "a most rigid examination into this affair should be made either by your Grace or by an impartial committee appointed by you." Such an inquiry would prevent immoral persons from entering their congregation and putting "a stain on themselves and all our Sisterhoods." Although McGivney pleaded that the sisters were powerless in such a delicate matter, he reminded the archbishop that "there will be no peace in the Community till this is settled."[14] It is unknown what, if any, action Hayes took on this matter. The contents and location of the other twenty to twenty-five letters is unknown, although McGivney believed that numerous people were aware of the letters and their contents. After this incident, the Gallens left little trace in the public record, and virtually nothing is known of their later lives.[15] The result of the anonymous letters was to stir up doubt about Margaret Reilly's reputation and suitability for a convent vocation, since they came to light precisely as she was trying to join the Good Shepherds.

At the time that the Gallens were receiving the poison-pen letters, the archbishop of New York, who ultimately would have to deal with the matter of Margaret Reilly, was occupied with gender and reproductive issues. Archbishop Hayes had recently taken up a public crusade against Margaret Sanger, the advocate of birth control. In 1916 Sanger had located her clinic in Brooklyn and was now organizing the First American Birth Control Conference, which planned to hold its final forum at Manhattan's Town Hall in November 1921.[16] She had invited several Catholic clergy to attend, including the archbishop. Sanger's activities proved to be a catalyst in the Archdiocese of New York that set the stage for establishing the church's position on the gender and sexuality debates of the twentieth century. Scant information is available on the sexual behavior of, much less statistics on abortion and the use of contraception by, lay Catholic women of this era, but family size did begin to decrease. The opposition of the American hierarchy to birth control was first articulated in a bishops' pastoral letter of 1919, written in response to the declining size of Catholic families in certain parts of the United States, even though it was still illegal at that time for physicians to even instruct women about birth control.[17] Despite this legal constraint, Catholic couples were obviously finding ways to limit family size.

Archbishop Hayes, learning of Sanger's plans, resorted to using "Church control" against "Birth control" to prevent the meeting from happening. Before the final forum could start, Hayes pressured the police captain through his proxy, Monsignor Joseph Dineen, to lock the building, disperse the audience already inside, and remove Sanger. Police officers complied by locking the audience inside the theater, ordering everyone to leave. When the police unlocked the doors for the evacuation, Sanger and her circle (which included a former member of the British Parliament, the keynote speaker) rushed inside. The police arrested Sanger and several other American Birth Control League members, although they had no legal sanctions to do so. The outcry against the Catholic Church as a "dictatorship of celibates" who attacked free speech and exerted "sinister" pressure to silence any public discussion of "enforced maternity" put Archbishop Hayes in an embarrassing position.[18] His actions in the Town Hall raid, once exposed to the public, had the effect of galvanizing support for free speech, family limitation, and Sanger's movement. The incident proved that Hayes was willing to espouse

unpopular opinions in order to preserve the church's belief in the importance of female purity and motherhood.

Yet Hayes, a cautious man of impoverished origins in the city's Five Points
slum, was a prelate on the way up, an aspirant to the cardinalate. Possibly,
he sensed that his defense of the church's official position on artificial birth
control must not appear weak. When Sanger's conference was rescheduled
a week later at another Manhattan location, she again invited the archbishop
and Monsignor John A. Ryan from Catholic University to be present. (Hayes
sent a representative; Ryan did not attend.) The public event, entitled "Birth
Control—Is It Moral?," took place without interruption. Apparently, the
pope was not swayed by the negative publicity against Hayes in American
media, as he awarded Archbishop Hayes the sought-after red hat in March
1924.[19]

Sexual Politics in Manhattan

The Sanger-Hayes debates of 1921–22 concerned the rights and freedoms
of women, which, on a much more private scale, also formed the crux of
the matter surrounding Margaret Reilly. When Margaret was applying for
admission to the Good Shepherd congregation, Father McGivney described
her to Archbishop Hayes as a liar and a megalomaniac and accused the sisters
of rigging an election in order to admit her. The sisters, according to Mc-
Givney, did not regard Margaret as malicious, only hysterical. "Those who
know her for years say she was always strange," he added. In his final word
to Hayes on the Gallen matter, McGivney defended the Good Shepherds as
a "fervent, most generous, most devoted" religious community, but he found
them at the same time "very sad and disappointed, and filled with a feeling
that they are almost abandoned in their trial."[20] At a critical moment when
the Good Shepherds needed his support and guidance, the archbishop had
chosen to marshal his energies to combat a "free love" advocate rather than
to investigate a report of a stigmatization. In fact, neither Margaret Sanger
nor Margaret Reilly were well served by the Catholic hierarchy. The gender
conflicts involved in these incidents demonstrated that the Catholic leadership of New York and its allies were determined to rebuke women whose
experiences were unorthodox or rebellious in order to uphold the power of
priests and the medical profession as the authorized spokesmen for women.

Because the Gallen episode was controversial in Margaret Reilly's life, it
is worth citing one of the letters to Gallen in full to give a sense of its rancorous tone and to imagine its impact on readers.

Dear Doctor Gallen:

Just to let you know that Miss Mahoney done up Miss Reily last night. But she is sorry for it now. Miss Reily would not let her fuck her—that was the cause. Miss Reily is a damn nice girl and I do not blame you to hold on to her. She is a model girl. I wish to God I was as pure. But one thing she can certainly keep secret: I know Miss Mahoney has told her some things and she has kept them from you, Dear Doctor, so much as I love you; Miss Reily does too. But how in Hell can she be good. I know she goes out with you. You can't hide it from me. She told me you are not her style—that Bull Shit. I Know Miss Mahoney is crazy over Miss Reily, as Miss Reily is so kind to her. She is so affectionate and forgives me so often. I am just waiting for her to tell some of the secrets I told her. But God help her. Miss Mahoney got 300 from her this week so far. But Miss Reily is doing it because she is afraid Miss Mahoney will give way on her for fucking Gallen. I told Miss Reily to lend me 1.00; if she doesn't, God help her. If I can't fuck you, Gallen, I get it from Miss Reily, and I have some of your ? [sic] in me. If Miss Mahoney ever goes back on me, God help her.[21]

The letter raises more questions than it answers. The typescript version in the Good Shepherd archives, labeled "Letter #1," closes with a note: "In the original there are mistakes in spelling which are not reproduced here. The punctuation is also different from the original." This indicates that McGivney had transcribed some of the Gallen letters in order to share them with Father Thurston across the Atlantic. Thurston's copy lacks several words that McGivney either could not read or chose not to include. In terms of the letter's content, the vulgarisms are in more common use today but still have the power to shock. Then, as now, "fuck" could be interpreted in a sexual way or in the metaphorical sense of ruining someone, as through blackmail. In addition, the verb's meaning seems to shift during the course of the letter, from the crudely sexual to the purely mercenary. The author's position is not entirely clear, either. Are these the ramblings of a woman who is angry because she, too, has an attachment to Dr. Gallen? Or is this a fight between three women over their complicated friendship? Or is the author looking to extort money from someone? Or if the author is Reilly, does she place herself at the center of the controversy because she was "always looking for notoriety"?[22] Finally, does the poor grammar of the letter suggest someone with limited schooling, an immigrant with a meager command of English, or a writer pretending to be uneducated?

The second letter in McGivney's packet to Thurston is dated thirteen days *before* Letter #1. More direct in tone, it begins: "Gallen, all I can say is that the letter I wrote you about that damn liar, I take it all back. She just as damn liar as ever lived. I met her with that nurse. And she thinks she was clever to let me see *your* ring on her finger by taking it off so often you damn sneak. The nerve of the damn nurse to eye me as she did. As big a liar as Miss Reily is, she has politeness; she knows her place." The author continues: "Oh, I am crazy. If it was Miss Reily you like as well as the [?], I not act so; but O God to think you are fucking Miss Reily, and me thinkg [sic] her so sweet. I will kill her yet. If I had been where she was, I smash her. I write her and tell her a few things. Gallen, you are one little cur and one damn sneak. How much do you pay Miss ?, ought to be ? for telling lies. Wait, just wait you and Reily."[23]

The emotional fury of the author is apparent, but again the context, motives, and goals are not. Was Margaret the writer, or was the sender an acquaintance who became disillusioned with Margaret because she had succumbed to Gallen and flaunted a ring from him, a detail also remarked upon by others?[24] Was the letter writer a woman who was also scorned by Gallen (who seems to have attracted a great deal of female attention)? Or was the writer trying to play all three figures—Reilly, Mahoney, and Gallen—against each other for financial gain? Finally, what are the "lies" told by Reilly and mentioned four times in the letter?

These questions are impossible to answer conclusively given the limitations of evidence, yet they invite speculations about the paradoxical environment of constraint and liberation that produced Margaret Reilly. According to her convent biographers, Margaret's Catholic girlhood was marked by self-punishment. The details of Margaret's penances and of her family's pious practices are convincing evidence of their attempts to achieve holiness in domestic and parish life. Indeed, Margaret's "precocious piety" recalls the strenuous asceticism of many medieval and Early Modern mystics.[25] Reilly's parents were daily communicants at a time when that was not the norm. Margaret's mother had aspired to be a nun, like her sisters. Mother Raymond recorded that "Mr. Reilly's family" said the Rosary every evening, disclosing the father's leadership of family practices that exacted a daily time commitment from each family member for the repetitive prayers. If the children wanted to go out, they had to say the Rosary first; if friends came over before the prayer was finished, they had to join the recitation or wait.

But in contrast to her sacralized and policed home life, Margaret had also grown up in a Manhattan where freer patterns of courting and mating had emerged among young men and women. She had worked as a stenographer and a domestic, and during the First World War, she had worked as a cleaner in the office of financier Bernard Baruch.[26] In the 1920s, the Modern Girl (not to be confused with the "New Woman" of the 1890s) had become a global phenomenon, as distinguished by her access to and use of mass-marketed commodities that allowed white women to express themselves as "modern." In New York, new behaviors accompanied that new look: a novel culture of sexual indulgence sprung up among "treating" girls or "charity" girls, namely, those working-class women who engaged in sexual relation-ships with men but in ways that carefully avoided prostitution (that is, they did not accept money for their favors).[27] These sexual practices and relations emerged among working women who were likely to roam the city *outside* of their own neighborhoods, frequenting the anonymous venues of the new commercial entertainments like dance halls, where they could find men, mingle freely, and enjoy the benefits of whatever perks they were offered. Their refusal of money from men for sexual "treats" related to their "sense of self-worth and how much treating as a practice had become part of their personal identity."[28] In the shifting sexual politics of the Progressive era, working women thus found ways to define themselves as "good girls" able to pick up men and deserving of sexual experience, but also as superior to the "bad girls" operating as prostitutes in the city. Charity girls enjoyed their independence and mobility but marked their own behavior as "good" by scapegoating others as prostitutes.

In similar fashion, the records of the Boston Psychopathic Hospital for the early twentieth century demonstrate that Irish-Catholic girls and young women had wider sexual experience than has traditionally been attributed to this population.[29] Thomas Hine's history of the American teenager like-wise found that during the 1920s, the diversity of sexual behaviors of young persons rose, such that it was possible for "nice" girls to do a lot of things short of intercourse.[30] The large numbers of drug users and pregnant adoles-cents in the care of the Good Shepherd sisters provide evidence enough that behaviors that were being defined socially as "delinquent" existed among young women in New York during Margaret's lifetime. The RGS had to be careful to avoid the Vice Commission's tendency to assume a direct link between immigration and prostitution, since many of the girls in their care were the children of immigrants. The speakers at Sanger's American Birth Control Conference likewise acknowledged "the problem of the delinquent woman,"[31] and even a Catholic woman submitted an editorial for Sanger's *Birth Control Review* in which she chided the church for failing to forcefully oppose prostitution.[32] Margaret herself may have had some sexual encoun-ters before entering religious life in her late thirties, although the Gallen love triangle remains opaque. While the Reilly family's rather severe piety points in a direction that continued post-famine Irish traditions of gender segregation in public and private life, the Gallen letters hint otherwise at unruly experiences in Margaret's life that may have left a residue of unresolved feelings of uncleanness or sexual sin when she entered the convent. Although it is impossible to know definitively what Margaret did, the Gallen letters offer a possible explanation for her persistent need to atone, for the abortion rumors that attended her connection with Dr. McParlan, and for her insistence upon leaving Manhattan for a convent far from the one in her neighborhood.

In addition to personal details that are unobtainable, it is impossible to ascertain what social circles Margaret inhabited as an employee before entering the convent, but the author of the Gallen letters sounds like she would recognize the racier side of urban youth culture and sexuality represented by bravado, "treating," vulgarity, and greed. Were the payments referred to in the Gallen letters payment for keeping sexual secrets? If so, this form of blackmail was teamed with a softer yearning for romance, marriage, honesty, and true friendship—the domestic arrangements sought by "good" Catholic girls. The "charity girl" and the Catholic nun or mother offered competing images of womanhood in 1920s Manhattan.

As the Gallen letters illustrate, Margaret and her generation of women seemed poised to succeed or fail dramatically. Her family had entered the liminal state of many Irish American Catholics of the 1920s who aspired to "lace curtain" status and who clung to the church as the source of moral norms and identity, but who could also suddenly be brought low by "bog Irish" behaviors that threatened to destroy their hard-won social and financial gains. As historians have considered the plight of the Irish who veered between achievement and failure, they have asked, "Were the Celts successful because most worked their way out of degrading poverty, or were they failures because too many of them seemed to get stuck in the lower middle class too long?"[33] And did Catholicism contribute to a lack of economic initiative or to the protection of those engaged in the struggle by enforcing middle-class standards of morality and gender roles?

Within this fragile milieu, it is understandable that the Reilly family would choose to identify with white America and the church's clear-cut moral positions in order to associate themselves with New York's social elites rather than with its struggling immigrants or African Americans. Given the fragmentary evidence about Margaret's behavior in the Gallen matter, we cannot know if her failed romance with the surgeon, which coincided with the death of her parents, led her to abandon her hopes for marriage and to enter religious life, which offered financial as well as spiritual refuge. Nor can we be certain whether she was the perpetrator or a target of the anonymous letters, which happened to overlap with her reports of demonic attacks on her body at the convent. Evidently, enough Good Shepherd sisters discounted (or ignored) the importance of the Gallen letters when they voted to accept Margaret as a member even after the disquieting letters and related pregnancy rumors surfaced during her postulancy.

The Medicalization of Mysticism

As previously mentioned, one of the staunchest supporters of the mystical experiences of Margaret Reilly was Thomas F. McParlan (1870–1928), the second New York physician who treated her. He lived on East 96th Street just two blocks from the Reilly family, and, like them, he worshipped at St. Ignatius parish. He received his medical degree from Bellevue Hospital Medical College in 1891 and interned at St. Francis Hospital. Later, as a visiting physician there, he oversaw electroshock treatments, which were a novelty in the management of nervous diseases.[34] Although a specialist in gynecology, McParlan also served as the private physician for two prelates of New York: Bishop John Farley and Archbishop Patrick Hayes. He attended several orders of nuns and donated free medical care to the poor in the care of city institutions. For his services, he was named a Knight of St. Gregory by Pius X, one of the youngest Americans so honored.

As a privileged witness in the Reilly matter (he was the only lay observer at Margaret's 1925 Peekskill vows ceremony) and as a pious foil to Dr. James Walsh, McParlan became the major conduit of information on Sister Thorn's health, reporting regularly to outside visitors, including Brother Lukas Etlin and Sister Carmelita Quinn. Not only did McParlan offer diagnoses, but his letters also provide details of her illnesses not mentioned elsewhere, such as her bloodshot eyes (which he attributed to lack of sleep from the devil "beating and abusing and tempting her"); an appendicitis attack; a diseased pancreas; and swelling of the right side of her chest, arm, and hand.[35]

Immune to his contemporaries' interest in hysteria, McParlan found great rewards in the cult of suffering, as revealed in his correspondence with Brother Lukas. After a visit to Peekskill in 1926, the doctor reported: "MR is much improved today Deo Gratias. . . . I feared very much for her life a few days ago and had she been any other person would have had her operated on at once, but feel that this is an evidence of our Dear Lords love of her, in purifying by suffering every organ of her body so she will be truly consumed with love of Him. Some day I hope to talk to you over my ideas of this phase of the saints."[36] Later that same year, he reported to Etlin: "Our little Thorne [*sic*] has had a most severe attack, but is wonderfully recovered and yesterday looked well was up at work and doing fine. The poor old doctor Tom is awfully mixed at times. There is a positive painful and cruel disease there but I am powerless to interfere for Our Dear Lord has told her I must not have any operation and still when it flares up I am in a quandry [*sic*] what to do; so I use the simplest preparations and try to be obedient."[37] Where Walsh found hysteria and possibly fakery, McParlan saw only divine love and "the hand of God for some great purpose."[38]

McParlan's religious outlook led him to withhold treatment from an obviously ill patient, although he confided his unease to Brother Lukas, Sister Carmelita, and Mother Raymond about failing to address Margaret's pain and suffering. Not wanting to disobey a divine command, McParlan contented himself with the role of supplicant at Sister Thorn's bedside. The doctor's feelings of impotence (which he described as a supernatural force preventing him from doing anything) toward Margaret's physical pain hint at psychological factors at work: his unconscious desire to see her suffer? An egotism that was masked by religious sentiment? A lack of medical competence to treat this case? A voyeuristic desire to see if Margaret would work miracles like those he had read about in the lives of the saints? An identification with the abject dimensions of femininity?[39] In contrast to "poor old doctor Tom," who described himself as "awfully mixed" and often "muddled," other doctors were undoubtedly puzzled by McParlan's passivity, which he defended as his assent to Margaret's claim that God told her not to seek treatment.

As a medical practitioner, McParlan relied on empirical evidence to guide his treatment of patients. Yet in Margaret's case, he persistently identified with religious factors. In Margaret's spiritual victimhood, he repeatedly stated his belief that God purifies people and saints through suffering. Evidently, McParlan's outlook resembled that of Father Bradley, who commented that God had "humbled [Margaret] to the very dust. But she enjoys it."[40] All of Margaret's advocates imagined that she must suffer in order to be "truly consumed with love of Him" in preparation for furthering God's plan. Her mission, they believed, was to reform the American priesthood, which was jeopardizing the souls of the laity in the United States.[41] McParlan's consistent comment about Margaret's ordeals was that her pain was proof that she must be one of God's chosen. The doctor's belief in her sanctity was only bolstered by the subsequent reports of miraculous cures effected by Margaret's blessed Sacred Heart badges, which she began distributing from the convent.

Rather than respecting the customary distance between physician and patient, McParlan seemed to revel in his own identification with Margaret in order to portray himself as a similar prisoner of divine will. For example, when Brother Lukas went to lead a spiritual retreat for the sisters at Peekskill in 1926, McParlan traveled from Manhattan to meet him there, confiding: "You may not know how at times I am torn before what I feel to be the supernatural and what my common sense says, only natural. To see Thorne suffer from a purely natural disease and feel powerless to even help because of the imposing and above all supernatural cause, leaves me in an awful muddle, so please pray for me."[42] Until his premature death in 1928, McParlan believed that the terrible, purgative suffering of Sister Thorn was serving God's inscrutable plan for the world.

McParlan expressed these sentiments after spending time with Margaret at Peekskill in 1927:

> I was up to see Sister Thorn last Saturday and it seemed to me she was a little better. God's ways are wonderful and His work in her is to me a miraculous purification of her every organ with suffering for Love of Him. What will be the outcome I know not. In another 15 months she can receive her complete vows and then His Eminence intends to lift the strict seclusion he has thrown around her and leave her free for whatever Mission Our dear Lord intends. His Eminence often told me he is holding in this strict manner in order that her enemies cannot appeal to Rome to put her out of the order.[43]

In his encounters with Margaret, McParlan was frozen into inaction with her, adopting a bullying posture toward others who did not believe in her. Through her parochial school and convent training, Margaret was shaped by a religious system that encouraged, rewarded, and even expected the constant self-sacrifice, and even anguish, of women. In the reckoning of McParlan and Hayes, hysteria was not the issue. In their view, her quest for salvation, like that of all Christians, demanded and legitimated physical suffering in pursuit of eternal spiritual rewards.

The third physician with close connections to Sister Thorn was the aforementioned James J. Walsh (1865–1942). During Walsh's physical examination of Margaret in 1922, as he flexed her limbs and pressed her hands and feet with his own, he waited for her to display the heightened sensation that was attributed to hysterics. He soon confirmed that her "sensitivity" in those areas seemed to wax and wane with how closely she was interested in what he was saying to her at that moment. Walsh's diagnosis of her stomach problems as "hysterical" anticipated his subsequent judgments about her stigmatization.

Walsh was one of New York's most distinguished Catholics. In addition to being a neurologist and a former dean and professor of medicine at Fordham University, he was a recipient of the 1916 Laetare Medal, awarded by the University of Notre Dame to honor the achievements of one notable layperson each year since 1883. Walsh was also a Knight of St. Gregory and a Knight of Malta, papal honors awarded for service to the church. By the time of his death, Walsh had authored over forty books and 500 articles on Catholic medicine, history, and science. Described as an "entrepreneur" and a "controversialist," Walsh can be credited with elevating the quality of medical education at Fordham and of setting high standards for his wide-ranging academic interests.[44] He was also regarded as an expert on "feminine education" in Catholic tradition, defending it against critics who regarded the church as opposed to the intellectual growth of women. Still, he was hardly a feminist, since he opposed woman suffrage and believed that women were "destined to be 'helpers' of men."[45]

As he observed Margaret, Walsh found no trace of stigmata on her body, nor did he see a raised crucifix on her breast. For Catholics, this was not necessarily conclusive proof against stigmatization, as the location and duration of stigmatics' wounds often varied. Some stigmatics reported a full stigmatization—all five wounds of Christ; others endured one or several marks at various sites; and some stigmata lasted decades, while others lasted for shorter periods. Walsh was told that Sister Thorn's stigmata had lasted only about ten weeks, between September 4 and November 18, 1921. "There has been no sign of them since and no marks of any objective kind remain, though subjective feelings with regard to them are complained of," he wrote. The fact that the wounds did not reappear during periods when someone was constantly with Margaret supported Walsh's opinion that she was involved in some fakery, since he believed that the presence of witnesses was "sufficient of itself to prevent the manifestations."

Despite beginning in a one-room schoolhouse in Pennsylvania, Walsh's education and medical training exceeded that of many American Catholic physicians. After earning his medical degree at the University of Pennsylvania in 1895, Walsh had gone abroad to continue his studies in Paris (at the Pasteur Institute and the Salpêtrière, like Freud), followed by one semester of study in Vienna and two semesters in Berlin at Rudolf Virchow's laboratory. In 1897 he traveled to Russia with his brother to cover the International Medical Congress for several American journals. During these years abroad, he also visited the Catholic shrine at Knock in Ireland, and at Lourdes, he met Gustave Boissarie, the physician responsible for verifying cures reported by pilgrims who cast themselves on the mercy of Saint Bernadette and the Virgin Mary.[46] When Walsh returned to New York City, he taught neurology at Fordham and eventually became acting dean of the Medical School. In 1913, however, he resigned his post following a dispute over differences with the Jesuit president of the university about maintaining high standards of quality at the medical school.[47] Hampered by lack of endowments that could sustain an upgraded curriculum, Fordham's medical school closed in 1921.

As he diagnosed Margaret in 1922, Walsh emphasized stress as a factor contributing to her stomach ailments because of the family's emotional and financial anxieties. In his written report to Archbishop Hayes, Walsh repeated the story of Margaret's father, who faced financial ruin in 1911 after a dynamite explosion killed a passerby at his construction site. Walsh even remembered the noise of the explosion since he lived just two blocks away. Following that tragedy, Mrs. Reilly developed a cataract. Nursing care fell heavily on Margaret, as Walsh recalled: "A brother enabled her to care for her mother at home, but she seems to have been tried rather severely." These anecdotes suggest that he believed family crises caused Margaret's own health to decline. Walsh hinted further, but inconclusively, that Margaret's conviction that she had ulcers came from life-cycle changes. As he came to learn that Margaret was older than he had been told, he became convinced that she was experiencing hysterical episodes that he regarded as typical of adolescent and menopausal women. (At age thirty-eight during their 1922 meetings, however, Margaret fit neither stage.) In his diagnosis, Walsh adopted the discourse of hysteria that was common to medical men for centuries: women were more prone to suggestion, emotionalism, and fantasy because of their sex.[48]

If Walsh accepted biological roots for hysteria, he was also content with natural explanations for many allegedly supernatural events. Searching to account for the unusual incidents reported after Margaret's arrival at the Peekskill convent, Walsh compared them with the recent poltergeist scare during the winter of 1922 at a farmhouse in Antigonish, Nova Scotia. The case had drawn attention for over a month in the *New York Times* and warranted a sponsored visit from Dr. Walter Prince, director of the American Institute for Scientific Research in New York City.[49] Although this rural melodrama of mysterious house fires and runaway cattle convinced many, including Arthur Conan Doyle, of the reality of spirits and haunted houses, Prince ultimately traced the phenomena to human hands, prompting Walsh to compare Antigonish and Peekskill as "the same sort of thing."[50] When the Antigonish "ghost" proved to be a hoax improvised by the adopted teen-age daughter of the Macdonald family, Walsh extrapolated that poltergeist events are often traced to hysterical persons—of whom, again, pubescent and menopausal women are the most acute cases.[51]

At Peekskill, Walsh found echoes of the "poltergeist work" at Antigonish: "The veils [belonging to Margaret] are not torn, they are cut with a scissors when folded and that gives these irregular appearances." The breaking of glass and crockery, the thrown inkwells, the cutting of clothes, curtains, and even veils, in Walsh's mind, were no more than mortal trickery. No demonic forces were at work at the convent, and Walsh scoffed at the press sensationalism about spirit rappings and spiritualism.[52] As he continued to try to sift fact from fiction in the details of Margaret's life, he found that she had a pattern of self-aggrandizement, as when she declared herself to be the confidant of her employer, "Barney" Baruch. When she later admitted that she was merely Baruch's weekly office cleaner, Walsh sniffed: "I doubt if he ever knew of her existence."[53] Walsh soon discovered that most of the rumors surrounding Margaret tended to be outsized, like the story that all of the Peekskill convent's 3,000–4,000 chickens had died on the day of the archbishop's exorcism of the property. In fact, only three or four squabs had died, as Mother Raymond corrected him, shocked by the absurdity of the anecdote.[54]

Reading the Stigmatic Body

Access to Margaret Reilly could not be taken for granted, even for the renowned Dr. Walsh. On his first visit to Peekskill, Walsh had forgotten his permission letter from the chancery office of the archdiocese. Fortunately, Mother Raymond was able to reach the archbishop by telephone to ascertain the doctor's bona fides. "After that," Walsh reported, "she gave me every facility with the most engaging frankness." Following his examination of the "patient," the physician took time to present a lecture to the congregation on Saint Teresa of Avila, seamlessly merging paternal, medical, and didactic authority over the assembled sisters. In Walsh's summary to Archbishop Hayes about his June 1922 visit to Peekskill, he noted that "the Good Shepherd [*sic*] here and in Pennsylvania are very good friends of mine."[55] He suggested further that "it would be quite rash and entirely imprudent for me to attempt to make any decision in the [Sister Thorn] matter. This sort of case requires careful study and I should probably have to see her at least two or three, perhaps half a dozen of times."[56]

When Walsh made a second examination of Reilly six weeks later, he found her "in very good physical condition." He described Margaret as having put on some weight, exhibiting a good appetite, sleeping well, and experiencing no loss of power in her limbs, despite her paralysis of six months. "She is able to stand now," Walsh wrote, "though not able to walk. Her standing is made somewhat difficult by tenderness of her feet which she thinks due to the after effects of the stigmata, though there is absolutely no sign of them in her hands nor anything by which there could be the least suspicion of there having been a deep lesion of the soft tissues of the palm." For Walsh, the absence of cuts or scars on Margaret's skin were evidence against her stigmatization.

Acting on a suggestion that he repeated in his letter to Archbishop Hayes, Walsh scheduled a follow-up examination for Margaret with eye specialist Dr. John B. Lynch in August 1922. Since the nineteenth century, especially from the eye examinations of stigmatic Louise Lateau, religious officials concluded that religious ecstasy produced insensitivity to pain and restricted vision—symptoms that also appeared in the medical reports of numerous hysterics. Limited vision was upheld as proof among Catholics that a mystic had achieved the deepest state of contemplation. For doctors, eye tests presumably could settle the question as to whether trances were states of ecstasy or hysteria. They shone high-wattage lamps in the eyes of Margaret Reilly's contemporary, Therese Neumann, to measure the anticipated reaction of her pupils to the light, observing that no change occurred there when she had entered into an ecstatic state. When Dr. Lynch visited Peekskill, he likewise found in Margaret's eyes "an absolutely insensitive" cornea, a retina that did not respond to light, red/green colorblindness, and an overall diminished vision field.[57] But was this evidence of any supernatural event?

The eye specialist did not remark on the absence of skin abrasions that might be expected from stigmatization, although he did find Margaret prone to hives in the form of a white line (perhaps denoting a thyroid gland problem, he said) appearing on the skin surface after it had been irritated. Walsh declared this symptom "quite common in nervous people" and "marked particularly in hysterical people." He also diagnosed Margaret's inability to use her lower limbs as "astasia-abasia," a condition that "occurs in connections with what are known as hysterical symptoms." The term appears frequently in Freud's case studies of hysteria to describe paralysis of the lower limbs and, indeed, in the histories of numerous stigmatized women of Margaret's generation. Although Walsh also employed the term "hysteria," he had expressed dissatisfaction with the term's sexual connotations. In his textbook *Psychotherapy* (1912), Walsh noted that although patients who develop organic symptoms from neurotic causes were often diagnosed as having "hysterical stigmata," "the word hysteria carries an innuendo of imaginativeness or occasionally of affection of the sexual organs that is un-fortunate." He suggested that "it would be better, therefore, not to use the term in any way," although he clearly ignored his own advice in applying it to Margaret.[58]

Lynch and Walsh thus concurred that Margaret's symptoms were con-sistent with "nervous trouble," and even hysteria, which it often accompa-nied.[59] Throughout his career, Walsh drew connections between hysteria and stigmata, as in his comparison between Margaret Reilly and Therese Neumann, the Bavarian stigmatic: "The Konnersreuth case has many of the earmarks of hysteria. The injury at the beginning in the midst of excitement, the paralysis and loss of sight developing afterwards and then completely cured, are frequent in hysteria." He referred to Therese's severe back injury, which she suffered while helping carry water buckets to put out a village fire. In considering Neumann as a hysteric, he also reminded Catholics that the last six or more stigmatics investigated by the church had "proved to be either deliberate fakes or hysterical individuals producing their own phe-nomenon." Despite these misgivings, the physician was intrigued enough by Margaret to ask the archbishop's permission to visit her again at the convent: "There are half a dozen of points now that I have thought over the case that I should like to clear up a little bit, yet without disturbing her. I think Reverend Mother will tell you that neither Margaret nor the routine of the religious life was perturbed."[60]

Walsh conjectured frankly that Margaret's stigmata were self-induced, and that a stamp and red aniline dye had created the image at the Peekskill convent: "As to the picture of the crucifixion on the wall I must frankly say that I was very much disappointed. Probably through my own fault, I had conceived the idea that the picture was an interesting work of art. . . . The picture looks as though it were made by a rubber stamp or by one of the decalcomanias which we used to have as children and which transferred pictures. I think that I remember in Paris that they had pious pictures also in this order."[61] "In the meantime," he continued, "I am having some of the Barclay Street people quietly look into the question as to whether there are any decalcomanias of this kind or whether perhaps there are any rubber stamps of pious objects."[62] "Barclay Street people" undoubtedly refers to the several Catholic import houses in that area, which since the late nineteenth century had marketed the American equivalent of the Catholic bric-a-brac sold near the church of Saint Sulpice in Paris.[63] Because Barclay Street was also home to numerous craft industries, the doctor could easily have con-tacted a vendor of rubber stamps, decals, and inks to verify his hunch. He already knew that Margaret had worked as a stenographer in the city, giving her familiarity with office supplies, and that the Good Shepherd printing operation at Peekskill provided access to stamps and dyes.

The Struggle for the Soul: Psychoanalysis vs. Catholicism

In New York professional circles, Doctors Walsh and Lynch were a hard team to discredit or ignore. From the perspective of neurology, their statements about Sister Thorn reflected the views of Charcot and of his American counterparts, George Beard, A. P. Rockwell, and Silas Weir Mitchell, who had popularized the catchall syndrome of "neurasthenia" some decades earlier.[64] Walsh's conviction of the link between menopausal women and hysterical behaviors was a misogynistic view of women shared by the best European physicians and investigators of modern mystics, including Walsh's own mentors and clergy friends. In reviewing a book about stigmatic Therese Neumann, a Jesuit's comment was typical: "The stigmata of themselves can never be taken as a sure sign of the supernatural. They may follow naturally from high, religious sensibility in an hysteric temperament."[65]

It seemed nearly universally agreed upon among men that hysteria "naturally" produced certain symptoms in an individual, including even stigmata, although no one had actually documented it. Ironically, in 1933 it would be a psychoanalyst who was able to get a patient to reproduce bloody marks on her skin under hypnosis. Walsh's disbelief in Margaret's stigmata represented sentiments that echoed the European experts who were his professors, a generation of physicians who saw their work as "combat against malingering women who had to be forced into their social roles as wives and mothers, serving their family, nation or race."[66] Although Walsh clearly accepted the presence of Catholic nuns and sisters as women who embraced social roles outside the norms of marriage and maternity, he still regarded Margaret as a hysteric who was suffering from the universal weaknesses of womanhood made worse by fatigue.

Doctors and clergy presented themselves as privileged interpreters of the body, but now their medical expertise was being challenged by the new field of psychoanalysis, which looked beyond the visible evidence of the body to the invisible world of the unconscious. When Walsh described Margaret as hysterical, he notably did not rely upon the groundbreaking publication of his day, Sigmund Freud and Josef Breuer's *Studies in Hysteria* (1893–95).[67] Walsh opposed Freud's conception of the unconscious, not on medical grounds but on moral ones, since the Catholic Church had objected to the Viennese doctor's alleged "sex-obsession," his antireligious opinions, and his refusal of revealed truths. The pope had characterized these enemies of the faith in his 1907 condemnation of "Modernism." Moreover, in contrast to Freud's belief that religion was a reflection of neurotic behaviors, Walsh instead contended that it prevented them: "There is no doubt that an abiding sense of religion does much for people in the midst of their ailments and, above all, keeps them from developing those symptoms due to nervous worry and solicitude which so often are more annoying to the patient than the actual sufferings he or she may have to bear."[68] Further hints of Walsh's animus against psychoanalytical explanations for human behavior appear in his self-authored biographical entry for the *History of Medicine in New York*, in which he classified Freudian psychotherapy as one of the faddish "cures that fail,"[69] a phrase that became the title of one of his books. In a preceding publication, Walsh had rejected "the talking cure," which he compared unfavorably with hypnotism. But Walsh had also reversed his opinion of hypnosis between 1911 and 1923.[70] An earlier fan of hypnosis, he later saw it as no different from psychoanalysis, as he commented to Father Wilfrid Parsons, the Jesuit editor of *America* magazine: "Of course for me psychoanalysis is just exactly the same sort of thing as hypnotism. Hypnotism cured lots of people. Now we know that it is only induced hysteria. Psychoanalysis cures lots of people but only because it produces a state of suggestion under which some of the psychoneuroses disappear."[71]

While unconvinced of the usefulness of the analyst-analysand relationship in permanently restoring the patient's health, what Walsh did endorse as helpful to the "cure of souls" was the power of mental suggestion to modify or relieve symptoms and to encourage the patient. His ongoing interest in the relationship between physical and mental healing is suggested by two of his books, *Health through Will Power* and *Religion and Health*.[72] Instead of addressing himself to current psychoanalytic theory emanating from Europe, Walsh framed his objections in the context of mind cure, a late nineteenth-century American movement dedicated to curing pain by eliminating the power of evil, following the conviction that mind controls matter. Mind cure influenced the formation of Christian Science, New Thought, and other nonmainstream religious traditions of the early 1900s. Sidestepping Freud, Walsh aligned himself with the defense of mental religious therapies professed by mind cure and its proponent, William James. Walsh did not dismiss theories of the unconscious in order to endorse mind over matter, but neither did he accept uncritically the reports of demonic possession, miraculous cures, exorcisms, or spirit mediums that came across his desk. Walsh stood with the consensus of American medical opinion of his day, but by integrating vitalist principles into his work, he achieved "a means to bridge medical knowledge with practical moral teachings stemming from then-current Catholic teachings on the will." Walsh gave his own views a Catholic twist by interpreting the "vital force" that controls the human body as referring to the soul.[73]

At the same time, Walsh showed some professional interest in Carl Jung, whose relationship with Catholicism, while not completely hostile, has been characterized as a dance of "approach-avoidance."[74] Following the much-publicized visit of Freud and Jung to America in 1909, Fordham University expanded its work in "nervous and mental diseases." In 1912, to promote a new clinic and new curriculum at the university, Walsh invited Jung from Zurich, along with neurologists Sir Henry Head (1861–1940) and Sir Gordon Holmes (1876–1965) from London. The high-profile guests received honorary degrees and taught a Fordham extension course in New York City.[75] Jung received his award in absentia since he arrived in New York a week late for the festivities. When he delivered a series of lectures titled "The Theory of Psychoanalysis," he surprised his listeners by attacking the Oedipus conflict and other keystones of the Freudian edifice. Upon Jung's return to Europe, his break with Freud became definitive because of his remarks. Although Jung's writings did not attract significant Catholic audiences until after Vatican II, when his impact on Catholic spirituality was felt in the spiritual retreat movement, Catholics through midcentury would continue to favor Jung over Freud.[76]

Walsh embodied the church's "off-modern" position that everything regarded as modern in the twentieth century had been anticipated in medieval times by Catholic philosophy and theology, while at the same time, he mixed his Neo-Scholasticism with the uniquely American innovation of mind cure. Miraculous cures became the subject of intense professional medical and religious scrutiny in the early twentieth century, since the healing of the sufferer could be regarded as the result of either natural or supernatural processes. When it came to stigmata, Walsh recommended investigating allegations on a case-by-case basis, putting himself at odds with Catholics who preferred to accept all reports as valid. Because Walsh believed that Christian faith did not depend upon signs and wonders, he affirmed that "in fighting miraculism we defend the Faith."[77] He also worked energetically to debunk miraculist frauds wherever he found them. On his list of "cures that fail," Walsh had placed the "so-called shrine cures" of Catholics alongside Arthur Conan Doyle's belief in communication with the dead. These debates among Catholics, and the boundary wars between Catholics and the emerging sciences of the mind, demonstrate that there was a period of optimism and receptivity toward psychoanalysis in the 1920s and 1930s, when the borderland between natural science and the supernatural appeared to coincide in the newly discovered category of the unconscious. These conversations were not resolved by mid-twentieth century, when they were abruptly halted by church leaders. In 1947 Monsignor Fulton Sheen of New York sharply attacked the psychoanalytic and psychiatric professions for attempting to usurp the functions of the confessional, retreating from the quest for common ground between Catholicism and the behavioral sciences.[78]

Walsh's education, professional training, and religion molded his judgment of Margaret Reilly. He was aware that nuance did exist in the church's position that hysterical symptoms did not necessarily preclude supernatural causes for them, as he explained in a letter to Archbishop Hayes. "It is perfectly possible that there may be both divine and diabolic intervention in the case, that is what Margaret herself declares," he wrote, "and yet these symptoms of hysteria be present. . . . If, as is said in the lives of the saints, the Lord permits the natural reaction to take place in order to keep his loved ones humble, then one might have even what is present in Margaret's case."[79] Yet Walsh remained convinced that if Margaret were moved to a less-sympathetic environment than the convent, "the case would take on a very different aspect." Without an appreciative audience, he believed, her theatrics would cease. Walsh's report about Margaret to Archbishop Hayes was less candid than his comments to Father John W. Cavanaugh, a Holy Cross priest who had recently served as president of the University of Notre Dame. With the archbishop, Walsh observed a degree of formality and restraint that was necessary in such situations. Walsh's reticence, moreover, signaled the deference of the lay professional to the church, an approach that politely left the door open for the archbishop to defend purely supernatural explanations of Margaret's experiences.

Walsh was also in contact with his respected British friend, Father Herbert Thurston, whom he had reminded to avoid public discussion of the Reilly case.[80] Walsh had advised the archbishop of Thurston's opinion "that these cases of stigmatization, even when not factitious, are merely neurotic manifestations because they occur in people rather noted for nervous symptoms, but not particularly for sanctity."[81] Thurston, too, had evaded a Freudian vocabulary, not out of ignorance (which was unlikely given his voracious reading habits, his continental contacts, and his membership in the Society for Psychic Research), but because Freudianism was tarnished by its association with Modernism, which the church had condemned. Like Walsh's, Thurston's understanding of hysteria was limited to an already outmoded Charcotian model that labeled the symptoms of the neuroses through observation.

Walsh's diagnosis of Margaret, ultimately, seemed to progress no further than seeing and naming what was believed to be hysterical behavior. This had been the technique of Charcot at his public displays of patients' hysterical fits as they progressed through the four stages that he had identified. This biological model of hysteria had largely fallen out of favor by the late 1920s,[82] supplanted by a method of listening to patients pioneered by Charcot's student, Sigmund Freud. For the reasons discussed above, however, Walsh was unlikely to endorse psychoanalysis.

Doctors McParlan and Walsh shared certain limitations as investigators and healers despite their different outlooks as Catholics. As noted, it is surprising that they did not insist on a more thorough medical study of Sister Thorn's stigmata after being permitted to visit her multiple times. Unlike McParlan, Walsh classified Sister Thorn as a hysteric, yet he offered no treatment for this diagnosis. Walsh regarded the careful investigation of all disputes about supernatural claims as acts of strengthening the Catholic Church, yet he was not inclined to dismiss Sister Thorn's reported symptoms altogether. But he did not make the intellectual shift to studying the sources of her so-called hysterical symptoms, the very shift that defined the breakthroughs of Freud and Breuer. In *Studies on Hysteria*, Freud and Breuer argue that hysterics characteristically cannot recall the origin of their symptoms and cannot connect them to any prior life events. Repressed affect produces ideas that the analysand needs to learn to reconnect to their sources. Through hypnosis, Freud believed, the hysterical patient can bring repressed events to consciousness, realigning idea and event and discharging the affect that was disallowed by the patient's repression.[83] As Freud put it, "Psychical trauma or more precisely the memory of the trauma—acts like a foreign body which long after its entry must continue to be regarded as an agent that is still at work."[84] Beyond identifying stressful conditions in Margaret's social environment, however, Walsh was not interested in following the psychical causes of trauma in her memories.

Freud's understanding of hysteria as the major contemporary alternative to Walsh provides a counterreading of Margaret Reilly's symptoms. According to Freud, most hysterics are women, while men are likely to be obsessional neurotics. In brief, this means that in their clinical practice, analysts and therapists since Freud have found that a majority of women patients will turn their traumas against their own selves or bodies (as in anorexia, bulimia, and self-cutting), whereas men will more likely act out their anxieties in forms of physical and verbal aggression against others. In the predominantly female cases of stigmatization, extreme fasting and self-cutting practices were documented as part of the repertoire of mystical phenomena.

If "hysterics suffer mainly from reminiscences," as Freud believed, and paralysis and amnesia were typical "stigmata" of hysteria, as Pierre Janet believed, then Margaret's loss of both parents, her unrequited love, her flight to Peekskill, and her subsequent paralysis reflected her inability to face disturbing memories that left her feeling powerless (and literally immobilized) to change her present situation. Altering the approach that he had pursued in the rest of the book, Freud, in the final chapter of *Studies on Hysteria*, associated women's hysterical symptoms with premature sexual experiences, usually in the form of assaults by a parent, relative, or acquaintance. While no evidence links this kind of event to Margaret, there were rumors that her mysterious hospitalization and her ongoing connections with a gynecologist, Dr. McParlan, involved an abortion. Furthermore, a large percentage of stigmatized women were victims of rape or attempted rape. Among Margaret's contemporaries, Alexandrina da Costa of Italy and Therese Neumann of Bavaria were both sexually assaulted in their teens by their employers, after which they suffered spinal injuries and inedia and reported being attacked by demons. If hysterical symptoms are the residues of trauma, and hysterical conversion symptoms are the body's way of both evading and expressing some original trauma that could not be confronted directly, then Sister Thorn's paralysis, food revulsions, and reported demonic assaults on her skin and genitals are consistent with topoi in the annals of psychoanalysis and psychiatry for conversion symptoms. Freud had discovered that "a repressed memory can become traumatic by virtue of deferred action and belated reencoding."[85] A Freudian treatment of that era, when the approach was still quite eclectic, would have combined hypnosis and talk in an attempt to trace Margaret Reilly's symptoms (paralysis, demonic fantasies) to some original trauma(s). As it was, she used the cultural symbols available to her as a devout Catholic woman to convert her fantasies into bodily form, producing her versatile identification with the bleeding, traumatized Christ; her inability/refusal to leave the shelter of the convent when threatened; her choice of a restrictive moral code for living; and her oscillations between masculinity (Jesus, the innocent victim-priest) and femininity (herself, the innocent victim-nun).[86]

As noted earlier, in the Freudian model of hysteria, a fixed idea becomes elaborated into a symptom (in the body) or into a sign (in the psyche) that lives on in the unconscious until brought to consciousness through speech. Thus Freud's concept of the return of the repressed, even when manifested in what might seem like an unrelated form, offered Walsh and other Catholic physicians a way to understand the "conversion symptoms" of Sister Thorn: her paralysis, bleeding, food revulsion, skin markings, and inexplicable maladies. Freud was, of course, hostile to religion and regarded religious mania as one form of hysteria, a view not shared by Walsh. But Walsh remained uninterested in Freud's breakthroughs in theorizing hysteria as the failure to overcome trauma and in the psychical workings of hysteria, and thus he seemed content to rest upon his diagnosis of Margaret. Although Catholic theologians and clergy might have adopted some of the terms of the already outmoded neurology of the late nineteenth century in order to explain the fits and visions of mystics, they opposed an essential tenet of psychoanalytic theory that sought to explain human actions as determined by forces not always known to the conscious mind. From a Catholic standpoint, God might work through the pathological as well as the "normal," but Catholics also maintained that God had created a human mind that presented humans with choices for their actions based upon free will.

Outside of hysteria, Freudianism, and behaviorism, what diagnostic choices were available to Margaret's doctors? It seems surprising that no one proposed the copycat syndrome to interpret Sister Thorn as someone obsessed with imitating the saints or other stigmatics. After all, Herbert Thurston had freely applied the term "Christ complex" to some of the cases he studied, citing evidence from the recent crop of European *stigmatisées* who had produced their own imitators: Frenchwoman Blanche Wittman had modeled herself on Louise Lateau in neighboring Belgium, as did Genevieve in Paris, one of Charcot's famous patients, who imitated Lateau's ecstasies and even thought of Louise as her sister. The odd events that Margaret Reilly reported in the convent clearly reprised scenes from the lives of holy women familiar to her, including Anne Catherine Emmerich, Gemma Galgani, Rose-Virginie Pelletier, and Saints Colette and Gertrude.[87] Neither Walsh nor McParlan had considered Margaret's education in Catholic schools as contributing to her familiarity with mystical saints, even though Europeans had not hesitated to make that connection. One study of the patients at the Salpêtriére in Paris already had found that many of the women who were brought up in convent schools went through periods of deep religious inspiration. Two of them were even former nuns.[88] Their "illness behaviors," which became fodder for the hysteria doctors, may have been learned from this background.[89] But even if Sister Thorn did not consciously imitate one particular figure, she was acting out elements of a familiar composite role, suggesting that socially constructed categories scripted the forms of behavior expected of a mystic and shaped how Catholics interpreted the phenomena of suffering and stigmata. Like the stigmatics before her, Sister Thorn could find support from a Catholic milieu that venerated mystical women who claimed extraordinary gifts—in contrast to the medical professionals who generally dismissed stigmata and other physical phenomena as evidence of women's natural excitability, as illnesses whose contagious potential was only increased by the convent environment.

The Camera and the Stigmatic

A notable gap in Catholic engagement with modern technologies to investigate and document stigmatization is the absence of photography. From its emergence in the 1840s, the technology of photography added a new possibility for validating stigmatization, but it was never embraced systematically by the Catholic Church. (The first type of image creation, the daguerreotype, preceded the photograph, and it took at least four decades after that before the photograph could be reproduced for the mass readership of newspapers.) On the contrary, after the advent of photography, witnesses to stigmata seemed to be rarely if ever present when the bleeding began, and thus instead of visually documenting the onset of the wounds, the devotional focus shifted to the theatrics that followed the appearance of the marks, much as Charcot had focused his audiences on the hysteric's convulsions. Notably, stigmatics who bled each Friday often enacted Christ's Passion with bodily gestures while they were entranced, and it was these spectacles that received the most attention, though not in mainstream media.

The Catholic Church did not engage debates on the evidentiary values of photography of stigmata and stigmatics, which it could have used in its favor by confronting the viewer with the "reality" of Christ's Passion and as a rebuke to modern materialism and atheism. Embedded in the church's critique of positivism was its implicit belief that sanctity could not be located or captured in the body's appearance by the camera. Instead, photography served the cults of stigmatics by invoking aesthetic, rather than scientific, traditions of representation. In general, photographs of stigmatics circulated among Catholics like holy cards, copying iconic pious poses of the saints in Western art: the uplifted face with eyes rolled heavenward and hands clasped in prayer, or the sickly stigmatic lying bandaged in her bed, cradling a crucifix in her folded arms.[90] These scenes were not novel, being essentially derived from engravings or paintings of nineteenth-century mystics like Anne Catherine Emmerich and Maria Mörl. Rather than attempting to establish an empirical record about the appearance or health of the women, the images were meant to encourage devotion. There are no photographs of Margaret Reilly "in ecstasy" or displaying her stigmata, nor is there any evidence that such photographs were taken, even though images were evidently made of the crucifix mark on her wall, and there are some casual solo

Maria Domenica Lazzari di Capriana.

This 1840 engraving of Maria Domenica Lazzari (1815–48) shows her in what would become a familiar representation for stigmatized women. She took to her bed with influenza in 1833 and never left it. She received the stigmata in 1835 and was able to live without sleep or food. (Courtesy of the Wellcome Library, London, UK)

Maria Mörl (1812–68), who remained in a nearly continual ecstatic trance, was among the first stigmatics to generate a tourist audience and mass-produced images that were sold to her devotees. One of her observers, German writer Johann Joseph von Görres, concluded that "God put her like a living crucifix on the crossroads, to preach to a godless and dissipated people." (Courtesy of the Wellcome Library, London, UK)

photographs of her at Peekskill and several images where she poses with other sisters at the convent.

While physicians like Walsh were eager to dismiss Margaret's physical symptoms as hysterical fantasies, Catholic leaders were curiously lax about acquiring photographic evidence of her mystical wounds that could help validate or negate their supernatural origins. This omission may have been less about the embrace of technology and more about an unspoken strategy of the church to protect itself from the embarrassments and exposés recently visited upon the spiritualists for their alleged spirit photographs, or evidence of the church's attempt to distance itself from the sensationalist use of photography by figures like Charcot to display hysterics in his "museum of living pathology" in Paris. As he recorded the "*attitudes passionnelles*" of his patients, Charcot then used the photographs to illustrate textbooks on hysteria, juxtaposing the women's enactments of traumas from their past with displays of the female body positioned in the form of a cross, suggesting that insanity and religious mania were related. Charcot's notions influenced U.S. gender ideology, which likewise came to regard women as prone to confusing sexuality and religion. (Madame Bovary did not reside in the French imagination alone.)

The Catholic Church's response to modern stigmatization, therefore, included its limited support for the scientific study of mysticism specifically to undermine rationalism, positivism, and the other components of Modernism that were hostile to the supernatural. Otherwise, the church only "inadvertently" adopted modern scientific methods of recording data for proof, as seen in its investigations of miraculous cures at Lourdes.[91] Stigmata were less systematically treated than Marian apparitions and alleged healings, however, perhaps because they were incidental to the modern canonization process, appearing as testimony in only one modern saint's dossier: that of Gemma Galgani. In this regard, the relationship between the church and modern science became one of cautious opportunism, even when certain technological innovations could have helped establish the genuineness of stigmata as support for Pius X's condemnation of disbelief in miracles as a heretical facet of Modernism.[92]

Clergy and theologians also embraced some uses of psychology in order to help the church separate true from false forms of mysticism. The church did not, however, enlist photography or film to help validate or study mystical phenomena, nor did it endorse psychoanalysis as a potential way of understanding the role of the unconscious mind in religious fantasies or practices. But by not issuing formal rejections of the stigmatizations claimed between

1820 and 1950, the institution represented its position ambiguously. Catholic leaders, wanting to put the best face on things, reassured the public that the church judged reports of visions, miracles, and mystical events by the exacting standards that Pope Benedict XIV set in the eighteenth century and through the relevant Vatican congregations on miracles and canonization.[93] A new study that has painstakingly reviewed medical miracles recorded in the Vatican archives in relation to the canonization process over four centuries has concluded that this self-image was generally true: clerics had no problem deferring to scientific opinions, whereas scientists were less likely to agree that miracles may possess divine origins. It may be the case that "religion sits more comfortably with medical science than vice versa."[94]

A Friendlier Relationship in France

The sparring match between the Catholic Church and modern medicine was renewed after the First World War, yet some within the church forged connections between Catholicism and psychology. In France, for example, the Carmelites imagined a warmer relationship between religion and the human sciences and even directed their energies to the study of stigmatization. The French had already learned from the Spanish Carmelite tradition how to emphasize spiritual suffering and victimhood. By renewed reflection on the distinctive spiritual tradition of their founders, Saints Teresa of Avila and John of the Cross, the Carmelites began to use the autobiographies and spiritualities of the saints to trigger new studies of the "psychology of the human soul." Soon, the order began to host conferences with the hope of establishing religious psychology as a bridge between spiritual experience and the new sciences. During the 1930s, the French Carmelites brought together distinguished Catholic faculty, doctors, and journal editors from the ancient centers of Catholic learning in western Europe, including Paris, Fribourg, Lille, Louvain, Lyon, Münster, Reims, Rome, Salzburg, and Würzburg.

In 1935, for the 300th anniversary of its Paris province, the Carmelite order sponsored a conference at its monastery at Avon-Fontainebleau to address the intersection of religion and psychology. The topic was pain and stigmatization. Eventually, the meeting would establish itself at the monastery for three days of papers on a prearranged topic.[95] Proceedings of the congresses were published in a well-received periodical called *Etudes Carmélitaines*.[96] In the second volume of 1936, contributors discussed medieval and modern stigmatics, including Maria Mörl, Louise Lateau, and Therese Neumann. (The journal's editor, Father Bruno de Jesus Marie, had visited

Neumann in the previous year.)[97] Together, the collection of articles from this volume provide an index of the state of Catholic scholarship in the interwar decades on the topic of stigmatization.

Ultimately, the philosophers, theologians, physicians, and scientists gathered at Fontainebleau were unable to agree upon a general definition of mysticism, except as a "desire" for beatific union with the divine. Nor could they agree that dissecting mysticism rationally is a good idea, since, following William James's categorizations and drawing upon earlier Christian sources, they affirmed that the attempt to intellectualize mysticism misses the whole point—namely, the believer's ineffable experience of divine union. Besides, as Catholic scholars pointed out in their own defense, scientific experiments had failed so far to prove anything conclusive about mysticism. When the 1936 issue of *Etudes Carmélitaines* appeared, one author lamented that despite decades of study, science was no closer to explaining stigmata: "Contrary to those who, under the cover of experimental science and of so-called positive facts, maintain that we can apprehend the *processus* of mystical stigmatization in one of its parts, we claim that, in spite of a few very deficient data given to us by experimentation and clinical research, we are as far from the explanation of the stigmata as in the days of Charcot, Bourneville, Bernheim, and Virchow."[98]

Rejecting the materialism and determinism of Freudian psychoanalysis and of its predecessors, these Catholic scholars stood against the psychoanalytic profession. Even though the French conference made no definitive connections between psychology and religion, bonds between academicians, psychologists, psychotherapists, psychiatrists, and Catholics became better articulated there than among their American counterparts. The Roman leadership of the Catholic Church, however, displayed no special tolerance for psychology or psychoanalysis, even at the end of the twentieth century. The church maintained its theological position that the universal need for repentance came from original sin, not from neurotic guilt. Even today, the Vatican remains opposed to using Freud even as a provocation toward critical thinking about the workings of the unconscious mind. According to a priest who serves as a Vatican consultant, "The difficulty is that in Rome they don't know what to do with Freudian psychology. Most of the consultants have yet to assimilate his theory of the unconscious. . . . The trouble is, we have very little dialogue between psychology and religion."[99]

Catholic doctors and psychologists in Europe and America displayed a range of responses to modern claims of stigmatization. Catholic tradition taught that direct contact with God was possible through mystical experience and that such immediacy was a charism available to any Christian, though not proof of an individual's holiness. Throughout Catholic history, this idea has enabled Catholic visionaries, saints, or the institutional church to use experience of the divine to attack "secular" society and its sinful self-ishness, as well as to reproach the church itself and its clergy representatives for not living up to Gospel expectations. Doctors suggested, though, that upon closer examination, a mystic's claims might turn out to be the product of human invention. From London, neurologist F. M. R. Walshe made an example of the spiritual director of Teresa Higginson, who injudiciously foretold Higginson's mystical marriage and who read to her from mystical literature about women favored by Christ with special gifts. It is no wonder that Higginson went on to concoct letters describing her own experiences that closely mimicked what she had heard from her confessor.[100] Walshe conceded that not all fake stigmatics were conscious deceivers, however: "The capacity for dramatization that the hysteric possesses tends to blind the subject to the significance of her conduct until she may ultimately ac-quire the same conviction of their preternaturally imposed character that is enjoyed by those around her."[101] Like Herbert Thurston before him, Walshe suggested that the symbiotic relation between a stigmatic and an audience may foster unconscious deception on the part of the stigmatic, much as a child may tell a lie out of a wish to please her or his parents. He defined the hysteric's conduct as the product of two factors: "innate qualities and her environment." By the latter, he meant the reciprocity between the subject and an already desiring "client." He underlined this claim by noting that the hysteric's physical fits stop when the audience leaves, as James Walsh had remarked about Margaret Reilly. The hysteric therefore interiorizes her role as an actor in a performance. If, as Walshe found, most hysterics perceive their own agency in producing their symptoms—shown by their rapid abil-ity to adapt to changing circumstances—then "the hysterical fit is what we make it."[102] By this reasoning, the burden for explanation shifts from the performer onto her receptive audience.[103] Yet if the audience is complicit, then how can it impartially judge the virtues of the hysteric?

Investigations of Masochism

In the convent, Sister Thorn acquired a new role: that of a "victim soul," a term for religious suffering that invites a comparison of psychological and spiritual interpretations of her experience. Victim spirituality gained strength in the closing decades of the nineteenth century and suffused pre–Vatican II Catholic devotional practices and thought. Of course, this period was also the "golden age" of hysteria. As Mark Micale has described the cult of miracles at Lourdes as "a kind of popular nonmedical counterculture of hysteria," stigmatic cults may have served a similar role.[104] Yet in the context of psychological study, spiritual victimhood can be said to represent a type of "moral masochism," a term associated with Freud, who initially believed that it had a biological basis. In Freud's understanding, the moral masochist is not a person who takes sexual pleasure in pain.[105] Rather, the moral masochist identifies with a strong ideal and is willing to submit to great trials in order to meet the "demands" of that ideal. Although Freud *had* initially described masochism as sadism (the aggressive drive) turned against the self, he revised his theory and his entire concept of the drive.[106] Freud's successors, including Leonard Shengold, Alice Miller, and Nancy McWilliams, have further refined Freud's notion to suggest instead that women expressed rebellion against their subordination through masochistic behavior. As supplements to Freud's case studies, their clinical data also accounts for the spiritual victimhood that attracted Catholic women like Margaret Reilly.[107] Elaine Showalter's question about the treatment of hysterics could equally be directed at Margaret: "Instead of asking if rebellion was mental pathology, we must ask whether mental pathology was suppressed rebellion."[108]

Catholic theology's elaborate system of rewards and punishments and the strict rules governing convent life would seem to be prime sites of moral masochism. Sister Thorn did not spell out her personal understanding of the church's system of spiritual accounting, but we do find plentiful evidence of moral masochism in her remarks and actions and in the words of her acquaintances. Employing moral masochism as one lens to interpret stigmatization in a post-Freudian frame, we may ask why extreme suffering was necessary, in Margaret's view, to expiate the suffering of others? One answer appears in a remark she made about God while she was telling Father Bertrand of her painful stigmatization: "How good He is! How much He loves! How little He asks!"[109] Together, the priest and the postulant defended "what was planned by Heaven," interventions in which the torments of one soul were necessary and certainly not cause for complaint. They did not challenge the notion of vicarious suffering or "mystical substitution," which had become ubiquitous in the piety of Catholic religious orders.[110] Nuns and sisters learned that their physical suffering was worthwhile because it removed pain and suffering from someone else, often from priests or from the "suffering souls in Purgatory." Laypersons were equally accustomed to personal gestures of "giving up" something in order to spiritually benefit someone else, but the embrace of physical pain signaled a deeper participation in victimhood through the imitation of Christ. When emphasis on Purgatory disappeared in Catholic teaching around Vatican II and the chase after indulgences declined, so did the rationale for this kind of vicarious suffering. Its partisans persist today, we are told, in peasant societies, in rural communities, and in localized cults of the victim souls and visionaries of the Catholic devotional universe, which, in psychoanalytic terms, remain harbors for masochistic emotions.[111]

Why did women like Margaret hurt their bodies, stop walking or eating, or suddenly flee their familiar lives to commit themselves to rules of conduct that severely constrained behavior and movement? Today, psychotherapists recognize superficial self-injury, such as pricking a circle of cuts around the forehead, as a symptom of borderline personality disorders. In this model, Margaret's hypersensitivity and skin torments would represent a psychic defense against the threat of being returned to Manhattan. But whether or not she was unconsciously defending herself against worse harm, those who knew Sister Thorn repeatedly praised her suffering for others—a reminder that the position of victimhood, even if self-induced, was psychically and spiritually rewarded in Catholicism. It was a phenomenon produced and affirmed by the combined efforts of the spiritual advisers, confessors, and male and female religious leaders guiding Sister Thorn's vocation, and it would continue to discipline women's experience and spiritual style for at least another generation.

Margaret Reilly's spirituality expressed numerous masochistic features, notably, the self-imposed physical mortifications of her youth (ashes in her shoes, the hair shirt and whip), her voluntary undernourishment, and the physical assaults upon her at the convent (possibly self-inflicted) that were projected onto demonic forces outside herself. In this regard, she illustrates a complex layering of past and present in early twentieth-century Catholicism. Female moral masochism corresponds to an entire Christian tradition of victimization for others, a tradition especially prevalent among Catholic women (many of them in religious orders), who embraced this outlook in varying degrees of intensity from the Middle Ages through the mid-twentieth century. Such behaviors by women also expressed their general subordination in society, according to modern historians of gender.

Further explanations for self-hurt exist outside of Freudian and Lacanian psychoanalytic theory. (The latter is named for French psychiatrist Jacques Lacan, discussed below.) In Ariel Glucklich's 2001 study, *Sacred Pain: Hurting the Body for the Sake of the Soul*, among his examples of "sanctioned 'masochism'" is a sixteenth-century stigmatic whose imitation of Christ had parallels in Margaret's life: a combination of self-inflicted pain, attacks from demons, and natural pain from illness.[112] Glucklich cites the tortured life of Saint Maria Maddalena de' Pazzi, a Carmelite nun of Florence, to explain

both "pathological" and "sacred" pain as forms of violence that unexpectedly "revolve around a sense of empowerment and a positive affirmation
of some sort." Although Glucklich focuses on self-cutters, whom he regards as "like religious self-mutilators without the theology," he objects to
Freudian theories that are too reductive in tracing every case of self-injury
to the same perversion. In Glucklich's view, Freud's approach ignores the
individual's cognitive interpretation of her pain and cannot explain the fact
that the cutter's self-image never matches what others believe about her.
Freud's concept of the pleasure principle also assumes that every human
always desires to avoid and eliminate pain. Because Glucklich regards pain
as a category that is multiple—that is, experienced differently by different
persons—in his view, "mystics like Maria Maddalena cannot be reduced
to the perversion of enjoying something hurtful that they inflict on their
bodies." Rather, her pain and self-injury became "a meaningful experience
rather than a problem she had to resist and reject." Applying Glucklich's
insights to Sister Thorn, any erotic satisfactions or defense mechanisms
that were thought to be derived purely from masochism can be reread as
her attempts to value pain in the context of cultural meanings that are not
the result of mental illness or imbalance. In this understanding, Glucklich
seems close to Antoine Vergote's formulation that "the central elements in
mystical phenomena seem to be that they constitute God as an object of
desire and that they mobilize an entire apparatus to liberate this desire, to
formulate it in authentic terms, to accomplish its fulfillment in love, and
to perfect the quality of joy experienced through this love."[113] Therefore,
rather than pathology, one discerns in Sister Thorn's practices a powerful
desire to make the divine present by using her own body, concentrated
through the experience of pain. The actualization of the divine in human
flesh is the inescapable message of Christianity.

The colonization of women's bodies by asserting a connection between
punishment and reward of the sort that characterized preconciliar Catholicism has not disappeared. In her clinical practice, therapist Nancy McWilliams continues to encounter masochistic personalities, whom she describes
in this way: "It is common for self-defeating people to have magical beliefs that connect assertiveness or confidence with punishment, and self-
abasement with eventual triumph. One finds in most religious practices and
folk traditions a connection between suffering and reward, and masochistic
people often support their pathology uncritically with these ideas." She perceived that, among her clients, "omnipotent fantasies behind masochistic
behaviors die hard. One can always find evidence in random events that one's
successes have been punished and one's sufferings rewarded."[114]

In Margaret's day, masochistic behavior was labeled hysterical and attributed to women's demands for recognition. In our time, by invoking a hermeneutics of suspicion combined with post-Freudian psychoanalytic theory and case studies that address the shortcomings of neurology and dogmatic Freudianism, we can sketch a more nuanced psychic portrait of Catholic women like Margaret who experienced exaggerated shame and guilt that led them to self-punishing actions. For Christians, the goal of perfection, such as achieving sainthood, is an impossible psychic ideal. Therefore, a human's relationship to God is always asymmetrical: He is complete without me, but I am nothing without Him. This gap explains the enduring psychological power of atonement theory in Christian theology—the belief that humans must humble themselves in order to exalt God, who delivered up his only son; and that only by such sacrifices can humans attempt to redress their eternal unworthiness. Sister Thorn lived in an era when this model of sacrificial victimhood was thriving, perhaps because it was so compelling for Catholic women inundated with conflicting social messages about their opportunities and abilities and afflicted by the presence of genuine emotional and physical trauma that led to consequences tantamount to soul murder.

The methods of psychoanalysis for understanding suffering have continued to evolve since Freud. Whereas psychoanalysis and psychiatry rely upon analyst-centered models, patient-centered evaluations have emerged in recent decades to support and advance a biocultural model of suffering. In this field, the work of psychiatrist and anthropologist Arthur Kleinman has been pioneering. Twenty years ago, Kleinman argued that suffering affects identity and should be addressed through the various lenses of ethnography, biography, history, and psychotherapy because the experience of pain is a socially constructed one.[115] Although pain can now be regarded as a biocultural phenomenon that possesses meanings drawn from physiological and social influences, the reigning model for the medical profession during Margaret Reilly's lifetime was Descartes's dualistic model of pain as a highway that carries sensation from the body directly to the brain.[116] This strictly biological model that imagined the senses projecting pain onto the mind, and even later nineteenth-century variations upon it in psychology and medicine, had greatly, if not entirely, ignored the individual and cultural contexts that are now understood as important contributors to the experience of pain. People perceive pain differently in different circumstances. As Ariel Glucklich found, "The perceptual ambiguity of pain undoes psychological theories of masochistic pain—such as Freud's—which interpret it as the bringing on oneself of something hurtful and vindictive."[117] From Kleinman's perspective, the telling or sharing of one's personal story of pain as a narrative mediates suffering by ending the isolation of the sufferer and giving the afflicted a sense of empowerment. In this sense, except for Dr. McParlan, Margaret's physicians only addressed her biological symptoms and disregarded her narrative of mystical experiences. On the other hand, the convent community that did care for her for sixteen years helpfully listened to her "illness narrative," which represents, in Kleinman's view, a helpful form of compassion. Nevertheless, her fellow sisters matched Sister Thorn's personal experiences to a master narrative of spiritual pain: the Passion of Christ. That is to say that while Margaret's suffering, which included chronic illness, may have been purely explicable as natural disease (as Walsh believed), in the end, her religious congregation (and McParlan) understood pain as the inescapable result of human sinfulness and insisted upon a spiritualized interpretation of it. Margaret's pain was meaningful to them because it was the necessary contrast to the ultimate triumph of the body over suffering and death that was accomplished once and for all through the sacrifice of the Son of God.[118]

In the 1920s, the Catholic Church in New York had its own understanding of pain as a social force. As it waged war against perceived enemies on several cultural fronts, the church enlisted pain as a moral lesson in the cosmic battle between sin and salvation. Sister Thorn's pain, it turns out, was less interesting for its lessons of the self than for how it served this greater narrative of the Church Triumphant. Tales of larger-than-life battles have a long tradition in New World Catholicism stemming from American colonization in 1492, after which new literary genres emerged to represent the conquest of the New World as an epic battle between the forces of God and those of Satan.[119] In Margaret's lifetime, the church revived this Manichean rhetoric in its fight against the modern Satan of materialism to resist the appropriation of pain by physicians as a purely medical problem to be solved by the treatment of the physical body.

At the same time that the church was combating the medicalization of pain, it also was opposing new psychological models that construed physical pain as mental and even unrecognizable to the conscious mind and as a category that was separate from the pain caused by trauma or injury. Finally, the church refused the wholesale disenchantment of the world by challenging anyone who trusted in reason and materialism alone and denied humans' spiritual side. By committing itself to defending the supernatural and the world unseen, but without appearing to be gullible, the church for the time being was obliged to reject determinist theories of the effects of the unconscious mind on religious experience. In fact, during the following decades, American Catholic doctors "regressed" to discredited neurological explanations for mystical behaviors. While the Catholic Church was not decidedly antipsychoanalytic in the 1920s, it became so during the next thirty years. The example of Italy, where the Catholic Church was the dominant political and cultural force, proved to be a bellwether. As the church became instrumental in negating psychoanalysis there, during the Fascist era, it strove to eliminate academic psychiatry and psychology as well, declaring itself "almost entirely . . . in favor of neurology."[120]

The Catholic leaders of New York moved in this direction during the 1920s, when the hierarchy increasingly flexed its muscles on the issues of abortion and contraception, which likewise could not tolerate threats to natural-law principles. Tellingly, the church entered the public arena to comment on the need to preserve stable categories of gender identity and to regulate consumption habits rather than to consider the positive contributions of psychoanalysis. Any tentative bonds formed between Catholics and analysts in the 1930s were surely ruptured in the next decade by Fulton Sheen's denouncements, which angered several New York Catholic psychiatrists and analysts enough to lead them to resign from their positions at Catholic clinics and hospitals in protest of his remarks.[121] Sheen epitomized the church's inability to consider that its own categories of understanding, including the mystical phenomenon of stigmata, could be related to unconscious forces, or that religious feelings sometimes can have pathological derivatives.

Hysteria and Stigmata after Freud

Margaret Reilly's examiners confidently labeled her as a hysteric, but was there agreement that she displayed the neurotic behaviors that characterized hysteria? Even her supporters were unclear on this question. Father Cavanaugh stated that no evidence of neurosis existed and first called her case "baffling." He then went on to contradict himself by conjecturing that "the girl is evidently neurotic but any normal girl might well be after 8 years of stigmatism of the cross on her bosom and after the experiences of the last four months." His comment implied that stigmatization causes neurosis rather than being an effect of it. Neurotics were supposed to be clever at faking their symptoms, but Cavanaugh found Margaret quite genuine. But he again qualified himself: if she was faking, she was unconscious of it. This diagnosis of unconscious deception fits Dr. Walshe's findings, cited earlier, as well as data provided in a classic study of neurotic behaviors published in the 1960s.[122] Dr. Gallen, however, had reported that he was able to relieve Margaret's pain in the hospital by injections of water. Like Walsh's examination of Margaret's feet and hands, Gallen's experience indicated that the patient's symptoms were histrionic, reflecting Margaret's desire to be the center of attention.[123] Such reports satisfied the physicians regarding her hysterical symptoms and, in doing so, endorsed Charcot's circular logic that mystical experiences are often neurotic and inherently feminine.

Margaret Reilly's Catholic examiners therefore diagnosed her as a hysteric according to pre-Freudian categories. Consequently, Sister Thorn provides an American example of Catholicism and science working in concert to marginalize the feminine, as both priests and doctors accepted the intellectual authority of medicine to affirm the ancient association of men with the mind and women with the body. American doctors of this generation tended to classify women as occupying one of two poles: oversexed or naïve. "Just as hypersexuality was the bad girl's ailment," Elizabeth Lunbeck documented in her study of the patients at the Boston Psychopathic Hospital, "hysteria was the good girl's."[124] In this regard, Margaret's Catholic circle was determined to group her with the good girls. Nevertheless, Margaret's reported aggression toward Gallen does not quite match the definition of the hysteric woman as someone who was unwittingly seduced.

One arena where Margaret Reilly and the Catholic nuns and sisters of her era could legitimately identify themselves socially and psychically as victims was in their identification with the broken body of the sacrificed Jesus. The social pressure upon women to conform to Catholic norms of chastity and purity, combined with a spiritual emphasis upon the tortured, powerless Christ, rewarded a personality that embraced suffering—illustrated in women's refusal to attack the authorities (God, priests, religious superiors, parents) who were responsible for inducing those feelings of unworthiness. Consistent with findings from the clinical study of masochistic personalities throughout the last century, it is also understandable that Margaret believed that her humiliation would result in her ultimate vindication, as Jesus Christ had triumphed over sin and death.

Gallen, McParlan, Walsh, and Thurston did not invoke Freudianism to assess Sister Thorn. Still, examining her experiences through neo-Freudian psychoanalytic theory and case studies from its clinical practitioners deepens the interpretive possibilities for understanding the roots of religious desires and the positioning of men and women relative to each other and God. In the post-Freudian era, the psychoanalytic study of culture was revolutionized by the work of Jacques Lacan (1901–81), a Jesuit-trained French renegade in the clinical field who developed an idiosyncratic system using his revisions to Freudian theory, Saussurian linguistics, Marxist categories of ideology, and graphs and algorithms to explain the formation and psychic structuring of the human subject.[125] He even sought the help of his younger brother, a monk, to secure the pope's endorsement for his own version of psychoanalysis as he broke with the French establishment, though his longed-for papal audience never took place.¹²⁶ Despite Lacan's deliberately obscure and enigmatic discursive style and his cultic posturing, he is useful to students of religion because he explored the complex relationship that humans have to images and ideas of identity, including his own identity as someone from a Catholic milieu who broke with it to embrace modernity via all of its revolutionary currents: surrealism, Dada, anthropology, psychiatry, communism, and structuralism.

Although Lacan's influence has been felt mostly in literature and film departments as a tool for cultural theory and critique, several prominent scholars have successfully assimilated Lacan to the study of religion. Among them, Antoine Vergote, a professor at the University of Louvain who studied in Paris with Lacan, Claude Lévi-Strauss, and Maurice Merleau-Ponty, has published the most complete Lacanian study of religious attitudes and their pathologies. Vergote explored the two motives at the heart of religious neurosis: *debt*, by which he means conscience and feelings of guilt and sinfulness; and *desire*, which includes erotic as well as mystical forms of longing. He names debt and desire as "two basic dimensions of existence, hence the two are at the heart of both religion and psychoanalysis." Debt and desire exist as essential parts of human life due to the logic underlying all guilt feelings: the notion that we feel guilty because all pleasure is stolen from God or that we do not deserve to occupy a space in the universe with God.¹²⁷

Christian existence, as Vergote describes it, embraces the two poles of guilt and longing, the former leading to the desire for self-punishment. Vergote's discussion of stigmata, therefore, stems from his consideration of the masochistic elements of Christianity. Absent any extensive therapeutic analyses of stigmatization, Vergote acknowledges that we can only make inferences from the evidence available, as I have done with Sister Thorn.¹²⁸ "In the domain of religion," he writes, "we can interpret the celebrated phenomenon of religious stigmata (whose hysterical character has frequently been noted) as an example of affect speaking through the body."¹²⁹ Stigmata, like hysterical symptoms, might be seen as the realization of a feminine desire to be wounded, making the wounds the means "by which love marks the body of its choice." Vergote continues: "The mystical wound, then, could be seen as the realization—in religious terms—of an initiating wound that is itself the sign of a feminine desire that has been assumed by the subject. It can also be supposed that the displacement of the wound onto the body as it is portrayed in Christian iconography is the result of a hysterical repression of a feminine fantasy."¹³⁰ Vergote's explanation still relies on hysteria, but upon an understanding of the condition that has been significantly expanded and nuanced since Charcot.

Vergote studied the stigmatization and visions of Therese Neumann, Margaret Reilly's contemporary, carefully situating her experiences in their cultural frame.[131] He observes that Neumann's visions became a source of pleasure, as Freud theorized, by allowing her to repeat and express a traumatic experience and then to repress it through the manifestation of a symptom. Therese's spinal injury when she was young was reproduced in subsequent paralysis and convulsions; her reenactments of Christ's Passion allowed her to replicate that and other experiences of aggression and rejection (including her possible rape by a neighbor). As Vergote suggests, "Anyone with a smattering of clinical understanding can see that this way of actively repeating a traumatic experience has a particularly curative effect on the subject."[132] Through her bleeding wounds, demonic attacks, and food refusals—all possibly self-inflicted—Sister Thorn likewise may have engineered the repetition of her own traumatic experiences.

Toward a Feminist Reimagining

This chapter has explored Margaret Reilly's experiences as interpreted by her Catholic doctors—Gallen the would-be suitor, McParlan the pietist, and Walsh the rationalist. It has contextualized the responses of these men by tracing the medical and psychological reception of hysteria and of women's mysticism from Charcot to Freud to Lacan, and through the eyes of Catholic medical experts from Thurston to Vergote, who had varying degrees of investment in those theories. Neurology and early psychoanalysis generally dismissed women's excessive mystical experiences as expressions of nervous exhaustion or of hysteria. Taken together, models of the unconscious mind have often pathologized mysticism and failed to adequately address gender—notably, the subjectivity of women, a gap that Glucklich attempts to remedy by theorizing pain as combining suffering and deep meaning. His formulation, however, seems to imply that women's suffering somehow conveys concentrated spiritual meaning, as though in answer to the projections of men who are searching for it.[133]

Often indebted to and in debate with the psychoanalysis of Freud and Lacan, feminist theory has challenged these theoretical formulations of women's experiences to offer yet another lens upon the interpreters of Sister Thorn. As Phyllis Chesler has rightly pointed out: "Although the ethic and referent of mental health in our society is a masculine one, most psychoanalytic theoreticians have written primarily about women."[134] Other feminist critics have noted the irony that Freud experimented on women by pioneering his theories of the "talking cure" with them and yet devised a theory that presumed a male subject as the model of humanity. Alice Jardine has correctly identified the "strange gap between the female bodies at the inceptions of psychoanalysis and the male subject taken as its norm, and especially within the resultant syntax, [within which] lies the power and, for some, the faults of psychoanalysis itself."[135]

The omission of women's subjectivity in classic psychoanalytic theory was first addressed by object-relations theorists, who built upon Freud to address women more usefully by looking at the pre-Oedipal bond of infant and mother. More recently, feminist scholarship has called for an "analytical critique" of Freud of the sort imagined by Diana Jonte-Pace in her study of Freud and feminism.[136] By this term, Jonte-Pace means developing a partnership between psychoanalysis and feminism that does not reject or shy away from Freud but that builds on the work of feminist psychoanalytic theorists like Juliet Mitchell, Julia Kristeva, Judith Van Herik, and Sander Gilman—all of whom value Freud as someone who began to speak the unspeakable, even when it was disturbing.[137] Feminist critics of this tendency in psychoanalysis to pathologize women have presented overwhelming evidence of masculinist bias in notions of women's experience;[138] similar critiques could be made of some of Margaret Reilly's interpreters, who tended to perpetuate dominant religious and social outlooks on women, even when the interpreter was herself a women.

The cultural appeal of spiritual victimhood, tied intimately to the need to abject (or cast aside) the maternal body, did not end with Sister Thorn's generation. It endured at least until Vatican II steered Catholic theology away from formerly dominant sacrificial notions of Christology. Sister Thorn's conscience was constantly torn between her flawed self and her idealized other. Guilt and self-loathing were reinforced by her Catholic upbringing, from inside her family circle by her parents and siblings; at school by the sisters; and in the convent by the superior, the other sisters, and her confessor. As Sister Thorn tried to come to terms with an oppressive ideal of femininity at the same time she tried to live up to it, she inhabited a constantly divided set of desires.

American Catholic women of Sister Thorn's era were not ready to revolt, as certain feminists would do fifty years later. Rather, the church enlisted women to withstand the forces of modern change, which in the broadest sense meant rejection of the paradigm shift toward a new understanding of the body as something created by social forces. If the body has gradually become accepted as a culturally constructed entity over the past 150 years,[139] in Catholicism it retained its Aristotelian-Thomist associations with the categories of the natural and the eternal well into the twentieth century. No wonder the first wave of Catholic gender upheaval of the 1920s became a battleground for the church, as it tried to defend fixed gender roles founded in "natural law," to reject contraception as attempts to interfere with nature, and to organize a national campaign against birth control.[140] As discussed, Archbishop Hayes's attempts to prevent public conversations on the topic in New York had the effect of marking the Catholic Church as the major antagonist of the birth-control movement. In the changing gender norms of the 1920s, the Catholic Church also resisted anything that undermined clear-cut distinctions between the sexes by confusing their separate social roles and physical distinctions—notably, woman suffrage and the "flapper," who became a global phenomenon in the twenties with her boyish figure, bobbed hair, and makeup. Nevertheless, the increase in religious vocations for women over the next forty years, even at the ratio of four to one of women religious to priests, suggests that the convent retained considerable appeal, even for the "modern girl," as a place where women gained status, skills, and satisfaction through serving others, united in their attraction to self-sacrificing victimhood.

Raised in an ethnoreligious enclave in New York City, Margaret Reilly was far removed from the Parisian hospital theater of Charcot, the Berlin laboratories of Virchow, and the Viennese office where Freud treated afflu-ent (and mostly Jewish) neurotics. Yet by the 1920s, psychoanalysis had made significant inroads in the United States, establishing a home in New York despite Freud's dislike of all things American. Manhattan hosted about 500 analysts even before psychoanalysis flourished in America in the late thir-ties.[141] While Freudianism had "eclipsed the Protestant pieties sovereign in America's official life,"[142] Catholics provided a barrier to its unopposed progress. The Reilly family represented the situation of many Catholic fami-lies. Within a large urban population of Roman Catholics, the Reillys had little recourse to therapeutic help and little impetus to seek it. Catholicism was a major source of comfort and existential meaning for millions of Irish Americans like them. Prayer was the means to resolve a desperate situation, and existential comfort came via the confessional, not from talking to an isolated (and possibly godless) clinician who had no business prying into the private matters and feelings of others. Suffering was to be cherished, with Jesus and the martyrs providing glorious inspiration. Moreover, in the church's official statements, psychoanalysis was tainted by its connection to Freud's Jewishness and to its advocacy of sexual freedom. In the American Catholic Church's struggle for legitimacy in the twentieth century, it was not hindered in its fight against novelties like psychoanalysis by the rancorous anticlerical politics and social relations that divided the Catholics of France, Belgium, Italy, Austria, and Germany. The absence of these constraints in New York City allowed the American church to support Rome's position and to lead American Catholics to function as an international voice of resistance to psychoanalysis.

For the skeptic, the obvious explanation for the events at Peekskill was the "subtle and seemingly purposeless fraud" that Father Thurston associated with many reported stigmatizations. If Margaret was a fake, then her stigmata were the products of conscious (rather than unconscious) activity, involving an ink stamp or decal to manufacture the crucifix on her chest and wall and using knives, needles, or shards of glass to poke holes in her hands and forehead. Her access to such materials at the convent's printery, her former employment as a clerk, and her penchant for telling tales make this explanation plausible. When it came to finding mystical phenomena, the several physicians (except Thomas McParlan) who examined or studied Margaret were dubious of her claims, invoking accepted but dated scientific language and methods to explain what was going on. Furthermore, the doctors who examined Sister Thorn found no bleeding marks or evidence of abraded skin, but instead only chronic digestive illness, mild vision irregularities, and hysteria. Catholic doctors, unlike Protestant critics, did not brand nuns as abnormal women for rejecting marriage and motherhood, but they did reiterate a pre-Freudian neurological model that regarded hysteria as an implicitly universal female condition. Accordingly, Reilly's commentators contented themselves with hearsay that she had colored the cross on her wall with menstrual blood and that her hysteria was related to being jilted, to a secret pregnancy, or to menopausal moodiness. Following European trends where hysteria removed mystics from the discursive power of religious authority only to deliver their symptoms to a new master, likewise the American Catholic medical elite embraced the etiology of hysteria to dispute Sister Thorn's mystical experiences.

This chapter has worked to connect cultural and psychological interpretations of Sister Thorn's experience without trying to insist that mystical experiences can be reduced to either. Even though revealed religion had been vigorously challenged by materialists since the Enlightenment, faith and medicine were finding numerous points of overlap in the 1920s, as happened in the circle surrounding Sister Thorn. As a woman seemingly innocent of any sordid sins, Margaret Reilly nonetheless held strong feelings of anxiety and shame that she had turned on herself from a young age. Inflicting pain upon herself became a psychic strategy to restore purity that also allowed her to continue to express disgust with the imperfections of the world. The church provided her with plenty of world-hating messages, and she had been able to internalize its strong demand for obedience to authority as a call to the convent. At least one episode in Margaret's life, her relationship with Dr. Gallen, hints at darker moral dilemmas prior to entering the Good Shepherd sisters. As Sister Crown of Thorns, Margaret may have felt that a lifetime of suffering for others modeled on Jesus Christ would balance the score for any of her real or imagined transgressions.

As medicine became ever more "rationalized," it sought to colonize women's experience, and some of its practitioners hoped to take possession of religion itself in order to discredit female visionaries and stigmatics. The Catholic doctors who encountered Sister Thorn upheld routine standards of empirical study and scientific explanation, but they were unwilling to abandon the Aristotelian-Thomist categories of Catholic tradition. That is, they believed that hysteria and sanctity could coexist, and they used both categories to dismiss women's experiences. Although Walsh differed from McParlan, whose piety overrode his clinical judgment, even Walsh had merely exchanged a religious elite for a scientific one, adopting the discourse of female hysteria from doctors and neurologists who regarded women as histrionic and easily confused. His approach was medical rather than psychological. While European Catholics had begun efforts to institutionalize cooperation between religion and science, in America the Catholic animus against Freud generated by the clergy prevented his theories from being taken seriously and certainly slowed the integration of subsequent post-Freudian approaches as well. This chapter has suggested that recent religious and psychoanalytical scholarship on mystical phenomena challenges the ideological positions at work among clergy and doctors during Margaret's lifetime—especially in light of theories about female subjectivity and actual women's demands to achieve it—and expands the range of possibilities for understanding such extraordinary phenomena.

{5} Cor Jesu Regnabit

Devotional Culture in American Catholicism

> The Cross is our food. Happy are those souls who
> desire only this bread.
>
> —Message from Jesus to Margaret Reilly for a priest,
> June 29, 1925

> O Jesus! my most sincere Friend! I expose to Thee all my
> wants, I discover to Thee all my miseries, my weakness,
> my tepidity and sloth—in a word, all the wounds of my
> soul, and fervently implore Thee to let Thyself be moved
> to pity by them, and that Thou wouldst come to my aid
> according to the magnitude of Thy mercies.
>
> —Devotions to the Sacred Heart, prayers of Blessed Margaret
> Mary Alacoque, in *The Pious Child: Instructions and Prayers for
> Catholic Children* (1894), 176

As Margaret knelt in prayer before the splendid new altar to the Sacred Heart of Jesus in her parish in Manhattan, this addition to St. Ignatius Church impressed her and all who saw it. The altar features a statue of the Savior displaying his heart to Margaret Mary Alacoque, a French nun who was canonized in 1920.[1] This Catholic Reformation stigmatic and visionary professed the motto *Cor Jesu Regnabit* ("The heart of Jesus will reign") and is venerated as the creator of the modern devotion to the Sacred Heart. Opposite this statue stood Margaret Mary's Jesuit confessor, Claude de la Columbière, offering his services for the devotion that she established. During Margaret Reilly's lifetime, the Sacred Heart cult was undergoing a revival thanks to a determined advocate, Father Mateo Crawley-Boevey, and to Pope Pius XI, who identified the Sacred Heart with the "spirit of reparation" so crucial to victim spirituality.[2] Margaret Reilly's lifelong engagement with the Sacred Heart showed how individuals took up and mediated this significant dimension of the Catholic International.

This chapter regards Sister Thorn and women religious as producers and consumers of devotional and religious goods that served the intimate needs

189

of Catholics in crisis situations and established connections between the local and the universal church. Margaret not only joined in the Sacred Heart devotion at the parish level, but she also made badges of the Sacred Heart at the convent. These were applied to health emergencies and for healing purposes but did not exist for profit purposes. The badges did not have an uncontested existence, however. They soon met with resistance from the archdiocese because they challenged the authority of the hierarchy and clergy as the sole mediators of divine power. Unlike a scapular badge, which required a priest's blessing, Margaret's badges came already blessed, she said, by the Lord himself. But as a priest pointed out to the archbishop: "Our Lord has instituted His priesthood to be His ministers even in blessing."[3] The handmade badges also occupied an imprecise position within the American economy, representing an alternative to consumer capitalism and produced by a woman who was isolated from the market. (More accurately, as we shall see, the badges were hybrid objects that relied upon mass production for its components, which were then reconstituted in the hands of Sister Thorn as vernacular items.)[4] In the Roaring Twenties, the handmade item was already being overtaken by mass production, a process that challenged the survival of many convent handmade goods as the twentieth century progressed. In this brief interim decade before the marketing of religious products for profit made lasting inroads in American Catholicism, Sister Thorn became a devotional entrepreneur, dispensing the promise of divine help through her badge apostolate, which furnished a perfect example of the church's "off-modern" outlook (the term coined by Stephen Schloesser). Throughout the chapter, we will consider the personal, economic, institutional, and therapeutic effects of her Sacred Heart badges.

Returning to the devotional sites that produced Margaret Reilly, we begin at St. Ignatius parish. Originally named St. Lawrence O'Toole in 1851 when it was founded for the largely Irish immigrant population of Yorkville in Manhattan, St. Ignatius was turned over to the Jesuits in the 1860s, who have continued to staff it to the present day. In the early twentieth century, St. Ignatius became the Jesuit's "flagship" church, decorated in an opulent Italian Renaissance style replete with marble, gilt, bronze, and enamel thanks to financing from wealthy (and sometimes anonymous) donors. The Sacred Heart altar frequented by Margaret, installed to the left of the main altar, was funded and constructed in the early 1900s by affluent parishioners.[5] As was typical for such projects, the statues began as plaster casts, to be replaced by white Carrara marble. Somewhat later, bronze doors symbolizing the saintly virtues were added to enclose the altar space.

From childhood, then, Margaret experienced the art, statuary, and stained

The richly decorated interior of St. Ignatius Church testified to the generosity and growing affluence of Catholics in Manhattan by the 1920s. (Courtesy of the archives of St. Ignatius parish, New York, N.Y.)

The Sacred Heart altar at St. Ignatius, one of the parish churches frequented by Margaret Reilly, with the marble statue of St. Margaret Mary Alacoque, the founder of the devotion. The sculptor, Joseph Sibbel, was born in Germany and active in Cincinnati before coming to New York, where he contributed sculptures for St. Patrick's Cathedral and St. Ignatius parish. Ironically, in a review of the St. Ignatius statuary, the *New York Times* commented: "Catholic churches are so often decorated with work by Italians and Germans that it causes remark when Americans are found contributing to their adornment.... It is one more sign of the spread of art in America to find that congregations discover at home the artists and artisans who are capable of carrying out the finest conceptions for religious houses" (June 28, 1901). (Courtesy of the archives of St. Ignatius parish, New York, N.Y.)

glass at her several Manhattan parishes—Blessed Sacrament, St. Francis de Sales, and St. Ignatius. As Catholic sacred art had done for centuries, these church interiors were teaching agents for Catholics to learn about the lives of the saints and an inspiration to perform devotional practices. By the time Margaret attended St. Ignatius, its partiality to the Sacred Heart devotion had been firmly established. Rites began there in 1871, when the sodality of the Sacred Heart was introduced during a mission preached by a Jesuit.[6] It was a hugely successful event, enrolling thousands of Catholics as promoters. They showed their fervor by attending novenas and observing First Fridays by kneeling on the special benches placed for them near the altar to receive Communion and to revere the consecrated Host through prayer. Soon there were so many Sacred Heart devotees that a system of promoters and archpromoters emerged to organize attendance at sessions by alphabetical order. A corps of laywomen attended to the "petty details" that would have interfered with the clergy's "more urgent duties."[7]

The success of the sodality led St. Ignatius parish to be formally dedicated to the Sacred Heart in 1872, and the altar familiar to the Reilly family was built thirty years later. Unlike the parish's other altars that were financed by individual donations, the Sacred Heart altar was a group gift from the League of the Sacred Heart. When Father James Conway, as its director, broached the subject to its members in 1900, they raised more than $10,000 in an astonishingly short time. During Margaret's years as a young parishioner and sodalist (as discussed in chapter 2), Father William Ennis presided over the parish novenas, especially those to the Sacred Heart.

If the Sacred Heart became a core symbol for Catholics of Jesus's presence in the world, it is by now well established that the lived religion of Catholics prior to Vatican II involved a highly visual and sensual encounter with religious objects that equipped Catholics to establish that presence everywhere.[8] In the nineteenth century, material religion signaled the theological difference between Catholics and Protestants; by the twentieth century, devotions became a way that Catholics marked their distance from modernity. Labeled as "off-modern" by Stephen Schloesser, this Catholic relationship to modernity has also been described as "non-modern" by Robert Orsi. Schloesser traces the efforts of Catholics to synthesize their heritage with the present after the First World War by making recovery of tradition itself an act of reparation.[9] In Orsi's formulation, "the clearest sign of Catholic difference from modern culture was devotionalism, that array of practices, objects, liquids, images, ceremonies, and gestures by which Catholics engaged the presence of God and the saints in the spaces and the times of everyday life."[10]

The "off-modern" or "non-modern" Sacred Heart cult had emerged from the visions of a seventeenth-century stigmatized nun, the source of its distinctive iconography. Between 1673 and 1675, Margaret Mary Alacoque beheld Jesus's heart on a throne of fire surrounded by rays of light. Encircling the heart was a crown of thorns, and above it rested a cross. The practice of venerating an image of the exposed heart of Jesus by gazing upon it while offering certain prayers stems from the Counter-Reformation, but it regained intensity during the nineteenth century.[11] Although rejected by the Council of Trent before Alacoque's lifetime, the feast of the Sacred Heart was finally recognized by the Catholic Church in 1856.[12] Especially in France, the Sacred Heart devotion took on monarchist and antirevolutionary political associations after Jesus revealed that the "wound" in his heart was the official atheism of the French nation. Two centuries later, when French Catholics renewed their appeals to the Sacred Heart, they asserted that national disasters such as the military defeat at the hands of the Prussians in 1870 and the Paris Commune were consequences of France's continuing failure to nationalize the devotion. The proponents of the Sacred Heart cult hit upon a powerful rhetorical strategy by claiming that the decline of Christianity throughout France represented a new crucifixion.[13] This political context was not easily transferred to the United States, however, where throne-and-altar politics did not hold sway. Margaret's efforts on behalf of the Sacred Heart, therefore, were put to personal, usually thaumaturgic, purposes. Separated from its French royalist overtones, yet allied with the French origins of the Good Shepherd sisters, the energies of the Sacred Heart flowed from Peekskill as a healing device, a form of solace, and a call to reform one's daily habits.

The Sacred Heart devotion involved the activity of concentrated looking. For Catholics of Sister Thorn's generation, the foremost ritual of "looking at" the body of Christ was to regard the consecrated Host as it was elevated during Mass and to revere it in the tabernacle at Benediction, while saying a novena, or during Forty Hours devotions. By contrast, the Sacred Heart devotion concentrated the gaze upon the bodily organ associated with the emotions in order for Christians to comprehend how their sins wounded the heart of Christ. Its image quickly became ubiquitous due to the technique of chromolithography, which enabled the cheap color reproduction of the Sacred Heart on holy cards, enthronement certificates, and wall hangings.

Confraternities of the Sacred Heart spread the devotion sporadically in eighteenth-century Europe, but the cult grew dramatically under Jesuit sponsorship after the Napoleonic Wars, attracting many French and Irish Catholics—hence the appeal at Yorkville in New York City, where those immigrant groups had clustered. As noted above, in France, the Sacred Heart served the church by securing the loyalty of the masses against the influence of secular ideologies, including republican and socialist forces of the nineteenth century and, later, the Central powers and Nazi armies. In Manhattan, the Sacred Heart had no such political overtones. The widespread appeal of the cult stemmed instead from the fact that it promised the success of petitionary prayer to everyone: because Jesus promised to Margaret Mary Alacoque that he would bless each home where the image is venerated, Catholic supplicants needed only to implore Jesus by reciting the Sacred Heart prayers and by displaying the image. Sister Thorn's congregation had embedded itself in the history of the cult of the Sacred Heart by claiming that Pope Leo XIII's consecration of "the entire human race" to the Sacred Heart of Jesus in 1899 resulted from the promptings of a Good Shepherd sister. The order's histories highlight the pope's choice to perform this rite of consecration only a day or two after the sister's death.[14]

In the United States, the Sacred Heart was a useful and democratized devotion for immigrant Catholics that also preserved ties to Europe and to the universal church.[15] To some degree, it also offered the same "comprehensively feminized image of Christ" that Europeans experienced as part of a general feminization within Christianity.[16] The best-known precedent for devotional connection to the Old World was the popular sale of Lourdes water in America in the nineteenth century, derived from the sacred spring identified by Bernadette Soubirous in France.[17] Now, the Sacred Heart offered a new cult that beckoned lay and ordained Catholics to deepen their love for the Lord. Its rituals center upon making reparation for human sinfulness, understood as injuring Jesus through lack of attention to the Eucharist, by swearing and failing to observe the Sabbath, and by disobedience to father figures generally. At the institutional level, the cult of the Sacred Heart defended patriarchy beginning with the pope, whose paternal authority had suffered repeated blows in the nineteenth century, and ending with the family.[18] In the home, fathers led the enthronement of the Sacred Heart ritual, making explicit the godly authority of men. For each devotee, the cult provided the opportunity to reflect upon and embrace Jesus's sacrifice of his life for the sins of humanity. Brother Lukas Etlin, for instance, preached this sermon on the Sacred Heart to convent women: "Jesus is all mine in His agony. Oh, what that means to the loving soul! She participates in His sufferings as also in His merits. Jesus is all mine sweating Blood for the sins of the world, for my sins! He is agonizing because of the crimes of men, my sins! Jesus in His sweat of Blood is all mine! He wishes me to compassionate Him in His suffering. Jesus, my love, is all mine!"[19]

The possessive (and fetishistic) combination of agony and bleeding, pain and possession, were major ingredients in the victim spirituality that was commended to the women who heard these sermons.[20] In Margaret's congregation, the Good Shepherd foundress had died a painful death from an ulcerated sore that she kept secret in order to suffer for others, while another Good Shepherd leader took the motto "More suffering, more love." In family and parish settings, the patriarchal role predominated the Sacred Heart rituals: the father led the service that enthroned the image in the family home, while the priest, serving as an *alter Christus*, embodied the theological connections between manliness, authority, and divinity.[21] Even in convent settings, a male presence was important to Sacred Heart events. Since Vatican II, the emphasis in Catholic teaching about this devotion has shifted dramatically away from the notion of self-abasement as reparation for sins to an emphasis upon the great love of Christ for all.[22] Yet during Sister Thorn's lifetime, the liturgical emphasis on sacrifice (by priests and religious as tantamount to the Mass itself) lent itself well to interpreting stigmatic phenomena as intensified dramas of the suffering of Christ.

Margaret's veneration of the Sacred Heart at home and at her parish was part of a range of other pious activities that absorbed her, such as offering nine days of prayer known as novenas (after *novem*, the Latin word for nine), participating in adoration of the Eucharist, and receiving Communion on the first Friday of each month. Her spiritual posture was one of constant atonement, and the popularity of the "victim soul" during this era made explicit connections between the sacrifice of the Eucharist and one's own spiritual victimhood. Although the term "victim soul" is no longer prevalent in the literature of devotional Catholicism, its emergence in the late 1800s gave it special currency in the decades between the two world wars, a period when the vicarious power of extraordinary suffering was represented to Christians as a personal and heroic spiritual response to the massive trauma of war. Celebrated as the destiny of a chosen few, the task of the victim soul is to plead with God to make reparation for the sins of others by voluntarily embracing and enduring pain. Obedient submission to suffering, rather than the suffering itself, is the redemptive act and imitative of Christ's complete acceptance of God's will.[23] Since the Counter-Reformation, French piety has especially exalted the role of Christ as priest and sacrifice and advocated various forms of contemplative prayer, mysticism, and reparation as the core of spiritual life. The Good Shepherd congregation, with its roots in France and its array of confessors, communicated the value of vicarious atonement to aspiring nuns like Margaret.

A system of suffering makes no sense without compensation. The incentive for Catholics to perform rituals of self-sacrifice was to gain the reward of prayers known as indulgences as established by various papal decrees since the Middle Ages. Indulgences depended upon belief in Purgatory, a concept no longer emphasized by the Catholic Church after Vatican II.[24] In the 1920s, however, indulgences were sought in order to lessen time in Purgatory, that halfway place between earth and heaven for those who died without having fully atoned for their sins during their lifetime. The living continued to pray for the souls of the dead, certain that God would hear their prayers and shorten the sentence of those languishing in Purgatory. A recitation of the Litany of the Sacred Heart, privately or publicly, received a 300-day indulgence, giving further weight to the merits of the Sacred Heart badge. Praying the Stations of the Cross, receiving Holy Communion on nine First Fridays, and praying for the dead in a cemetery were likewise rewarded.

Sacred Space and Devotions

The spiritual rewards sought by Catholics through acts of atonement were balanced by the practical concerns of the institutional church to secure funding for the construction and maintenance of its physical infrastructure. In this regard, the swelling numbers of immigrant Catholics in New York City (before the passage of the Johnson-Reed Act in 1924 effectively curtailed new immigration) put pressure on all forms of archdiocesan services. In some cases, it led Manhattan parishes to attract financial donations by offering a unique experience to pilgrims visitors—a relic, a novena, a shrine, the tomb of a holy person. The United States was mostly deficient as yet in these sorts of vernacular traditions. As Nathaniel Hawthorne had famously lamented about America at mid-nineteenth century, it was a nation entirely lacking in shadows, mystery, and antiquity. Still, American Catholics did not lack a sense of sacred space. As Jon Butler has noted, "From the provision of chapels in early Maryland to the development of the first shrines in antebellum America to the construction of the great American basilicas and cathedrals in America between 1840 and 1940, Catholics have demonstrated that the sacralization of space in America has been as important as the sacralization of space in Europe and elsewhere."[25]

During the construction boom in Catholic churches that began in the late nineteenth century, the effort to install certain practices that would have appealed to Hawthorne's desire for a properly mysterious environment took root. While taking care to avoid being cheapened by the term "marketing," Gilded Age Catholic pastors, patrons, and congregants contributed to the work of making and extending sacred space throughout the nation by fostering devotional sites in the newly built churches with an eye to gaining revenues by appealing to pilgrims. The case of St. John the Baptist parish at 76th Street and Lexington Avenue is illustrative. St. John's had been founded in 1882 as a national (that is, ethnic) parish for French Canadians, the second such parish in Manhattan. The Yorkville neighborhood, just to the north of St. John's and populated by German and Irish Catholics, hosted four other churches, including the two parishes of the Reilly family, St. Ignatius Loyola and St. Francis de Sales. When St. John's sought to expand from its initial building, it received an unplanned visit from a priest traveling from France to Saint Anne de Beaupré, the popular pilgrimage shrine to the mother of Mary on the outskirts of Quebec. The priest was carrying a relic of Saint Anne from Europe. When the relic was displayed publicly for a short time at St. John's, an epileptic was cured by contact with it, leading to an upsurge in pilgrims to the parish, many of whom pleaded with the visiting priest not to depart with the relic. After reaching the Canadian shrine, he received permission of the archbishop of Quebec to divide the relic in order to share it with St. John's in New York. The relic of Saint Anne was reinstalled in a shrine on the south wall of the church, and a novena soon began there. But St. John's did not stake its reputation entirely upon the relic. The parish also worked hard to establish devotion to the Blessed Sacrament by installing the priests of the Blessed Sacrament Congregation to manage the parish and to oversee the perpetual adoration of the Eucharist. Eight blocks away, St. Ignatius parish would need to redouble its Eucharistic devotion and Sacred Heart Leagues in order to keep up with the appetite for devotions and to preserve the donations of its faithful. Other Manhattan parishes began to draw crowds and recognition for their relics, such as pieces of the True Cross displayed at St. Patrick's Cathedral and at St. Vincent Ferrer, which also acquired relics of all of the Dominican saints.

As a friendly, unstated inter-parish competition in New York City increased the demand for holy objects to attract donors and pilgrims, the church's many cults could at times rival each other. For centuries, Mary and Jesus had coexisted in popular devotions with the cults of saints, but by the late 1800s, Christocentric practices were being emphasized by the institutional church to reflect its new theological emphases. The fervent Marianism of the nineteenth century, described by historians in recent decades as a symptom of the "feminization" of Christianity, was now being countered by devotions centering upon the body of Jesus in the Eucharist and in his sacrificial death. Sister Thorn's devotional work with the Sacred Heart badges is testament to the success of this shift toward Jesus.

Jesus combined these two concepts of the Passion and the Eucharist when he told Sister Thorn in a vision that "the Cross is our food." In Thorn's lifetime, the possibility for Catholics to partake of Communion on a daily basis came from the impetus of Pope Pius X, who shifted the emphasis from adoration of the Eucharist to frequent consumption of it. Pius's actions affected the church's new off-modern position in the early twentieth century by implying that the sacraments were a creative blending of tradition and the present, and that they were necessary to the modern world without being mired in its snares. As the author of a popular history of Eucharistic devotion put it, "The antidote for modern, up-to-date life is the Eucharist."[26] The increasing emphasis on the Blessed Sacrament could be seen in the devotions mentioned above and in the religious education of Catholic children. While preparing for their first Communions, Margaret and her siblings were instructed by the highly legalistic manual theology of the day, which readied children for the sacrament by fostering the notion that their sinfulness had required the atoning act of Jesus's death. Although family photo albums of this era customarily display innocent, smiling children in pure white costumes on their first Communion day, the somber side of preparation for the sacrament was this new burden of guilt impressed upon the young. A major consequence of the pope's endorsement of more-frequent reception of Communion as "the shortest and safest way to Heaven" was to lower the age of moral responsibility for children.[27] In Margaret's case, preparing for Holy Communion affected her at a young age with the need to avoid sin and gave her the devotional tools to do so by recasting tradition as an essential ingredient of the modern.

Heightened Catholic reverence for the Host at Communion and in paraliturgical events also intensified the ascetic practices followed by women. Among the Catholic mystics who had survived by consuming only the Host were a significant number of stigmatics known for this type of inedia. Because Catholic theology comprehends the Eucharist as the source of eternal life, Christian mystics have often signaled their desire for union with God through the act of incorporating the body and blood of Christ. Furthermore, "by avoiding foods that are 'not God,'" Rebecca Lester suggests, fasting women "limit and control the process and create an intense Eucharistic craving."[28] Ascetics believe that the more one incorporates God, the faster the union will occur. Through food, "holy ascetics were able to enact, express, and to some degree resolve the central issues of the autonomy/dependence struggle, and the antecedent concerns of self and identity, through a specific cultural and ideological system."[29]

After 1905, when the pope encouraged more-frequent Communion among Catholics, women's eating and spiritual practices joined this chase for holiness. Margaret Reilly's extreme fasting practices have already been

noted, and during her lifetime, reports of Eucharistic inedia were prominently featured for stigmatics. Among American instances of such practices
was Marie Rose Ferron of Rhode Island, who never ate solid food after age
twenty-two, when she refused some freshly baked bread offered by her
sister.[30] For the next eleven years, Rose only ingested liquids and the consecrated Host. Although she did "suck on some foods, candies and drink
some Moxie (an American soft drink)," it was reported that she was not
able to digest them.[31] Absent the junk food, Ferron reprised the Eucharistic
miracles that abounded in the lives of female saints and stigmatics since the
Middle Ages, including miraculous reception of Communion from a distance, saints ingesting no food except for the Host, their ability to preserve
the Real Presence of Christ between Communions, and so on. In every
anecdote about the eating habits of holy women, the refusal of earthly food
was contrasted with desire for divine bread, which in turn was equated to
Christ's suffering on the cross.

Another type of Eucharistic miracle often recorded in the lives of stigmatics told of mystics who were miraculously enabled to keep a small piece
of the Host undissolved in their mouths between acts of Communion. Margaret's contemporary, Therese Neumann, professed this gift, along with her
ability to swallow and digest the Host without any visible movement of her
throat. (Catholics even devised a precise term for this phenomenon: mystical deglutition.) Through these phenomena, mystics reminded the faithful
that God truly was incarnate in the body of Christ, whose powers overrode
those of mere nature. Surely the Good Shepherds' Host-making operation
at Peekskill was a constant reminder of this belief.

The church's anxiety to establish the Host as central to Catholic practice
was evident in Margaret Reilly's generation, although it was not new to Catholicism. From the Protestant Reformation, mystical phenomena involving
the Host had been crucial to polemics against the reformers, since interpretation and comprehension of the Host defined the theological boundary
between the Catholic and Protestant factions. Even four centuries later,
affirming the Real Presence of Christ in the Host through a variety of popular devotions in America renewed this sharp distinction between Catholic
and Protestant as a way for the former to establish their own "real presence" in the United States. From her childhood, Margaret participated in
the common Eucharistic devotion of the early twentieth century known as
the Forty Hours. It consisted of uninterrupted prayer before the consecrated
Host from Thursday to Saturday, usually in a side altar within the church.
Volunteers kept shifts of up to eight hours, usually on their knees in silent
prayer. In her school days, Margaret took an afternoon shift, and as an adult,

she observed the so-called Holy Hour on Thursday night until midnight. As with the Sacred Heart devotion, the establishment of the Forty Hours in America points to the successful transnational diffusion of a practice that originated in Europe. As seen in the stories surrounding Sister Thorn, the Real Presence was everywhere and at all times ready to battle Protestants and Satan in order to strengthen the bonds between Catholics of the Old and New Worlds. In the ardent veneration of the Eucharist, Catholics could overcome any sense of inferiority to the faithful of Europe and proudly claim their place in America.

My encounter with a Sacred Heart badge sparked the investigation for this chapter. The badge is a small item in the vast museum of Catholic material culture, which has grown since the Catholic Reformation had encouraged the use of rosaries, holy medals, statues, and printed prayer and saint cards as devotional aids. Among Sister Thorn's items at the archives of the Good Shepherd Sisters are several square pieces of cloth or paper about two inches wide, each containing a mass-produced color print of the Sacred Heart of Jesus. The image is covered in transparent plastic and held in its envelope by a crocheted thread edging of red or white silk. Margaret Reilly began to assemble this item by hand soon after her arrival at the convent of the Good Shepherds in Peekskill. As she progressed to the stage of postulant and then novice in the community, hoping to enter the congregation fully, she began to promote badge making as her special commission from Jesus.[32] She claimed further that the badges had been held in the hands of Jesus or Mary and personally blessed. As Sister Carmelita Quinn explained: "One of the special apostolates of Sister Mary Crown of Thorns was to distribute Sacred Heart badges around which she had personally crocheted. Most badges were stitched in red, a few in white. Sister explained; the ones in red and white were all 'held in Jesus'[s]' hand and blessed. The ones in WHITE (which Jesus asked her to stitch differently) were also held in the hands of our Bl.[essed] Mother." The badges finished in white thread, Jesus instructed, were to be used in the rarest cases of illness or catastrophe.[33] Margaret claimed that a saint helped her thread the needle, while Jesus obligingly kept her hands from perspiring on the tricky isinglass.[34] Only one Good Shepherd sister was permitted to help her in the production process by inserting words of the Gospel on a scrap of paper inside the badge. The Evil One showed up from time to time to frustrate their efforts, once setting fire to the piece of cloth, creating "smoke and a stench."[35]

Besides serving as portable reminders of the overburdened heart of Jesus, Margaret's sewn badges joined a long-established convent economy of hand production. This tradition has been sadly neglected in art history by dismissing it as the toil of anonymous women obliged to avoid the trap of idleness.[36] The painting or printing of holy cards; the weaving and needlepointing of tapestries; and the embroidering of badges, banners, liturgical vestments, altar cloths, and kneeler covers have regularly been overlooked as handiwork that displayed what were merely women's natural domestic talents. In the needlework created by the sisters, they did indeed find ways to domesticate sacred symbols, but their productions need not be understood as failed imitations of high art. Not only as individuals but as a cooperative, women in sisterhoods combined economic necessity with craft: needleworking was one among several activities that sustained them financially, including baking Communion wafers, bookbinding, printmaking, fashioning liturgical vestments, typesetting, and metalwork. Most of the sisters learned by doing, and not always by choice, since tasks were assigned. Having such income-generating projects at a convent allowed congregations like the Good Shepherds, who baked Hosts and printed religious cards at Peekskill, to sustain their ministry to delinquent girls and women.

Handcrafted items associated with Sister Thorn are dispersed throughout the United States. At the Benedictine convent archives in St. Louis, I saw a tiny puffed silk heart crocheted in pink thread with a circular white object (the Host?) attached below, identified as one of "Thorn's treasures."[37] The antecedents to such miniature objects and to Sister Thorn's Sacred Heart badges lay in the great medieval convents, such as Eichstatt and St. Walburg in Bavaria, where nuns and sisters fashioned intricately patterned tapestries and needlepointed clerical vestments. The scale of their handiwork ranged from the enormous wall hangings of earlier centuries to pocket-sized items. It was particularly during the Renaissance, however, that nuns became known for producing miniature images, a practice that flourished in Italian convents and convent schools. These handmade *immaginette* helped Catholics to keep the saints close at hand—in pockets, purses, and on chains or strings hung next to their body.[38] The portable images could be given to friends and family on sacred days in the church calendar, such as saints' days, feast days, and the celebration of a first Communion.[39] The making and sharing of religious objects, no matter how small, sustained intimate relationships among Catholics. In this important role, the objects disclose the history of emotional connections and gestures among Catholics that kept alive the cult of the saints and recognized the bonds between the living and the dead in the rhythms of daily practices.

Handiwork thus performed several functions for women religious by helping them observe the discipline of their convent rule, providing needed income for the religious congregation, and marking continuity with their monastic ancestors. The Good Shepherds continued to develop their skills in the same way sisters had throughout the centuries. In Europe, for example, nuns and sisters sold their sewing, embroidery, and lace along with sculpture, hand-gilded frames, liturgical clothes, and linens for trousseaus. Religious women also made miniatures of their own design that were painted, embroidered, or collaged.[40] American sisters followed this tradition at Peekskill by preserving the titles of "needleworker" and "sewing mistress" for sisters who taught crocheting and fine embroidery to the convent's inmates into the mid-twentieth century. Census records for Peekskill in 1920 and 1930 reveal the dozens of girls whose skills were dedicated to "industrial" sewing to give them marketable skills once they left convent care. In more ephemeral ways, the Catholic sisters showed off their handiwork on feast days by decorating the convent altars—for example, the shrine to the Good Shepherd foundress in the foyer of Mount St. Florence—and by ornamenting the chapel altar to reflect the liturgical seasons of Advent, Lent, and ordinary time. Convents performed plays and other entertainments as well. The Philadelphia Good Shepherd house reported with satisfaction about a tableau presented to the Visitor (Mother Hickey) in 1920, which enacted the purgative way, the illuminative way, and the unitive way of spiritual growth.[41] Such activities, however didactic, provided sisters with an all-too-rare chance to employ their creativity, as well as an occasion to recall the bond between the American sisterhood and its French origins and to reaffirm the core symbols of Catholicism that linked the observances at the convent to those of the universal church.

Embroidery and needlework were not limited to religious women or to Catholics. In Euro-American culture, girls were commonly taught these arts so that they would use their time productively. For some, it took on spiritual meaning. Marie Rose Ferron, an alleged stigmatic and visionary, "busied herself as well she could with her 'little crafts.'" Turning even her insomnia to pious use, she occupied herself in her sleepless hours after midnight making bookmarks and braids and repairing rosaries.[42] Like Margaret Reilly, Rose claimed that she had supernatural help, as she only had the use of one hand and her mouth for sewing. With the Lord's help, Rose managed her ailments, proved her domesticity, and produced religious artifacts. When similarly confined to bed, Margaret Reilly joined the ranks of dependent women who ate and slept little but proved to be model invalids and industrious needleworkers who transported the ideals of late Victorian womanhood into the next century.

By the time the archbishop of New York ordered Margaret to cease production and distribution of her Sacred Heart badges, she had already completed about 4,000 of them. The chancery further directed the convent to request the return of all badges already dispersed. The fact that many badges in circulation were not returned shows that in matters of local and private devotions, the church could not enforce its authority absolutely. When it impinged too closely on folk piety, the church encountered resistance.

When Archbishop Patrick Hayes demanded the recall of the badges, he had several reasons to worry about the rising demand for them. First, he was uneasy about the miraculous healings already being attributed to them, not to mention Sister Thorn's unsupported claim that Jesus himself took the finished badges and delivered them to the Virgin Mary to be blessed. Catholics understood that they were not being saved by Margaret Reilly or by a bit of embroidery, but by the power of the Sacred Heart of Jesus; yet because the church forbids veneration of a living figure, Hayes took steps to prevent Sister Thorn from attracting undue attention to herself. The recent sensational article about Margaret in the *New York World* had made matters worse in the region by singling her out as a curiosity. In Max Weber's conception of charismatic power, "If virtuosi are allowed to operate unchecked, the church may forfeit valuable political patronage, wealthy funding sources, and social respectability."[43] These very concerns led New York's archbishop to eliminate contact between Margaret and outsiders through her badges. In addition, he was wary of the money-making schemes that often accompanied such situations, an implicit rebuke to capitalism in defense of Catholicism's distance from the market.

Sister Thorn was a rare instance of an American stigmatic, but hunger for miraculous events was seemingly on the rise in the United States in the 1920s. Although miracles usually attracted populist support from laity, the Catholic hierarchy took severe measures against most allegations, as it did in the Archdiocese of Boston when a cult emerged at the grave of Patrick Powers, an Irish-born priest. Powers had been buried in Malden after his death from tuberculosis in 1869.[44] During the week of the stock-market crash of 1929, rumors began to circulate that a miraculous cure had occurred there. After thousands of pilgrims hurried to the cemetery to take dirt from the grave, the chancery blocked any profiteering attempts of locals, while Archbishop William O'Connell closed the cemetery for a time to eliminate the crowds and to exhume the body of Father Powers. Although the archdiocese said that it was investigating the miraculous claims at the site, it provided no further information, hoping the furor would die out from bureaucratic neglect.

Just as intriguing as the details of this spontaneous cult in New England was the contrast between the church hierarchy's fear of the contaminating effects of commercialization—as Archbishop Hayes had tried to avoid in Peekskill—and the laity's newfound urgency about the possibility of profiting from American saints. In Boston, one businessman had begun to sell a medallion of Father Powers after intuiting that "people seem to feel the time is right for a Catholic Irish American Saint."[45] In a separate letter, however, the salesman expressed fears about his rivals in the devotional marketplace: "The earlier we started the better, rather than wait for the Jews, who have strangled the religious goods market to get into it."

Whether official or underground, Margaret's badges needed help to make their way into the world, where they occupied a territory closer to folk production than the fine arts. Among her circle of friends, however, were successful middle-class Catholics who aspired to the Beaux Arts tradition through their investment in the religious-art market in New York City. Margaret's physician, Dr. Thomas McParlan, was a case in point. Sustained by devotional culture, he reveled in its images and objects, but he also enjoyed being regarded as a patron of serious Catholic artists. He discovered and began to promote the work of Charles Bosseron Chambers, who arrived in Manhattan in 1916. In November 1926 McParlan wrote to Brother Lukas Etlin, with whom he had shared one of Chambers's popular works: "So pleased that you liked the 'Light of the World.' Mr. Chambers is such a staunch, loyal Catholic and his whole heart and soul are in Religious subjects."[46] Chambers (1882–1964), born in St. Louis and trained in Berlin, Vienna, and Dresden, became known as the "religious Rockwell" for his fashionable paintings and illustrations of Jesus, Mary, and biblical scenes. *Light of the World*, a sentimental portrait of the boy Jesus, was called the most popular religious painting of the time. Chambers, who added his middle name of Bosseron in order to evoke his French ethnic heritage, had married the niece of Patrick Feehan, the first archbishop of Chicago, and the couple moved to New York, where the artist occupied a splendid atelier in the Carnegie Studios at Carnegie Hall.

The lucrative career of Chambers, enabled by the support of his patrons, exemplifies the successful marketing of religious art from the twenties to midcentury as a result of a growing interest among wealthier American Catholics in oil paintings and prints and among ordinary Catholics in the religious themes of holy cards, calendars, and chromos. Chambers's literal and pious style seems saccharine to modern tastes, yet his devotional images live on in poster art and framed prints distributed by Catholic publishers, where he is often compared favorably with painter and illustrator Maxfield Parrish (1870–1966). McParlan declared that Chambers had "that power of imparting the pure and spiritual to his work."[47] Art critics remarked on his "softly appealing color and a smoothness of finish that is especially marked in the drawings." In 1933 Chambers was enlisted to help the Good Shepherds with a benefit gallery exhibition, the entrance fees of which were donated to establish a reception house for the congregation in Manhattan since the Peekskill convent was too remote to serve as a headquarters for the sisters' work in the city.[48] The artist also donated a crucifixion altarpiece to the sisterhood for their convent. McParlan's connection with Chambers marks the beginning of Catholic professional support for Catholic artists in New York and of a financial connection between artists, favored charities often led by society women, and religious orders.

McParlan's interest in promoting religious art encompassed both high and low ends of the aesthetic spectrum. In addition to his efforts in publicizing painters like Chambers, McParlan spent many hours trafficking in religious goods, especially rosaries, which he ordered from Brother Lukas, Sister Carmelita, and others and then dispensed to convents and monasteries to be blessed before distribution. He commented with satisfaction that "the lay people I have given them to all tell me the same story—an increasing love of the Blessed Virgin and longing to keep on reciting the rosary."[49] McParlan's letters reveal him to be a tireless retailer of Marian piety, his own role pointing to the growing importance of laity in furthering devotions in symbiosis with religious orders of men and women. His efforts show that in New York, Catholic piety of the twentieth century was sustained by the combined efforts of clergy and laity, a strategy made easier by the fact that the bonds between families and religious orders were quite strong. On one occasion, McParlan mentioned that his daughter, a convent-school student, asked him to send her "those Holy Land Indulgence rosaries," acquired by Brother Lukas through special papal permission, "as my gift to the girls, they will go crazy with delight as they all love them so."[50] McParlan's wife reported being moved to tears by Brother Lukas's gift of these blessed rosaries, which she arranged on her desk in order to view them every day. After the death of Lukas, McParlan himself sought comfort in holy objects, as he petitioned Sister Carmelita: "Could you not send me some little relic of Father[,] even a button from an old coat I would highly prize."[51] The trade between Catholics in objects of elite and popular culture worked to transmit reassurance of the presence of the loved one, whether it was the boy Jesus cradled in the arms of Saint Joseph in *Light of the World* or the aura from a coat button of a venerated monk.

The particular image of the Sacred Heart used in the badges made by Margaret was a German print distributed by the Benedictine Convent of Perpetual Adoration in Clyde, Missouri. It was a gift to subscribers with each renewal of the magazine *Tabernacle and Purgatory*, founded by Brother

Lukas. Margaret removed the metal rim from the badge and added her own crocheted border. Belying their simple appearance, her badges established a bond between her and several other religious congregations in the United States—the Good Shepherds in New York, the Benedictines at Clyde, and the Jesuits in New York and their counterparts in France, Germany, Ireland, and even Peru. The circulation of the Sacred Heart image by dozens of Catholic printing houses worldwide and the translation of its prayers into many languages contributed to the internationalization of the cult.

As an artifact of devotional life, Sister Thorn's badge was a refurbished item that converted a mass-produced image into a handmade one, using both traditional and manufactured materials of silk and isinglass. By converting mechanically made items to spiritual purposes, individual Catholics helped the church to promote Christian iconography and to resist commodification by directing the circulation of the badges in patterns that did not follow purely economic laws.[52] The recycled badges, given as gifts, allowed Sister Thorn to reach persons who were seeking the power of divine healing and who would, in time, help to nationalize her influence.

Margaret followed the conventual norms of humility in resisting credit for the Sacred Heart badges, noting modestly that they represented the combined efforts of humans and the saints. As she doggedly punched her needle and thread through the isinglass and cloth, she was assisted by Colette of Corbie, a fourteenth-century French saint who had been her companion since childhood, helping Margaret with family chores and cooking. "Everywhere Coletta is her assistant," Brother Lukas agreed.[53] Sister Carmelita recalled that Colette was special to the Reilly family because, "after much prayer, this saint was a gift to her parents after long years of being childless." Margaret called Colette the "Patron of Parents desiring children" and gave Sister Carmelita some holy medals of the saint to take to Clyde, where the sisters could enclose them in letters to persons praying for "safe pregnancy."[54] After she was stigmatized, Margaret experienced events recorded in Colette's life, such as visions of the Passion, endorsement of strict rules of cloister, attempts to reform convent life, and her prediction of her own death. At Peekskill, Saint Colette became so busy repairing broken plumbing, putting out fires, and restoring lost articles that she merited her own shrine there, drawing an audience of Catholic parents who came to give thanks for the safe birth of their children.[55]

For several centuries, the Sacred Heart devotion commemorated by the badges revolved around performing rigorous acts of reparation for sin. Since the mid-twentieth century, in the generation that followed Sister Thorn, the devotion has shed much of that severity.[56] Karl Rahner (1904–84), one of the

most influential theologians of the twentieth century, downplayed the notion of reparation and supported the pope's insistence that Alacoque had not
founded a new devotion but instead had revived an ancient continuous tradition. "There has always been a devotion to the Heart of Jesus," wrote Rahner,
"since the earliest days of the Church and there always will be one."[57] When
Sister Thorn became active in promoting the Sacred Heart through her
badges, the cult had already achieved favor throughout the Catholic world,
but it was still closely associated with atonement. Sister Thorn identified
strongly with Saint Margaret Mary Alacoque, an association that resulted
from the publication of several English translations of the visionary's life
between 1890 and 1915 and from the connection established between Pelletier (the Good Shepherd foundress) and Alacoque when the canonization
of the two women occurred on the same day in 1920.[58] Certainly, as she faced
criticism and gossip at Peekskill, Margaret Reilly could not have failed to
notice that Saint Margaret Mary had received private messages from Jesus
that helped her endure her enemies in the convent.

But as Catholic history demonstrates, new cults do not always survive,
and only a few have achieved the staying power of the Sacred Heart, which
has benefited in the twentieth century from the canonization of its promoter, the support of the Jesuits, and the populist family "enthronement"
ritual that spread around the world thanks to the traveling "revivals" of
Father Crawley-Boevey. By contrast, in the same era, the alleged stigmatic
Teresa Higginson had failed to establish a devotion to the holy head of Jesus
in Great Britain, apparently because it imitated too closely the cult of the
Holy Face created by her contemporary Thérèse of Lisieux.[59] But even the
Sacred Heart had not succeeded in gaining the approval of the church at first.
Instead, it foundered before taking root through the persistence of a nun—a
detail overlooked in most theological deliberations, but perhaps one that
was inspirational to Sister Thorn and to the Good Shepherd congregation
in their promotion of the Sacred Heart through its ever-present symbol.

Historians of Europe have noted the rise and success of the cult of the
Sacred Heart of Jesus, especially in Counter-Reformation France and during
the Second Empire and Third Republic, where it rallied royalists dedicated
to the restoration of the monarchy against republican forces.[60] Margaret
Reilly did not set out to become a messenger of the Sacred Heart in any political vein, but she nonetheless helped spread its cult in America. By sewing
and distributing Sacred Heart badges from the Peekskill convent, Margaret
was doing more than occupying herself with embroidery: she was continuing a historical tradition of convent-based hand production, participating in
a spiritual economy of gift exchange, patronizing the Sacred Heart cult, and

affirming Catholic beliefs in sacramentals and the thaumaturgical power of blessed objects. From one perspective, Sister Thorn's improvisations came toward the end of the growth spurt for the Sacred Heart cult. She was help- ing to intensify the cult in the United States after the First World War, drawing connections to its European origins, to the "martyrdom" of the soldiers, and to the origins of her own religious order in France.[61]

The holy cards, embroidered badges, medals, relics, and rosaries that were significant in the life of Sister Thorn testify to the importance of objects in Catholicism and to the rich interactions among Catholics inside and outside religious communities. Some of the commonplace objects that were made in convents and given as gifts among sisters and to the outside world included greeting cards, holy cards, rosaries, needlework, tapestries, and even dolls. By choosing these as gifts, the sisters contributed to the communal whole of their faith by honoring them as signs of mutual obligation and affection. When these items passed from the enclosed world of the convent to public spaces and then again to the private spaces of family homes, they fulfill folk- lorist Kay Turner's insight that in many cultures, women are responsible for building relationships with institutions and between people.[62]

The back-and-forth transfer of practices honoring the saints between parish, home, and convent suggests that devotional culture has a circular flow. Catholics did not merely perform devotions like automatons; they also improvised, innovated, and made something of them to suit themselves and passed them on to others. The Reillys, like many Catholic families, maintained a home altar in an empty bedroom—a perfect embodiment of their seamless understanding of the parish as home and the family home as a church.[63] For Catholics living in crowded conditions who found it hard to dedicate domestic space for an altar, rosaries, printed images of a cru- cifix, or pocket-sized prayer cards became inexpensive substitutes. In the expanding cities of the industrializing United States, the portability of devotional objects like the Sacred Heart badge served Catholic immigrant and postimmigrant populations well, making it possible to make connec- tions with Jesus, Mary, and the saints even in the middle of a workday, in a store, or on a streetcar or train. The reduced size of the objects originated centuries earlier in the historical conflict between clerical and lay interests. Ordained clergy perceived their vocations as superior to those of the laity, who were commonly enjoined to take up pious practices that imitated the rituals of monastic or religious life. Herbert Thurston commented insight- fully how this process led to the miniaturization of many monastic rituals for ordinary persons. In his study of the Benediction ritual, for example, Thurston suggested: "Just as the Rosary was a miniature Psalter (with 150

Hail Marys instead of 150 psalms), just as the scapular was a miniature religious habit, just as the Stations of the Cross were a miniature pilgrimage to the Holy Land, just as the morning and evening *Angelus* are probably a curtailment of the *Tres Preces*, the morning and night prayers of the monks; so the *Salve* which has by degrees developed into the *Salut* and Benediction of the Blessed Sacrament, was originally a lay imitation of the most popular feature in the monastic Office."[64]

In this passage, Thurston touches upon a now-familiar theory of popular Catholicism as a form of lay engagement with its "Great Tradition" (to use anthropologist Robert Redfield's term) in ways that produce so-called little traditions. In historical writing about popular piety, credit was given to the elites as the source of religious activity, whereas today's theorizers more commonly understand the process as involving laypersons confronting theological or doctrinal issues and improvising or elaborating them on their own terms, or as part of a shared clerico-popular culture. As a priest, Thurston claimed that through the act of miniaturizing, ordinary Christians captured the elite dimensions of their faith in texts and objects that are reductions of longer or larger originary practices. But the miniaturized symbols used by ordinary Catholics (badges, holy cards, rosaries, scapulars) have also proved to be highly adaptable to the lives of laypersons and to new technologies. In the age of the automobile, the dashboard saint served the needs of creative popular piety, as does my plastic Sacred Heart iPod cover today.

Nicknaming is a verbal form of miniaturizing, and it also played a role in Margaret's life. Before entering the convent, she received the nickname of "Thorn" from Jesus. During her religious life, despite her advanced age as a postulant, Sister Thorn was called "Little Sister" by the nuns and priests who knew her. Brother Lukas called her the "Little Friend of the Master." Among other holy prodigies of Margaret's generation, the pattern of affectionate miniaturization prevailed. In New England, Rose Ferron became "Little Rose." In Portugal, Alexandrina da Costa became the "Little Saint of Balthasar." In Ireland, Nellie Organ became known as "Little Nellie of Holy God" or "Little Violet of the Blessed Sacrament."[65] Marie-Thérèse Noblet, a French missionary-stigmatic in New Guinea, became "Little Mother of the Papuans." These diminutives imagine sacred figures as innocent, trusting, and childlike; they are terms a parent might use. The gendered dimension of this process, however, risks marginalizing girls and women by diminishing them, just as female mystics and visionaries were often rejected by bishops and clergy for professing "simple" or "little" or even fantasized forms of piety. The new exception to the rule was Thérèse Martin of Lisieux, the "Little Flower of Jesus." The success of her "little way" of piety constitutes the beginning of a countertrend toward democratization of sanctity in the twentieth-century church and a turning point in Catholicism leading to an increase in the canonization of women. Prior to the twentieth century, less than 19 percent of the total Catholic saints were female.

Sister Thorn's piety, as it unfolded, was not an instance of the "little way," however. Indeed, in contrast to Thérèse's contribution to spiritual life, Sister Thorn's path remained utterly conventional in devotional culture. Margaret was not an innovator with respect to her interest in excessive fasting and penances, her desire to humiliate herself, and her desire to safeguard religious vocations. Even her task of reforming religious life had already been assigned by Jesus to scores of European female mystic-saints, including those whom Margaret emulated: Colette of Corbie, Catherine of Siena, and Margaret Mary Alacoque of Paray-le-Monial. "Thorn," Jesus said, "you are to bring back your illustrious Order to its ancient rigor. I have given you the spirit of wisdom and filled you with understanding. I command you, make use of it. You will face constant opposition. By penance and prayer you will draw My blessing upon the Church and your Community." The formality and generic quality of this language suggests that the anecdote itself may have been fabricated by Lukas Etlin, who wrote the narrative of Margaret's life in which these words appear. Her "little talks with Jesus" conclude conveniently with the Lord's prediction on August 25, 1921: "Jesus tells me I am to go to the Convent of the Good Shepherd at Peekskill to make a retreat beginning September 1, 1921."[66]

Margaret's embroidered badges miniaturized the rites and public activities surrounding loyalty to the Sacred Heart and represented a gift economy inside Catholicism rather than dedication to a capitalist ethos. Gifts of holy objects between Catholics linked Margaret Reilly and her convent family to local, national, and even international audiences of persons whom she had never met but who sought divine favors through her. In defiance of the encroaching impersonal capitalist relations that defined modern American society, Margaret's badges channeled a spiritual force not subject to quantification or marketing: they became sacred articles in their own right because they transmitted healing powers from Jesus and Mary. Margaret's gift giving and gift reception defined a "holy economy" that ran counter to American consumerism and produced rewards that were mostly intangible. Devotional practices, therefore, are not antimodern solely because they concern the presence of supernatural beings, but also because they highlighted a countercultural tendency in Catholicism to reject competition and profit.[67] During Margaret's badge episodes, however, the opposite intention was surfacing. American Catholics were beginning to perceive the economic potential behind religious retailing, even in monetary exchanges at these very local levels. Lay Catholics purchased items from monasteries and convents to help sustain them as nonmaterialist islands within a capitalist ocean, but soon these transactions would give way to a nationalized marketing of religious goods, sometimes sponsored by those very monastic communities. The gift economy, too, would be pressured to yield to a profit-driven model, even if for the survival of monasticism.

At Mount St. Florence, Sister Thorn gave gifts, but she also received them. The most astonishing and valuable object to enter the convent on account of her was a crucifix sent by Father Lukas Etlin for Christmas in 1922. It was a carved wood reliquary cross containing the relics of fourteen saints and a piece of the True Cross, with authenticating papers. A carved image of Mary as the Sorrowful Mother appeared underneath the cross, with ivory caps decorating the ends of the cross. Margaret "always felt that this treasure came to her as a reward for her blind obedience," and she used it as "her shield from the attacks of the evil spirit."[68] When the crucifix arrived at Peekskill, Margaret raised herself from her chair to a standing position by supporting herself on a table "and cried." With her face "all inflamed," she kissed the cross; two other sisters who entered the room did likewise.[69] Sister Carmelita declared that Etlin's present "brought a close union between Thorn and the saintly priest," as well as between herself and Margaret.[70]

Father Bradley regarded being in the presence of Etlin's crucifix so gratifying that he refused payment for his spiritual retreats at Peekskill. But he did help out his fellow Benedictines by purchasing religious pamphlets from the Clyde printery to dispense, in this case 100 copies of *Enthronement of the Sacred Heart*.[71] He also ordered Lukas Etlin's pamphlet on Saint Gertrude the Great for the Good Shepherd convent, to be sent directly to Margaret for her to distribute. Bradley did not miss the opportunity to point out the connection between the lives of Gertrude and Margaret: "All you read in the lives of the saints about the attacks of the devil, one can see here."[72]

When the Vatican confers a precious relic on a mystic or visionary, the gesture is often interpreted as marking papal approval of a controversial case, such as that of Therese Neumann, who received a first-class relic of Francis of Assisi from Pius XI in 1938 and a bit of the True Cross from Pius XII in 1955. Because the latter gift came shortly after the publication of the first scholarly book attempting to debunk her case, Neumann's devotees interpreted the papal offering as a sign of Vatican endorsement for the Konnersreuth cult. Etlin's presentation to Sister Thorn was seen in the same light.

In Sister Thorn's milieu, Catholics exchanged saints' cards, holiday cards, and handmade devotional items for many reasons and occasions: in thanks for donations to the church, in recognition of prayers offered, as devotional objects in themselves, as didactic tools, as rewards at school, as relics at funerals, and as objects charged with miraculous healing power. Since semicloistered sisters like Sister Thorn were largely invisible to the public during their adult lives, the act of exchanging such items allowed them to be remembered by their families and friends.[73] In 1924 Margaret sent a Christmas card to Sister Carmelita, for example, with the message: "Let us meet each other at the Crib Christmas Morning. . . . To the Little Dove of Jesus. Jesus has looked graciously on your Soul. He has loved you with a love of predilection because He saw in your heart the wish to be perfect. From your sister In Jesus Heart, Sr. Mary C of Thorns." The fact that Margaret's relatives have saved decades of holiday cards that she sent to them, often inscribed with only one line in her own hand, testifies to the importance of memories of shared holidays even when she could not be physically present.

Given the predominantly Irish American demographics of Good Shepherd congregations at this time, most Catholic families had daughters, sisters, or aunts in religious orders, making nuns and sisters familiar if not always accessible figures in Catholic life. Because nuns had to forsake all personal property and income when they entered religious life, the practice of giving and receiving religious tokens not only mediated between the cloister and the outside world but also served an important exchange function between the sisters themselves. Holy objects were among the few items that could flow in and out of convents without condemnation or question, for they did not threaten the solemn vows of chastity, poverty, or obedience.

Like most religious orders, the Good Shepherds performed the service of providing holy cards and spiritual "bouquets" to anyone who offered them a donation in exchange for prayers for an ill relative or suffering friend, or in thanksgiving for answered prayers. This form of spiritual "trade" continues to the present day and provides convents and monasteries with a regular (although not necessarily large) source of income. As noted, the Peekskill convent established its card-printing industry at a propitious moment when national Catholic publishing houses were forming. The Benedictines established a market presence even more quickly. In Missouri, the press at the Conception Abbey of Brother Lukas and Sister Carmelita went on to become a significant distributor of Catholic liturgical and religious objects in the twentieth century, akin to the Abbey Press of St. Meinrad Archabbey, Indiana, which had established its printing division in 1867, and the Liturgical Press of Collegeville, Minnesota, founded by the monks in 1926. All three printing houses stemmed from Benedictine foundations, which had established close ties to the Good Shepherd sisterhoods and to clergy in

New York. Cardinal Francis McIntyre of Los Angeles, for example, while teaching at St. Joseph Seminary in Yonkers as a young priest, recalled ordering booklets from Clyde for the book racks of local parishes in New York. Before long, American Catholic publishing became successful enough to support more specialized presses, such as the Leaflet Missal publishing company, which appeared in St. Paul in 1929 and soon established the *Catholic Digest* to reprint items culled from a range of Catholic journals. By the 1950s, the printing vocation of the Benedictine sisters at Clyde was invited to open a foundation in Rome to print English translations of church documents. The sisters were told, "If there is anything we need in Rome it is an extension of the Vatican polyglot press which will print English for us. We have to wait months and a year before getting anything printed in presentable English over here."[74] In the printing business, American Catholicism was coming into its own between 1920 and 1950, establishing its contribution to transnational Catholicism by pouring its efforts into serving the Vatican's needs for English-language publications and translations.

On a humbler scale, the Peekskill sisters exchanged holy cards and greeting cards among themselves to commemorate holidays and milestones in convent life. Even in this "academy of strict correction," decorative cards, paper cutouts, prints of crucifixes and saints, and the Sacred Heart made of paper, cloth, and thread gave vent to the sisters' creativity and feelings. Despite the admonitions against forming "special" relationships, each sister had her intimates. These small trinkets were signs of affection that drew upon a shared sacred sensibility and iconography. Among the only gifts permissible for Thorn and the sisters to share were handicrafts, since they had renounced and lacked personal incomes and the possibility of "going shopping." Still, the strict separation of the vowed sisters from the world of capitalist profit was blurred by several factors, notably the presence of the "outside" sisters arrayed in sturdy black habits and veils, whose task it was to purchase food and supplies for the convent. Similarly, the convent sale of holy cards joined them to a capitalist marketplace, as seen in the rapidly expanding demand for Catholic religious goods that would soon prove to be quite profitable for religious orders and secular entrepreneurs.

Devotional Catholics believe that objects have consequences. This final segment of the chapter considers how Sister Thorn, through her Sacred Heart badges (which traveled where she could not), built emotional and spiritual connections to lay and religious persons outside her religious community and effected changes in their lives. When her badges were put to use by their recipients for everyday needs, they were credited almost instantly with thaumaturgic power. A healing cult developed around the badges in circulation, supplemented by tales of the supernatural gifts that Margaret possessed. The archdiocesan offices and the Peekskill convent were deluged with mail requests for the blessed badges; other visitors fortunate enough to secure permission to visit Sister Thorn in person received them directly from her.

Cornelius S. Donegan was convinced that Margaret's badges cured illness, as he reported in a letter from Oyster Bay, Long Island, in 1950. In three incidents, Sister Thorn's badges had been victorious over an ailment: his own daughter had recovered from a mastoid operation through use of a badge from Thorn; a Dominican friar's eye was cured by application of a badge; and a neighbor was restored to perfect health since receiving a Sacred Heart badge. Donegan prayed daily for those in religious life, as Thorn had requested in answer to Jesus's frequent admonitions to her to help "battle with the worldly spirit in religious communities."[75] Years later, based upon his experience of witnessing these miraculous events, Donegan enthusiastically supported Sister Thorn's candidacy for sainthood.

Margaret's badges benefited strangers and her closest friends alike. When Dr. McParlan learned that Brother Lukas had fallen ill, he hoped that "he is wearing a Sacred Heart Badge from 'Little Thorn.'" The physician had already witnessed its healing effects firsthand: "I put one on a case in Hospital that was operated on and they had found Gangrene of appendix and large patches of it in intestines. General peritonitis and a large abscess. All there said there was no hope; that occurred 10 days ago. Today she is almost out of danger with intestines working naturally and all signs pointing to recovery and health."[76] McParlan learned of yet another miracle attributed to Thorn: a deaf patient was cured by placing a badge over her ear for nine days while making a novena to the Sacred Heart.[77]

From her midtown mansion, Lady Margaret Armstrong wrote to Archbishop Hayes with news of another miracle wrought by the badges: "Today I have to thank God for another 'coming back' thro [sic] a Peekskill badge—a man who has been five years away—he went to Holy Communion—and a grateful wife rang me up to tell me—I pass on this good news to you."[78] As she socialized with the upper-crust Ladies of Charity of Manhattan, Armstrong's pet project of these years was to convince affluent Catholics like the Vanderbilts to return to the sacraments, although, as she confided to Hayes, Mrs. Vanderbilt had not participated for twenty years. Determined to hook her fish or die trying, she even asked Archbishop Hayes on one occasion: "I am to have a major operation, and . . . if Our Lord should call me, will you look after Mrs. Vanderbilt?"[79]

Besides confirming Sister Thorn as a thaumaturge and a shepherd of lost souls, the Sacred Heart badges worked to credit her with saintly abilities, such as bilocation. A woman with appendicitis who received a badge from McParlan reported seeing Sister Thorn in a wheelchair at the foot of her bed, although the woman previously had never seen or met her. Sister Thorn advised her to "put the Sacred Heart badge on the pain." The woman recognized Thorn as the figure in her vision when McParlan brought her to Peekskill to visit at a later date.[80] In another anecdote, Thorn appeared to the Peekskill convent's attending physician, who occasionally drank too much. He felt three thumps on the back of his head and heard a voice say, "Sister Mary of the Crown of Thorns." It inspired him to "take the pledge" and stop drinking altogether. Nearly a half century after Sister Thorn's death, the badges continued to be valued gifts, moving around the United States through personal and family connections; they were never bought or sold. Sister Carmelita Quinn, for example, reported: "I gave the white one to Mrs. Louis Jeager in S. Louis in 1983 for her daughter Mary's use."

Sister Thorn's badges appeared in the religious landscape as the Sacred Heart devotion was growing dramatically. The First World War had only increased Catholic dedication to the comforting image of the tender heart of Jesus reigning over the world. In the postwar decade, Sister Thorn's Sacred Heart badges helped this popular devotion to flourish even more widely in the United States. Her badges demonstrate the continuity of European and American forms of vernacular religion and the flexibility of the cult, shorn of its French reactionary political overtones and nationalist crusade. When Archbishop Hayes put a stop to the production of Sacred Heart badges at Peekskill, his goal was not to inhibit a popular devotion but to gain control of a spiritual *virtuoso*. Sister Thorn's badges—like scapulars, holy cards, medals, and rosaries—challenge the belief that only the ordained may function as guardians of a religion's dominant images. From the perspective of her supporters, Thorn's authority came from her extraordinary spiritual graces and visions from Jesus, Mary, and the saints that others regarded as true. Following Max Weber, who first discussed charismatic domination as a form of power, sociologists have agreed that although the virtuoso gains an audience for seeming to possess exceptional abilities or qualities, she also presents a source of potential strife and disruption for the religious community by deriving authority from beyond the church and by claiming a parallel form of legitimation coming directly from God.[81] These debates engulfed Sister Thorn, whose spiritual revelations came from above for those who did not question their validity—but were possibly diabolical in the eyes of church officials, the official guardians of divine will.

If Marian visionaries generated what has been called "an apparitional script" in European Catholicism, surely a related "stigmatic script" spread during the same era through the same combined efforts of print culture (devotional literature about the Passion of Christ, allied devotions such as the Sacred Heart, narratives of the saints' lives, manuals for children, and sermons); visual culture (holy cards, greeting cards, paintings, statues, stained glass, and chromolithographs); the religious orders; and oral culture. By blanketing the world with holy objects—carried in the pockets of believers and displayed in their homes, schools, and hospital rooms—the church's stigmatic script disclosed a series of power/knowledge relations at work that pit the church and its theology against secular or scientific knowledge; established a contest between male, ecclesiastical, rational knowledge and independent female mystical experience; and exposed the mind-body dualism that has been a constant tension in Western Christianity. In these conflicts, devotional objects helped Catholics to narrow the gap between institution and individual and to imagine a universal frame for their actions that could be activated at any time, without the presence or sanction of clergy.

Among the many popular devotions of Sister Thorn's era—Benediction, Holy Hours, fasting and abstinence, novenas, missions, First Fridays, First Saturdays, the Rosary, and the Stations of the Cross—the Passion suffused them all. Through her own body, Sister Thorn manifested a kind of passionate agency that derived meaning from pain, although her experience was unlikely to create a fad for stigmatization. In the nineteenth century, American Protestants had successfully turned the Bible into an American symbol, yet because Catholics were as yet unable to do likewise with their rituals, they were forced to redefine "their devotional life as a 'family matter,' relocating it within the private sphere."[82] Sister Thorn's generation, however, represented the subsequent stage in devotional history by forming a bridge between the immigrants' "isolation from the dominant culture" and the growing strength of Catholic symbols as they were projected into the public sphere in the 1930s. Intimations of the passage to a more confident public Catholicism began to appear in Thorn's lifetime, derived in part from the power of devotionalism, including the Sacred Heart cult, that underwrote and energized these possibilities. While the formal qualities of the images involved in Sister Thorn's badges were not remarkable, and their relationship to more robust Baroque artistic traditions was rather diminished, the sentiments and resonances underlying them aspired to restore the lost potency of the symbol of Jesus's injured heart and to tie it to shifting Eucharistic piety as well. In Sister Thorn's badges, we can also see the overlap between immigrant and assimilating Catholics in the transfer and transport of holy objects that crossed freely among convent and home, convent and monastery, home and parish, convent and hospital, and home and school.

{6} It Is Beautiful to Live with Saints

The Americanization of Modern Sanctity

Our Lord is going to have an Irish American saint!

—Words attributed to Archbishop Patrick Hayes by Lukas Etlin
in a letter, 1923

One is never a saint except *for other people.*

—Pierre DeLooz, "Toward a Sociological Study of Canonized
Sainthood in the Catholic Church," in *Saints and Their Cults: Studies
in Religious Sociology, Folklore, and History*, edited by Stephen Wilson
(New York: Cambridge University Press, 1987), 194

It is beautiful to live with saints.

—Lukas Etlin to Carmelita Quinn, December 1927

Pious custom dictates that twelve stigmatics are alive at any one time in the world
in repetition of the number of Christ's apostles. Even if this tradition is suspect,
it emboldened the supporters of Margaret Reilly to make connections between
her and other spiritual *virtuosi* throughout "Christendom," a concept that the
church keenly hoped to revive in the wake of the First World War. From an
institutional perspective, stigmatic cults were helpful in affirming divine presence in support of the church's larger concern to reenchant the modern world
and to affirm the benevolent mastery of God and the redemptive sacrifice of his
son, even in the wake of the barbarism of 1914–18. This chapter considers how a
Catholic community that was already convinced of Sister Thorn's charisma was
preparing her as a potential saint by establishing her virtues and associating her
with a network of similarly extraordinary holy individuals. The chapter makes
a shift in perspective from Sister Thorn's personal experiences to her *audience*
by exploring how her advocates circulated stories and anecdotes about her. A
second goal of the chapter, one related to the theme of audience, is to argue
that within the Archdiocese of New York, the budding cult of Sister Thorn
created a "mini-Christendom" that reflected the values and beliefs propagated
from Rome—the institutional and moral center of the Catholic Church—but

in an American context.[1] Third, the chapter locates Sister Thorn in relation to the saint-making process as it existed prior to its revisions in 1969 and 1983. It remained to be seen what kind of saint Americans were seeking in the decades after her death—an ethnic symbol or a national one. Finally, I suggest that stigmatic cults continue to evolve in the post–Vatican II era, enabled by new communications technologies like the Internet that have altered the ways in which audiences encounter stigmatic and visionary cults.

Sister Thorn's followers hoped to provide the convincing background for a Vatican investigation for canonization. For a holy person's cult to succeed, however, the local bishop must first permit it. Sister Thorn's cult never received the unqualified support of Archbishop Hayes and therefore did not secure an official diocesan investigation. If an investigation had materialized, the mechanisms for opening canonization proceedings at that time followed a three-stage process. First, to establish Margaret as a Servant of God, the local investigation would be petitioned by the archbishop no sooner than five years after Margaret's death. (This waiting period may be waived or decreased by the pope, as Benedict XVI did in the case of the proceedings for his predecessor, John Paul II, and for Mother Teresa of Calcutta). If approved, the petition opened a Cause for Beatification and Canonization. The Vatican would assign a so-called Devil's Advocate whose task was to gather and present the case against canonization. (This position was eliminated in 1983.) Second, witnesses would attest to Margaret's heroic Christian virtues before a diocesan tribunal, and any written documents by and about her would be collected and read. Third, members of the general public would be invited to add information about the candidate. If the investigation result was positive, the local bishop presented the cause as a bound volume of documentation (*Acta*) to the Vatican's Congregation of the Causes of Saints, which assigned a postulator to the investigation.

Members of the American Catholic hierarchy who knew about Margaret Reilly and who helped to foster her cause included Cardinal Dennis Dougherty of Philadelphia, already an ardent promoter of the Little Flower cult in America; and Cardinal James McIntyre of Los Angeles (1886–1979), who was advantageous to Margaret's circle because of his local roots. Born in New York City, McIntyre was ordained by Patrick Hayes in 1921 and performed pastoral work in New York until 1923. He served as diocesan chancellor from 1923 to 1934 and became the auxiliary bishop of New York in 1940. Later, as the ultraconservative archbishop of Los Angeles (1948–70), he refused to implement the new Mass after Vatican II, embroiled himself in a power struggle with local nuns, and established himself as an enemy of feminism, communism, and labor unions.[2] His papers, however, contain no information on his contributions to Sister Thorn's dossier.

As in previous centuries, the success of local cults like Sister Thorn's depended upon the actions of her intimates and followers, the leadership of Catholic elites, perhaps a powerful patron, and the testimonies of an audience who believed in her.[3] This audience was built, as earlier chapters have shown, by reciprocal connections between priests and laity. Consider Father Bertrand Barry's dramatic tribute when he met Margaret: "Until something to discredit all I have seen and heard will come I will hold as being permitted to have spoken to a saint."[4] As his words imply, Sister Thorn matched an idea of sanctity that he already possessed. Indeed, his chain letter helped identify Margaret as a charismatic figure and spread news of her beyond Peekskill. Mystics are not canonized frequently, but since the Middle Ages, they had inspired local devotion as vernacular saints even if the church did not acknowledge them as such. After 1588, popular acclaim became devalued, however, as the Catholic Church formalized its canonization procedures by establishing the Congregation of Rites as the overseer. Henceforth in selecting candidates for sainthood, the church relied less upon popular acclaim and more upon religious and political elites, including "religious orders, municipalities, regional authorities, and the monarchy itself."[5] Since 1634, Vatican involvement in canonization proceedings has been required. Subsequent changes to the canonization process made in 1969 by Pope Paul VI and in 1983 by Pope John Paul II ultimately simplified the process and changed the name of the Vatican department in charge of saint making to the Congregation for the Causes of Saints. These actions further diminished the value of vernacular devotion and reduced the number of miracles required. (One miracle is now necessary for beatification and another for canonization.)

In Margaret's era, it was essential to establish her extraordinary virtue as attested by others. In this process, "sainthood therefore depends on a community's recollection of a dead person's past existence."[6] Margaret's religious community dutifully began to follow this template: her experiences were transcribed during her lifetime by several scribes at the behest of the archbishop and the superior of the Good Shepherds. Their commentaries were eventually molded into preliminary narratives of her life, which were further redacted to eliminate unorthodox elements, as well as to conform to an extant tradition of female stigmatics.

Sister Thorn's case became an accurate reflection of how women mystics undertook to become modern Catholic saints but rarely succeeded. Margaret satisfied some categories of sanctity by securing popular support and the report of at least one miracle after her death. In other categories, she fell short: healings during her lifetime did not count, she left no insightful spiritual autobiography, and she was not martyred. Her virtue was extolled by her advocates, but perhaps it was not exceptional enough. Soon after her death, new instances of her heroic virtue began to surface, as individuals began to form organized groups to petition for her cause to go forward. A prayer card was produced. Popular pressure began to build, both among the Good Shepherd sisters and the Benedictines and in the lay Catholic communities of New York and New Jersey. The Good Shepherds collected anecdotal information about Margaret's power as an intercessor who worked cures through her blessed Sacred Heart badges, which in the end did not match revised Vatican requirements for sainthood. In addition, demonstrations of her piety were duly compiled. From her death until at least the 1970s, Sister Thorn was being transformed from an individual wonder-worker into a hero for a community of the faithful.

Margaret's followers sought additional ways to gain wider approbation for her cause by linking her to other mystical women already revered by the church. Confident that they would soon have miracles as proof of her extraordinary holiness, devotees pointed to biographical commonalities between stigmatics and the saints (discussed in chapter 3), between Margaret and other stigmatics (discussed below), and between spiritual events in her life and sacred feast days of Christ's Passion. Contemporary stigmatics received the same treatment. Biographers of Therese Neumann never fail to mention, for instance, that her blindness disappeared on the day of the beatification of her namesake, Thérèse of Lisieux, and that her paralysis ended on the day of the Little Flower's canonization.[7] Louise Lateau's cholera was cured by making a novena to Our Lady of La Salette, a Marian apparition that was reaching an expanding cult in France and Belgium at that time. These stories of healing through the intercession of the saints were intended to authenticate the stigmatized women who sought their aid and to remind all Christians of their belief in the efficacy of prayer to the saints.

At the same time that the devout (on the periphery) looked for connections to impress church officials with their aspirants to sainthood, the church (at the center) found its own uses for vernacular piety. Because stigmatics represented the body of Christ and were closely tied to the sacrificial discourse of the Eucharist and of the reparation of sins, modern stigmatizations helped the church to redress the perceived imbalance in devotions that had favored Mary in the nineteenth century.[8] Marian traditions were nearly always sustained by lay folk as localized cults, but during the nineteenth century, the church had found it beneficial to vigorously promote Marian apparitions in protest of the social, economic, and political changes associated with "liberalism." Beginning around 1850, a pronounced emphasis upon the Sacred Heart of Jesus, sponsored by particular religious orders of men, began to compete with this politicized Marianism. Stigmatic cults served a similar function in focusing the attention of the faithful upon the body and sacrifice of Jesus Christ. Yet Marian phenomena did not disappear, even from stigmatic events, which often included them. The Virgin Mother frequently appeared to Margaret Reilly, for example, saying: "Thorn behold my Son."[9] In March 1923, Mary came at night "and let Margaret kiss her pure and sacred womb." The Virgin also comforted Margaret's fears about assaults from demons against her "holy purity."[10] Margaret's cult hoped to benefit from a strategy of accumulating as many supernatural advocates as possible, a practice pursued also by Marianists in the twentieth century.[11] From the church's standpoint, however, elements of local cults could be instrumental in enforcing orthodoxy. For this reason, stigmatic cults were often harnessed to affirm the Real Presence in the Eucharist as a rebuttal to Protestants and materialist philosophies. Just as the artistic avant-garde made its own uses of mystical Catholicism in modernity, so the church had its reasons for investing in popular devotions.

Only informal measures of gathering information about Margaret Reilly occurred, however, conducted in a preparatory way by the Good Shepherd congregation. Sister Clare Nolan compiled a list of eyewitnesses to Sister Thorn in the 1970s and held follow-up interviews with some of those individuals who were still living. The Good Shepherd archives that I saw did not document its internal discussions about promoting Sister Thorn, but its decision not to proceed suggests a lack of unanimity or enthusiasm for funding a canonization investigation. In Catholic circles, however, many stories continued to circulate about Sister Thorn, attesting to her miraculous wounds, combat with demons, and locutions from Jesus and the saints. Recipients of her Sacred Heart badges added their poignant healing testimonies as well. Yet within thirty years of Sister Thorn's death, the contingent details of her life had already been "smoothed" to fit a traditional narrative associated with stigmatics and visionaries. This process, which Paolo Apolito calls "the conventionalization of images," involves repressing the singular details of unusual events in order to replace them with items that supported official dogma, such as the centrality of the Eucharist in Christian tradition.[12] Ambrose Bierce's succinct definition of "saint" for his *Devil's Dictionary* seems quite apt: "A dead sinner revised and edited." Through such editing, conventionalization naturalized theological tradition and allayed the fears of church leaders about the potential embarrassment of endorsing a false mystic.

By the late 1960s, it became less likely that Margaret Reilly would become Saint Margaret of Peekskill, not only because of doubts among her congregation and lack of funds but also because the Catholic Church's standards for sainthood had shifted shortly after her death to focus less upon mystical marvels than upon choosing persons who epitomized virtuous living. (That the church had not lost interest in martyrs—that other path to sainthood—was exemplified by Dr. Tom Dooley, whose life during the 1950s was calculated to represent a "martyrdom in process."[13])

As Kenneth Woodward points out in his history of canonization, "the emphasis on spiritual uniqueness is very recent." For centuries, copying acceptable models of sanctity was the norm for saints, based on standards set by Pope Urban VII in 1642 that downplayed the saint as wonder-worker and replaced her with the "saint as moral exemplar." "To become a saint, therefore, was to imitate an acknowledged model of holiness. And to be declared a saint was to be recognized as such according to one of the acceptable patterns."[14] In this framework, Margaret's supporters needed to concentrate less upon the novelty of her bleeding wounds and demonic assaults than upon proving her heroic virtue, a shift that increasingly took the power of the popular fables of charisms and healing from the hands of ordinary folk and vested it in the Vatican's procedures for collecting the evidence of eyewitnesses. The pathway to sainthood began to rely less upon consensus and more upon judicial determinations about testimony.

But for reasons we have already explored, miracle workers and mystical women had been experiencing a surge in numbers during Margaret's lifetime, whether as a continuation of a tendency allied to romanticism in the mid-nineteenth century (evidenced by Anne Catherine Emmerich and Louise Lateau) or as a consequence of anxieties related to the political and economic crises of the early twentieth century (represented by Therese Neumann). Stigmatized women, with their related mystical gifts and powers of patronage, answered a popular craving for extraordinary beings and happenings beyond merely fulfilling the sober requirements of "static categories of the required virtues."[15] Precisely at the moment when the church was altering the standards for sainthood, Sister Thorn's potential candidacy revealed the tensions between the norms of the church, which judged her fitness by her virtues, and the *vox populi*, which celebrated the marvels in the candidate's life, even in an America that had not yet generated many such traditions.

In certain ways, the emerging circle of supporters around Sister Thorn demonstrates features of center-periphery theory, a model of spatial relations in which the distance from some cultural/economic/political center becomes significant, constituting a hierarchical relation in which the center exerts power over its periphery. This model, derived from the sociology of Edward Shils, had an impact upon economic thinking for world-system and dependency models in the 1970s and 1980s. Applying this concept to the highly centralized Catholic Church, Catholic peripheries around the globe should be loyal to and attempt to imitate Rome, acknowledging their subordinate position to the center. From the perspective of actual religious exchange, however, it may be more accurate to embrace a revised version of that model, such as the one proposed by Peter Brown in his study of the diffusion of Christianity in regions of the world in the first millennium. Brown suggests that the local variations on Roman Christianity generated many "micro-Christendoms."[16] In this light, Sister Thorn's story has at least two centers and one periphery: Rome and the Archdiocese of New York are its mini-Christendoms, while Peekskill lies on the outskirts. New York City, as the most populous Catholic center in the United States, helped the American church to overcome the nation's designation as a "mission" territory (retained by the Vatican as recently as 1908) and was building its own entire infrastructure and a top-down bureaucracy that emulated the power exerted by the Vatican. Peekskill (and its ally in rural Clyde, Missouri), lying on the periphery geographically and demographically, had nevertheless adapted the concepts promoted at both institutional centers of the Catholic faith, and the convent there served as a cultural subsystem inside the church that generated conflict when Sister Thorn's stigmatization fostered the unpredictable results that characterize localized religion.

Another factor in Sister Thorn's progress toward sainthood was the issue of the national character of Catholicism in the United States. She was first being considered for canonization in the 1940s at a moment when ethnically based cults were competing against candidates with universal appeal. The heretofore indistinct figure of Saint Jude who emerged during the Great Depression, for instance, offered solace that transcended all ethnic divisions among Catholics.[17] In the first decades of the twentieth century, two American Catholic women who became candidates for sainthood satisfied patriotic longings and helped to build national Catholic pride and identity, but they did not represent the western and southern European immigrant roots of most American Catholics.[18] The recently proposed Elizabeth Seton had British and Anglican colonial roots, whereas Kateri Tekakwitha was a native American whose U.S. citizenship was declared only posthumously. If Margaret's followers projected her to become the first American saint—following on the heels of Seton, whose cause was entered in 1911, and Tekakwitha, declared Venerable in 1943 (and canonized in 2012)—could they present Sister Thorn as more fully representing America?

Although American Catholicism resulted from the coexistence of many immigrant groups in the United States, it lacked the European tradition of village saints; hence Margaret Reilly's advocates would need to demonstrate her value beyond Peekskill and within the urban centers of New York, New Jersey, and Pennsylvania where her devout were located. Peekskill was a village in the American context, but Margaret's cloistered congregation was not permitted to advertise her unusual experiences and, after her death, had tried for some decades to erase her memory. Archbishop Hayes's confident prediction about Margaret that "Our Lord is going to have an Irish American saint!" is a noteworthy, but not necessarily convincing, merging of ethnic and national pride. To this day, no Irish American women have been canonized, nor any Irish American sisters, despite their predominance in religious life in the United States.

Every Catholic stigmatic has been connected in legend and in fact with other cult figures, a tactic that helped elevate local cults to national or global status. The following are examinations of the six individuals who were imaginatively associated with Sister Thorn through anecdote and narrative by her religious congregation and her biographers in order to enhance her credentials. Margaret's cohort included an Irish girl who inspired the pope to lower the Communion age for children, two lay stigmatics, two stigmatized women religious, and a stigmatized monk. This diverse group demonstrates that Sister Thorn, far from being anomalous, reflected a generational pattern and interest in the cult of suffering that affected mostly women but did not exclude children and men. Because the majority of stigmatics have been women (91 percent by Herbert Thurston's calculations), Sister Thorn was part of a group helping the Catholic Church to promote a divine mission for women over any earthly rewards. Aligned with the church's preoccupations after World War I, the suffering of women who experienced Christ's Passion was interpreted as an active force in defeating the forces of Satan. Even when confined to bed from illness and feebleness, as were many stigmatics, they were saving souls. Even as cloistered nuns, they could redeem others as spiritual victims and even suffer for the church itself. The chapter concludes with a discussion of a seventh contemporary stigmatic who illustrates how new communications technologies have changed the phenomenon of cult formation and the relationship between the mystic and her audience.

While a sickly Irish child who died at age four may seem only remotely linked to Margaret Reilly, the convergence of the two figures in vernacular piety and in Good Shepherd legend points toward the role of convents in serving as sponsors of devotions, as they had since the Middle Ages. At the same time, the cult of "Little Nellie of Holy God" anticipated future developments in Catholic theology and ritual by uncovering a surprising eagerness among laity and clergy in the early twentieth century to revise Eucharistic practices.

Ellen Organ (spelled "Horgan" and "Orgen" in some sources) was born in the Artillery Barracks in Waterford, Ireland, in 1903 and died at the Good Shepherd school in Cork in 1908. When Ellen's mother died in 1907 (her father had previously abandoned the family), Ellen and one of her sisters were taken to the Good Shepherd Industrial School at Sunday's Well. Since the girls had whooping cough, they were quarantined in the district hospital for ten weeks. Only afterward did they become wards of the Good Shepherd sisters in Cork, living at the convent. "Nellie," as Ellen was called, also suffered from curvature of the spine, causing her intense pain. She was subsequently diagnosed with tuberculosis, the disease that had killed her mother. To complete this pathetic list of unbearable ailments, Nellie had a tooth abnormally embedded in the root of the tongue that caused her agonizing pain. She started the practice of holding a crucifix in her hand and saying "Poor Holy God!" to ward it off, and when the tooth was finally extracted, the sisters reported, she endured the surgery without complaint.

Nellie was permitted to make her first Communion about eight years earlier than customary, after which the nuns enrolled her in the Children of Mary Sodality, where "her extraordinary devotion to the Blessed Eucharist became every day more marked." A Jesuit who visited Nellie at the Good Shepherd convent was impressed by her understanding of the sacrament: "Jesus comes on my tongue and goes down into my heart," she told him.[19] On February 2, 1908, four-year-old Nellie died and was buried in the public cemetery. Her grave became a local shrine visited by hundreds, and when her body was exhumed one year later, it appeared unchanged from the day of her burial, with her limbs flexible and her dress and Communion veil like new. Her body was transferred to the convent cemetery in 1909, where a plaque now marks the site. The legends that spread quickly about Nellie revolved around three topics: her many joyful Communions in her final months, the "smell of sanctity" that surrounded her death, and the discovery of her incorrupt corpse. Of these, it was the child's Eucharistic fervor that the church singled out in Nellie's cult.

"Little Nellie of Holy God" became known to Americans due to the superior at the Cork Good Shepherd convent, Mother Mary of St. Francis Xavier Hickey.[20] On her mission as Visitor General to the United States from 1920 to 1933, Hickey was obliged to conduct regular visits to RGS convents, where she met Margaret Reilly.[21] Soon the Good Shepherd sisters and Nellie's Irish supporters were claiming that the child's heroic suffering and piety inspired Pope Pius X to issue *Quam singulari* in 1910, the encyclical permitting the reception of first Communion by children earlier than the customary age of eleven or twelve. Stories told by the sisters and accounts of Nellie's exemplary life published by Irish priests attempted to establish these and other events involving the child as miraculous. Nellie was also soon enlisted by the international Eucharistic Congresses to "familiariz[e] the young with those rare souls whom God has raised up in our day to show that youth is no barrier to the fruitful reception of the blessed Manna."[22] Even in her short life, Nellie filled several roles as the pious child, frequent communicant, agonized patient, dying innocent, and apostle of the Eucharist. Yet it was the Catholic cult of suffering that linked Little Nellie, who overcame her physical agony by frequent Communion, to Sister Thorn, the stigmatic who fully represented the agonized body of Christ.

The premature death of a child is always tragic, but child mortality was so high in Ireland during Nellie's lifetime due to the presence of diphtheria, scarlet fever, and tuberculosis that few households were untouched. Within the Victorian tradition of sentimentalizing children's deaths, Nellie's tale was made even more pitiable by her father's abandonment, the family's poverty, and the nuns' charity. In the hagiographic template, following the Gospel stories of the childhood of Jesus that foreshadowed his adult mission, girls like Margaret Reilly and Nellie Organ did not have "normal" childhoods, either, since they had been chosen by God to serve more important ends. Biographers therefore fastened upon tales of young Nellie and Margaret dressing up like nuns and treating their crucifixes like dolls. Furthermore, the Good Shepherds drew connections between Nellie and the "childlikeness," sweetness, and simplicity of Margaret, who was commonly referred to by the nuns and others as "the little one," "dear little Sister," "poor little Sister," and so on. These diminutives function as terms of endearment, but they are also rhetorical devices intended to establish Margaret's naïve innocence. Margaret Reilly's age was consistently underestimated by ten to fifteen years by male visitors to the convent, who continued to refer to her as "little" and "young" even after they learned that she was in her forties.[23]

Finally, Nellie Organ illustrates a variant on the center-periphery dynamic that defines vernacular Catholicism as a continuum between a localized cult that thrives upon lay momentum and a distant institutional authority that demands loyalty to its universalized beliefs and rites. From the margins, Little Nellie's desire for early and frequent Communion was said to convince the pope to overturn the Jansenist attitude of reserving the Eucharist as "a reward, rather than a remedy for human frailty,"[24] anticipating by fifty years the shift in the theology of the Eucharist that accompanied Vatican II.[25] Although sickly, insignificant, and far removed from Rome, Little Nellie, thanks to her Good Shepherd advocates, was credited as the inspiration for a papal decree that expanded the availability of Communion for children, a triumph of the periphery at the center. Her achievement gained wide currency through the intermediaries whose work allowed them to influence the center from the margins, namely, a combination of traditional Catholic elites (bishops, priests, and sisters) and new elites (the journalists and biographers who publicized the life of Nellie in print). The bishop of Cork and the Good Shepherd sisters were careful to highlight elements of "heroic suffering," one of the criteria of sainthood, in Nellie's pain-wracked childhood. Brother Lukas Etlin profiled her for similar purposes in *Tabernacle and Purgatory*, his monthly periodical devoted to the Blessed Sacrament. By such print publicity, derived from the personal anecdotes transmitted within and between convents, Little Nellie gained local and transnational audiences that were later linked to Sister Thorn via the tropes of youthful innocence, heroic suffering, attachment to the Good Shepherds, and a hunger for the Eucharist. Only after World War II did a "bumper crop of Catholic life-writings" appear in print, representing "the culmination of American Catholic confidence"; but as was evidenced by the literature surrounding Little Nellie, the trend was "already evident by the First World War,"[26] aided by the pressure from women's congregations.

Sister Thorn was firmly connected to Little Nellie and to metaphors of childish innocence through the Good Shepherds. Of the following six adults, three were contemporary stigmatics enlisted by Margaret's circle to support her potential sainthood and three were women whose lives had striking similarities to her own, although she never met them. Gemma Galgani, Therese Neumann, and Josefa Menendez represented the former group; Marie Rose Ferron, Padre Pio, and Maria van Beek illustrate local variations in mystical experience across the Catholic world that nonetheless contributed to its transnational currency.

The early twentieth century was a time of broadening roles and character traits for women. Unprecedented examples of female valor, athleticism, and patriotism were epitomized respectively by the international popularity of aviator Amelia Earhart, swimmer Gertrude Ederle (who in 1926 became the first woman to cross the English Channel), and nurse-spy Edith Cavell (who outwitted the Germans in World War I before being executed by them). Sexually liberated women were embodied by two sex symbols from

Brooklyn, Clara Bow and Mae West, who shocked film audiences as flappers and mantraps whose unconventional sexual standards differed strongly from those Catholic women who were being honored for their renunciation of the world. As if seeking to provide countercultural images of womanhood to compete with pilots, athletes, spies, and starlets, the Catholic Church singled out heroic women for Sister Thorn's generation who were remarkable for their extravagant suffering. They included Joan of Arc, canonized in 1920; mystic mothers like Anna Maria Taigi, beatified in 1920; saintly unmarried virgins like Gemma Galgani, Maria Goretti, and Thérèse Martin; and stigmatics such as Therese Neumann and Marthe Robin.

Gemma Galgani (1878–1903) achieved beatification during Margaret's lifetime; thus it is not surprising that Margaret's followers referred to her as "a second Gemma Galgani." Gemma was strongly influenced by her pious mother and a series of confessors in her impoverished family's home near Lucca, Italy. She planned to enter the convent but was refused because of her poor health, just as the Ursulines had twice refused Margaret Reilly. Determined to live by religious vows even without official recognition, Gemma dressed in all black, mortified her flesh by wearing a hair shirt and refusing to wear stockings in the winter, and penned copious spiritual reflections. She was stigmatized in 1898 while living with another family upon the death of her own kin, and she endured terrifying physical assaults from demons. She kept a diary in obedience to her spiritual director and died of tuberculosis at the age of twenty-five. The Passionist order of priests promoted her cause vigorously, and she was canonized in 1940.

Margaret's allies compared her to Saint Gemma for her strenuous suffering and her connection to the cult of the Sacred Heart. Both women embodied the ethos of self-sacrifice at the core of the cult of pain and suffering that suffused Euro-American Catholicism during the heyday of victim spirituality.[27] Because Margaret spent the last fifteen years of her life as an invalid, it was an obvious choice for others to praise her endurance as even greater than that of Galgani. There was a dark underside to the cult of pain, however, for sick persons who failed to use the experience of suffering to achieve saintliness. Catholic devotions could turn against their very patrons by spreading the notion that "if sick people would not subdue their own flesh as St. Gemma did hers, . . . it would be done for them." In contrast to what one might expect from Catholic tradition, at midcentury the sick were expected to be "cheerful, productive, [and] orderly," while the fascination with pain by their observers hid the actual physical experience of pain.[28] This sensibility at times defined the outlook of Sister Thorn's followers, who constantly praised her uncomplaining tolerance of affliction—a trait that connected her with the tradition of the suffering virgin-saint represented by Gemma Galgani—but also did not overlook her genuine illness.

The second connection made between Gemma and Margaret was the cult of the Sacred Heart, whose significance for Margaret has been noted in the previous chapter. It had also provided the energy behind Gemma's successful canonization campaign, which began during the papacy of Leo XIII. A strong advocate of that devotion, Leo believed that she had received visionary messages from its founder, Margaret Mary Alacoque, and was impressed by the endorsement of the Passionist order, whose emblem was the Sacred Heart. While Gemma's affective style of piety is similar to that of Alacoque, there are limits to imagining Reilly as Gemma's successor. First, textual evidence written by Gemma survives, whereas Sister Thorn has only second- and thirdhand gestures at a vita compiled by others. Second, Gemma was an impoverished laywoman who took up religious garb and vows but never gained entrance into a religious order. Sister Thorn achieved membership in a congregation, her troubled path echoing Gemma's life to the extent that she overcame several setbacks and her stigmata polarized her examiners. It was in her perseverance through obstacles where Margaret's followers heard the echoes of Gemma's spiritual journey.

Gemma left a written record through her diary and letters. The presence of personal writings was not always beneficial to a woman's cause, however. Often dismissed as infantile and sentimental, Galgani's diary and letters to her spiritual advisers were ignored in her canonization proceedings because they did not meet churchmen's standards of holiness and theological rigor.[29] Yet a recent scholarly study has taken Gemma's expressions seriously in order to rescue the female mystic from medicine's emphasis on physicality and the church's criterion of rationality. During the lifetimes of Galgani and Reilly, when women mystics were regularly dismissed as hysterics, the medicalization of female mysticism was accepted by both religious and social authorities. Contemporary social theory has shifted interpretations of hysteria from an emphasis on this assumed "essential feminine" to the study of the social construction of femininity. In her analysis of mysticism and hysteria, Cristina Mazzoni rejects hysteria as the sole or primary neurosis of the fin de siècle and shifts the focus once again by finding in it instead an opportunity for posing the problematic of constructing, even more than representing, the feminine.[30]

Considering this approach for Sister Thorn without her own testimony and without adopting her antagonists' hystericizing discourse is not an easy task. The church agreed that it was certainly possible to be a hysteric and also a saint, but opinion about Margaret proved to be divided between Catholics who were unquestioning believers (Thomas McParlan, Lukas Etlin) and those who adopted the medicalization model (James J. Walsh, Herbert Thurston). Sister Thorn's male evaluators, both doctors and clergy alike, continued the nineteenth-century pattern of infantilizing, hystericizing, or sexualizing women, often focusing on details of women's menstrual and reproductive histories as explanations for their strange behaviors. (The rumors of Margaret's abortion, the mistaken supposition that she was menopausal, and the notion that she had used menstrual blood to form the crucifix on her convent wall are just several instances.) In this light, the perception of the alleged mystical experiences of Sister Thorn followed familiar patterns of rejection of "vernacular theology" by the church and its proxies.

Therese Neumann (1898–1962) became the most famous stigmatic of the twentieth century, so it is hardly surprising that Margaret Reilly's followers sought to link her to the Neumann cult, which emerged a few years after Margaret's stigmatization but gained traction much more rapidly. My intention is not to review the complex biography of Neumann and its controversies, but rather to single out elements that disclose the transnational character of stigmatic phenomena in the twentieth century. As with Gemma Galgani's history, some elements of Therese's life corresponded to the church's universal ideals by transcending the differences between geographic locations (or center and periphery), while others expressed distinctive local flavor.

Therese was the eldest of ten children, born in the small Bavarian village of Konnersreuth in the Diocese of Regensburg near the present-day Czech border. She attended public school; in her teens, she was sent out to work at a neighboring farm, where her employer apparently tried to rape her. She also experienced a painful spinal injury while hoisting water buckets during a village fire. This event was followed by an episode of blindness, occasional deafness, and paralysis in both legs and then both cheeks. During these years of constant suffering, she lived at home with her parents. She claimed the miraculous cure of her blindness and an ulcerous foot due to the intercession of the newly canonized Saint Thérèse, whose holy card was brought home by her father from France after the First World War.

Neumann's stigmata appeared in stages in 1926 during Lent, after an abscess in her ear caused violent headaches that generated sleeplessness for a few weeks. Next, during a vision of Jesus in the Garden of Olives, she felt a stinging in the side of her left breast. This sensation was followed by the appearance of wounds in her hands and legs. From this point on, Neumann's dramatic wounds recurred nearly every Friday for the next thirty-six years, often featuring spectacular streams of blood from her eye sockets that flowed down her face and body and reddened her nightdress and bed sheets.

She received numerous mystical gifts, including detailed visions of biblical events and the ability to survive solely upon the Host and water from the onset of her stigmata until her death. Despite her claim of inedia, photographs and physical descriptions of Therese show a sturdy-looking woman who continued to perform farm labor when she was not bedridden. Because of the many prodigies reported at Konnersreuth, the Neumann family was asked to consent to supervised observation of their daughter. Only once, several nuns were permitted to live in the household for two weeks, measuring Therese's weight and excretions to see if they corresponded to food consumption. The results indicated that Therese lost weight then but regained it immediately afterward; therefore, she was most likely eating in secret at night. Attempts to follow up on these observations, however, or to repeat them in later decades, were refused by the family.

Neumann's extravagant mystical charisms—inedia, out-of-body travel, prophecy, and xenoglossy (speaking archaic tongues with no prior knowledge)—far exceeded those of Sister Thorn, who shared in them only in a cursory way. Whereas Neumann was reported to have eaten nothing but the consecrated Host for thirty years, Reilly's rejection of food never achieved this degree. Still, even Margaret's fasting was enough for one physician to find spiritual meaning in it: "Her food would not sustain a bird," he wrote. "With all this she is absolutely perfect in childlike simplicity and obedience."[31] Neumann experienced the ability to receive Communion miraculously; to be able to digest it without chewing or swallowing; and even to experience the grace of suffering for others during her reception of the sacrament, once vomiting up the Host on behalf of a particularly sick girl.[32] Margaret's followers attributed Host miracles to her, but these anecdotes have not been verified.

Interpretation of Neumann's stigmata and their significance has shifted over time, reflecting the preoccupations of more than forty years of political, economic, and religious priorities in Germany between World War I and the Cold War. For example, when the earliest pilgrims' accounts of Neumann appeared in print after her stigmata were first reported, the authors likened her agonized body to the recent casualties of World War I. Given the pilgrims' experiences with wounded soldiers, it is not surprising that they were reminded of the battlefield.[33] During the harsh economic depression of the twenties, the church used the Neumann cult to rebut criticisms from the socialist press that it was abetting fraud by supporting her. Religious and secular sources were called upon to provide testimonies of what they saw; thus the controversy produced scores of descriptions of Neumann's wounds and ecstasies. A typical report came from a biologist from

Bamberg who witnessed the blood flowing from Neumann's eyes in 1927: "The blood here flows several hours, as well as thrice during the Crucifixion ecstasy from the thorn stigmata, which open up at eight or nine points, mostly at the back of the head. One could perceive this quite definitely on the bloodstained shawl which Bishop Schrembs of Ohio and I handled."[34] F. X. Huber, who also witnessed Neumann's wounds, provided the kind of details that are generally lacking for Sister Thorn: "The stigmata formed gradually; first on the backs of the hands, then in the palms; they were at first open, then the wounds became covered by a scab and surrounded by scarring. But these wounds do not bleed outside the Passion ecstasies; neither do they moisten nor discharge; outside the Friday ecstasies they are absolutely dry. They are new growths, hard and horny, around which lies an elastic, delicate membrane which breaks and bleeds during the Passion ecstasy and at the end of it closes again."[35]

Visitors also drew analogies between Therese's stigmata and nearby Oberammergau, the site of a modern revival of the Passion play and of a deeply rooted German "blood mysticism." But, they contended, even that spectacle paled next to the experience of observing Therese in person. An American priest suggested that "those who have seen both Oberammergau and Therese Neumann during the Passion ecstasy have been far more deeply moved by what they saw at Konnersreuth than by the Passion Play at Oberammergau."[36]

Not everyone was impressed by the stigmatic, however: Carmelite father Bruno de Jesus Marie visited from France on August 28, 1935, and found not a "timeless" mystical setting but an ordinary Bavarian farmhouse full of pesky flies in the heat of summer. To him, Therese's "exalted states" were hardly profound, and after observing her, he remained unconvinced of any supernatural interventions. His voice was an important one because he was editor of the leading journal in Catholic psychology and espoused a democratized notion of mysticism as not defined by extreme manifestations. Because of the rise of Nazism in Germany, the Neumann case acquired a more political cast than most stigmatizations, yet Therese and her circle failed to mount strong public resistance to the Nazi regime in the 1930s and 1940s or to publicly oppose its anti-Semitism. Under the Third Reich, Neumann and her admirers, in fact, did little to condemn Nazi policies, although some of her strongest supporters were among its victims.[37]

After World War II, Neumann's cult became an international phenomenon thanks to religious tourism and journalism. News accounts focused on the sizable crowds who gathered each Friday at her home to witness her ecstasies, a group that often included American servicemen stationed in Ger-

many. Catholics began to construct Neumann as an icon against Nazi paganism, even naming her "the most influential figure in the postwar subculture
of German miracles."[38] After 1945, her supporters tried to enhance their
credentials as Nazi resisters—with mixed success, given their lack of active
protests against Hitler from their relative isolation in rural Bavaria. Even
the church's own position toward her was unclear. The local bishops were
initially hostile to the Neumann phenomenon, and the church has never
adequately addressed its incomplete scientific investigations of her, although
in recent decades, church officials have continued to use Konnersreuth to
shore up the church's reputation as a steadfast opponent of Nazism.

The advocates of Therese Neumann who had expanded her cult by appealing to local traditions—the blood mysticism of southern Germany and
the Passion play—also benefited from new technologies of photography,
journalism, and motion pictures. Marie Rose Ferron (1902–36) embodied
the hopes of an ethnic minority in exile, a group of people lacking a sense
of rootedness or a culture united through a common tongue but who were
also indebted to media in expanding Ferron's cult. Whereas Margaret Reilly
was promoted by Irish Americans who had an authoritative presence in the
American church, Rose represented the beleaguered French Canadians of
her native Quebec and New England.[39] In 1905, however, the Ferron family
(parents and sixteen children) left Canada for Massachusetts. In 1925 they
relocated to Rhode Island.

Like Margaret, Rose had constant stomach difficulties and experienced
preliminary marks on her body in the year before her stigmata manifested
themselves fully. Also like Sister Thorn, Rose's wounds accumulated over
time, starting around 1918 but becoming visible to others only in 1927. Her
stigmata began on Fridays in Fall River and became more pronounced during her adult life in Woonsocket, as visitors reported from the family home
where she was bedridden. The wounds returned each Friday for three years
until 1930, when they became invisible.

Beyond a superficial sameness, the ethnic patronage for Ferron and Reilly
was not as comparable as one might imagine. Margaret grew up within a
large community of assimilating Irish Catholics in the nation's largest city,
whereas Ferron represented the "unmelted" Franco-Americans of small-
town New England. Prior to World War II, French Canadians in the United
States were not only reluctant to abandon their cultural links to Quebec
(and to origins in the most royalist region of France), but they also saw
themselves as victims of an Irish-dominated Catholic Church. Convinced
that Irish American clergy were determined to suppress French-language
schools, the Franco-American faction took the bishop to court in Rhode

Island but lost its lawsuit. In this so-called Sentinelle Affair, Ferron gained heroic status as a victim soul whose vicarious suffering led the alienated French-speaking Catholics to reunite with the diocese. During this episode, Ferron was credited with "saving" fifty-six members of the dissident French Catholic group from permanent excommunication in the region.

Rose Ferron's efforts were not enough to prove her sanctity. After two diocesan investigations of Ferron's stigmata and saintliness, the case was closed by the bishop of Providence in 1964 because the findings were "predominantly negative." Critics charged that Ferron was a morphine addict who inflicted her wounds with needles and pins, and this unsavory testimony helped undermine her veracity. Until that point, Little Rose's cult had been forcefully promoted by Abbé Lionel Groulx, a Canadian historian and Quebec nationalist, and by her spiritual director, Father Onésime Boyer, who modeled her cult on Thérèse of Lisieux and championed Rose's "idea of victimhood" as superior to Thérèse's ordinary "Little Way."[40] Had Lukas Etlin lived, he would likely have performed a similar role in Margaret's life. Although Groulx declined to pursue Rose's cause, which led to a marked downturn in her cult following his death in 1959, her lay promoters formed "Little Rose" clubs across America. The members of these clubs were informed by Boyer's 1939 biography of her, *She Wore a Crown of Thorns* (published in French and English), which deliberately emphasized Rose's interactions with non-Francophones in order to Americanize her appeal.[41] In Detroit, one energetic woman who knew Rose started sixty-five Little Rose clubs in that city.[42]

Throughout the 1940s and 1950s, the Ferron cult grew through local clubs and by the publication of anecdotes from her devotees that appeared in national Catholic magazines like *The Grail*. Rose's cult soon became internationalized, aided by reports from Asia that Rose was appearing to Catholic missionaries—an attribute that became more pronounced during the era of communist persecution of priests in China. There, the clergy credited Rose for the extraordinary conversions taking place among the Maoists, suggesting a new Cold War vocation for stigmatics in battling atheistic communism. Today, despite the publicity efforts and the prayer clubs, the Ferron cult endures mostly on the Internet as one of many "unexplained mysteries" of New England, a regional curiosity for the audience of another would-be saint.[43]

All of the stigmatics profiled in this chapter were persecuted by malevolent forces, but torture was especially pronounced in the spiritual path of Josefa Menendez (1890–1923), a Spanish nun in a French convent. Her conflicts with demons during her convent postulancy so closely parallel those of Sister Thorn that it suggests a recognizable topos. According to Josefa's biographer, "All the demon's efforts, during a long period of nine months, were concentrated on the destruction of Josefa's vocation."[44] He continued: "Persecution by the devil was particularly severe before her first vows, which she took on July 16, 1922."[45] The repetitive tales of liminality and danger that recur in the biographies of nuns and sisters indicate that they served to help the church construct feminine heroism in the twenties and thirties, often against the secular models of celebrities and movie stars. The persecution narratives of Josefa and Margaret posed young Catholic women as warriors in an epic battle to "win" a convent vocation. With God's help, nuns could be spiritual superheroes who rescued many souls for the church. Like Sister Josefa's, Margaret Reilly's spiritual victimhood presented an alternative to secular heroism in an era of otherwise expanding gender roles and rights for women in America.

Josefa and Margaret shared the experience of influential spiritual directors who encouraged their profound devotion to Jesus and to his Passion. In the convent, although Josefa was assigned to the menial tasks of sewing school uniforms, cleaning chapels, and doing laundry, through her confessor she understood her new vocations as "messenger of Jesus to the world" and as a victim soul: "You will suffer to gain souls because you are the chosen victim of my heart—but you will come to no harm because I will not allow it," Jesus told Josefa. "It is not for you to choose, but to surrender." These messages from the Lord described "chosen souls" as individuals who collaborated with God by serving as his victims. "The greatest reward I can give a soul," Jesus said, "is to make her a victim of my love and mercy, rendering her like myself who am the divine Victim for sinners."[46] As with Galgani, Ferron, and Neumann, clerical promoters emerged to campaign on Josefa's behalf. A Jesuit compiled her voluminous spiritual messages as *The Way of Divine Love*, a book of revelations for the world that appeared "providentially" on the verge of the Second World War to advocate her prominence beyond the convent.

Whereas each of the previous stigmatics shared some similarities with Sister Thorn, Belgian Maria van Beek (Sister Rumolda, 1886–1948) was nearly an exact copy in terms of life span, vocation, and symptoms. This suggests that the existence of stigmatized women in convents was less uncommon in this era than we have realized, resulting from the successful diffusion of victim spirituality across the Catholic world. In 1920 Maria entered the Franciscan convent at Herentals near Antwerp, made her preliminary vows in 1921 as Sister Rumolda, and received the stigmata on November 18, 1922, accompanied by repeated demonic attacks. Like Sister Thorn, Rumolda was stigmatized by progressive degrees, and she achieved her religious vocation in her thirties only after a long struggle. Prior to that, she had been a Franciscan tertiary who filled her days with reading pious books and the lives of the saints and honoring the Holy Virgin and the Sacred Heart, her two favorite devotions. Like Sister Thorn, Rumolda favored excessive spiritual practices; even before entering religious life, she awoke during the night to observe a holy hour of prayer and imposed demanding physical penances on her body. During a vision of the Sacred Heart, Jesus told her that she would become a victim soul.

Sister Rumolda's followers performed the usual work of linking her to legends of the saints, notably Catherine of Siena. Bettering Catherine, Rumolda *twice* received the supernatural gift of an engraved wedding ring on her finger (once during her vows ceremony in the presence of Cardinal Désiré Mercier, archbishop of Mechelen), symbolizing her marriage to Christ. A letter in her own hand describes Rumolda's desire to assist the clergy and convert the "enemies of the church," both important roles of Saint Catherine—and likewise attributed to Sister Thorn, via Saint Colette. Since 1924 the five wounds of the Crucifixion, unusually, remained visible at all times on Rumolda's body, whereas her head wounds came and went every few days. She stayed in her convent cell during her years of stigmatization, connecting to the outside world only through letters. Like Margaret, she had limited physical mobility and slept little in her convent existence. Her days were spent almost entirely at prayer, contemplating Christ's Passion.

As Margaret was reputed to bear a crucifix on her chest that was miraculously transferred to the wall, Rumolda's improvisation on the stigmatic theme was to fashion paintings from her wounds by imprinting her blood onto cloth or paper items. The images that formed were interpreted according to Christian iconography. Rumolda's relics include blood-stained shifts, linen caps, and handkerchiefs, in addition to two albums of these blood "paintings," made by folding paper over spots of her blood. Reports about her from doctors and the vicar general to the archbishop are respectful, providing details of her wounds and of her reclusive but devout life, but her cult has not advanced beyond the local level, held back by the results of the investigation authorized by Archbishop Mercier.[47] In this, her stalled cult most resembles that of Sister Thorn, another dedicated but hidden sufferer who was destined to remain a local phenomenon.

As the stories above indicate, the nineteenth-century tradition of holy women who were revered for receiving the wounds of Christ persisted well into the twentieth century. Yet despite the fact that the vast majority of stigmatics have been women, the Catholic Church has recently chosen to

An example of scrapbooks kept of the blood "paintings" of Sister Rumolda of Antwerp, a purported stigmatic whose mystical experiences closely paralleled those of Sister Thorn. (Author photo; courtesy of the archives of the Archdiocese of Mechelen, Belgium)

In Belgium, Sister Rumolda represents a nearly exact mirror of Sister Thorn's life and role as a purported stigmatic and victim soul, suggesting the widespread appeal of the spirituality of suffering that characterized the interwar decades. (Author photo; courtesy of the archives of the Archdiocese of Mechelen, Belgium)

canonize Padre Pio, a stigmatized Capuchin friar.[48] (Gemma Galgani became an Italian saint, but her proceedings did not comment on or endorse her stigmata.) On the other hand, Padre Pio's spirituality and gendering shared much with Sister Thorn, marked by self-imposed penances and demonic attacks. In fact, the details of Pio's life—his chronic poor health, dramatic temptations, and strong sense of sexual shame—are comparable to the female "hysterics" of his era.

Born in 1887, Pio (Francesco Forgione) was three years younger than Margaret Reilly. He was a sickly child who, like Reilly, took up extreme ascetic behaviors—long fasts that (some claimed) destroyed his health and self-flagellation with ropes and chains. Pio closely identified with his mother, who nursed him through his many illnesses, did his laundry, and fed him, even after he entered the monastery.[49] Well before his ordination, he had alarmed his elders with his fainting, fasting, and beatings.[50] Like Reilly, Pio had only rudimentary education. Dr. Giorgio Festa, a Capuchin, judged Pio's knowledge to be "very modest, for because of his unstable condition of health, he has been hardly able to study that which is necessary to be a priest to celebrate the Mass."[51] Nonetheless, once ordained, Pio obsessively identified with the Mass and his own role in it. He was wracked by feelings of guilt, as he explained in a letter to his spiritual adviser about the new marks on his palms: "The reason [that I'm just now telling you about the pain and spots I have] is that I have always been overcome by that evil called shame."[52] Pio asked God to remove his stigmata, "not the wound or the pain, which is impossible since I wish to be inebriated with pain, but these outward signs which cause me such embarrassment and unbearable humiliation."[53] Well into his eighties, Pio was troubled by beatings from demons, a form of physical combat that "has a very long history in Christianity."[54]

Like Sister Thorn, Pio was allegedly examined several times by different physicians, who reached no agreement about his stigmata.[55] The evidence is even conflicting as to who saw him and when, where their transcripts are located, and if any credible eyewitnesses to the onset of his wounds existed, despite photographs of the marks on his hands and feet after the fact. Several distinguished scholars were called upon to evaluate him, including Amico Bignami (1862–1929), an outspoken atheist and a professor of medical pathology at the Royal University of Rome; and Agustino (Eduardo) Gemelli, a physician, psychologist, and Franciscan theologian who founded the first psychiatric hospital for Italian soldiers affected by World War I. Bignami's report of May 1919 found Pio's wounds to be "of neurotic origin," caused by "unconscious suggestion" and tincture of iodine.[56] He was amazed, however, that after Pio's wounds were bandaged for eight days and then uncovered, they bled as before.[57]

Father Gemelli evaluated Pio at the request of the Vatican. He claimed to see Pio in April 1920 just before the Vatican appointed Gemelli as rector of the Catholic University of the Sacred Heart in Milan, but others had said that Gemelli never received permission from the Capuchins for an official, rather than a private, visit.[58] It is contested that Gemelli was ever permitted to witness Pio's wounds alone or to carry out a proper medical examination. Gemelli himself complained that he was never allowed to complete a psychological study of the Capuchin. Nonetheless, he speculated: "It is my firm belief that Padre Pio da Petralcina produced unconsciously, and by way of suggestive action, the sores simulating those of St. Francis. I believe that Padre Pio is a psychopath, at this point without being able to say what type and of what nature his psychopathy is."[59] However, Gemelli in no way showed how Pio's concentration upon the wounds of Christ (or of Saint Francis) could mobilize unconscious forces to cause them to appear. Pio impishly suggested that Vatican officials visit a field and contemplate a bull to see if horns would grow on their heads.[60] Augustin Poulain had proclaimed confidently in his definition of "Mystical Stigmata" for the *Catholic Encyclopedia* of 1912: "There is not a single experimental proof that imagination could produce them, especially in violent forms."[61]

Yet during Pio's lifetime, such proof did emerge in the experiments of Dr. Albert Lechler on "Elizabeth K" in Germany between 1928 and 1932. With his patient under hypnosis, Lechler was able to get her to reproduce her tears of blood, proving to himself at least that "the key to stigmata lay in psychology, not theology."[62] World War I had presented an additional challenge to Pio's reputation. Pio's limited war experience (he was called to serve in the Italian army in 1915 but was soon discharged for poor health) was apparently devastating enough for him to share the neurotic symptoms of the disturbed veterans.[63] Yet Freudian theory seemed at a loss to explain the widespread presence of male hysteria in shell-shocked soldiers. It has been claimed that the observation of hysteria among so many veterans led to the disappearance of the term in twentieth-century medical discourse because practitioners could not face the threat posed to their notions of maleness by the feminized male.[64] Similarly, the Catholic hierarchy did not relish promoting a feeble, tearful friar for sainthood, so unflattering details of Pio's military career were eliminated from his official hagiography.

As a consequence of the controversial nature of Pio's wounds and behavior, his stigmata were ignored by the Vatican in his canonization documents, and Bignami's diagnosis was never rejected. With disquiet and even contempt, skeptics insisted that Pio, like deceiving women before him, inflicted his own wounds with carbolic acid and a sharp knife. In the eyes of the church, however, Pio's stigmata and "hysterical" symptoms did not affect his canonization campaign. Thus, when Pope John Paul II canonized Pio in 2002, he pointedly expressed no opinion about the stigmata or Pio's physical and mental condition except to make the customary aside that the wounds represented a sign of holiness. The Vatican has never endorsed the friar's stigmata, bilocation, or visions, although in a July 2009 speech at San Giovanni Rotondo, Pope Benedict XVI tried to "explain" their meaning. In order not to confuse mysticism with the miraculous, the church turned instead to emphasizing Pio's "heroic virtue"—the good accomplished by the hospital founded at the monastery of San Giovanni in Foggia where Pio spent most of his life after 1916.[65] Nonetheless, the periphery remains active as promoters of the worldwide cult of Pio, which thrives on the flamboyant tales of his wounds, bilocation, levitation, and encounters with demons. Pilgrims continue to flock to his monastery, shrine, hospital, and a new pilgrimage church despite their rural locale in the least touristic region of Italy—suggesting that the Capuchin satisfies an apparent need for saints who fit the vernacular tradition of mythomania as well as those who address the constant human need for medical care and healing.

As Pio's recent canonization demonstrates, the tendency of the universal church, centered at the Vatican, is to enforce orthodoxy through bureaucratic channels and to resist localized cults that violate the prohibition against venerating a living person. The controversies surrounding Pio illustrate the potential hazards that would have faced Sister Thorn if her cause had advanced. Yet, as Kenneth Woodward concluded about modern canonization proceedings, "Nowhere is popular devotion to the saints more at odds with the rules for making saints than in cases involving mystical phenomena."[66] When it has intervened in popular cults that are pursuing the canonization of a candidate with mystical features, the church has indeed followed its own regulations in an uneven fashion, as demonstrated by several cases in this chapter. Here, the Vatican's failure to sponsor reliable medical investigations of the wounds of Therese Neumann and Padre Pio, and its sometimes unfortunate choices of examiners—combined with the refusal of Neumann's family and Pio's religious order to make information available—suggests an institutional ambivalence about adopting scientific or psychological techniques in the event that they might expose frauds that could undermine the church, the monastic orders, or the faith of the laity.[67]

Further, the Catholic Church's unwillingness to endorse interpretations that called Pio's behavior pathological, even when professed by learned Catholic clergy like Gemelli, reveals its own uncertainty and vagueness about the category of the psychological. The church's coolness toward the investigation of the unconscious mind was similar to its failure to avail itself of scientific procedures and technologies such as blood typing, photography, and film to study stigmatization. It fell back on procedural details: was permission properly secured for the investigation? These refusals make the church's claims to scientific rigor about evaluating mystical phenomena less than credible, while supporting the observation of religious historians that the church adopted vernacular piety in the twentieth century only when it could be turned to serve its own purposes.

This chapter has shown how Sister Thorn's allies worked to generate a receptive audience for her by comparing her mystical life favorably to the saints and other charismatic figures who reported mystical experiences close to her own, and as an effort to connect "the old Faith and the new land."[68] I am not attempting to insist that all stigmatics share certain features, however, or that a composite biography is even desirable. For the last century, the church has tended to dismiss most claims of stigmata, except as general defenses of the existence of the supernatural. Predictably, reports of stigmata have declined in number since Vatican II, which downplayed mysticism, but a Catholic subculture of mystics and visionaries still endures. Contemporary stigmatizations continue to allude to past examples and replicate their details, but a more recent development—the presence of electronic media—has shifted the terrain again to make the local milieu immediately available on a global scale to anyone who has access to the Internet. In this new space, the relationship between a center and its peripheries becomes quite complicated.

A final comparison to Sister Thorn, therefore, is the case of a recent stigmatic who has achieved considerable popularity through the Internet. The cult of Fortunata "Natuzza" Evolo (1924–2009) of southern Italy has reached millions of people because she became the subject of a documentary and has appeared in interviews posted on YouTube.[69] From an illiterate peasant family in Calabria whose father sought work in Argentina before her birth, Natuzza was sent out to domestic service and never learned to read or write. At age ten, while working for the family of a lawyer, she began to have visions of a priest and was put in a psychiatric hospital. Her stigmata appeared in 1938 after her discharge from the hospital. In 1940 she was observed by Agostino Gemelli, who delivered the same diagnosis of hysteria as he had given for Padre Pio twenty years before. Later, Natuzza married and bore five children, but her husband claimed that they never had a normal life together due to the nearly constant supernatural happenings in her life.[70] Until her recent death, Natuzza lived in a building belonging to the Catholic Church with a chapel attached, housing a statue of the Virgin Mary as seen in one of her visions. Natuzza professed the ability to bilocate (with more than eighteen instances reported) and the gift of hemography ("miraculous writing in blood") in the form of words and Christian symbols appearing on her skin from her bleeding wounds that were transferred onto cloth or paper.

Natuzza's hemographies recall the most spectacular of the nineteenth-century frauds, Palma Matarelli (1825–88), an Italian peasant who was profiled by the century's chronicler of stigmatics, Dr. Imbert-Gourbeyre.[71] For doing so, the author was reprimanded by the Vatican, which had flatly rejected Palma's claims. Palma customarily displayed a crown of thorns, which she pressed onto cloth where the bloodstains formed shapes of hearts and swords, in seeming anticipation of the blood paintings of Sister Rumolda and Natuzza Evolo.[72] Natuzza's hemographies also possibly copied those of her contemporary and fellow Calabrian Elena Aiello (1895–1961), or they may simply represent new variations on the stigmatic tradition that continue to emerge at the local level as lay challenges to the church's "universally undifferentiated liturgies."[73] The blood that seeped from Natuzza's wounds in her wrists and feet, when wiped away, rearranged itself in shapes and letters, forming words even in Aramaic and Hebrew.[74] In her case, the blood serves *as* text, complicating the usual understanding of the wounds as signs in and of themselves.

The posting of photographs of Natuzza's wounds on the Internet presumably allows more viewers to see the "truth" of her stigmata and hemography, yet it lacks the crucial immediacy of the physical body that had formerly been a feature of events like Marian apparitions, where the Madonna addressed a specific audience in its dialect or was recorded by witnesses as expressing certain emotions related to that moment, such as anger or sorrow. But the disappearance of the body of Natuzza Evolo into the image on the screen hints at a far deeper change in mystical movements and their relationship to audiences. When a photograph of a supernatural event is posted on the Internet, the technology is strengthened while the human and divine subjects are weakened. Moreover, with the rapid pace of technological change, even photography and video are being supplanted. As modern creations like virtual reality and computer-generated graphics have been outpacing other "traditional cultural, political, and social processes," Paolo Apolito suggests, these changes affect religious cultists by "threatening to make photography and video obsolete in their capacity to offer stimuli for the world of visionaries."[75] Natuzza's audience, for example, is able to improvise and share legends about her that embrace the life stories of virtually every other stigmatic, since the accumulation of historical data about stigmatization is enabled on a scale as never before by the resources and audiences of electronic media.

Due to these changes, any images of Natuzza that are posted on the Web are now reshaping and organizing Catholic mystical culture itself, because the Web constitutes a new reality that is entirely self-referential. The pictures there refer to other pictures, not to any external "truth." This means, among other things, that visual technology has seized control of the experience from ecclesiastical authorities, making science and technology themselves the measure of truth and sidelining the role of faith and the human subject. Put another way, "Technology reduces the margin of subjectivity of those who are involved in its devotional use, in one way of another."[76] Viewed in this light, the technology used to "prove" the reality of Natuzza's wounds and predictions no longer appeals to the former belief that God allowed her wounds to be seen by privileged individuals who made a journey to see her, nor does it point to a collective group experience of faith as it had when Dr. Gemelli saw her in 1940. Rather, the supernatural becomes defined only by the technology of the camera and the Internet as accessed by individuals. And because far more information is available instantly to infinite online audiences, the church no longer has a monopoly on creating and distributing an official narrative about mystical prodigies or potential saints. It never exercised that power completely in the past, of course, but in a peculiar way, the very technologies that Catholic leaders might have used systematically to study stigmatization in a scientific manner have now bypassed its command in favor of an online reality that gives images an autonomy that refers only to other images rather than to validating a possible miracle affecting a corporeal body. The consequences of such developments remain to be seen; certainly, technology does not inherently destroy enchantment, but it does trigger "new and unpredictable processes whereby sacred status is conferred."[77]

What is the outcome, then, of the tension created between a center and a periphery in popular devotions and of the associative activity of cult followers? Margaret Reilly's cult produced an initial "effervescence," in a Durkheimian sense, but it did not expand widely enough to generate a thriving campaign for canonization, nor was it clear who might lead such a campaign after her death or where it might be located. The existence of similar "circles" devoted to stigmatics—at Lucca, Woonsocket, Konnersreuth, Foggia, Calabria, and elsewhere—have supplied the core for other emerging cults. But where would Sister Thorn's cult be centered? In Peekskill? In Manhattan? In Angers? Sister Thorn's immediate circle created a vital connection among people who cared about each other and believed in the worthiness of her suffering to achieve forgiveness for sinners, while her suffering body affirmed their conviction that illness provided an occasion to glorify God through an imitation of the suffering of Christ. As she suffered vicariously for others, Margaret was purifying the flesh from earthly distractions, the better to remind her devotees of eternal life.

Spirituality itself responds to historical forces, which help explain why the moment for this type of intimate connection with would-be saints has been eroding since Sister Thorn's lifetime. The dominion of Catholic sacrificial discourse endured at least until Vatican II, but around the 1930s, the personal suffering embodied by the stigmatics of Margaret's generation became translated into different social venues that offered alternatives to the world of private devotions. The Great Depression of the 1930s ushered in an age of mass economic misery, mass politics and labor, which the church met by a range of public strategies defined as Catholic Action: stadium gatherings, urban street processions, an anticommunist agenda, and an emphasis upon a collective experience of faith as a source of national religious identity. Opportunities for personal encounters with stigmatics and visionaries would of course continue for Catholics, but they would not be representative of the American church's goal by midcentury to establish itself as a respectable partner in "tri-faith America."[78] Despite the efforts of Sister Thorn's advocates to connect her story with those of other mystics and with the saints, these did not prove to be persuasive enough to be sustained in the new conventions of sainthood.

{7} Find Sweet Music Everywhere

Modern Catholic Supernaturalism

> We cannot change the world, taking out all its thorns, making
> its tasks easy and its burden light; modulating all its discord
> into harmonies, transforming its ugliness into beauty. But we
> can have our own heart renewed by the grace of God, and thus
> the world will be made over for us. . . . A soul of song will find
> sweet music everywhere.
>
> —Message from Jesus to Margaret Reilly

> The lesson of all which seems to be that mystical phenomena,
> visions and copious revelations, no matter how edifying their
> content, need to be scrutinized very, very carefully before they
> can be accepted as the seal set by God upon holiness of life.
>
> —Herbert Thurston, *Surprising Mystics* (1925; 1955), 217

When Sister Crown of Thorns died in May 1937, her community was hardly unprepared. From the moment of Thorn's first vows ceremony at Peekskill fifteen
years before, the Good Shepherd sisters had been anticipating her imminent
death. As the convent chronicles attest, her wavering health preoccupied the
sisters much of the time. By now, they were quite accustomed to the bloody
bandages, bedsores, laundry needs, wheelchair, and extra labor entailed in caring for a paralyzed invalid.

Beginning with a critical moment in December 1923 when a weakened
Margaret was "suffering intensely," the sisters placed "everything in readi-
ness though for her death bed Profession." Still, she clung to life. In January
1924 Margaret was about to receive the last rites, yet she rallied once more.
In February Archbishop Patrick Hayes visited the convent, reporting that
he scarcely recognized her since "she looks so very frail as if the lamp was
nearly burned out." At the close of 1924, she was still "suffering greatly and
growing weaker." In May 1925 she was frailer still and "suffering very much,"
and by December she seemed "supremely happy" although in great pain. In

1926 Margaret "suffered a great deal during Lent" and during that summer was disturbed by constant vomiting. "There are days when one wonders how she lives," remarked Mother St. Francis Xavier Hickey to Lukas Etlin.[1] In 1927 her "spine was attacked now as well as the pancreas. The pain in her head is awful at times." That year, Thomas McParlan reported on Margaret's new set of ailments: "Yesterday I saw Sister Thorn[.] [T]he mass in her abdomen which includes the pancreas is greatly enlarged and her sufferings are terrible. There is no position that gives her the faintest relief and she looks very badly. I am greatly worried over her condition and feel so powerless to anything for her."[2] By August, Mother Hickey feared "poor little Sister cannot last much longer. She is suffering so much, but always so sweetly and patiently."[3]

Yet despite her declining health, Margaret survived for another decade. She and the sisters believed that "her illnesses were supernatural," meaning not that God forced her to suffer but that her suffering served spiritual purposes "for her Sisters' other work"—namely, for God ("she suffers so lovingly for Him") and for the entire Good Shepherd community. "It is good for our Congregation to give us such a chosen soul," Mother Hickey declared with certainty.[4] McParlan added to the chorus by choosing not to operate on Margaret because he wanted to watch the Lord perfecting her through suffering. Lady Margaret Armstrong similarly recalled Thorn's miseries as "Our Lord's graciousness to her."[5] Through these metaphors of the Lord's wonderful infliction of pain, Margaret's community and cult clearly regarded her as a victim soul whose agonies were markers of her intimate relationship with the Passion of Jesus. As Father Bertrand understood it: "God permits that she is misunderstood and contradicted, opposed and ridiculed on every side; the story is questioned; the charge is made that it is all a fake and many seem to be ready to discredit the clearest manifestations of the extraordinary. No doubt, it is all in keeping with God's own plan and means greater perfection for this chosen soul and greater glory for the Master."[6] What makes these accounts remarkable throughout is their unquestioning belief that a holy woman's life must be marked by intense pain and unrelieved suffering as proof that God chose her to live out a special mission, no matter how dreadful.

This final chapter examines how Sister Thorn's prolonged illness and death represented this cult of suffering to its fullest degree and honored the special sensitivity of women's bodies to divine contact. In the details of her demise, Margaret's supporters sought confirmation of her chosen status and of the spiritual meaningfulness of her pain. But even more than her model death, Sister Thorn's claim to be a stigmatic-visionary was being prepared to furnish a grander narrative—namely, Catholic attempts to en-hance a relatively thin dossier history of mystical phenomena in the United States. By the 1930s, American Catholics had no national shrines nor any heritage of national pilgrimages such as the one that had evolved at Lourdes in France. Three factors—the legacy of the Great War, the social changes of the twenties, and the economic suffering that followed in the next de-cade—contributed to the valuation of affliction among Catholics and, for some, intensified a quest for signs of supernatural presence and for public expressions of that faith.

World War I had asked Catholics to suppress their ethnic loyalties in sup-port of the national cause and to share in the providential view of American destiny long associated with Protestants. However, the horrors of the war, as well as the resurgence of anti-Catholic activism afterward, led Catholics to focus less upon commonalities than upon differences; increasingly, they came to symbolize their enemies in the postwar era as satanic and demonic, a change illustrated by an exorcism case that gained national prominence as it followed closely upon Sister Thorn's stigmatization. In the twenties, American Catholics participated with their fellow citizens in most of the decade's characteristic trends: patriotic exuberance, a flood of consumer commodities, liberation of sexual and moral standards, and the stock-market boom and crash. The subsequent Great Depression made the thirties a piv-otal decade for Catholics in more ways than one. The economic hardships of those years made it a difficult time for clergy to enforce newly fortified church teaching that opposed contraception; and labor crises made it hard for embattled workers to turn the other cheek to capitalists. Yet the fragile prospect of material success led children of immigrant Catholics to respond to its demanding ethos through the idealization of pain.[7]

The set of witnesses dedicated to Sister Thorn took shape within Ameri-can Catholicism at a moment in its history that was especially affected by recent events in Europe. The prewar atmosphere of the universal church was one of world rejection created by the Vatican condemnation of Mod-ernism in 1907. The subsequent tragedy of World War I had only further convinced many Catholics of the arrogance and evil of human ambition and aggression, sentiments echoed by New York's archbishop in a postwar sermon condemning "a freedom of thought and action that knows neither the conventions nor the moral restraint of Christian society."[8] In Europe, the postwar decade filled the void in human experience of the sacred with a turn toward mystical and magical beliefs, including spiritualism and Catho-lic apparitional and visionary cults. These soothed various psychic needs of individuals, but real social demands were met by religion as well. Charitable projects sponsored by the Catholic Church were integral to rebuilding the religious infrastructure and artistic patrimony of western Europe, as its abbeys, convents, and churches lay in ruins. Much of this funding came from American Catholic donors who responded to requests from immigrant clergy like Lukas Etlin to assist even the vanquished Central powers.

In the United States, some of the closest associates of Sister Thorn were deeply connected to the tragedy of the Great War. As members of religious orders, they helped to fashion the Catholic Church into a transnational community in the twenties and thirties. More precisely, the war brought Irish Americans (who were generally pro-German as the war began) into contact with clerical leaders from Germany, Austria, Belgium, and France. Dr. McParlan of New York, for example, knew Michael Faulhaber (1869–1952), bishop of Speyer, who had been wartime chaplain of the Bavarian army and who became archbishop of Munich in 1917. Faulhaber was named cardinal of Munich in 1921 and remained so until his death after World War II. Faulhaber met Brother Lukas Etlin after the First World War when Etlin was directing the relief effort for Austrians and Germans through the Caritas program. In 1923 Faulhaber visited the United States for a Caritas conference, learning of Sister Thorn from Etlin. With much media fanfare, Faulhaber returned to America three years later to attend the Eucharistic Congress in Chicago. His entourage was met and escorted by Archbishop Patrick Hayes of New York, who, as the first appointed bishop of the American armed forces during the war, had served a parallel role to Faulhaber. These connections between European and American clergy led to a shared vocabulary of mourning that represented the war as Good Friday and the soldiers as fallen Christs, which had the effect of deepening Catholic investment in the Passion and in valorizing martyrdom.

The effects of the Great War upon American Catholics were particularly marked in two areas: the expansion of Catholic charities in the United States and the Catholic Church's attack on spiritualism. During the war, the church had cooperated with charitable agencies of Jews and Protestants to provide services to soldiers. Afterward, it converted the National Catholic War Conference into the National Catholic Welfare Conference to expand the reach of Catholic charities targeting immigrants at the diocesan and parish level, as well as the members of the armed forces.[9] Evidence of the church's own Americanization occurred in the postwar decades, an era when charity itself became big business and the church reaped huge financial benefits from payments by state and municipal agencies to its many charitable organizations and projects, including the Good Shepherds at Peekskill.

The church regarded spiritualism—one of a variety of alternative religions that arose to meet the whims of nonconformists of the twenties and to assuage the grief of families of the war dead—as heretical. Catholic theology rejected belief in speaking with the dead and opposed attending séances. Although spiritualist writings had been placed on the Index of Prohibited Books since 1864, the pope had felt obliged to denounce spiritualism twice more, once in 1898 and again in 1917.[10] In fact, Pius IX elevated its menace by condemning the "twin evils" of spiritualism and socialism.[11] This antagonistic position reflected the church's misogyny, as well, since most of the spiritualist mediums were women who challenged the ritual authority of the priest. As numerous scholars have noted, women played a leading role in the spiritualist community. It was not unusual, therefore, that the church "repeatedly anathematized the movement and especially the women within it."[12] Sister Thorn's stigmata appeared in the midst of these protests against the resurgence of spiritualism and renewed debates about the miraculous. Thus, as the church displaced women from the modernization process by condemning their right to employment outside the home, by discouraging their right to vote, by rejecting birth control, and by refusing them compensatory outlets like spiritualism, it found uses in a stigmatic nun to justify its countercultural ascetic ideals. In this sense, stigmatic women were not transgressive; what they revealed to the world was the suffering Jesus, not their personal demands for the independence or equality of women or unorthodox attempts to commune with the dead.

Because the Great War arguably had destroyed many of the old traditions and even the idea of tradition, after 1919 Catholic Church officials were concerned about restoring notions of authority and reestablishing Roman Catholicism as the guardian and fulcrum of Western Christendom. The church would accomplish this by absorbing the devotional energies that were flourishing in Europe and America since the nineteenth century and by striving to make monastic and conventual Catholicism the protector of tradition. In this context, the revisions to the Code of Canon Law in 1917, rather than endorsing the increased freedoms sought by young women in Western culture, greatly restricted the freedom of body and mind in convent life. The enclosed nun became the epitome of antimodern Catholicism and her mysticism its most esoteric treasure. What of the outlook of the nuns themselves, however? Even hemmed in as they were by protocols, a lack of theological training, male supervisors, and the local bishop, convents still possessed a kind of semiautonomy that allowed certain kinds of freedom to flourish inside its walls. Women religious leaders knew how to don the mask of the subservient nun when it was necessary to seek a desired result from the hierarchy, and most of the time, they probably never dreamed of being other than obedient. But when a member of a religious community started to profess visions and stigmata, such exceptional events often led to a loss of control over what followed, and a mystic nun could be made to serve a variety of clients and purposes. Sister Thorn may have been at once the longed-for icon of Irish Americans, the mark of successful integration of rising devotions to the Eucharist and the Sacred Heart of Jesus, a national saint, and the harbinger of the Catholic International, in which postimmigrant habits of faith in America were no longer tied to a specific European nation of origin. McParlan's buoyant analysis of Sister Thorn's role was capacious enough for all of these audiences: "I see in it all the hand of God for some great purpose."[13]

When Sister Thorn finally died, she was attended by the two women closest to her, Mother Raymond and Sister Carmelita. Raymond had left Thorn's room for two minutes to fetch a drink of water; when she returned, she found Margaret vomiting blood into the basin on her table. Sister Thorn died soon afterward. Crushed by the loss of her dearest friend, Mother Raymond at first could not bear to dictate the sad news to a secretary. A few weeks later, she penned a letter in her own hand to Mother Dolorosa at the Benedictine convent in Clyde, Missouri, describing how Thorn had suffered heroically "thru her ulcers, pancreas and other ills. Then the attacks of the evil one, her sweet pains [i.e., her stigmata]: some tests confirmed cancer of all the left side, also the bladder; she refused opiates, wanting to be coherent to make a good confession before communion." Raymond lamented: "I will miss her yes more than I can say but I am grateful He took her first. Memories crowd in daily and I thank Him for all He did for her and me."[14] The recorded cause of death for Margaret Reilly was pancreatic cancer with no mention of a diseased bladder or ulcers. If this was the case, then it is not unusual that no symptoms were observed. Pancreatic cancer possesses no specific early-warning signs, and symptoms often do not appear until the tumor grows large enough to afflict the stomach, liver, or other nearby organs.[15]

Convent legend has it that Sister Thorn foretold that her own death would precede her superior's by twenty-two months. In fact, Mother Raymond died of a series of heart attacks on March 19, 1939, three months before the prophesied date. On that occasion, one sister reported that Mother Raymond was buried near Thorn in the convent cemetery, adding: "But I am sure that in heaven they are even closer."[16]

Still, even Sister Thorn's death was not without controversy, and several variant accounts of it supplement or revise Mother Raymond's version. Archbishop Hayes told Lady Armstrong that Sister Thorn died peacefully

At Peekskill, Sister Thorn, seated, is flanked (top row, left to right)
by Mother Raymond, the superior; Mother Mary of St. John of the
Cross, the mother general; and Mother Mary St. Euphrasia, the assistant
general. The photo, taken in about 1932, may represent an unspoken
endorsement of Sister Thorn by the congregation's leaders. (Courtesy
of the Sisters of the Good Shepherd, Jamaica, N.Y.; permission and
photo provided in 1996)

from massive hemorrhages, not from cancer. Lady Armstrong, however,
wrote to Herbert Thurston maintaining that Sister Thorn "died from cancer—terrible agony, bourne [*sic*] with the greatest fortitude, took not opiates of any kind—and about an hour before her death, was able to receive
an entire Host—and retain it, altho' having been unable to swallow even
a drop of water for days."[17] Armstrong had seen Margaret three months
before her death, during which she enjoyed a "very happy visit and found
the wonderful little person able to sit up—after dreadful illness and agony."
She predicted confidently that "someday this Archdiocese will be happy
because she lived in it."[18]

During the week of Margaret's death—the news of which rated only a
brief notice in the *Newark Evening News* for the entire New York metro-
politan area—it was possible to see that new patterns of life were emerging
among local Catholics. For example, the newspapers remarked on several
mass gatherings of the faithful, such as the recent unveiling of a bronze
statue of Father Francis Patrick Duffy in Times Square, which drew a crowd

of 30,000. Duffy was the decorated chaplain who had served the nation in two wars. Yet the throng gathered in the square was not nearly as large as the Holy Name Society rally in Brooklyn that same month, which more than 90,000 Catholic men attended. These two events hinted that an era of public Catholicism and mass spectacles was gradually supplanting an era of intimate devotions, although the two would continue to walk together for a while.

In the summer that followed Margaret's death, as New York's *Catholic News* relayed, schoolchildren received diocesan awards for their anticommunist essays; Lucille Papin Borden's *Life of St. Francis* was serialized for Catholic readers; and Catholic children attended religious summer camps, such as Camp Acadia for boys and Our Lady of Lourdes Camp for girls. New Jersey beach resorts catering to Catholics promoted themselves as such. The Legion of Decency printed its weekly ratings of films, while plays were likewise neatly segregated into acceptable or unacceptable fare. The archbishop of New York was able to prevail on the license commissioner to deny renewals to fourteen burlesque houses, chalking up another victory over vice. For Catholic housewives, "In the Kitchen with Molly Gavin" furnished weekly menus and recipes for pot roast, stuffed peppers, rhubarb punch, and strawberry russe. At the dugout in Yankee Stadium, Margaret Reilly's cousin, Joseph McCarthy, was busy managing the Yankees. (Ten days after

The unveiling of the statue of Father Francis Patrick Duffy in Duffy Square, which occurred in the week of Sister Thorn's death, heralded a new public confidence among American Catholics and an increasing turn to public expressions of their patriotism. (Carl van Vechten Trust; from the collections of the Museum of the City of New York)

The gravestone of Sister Mary Crown
of Thorns in the cemetery at Peekskill.
(Author photo)

Margaret's death, McCarthy made headlines for chatting with his buddies
about the worst hitters they had known. McCarthy nominated one of his
own pitchers, Johnny Broaca, who hated batting practice so much that he
claimed he had learned how to hit only by reading about it.[19])

Despite these reassuring signs of normalcy in the press, ominous hints
were on the horizon for those American Catholics paying attention to European politics. Journalists gave notice of a fund drive by Catholics to aid
the Spanish victims of the Guernica air raid, and stories appeared with increasing frequency about Adolph Hitler's attacks on the Catholic Church in
Germany. The death of one nun in a convent on the Hudson River would
scarcely disrupt the lives of Catholics struggling amid the Depression or
compete with the iniquity of the rising fascist threat and a second world war
that would erupt in less than two years. In the circumstances of an unprecedented economic catastrophe and looming international political crises,
what attention did Sister Mary of the Crown of Thorns merit?

Sometimes events conspire to renew interest in relatively forgotten
figures, as the Great Depression had propelled the cult of Jude—patron
saint of hopeless causes but before then a relatively unknown figure in the
United States—into the foreground.[20] But as several homegrown aspirants
for canonization sprung up to join what was an admittedly short roster of
players, Catholic Americans grew hopeful that the time was ripe for native
contributions to the church's roll of saints. In fact, Americans seemed determined to put forward homegrown candidates as a matter of national or

ethnic pride. In New York, Margaret's followers were readying her for that very position. Dr. Thomas McParlan fervently expressed the wishes of her partisans by claiming that "in Margaret we are to have our first American (Irish-American) saint. In this day of materialism, it is no wonder our dear Lord is revealing His love for us, and as I have heard from others that are dear to Him, He begs for our love and affection."[21] His enthusiasm belied the difficulties in presenting Sister Thorn to the Catholic world within her several contexts of Irish American Catholic, New World revelation, and potential saint for the universal church.

Following Sister Thorn's death, numerous individuals came forward to present stories of miracles resulting from contact with her. On the day after her death, the *Newark Evening News* got the ball rolling with an incident from a few years earlier, when Thorn had been taken to the Cincinnati bedside of a nun suffering from a tumor. Shortly after the visit, the woman was restored to health when the tumor fell into her lap. The evidence was preserved at the convent.[22] A second healing incident involved the wife of a "well-known New York physician" who experienced a remarkable cure after a visit to the nun.[23] In a third event, a surgeon sought advice from the Lord through Sister Thorn before amputating a patient's leg. Thorn advised the patient to receive Communion and make a vow to Jesus, and on that same day, the patient walked out of the hospital, fully healed.[24] Sister Thorn was also credited with at least one miraculous healing by the imposition of hands. While traveling from New York to visit a Good Shepherd convent, Sister Thorn passed through Erie, Pennsylvania, where she healed a young girl by touching her and by speaking "words of cheer."[25] Even the New York Yankees benefited from Margaret's help. From the manager's office, Joseph McCarthy and his wife affirmed their belief that Thorn's prayers had helped the team, so perhaps she deserves some credit for the Bronx Bombers' seven championship seasons with McCarthy.[26]

As we learned in the previous chapter, Sister Thorn's local cult emerged somewhat haphazardly in oral tradition, and only preliminaries were set in motion to recognize her as a "servant of God," the initial step in the saint-making process. Although the hopes of beatifying and ultimately canonizing Sister Thorn did not coalesce, her supporters had shrewdly enlisted powerful leaders in the American hierarchy to help them, including Cardinal James McIntyre, a likely choice because he had served as the assistant chancellor of the Archdiocese of New York and had been ordained by Archbishop Hayes.[27] Given the death of Hayes in 1938 and of Lukas Etlin and Thomas McParlan a decade earlier, it was left to McIntyre, Sister Carmelita, and assorted clergy to advance Sister Thorn's cause. Mother Raymond and

Herbert Thurston died in 1939, further limiting the list of those who could speak knowledgeably to Vatican investigators. Perhaps the canonization of the Good Shepherd foundress in 1940 also relieved any urgent pressure on the congregation to produce another saint. Finally, the policy of several Good Shepherd superiors to suppress Sister Thorn in congregational memory certainly put a stop to in-house conversation about her.

Nearly forty years later, when Sister Clare Nolan of the New York Good Shepherds revisited Sister Thorn's life as part of an effort to improve the congregation's historical archives, her inquiries established many facts from the anecdotal evidence. According to Nolan's recollections and those of other Good Shepherd members, the congregation eventually decided following Vatican II that its service to at-risk women needed its limited resources more than an expensive canonization campaign. Saint Crown of Thorns or Saint Margaret of Peekskill never materialized for a number of factors that made her cause vulnerable: a lack of impetus and funding from the Good Shepherds, the failure of the cult to expand beyond the local level, not enough well-placed advocates, no officially recognized cures attributed to her after her death, and perhaps not enough evidence of her stigmata and visions that could be used to establish the "heroic virtue" necessary to the vita of the modern saint. As we have seen, victim souls were a familiar rather than extraordinary presence in the spiritual landscape before Vatican II, especially in monastic life. According to the documentation available to me, Margaret's stigmata seemingly lasted only ten weeks, from September 4 to November 18, 1921, although others claimed that she received other marks on her body throughout the following decade. Thus Margaret fit the contours of a particular style of expressive mysticism but failed to emerge as distinctive enough to merit sainthood among America's thousands of women religious. Of the evidence of holiness implied by her wounds, the very mention of stigmata was more likely to unsettle than mobilize Irish American Catholics. In the 1920s, a stigmatic was a curiosity in American Catholicism, but by the third decade of the twentieth century, Margaret Reilly's ethnic community was casting its lot with the American vision of success while at the same time pursuing a Catholic triumphalism. As James Fisher described it, the "Irish ascendancy had ultimately 'resolved' the Americanism debate by making the commitment to maintain Catholic distinctiveness inseparable from the commitment to pursue the American dream."[28] For Catholics, therefore, assimilation meant downplaying such countercultural oddities as bleeding wounds and visions from Jesus and instead earning one's place in American society by chasing worldly success, which in turn helped support purely Catholic institutions and organizations.

From Convent to Condo

Margaret Reilly's candidacy sputtered to a halt in the late 1960s, and the Peekskill community of Good Shepherds would endure for another twenty years. One recurring theme in Jesus's revelations to Margaret had been the need to protect religious vocations. Dubbing America the "grave of religious life," the Lord directed Margaret to call for increased purity in religious life and for prayers for priests to "convert." Her cautions about the worldliness and impiety of the clergy were consistent with a long tradition of nuns' visionary utterances but made her something of a maverick in the United States. From the date of her vows ceremony until the midsixties, religious vocations only increased; hence, dire warnings about the demise of religious life seemed overstated, especially for sisterhoods. The ideological value of drumming up a climate of fear about the loss of vocations, however, trumped the actual state of affairs in order to commit women religious to serving the clergy as well as their own congregations.

In the end, the Good Shepherd convent at Peekskill closed not from a lack of dedication to religious vows but rather from American demographic change and demands by urbanites for real estate to satisfy their pastoral yearnings. In 1978 the Peekskill convent was abandoned, and in the 1980s Mount St. Florence and Saint Germaine's Home were sold. The convent was later listed on the State Register of Historic Places in recognition of the sisters' service to New Yorkers for a century. In the following decade, the convent property where Sister Thorn had lived was slated to be demolished and converted into condominium projects called "Villa at the Woods" and "Chapel Hill Estate." However, in response to pressure from the city of Peekskill, the Saint Germaine Home and the convent chapel were preserved and adapted to modern use as loft apartments and a recreation center. The conversion of sacred to commercial space signals a downsizing phase in the life of the congregation that has become all too common for many American women's religious communities.[29] Like the Good Shepherd sisters, many orders of American nuns and sisters are being forced to sell portions of their property in order to meet the health-care and pension needs of their declining and aging membership and because of the lack of new vocations to replenish their dwindling communities.

The present-day work of the Good Shepherds, who number about 4,020 worldwide (or less than half as many sisters as at the time of their founder's death in 1868), continues the order's original ministry by running rehabilitation programs for women in family and social difficulties, including unwed mothers, battered wives, drug addicts, women prisoners, HIV-positive patients, prostitutes, and exploited women.[30] In New York City, for instance, Good Shepherd Services works with over 20,000 children and families to sponsor programs for child care, after-school activities, job placement, family counseling, and a food bank and a thrift shop. Since the 1980s, the Good Shepherds have closed certain houses in order to expand their work to include participation as a nongovernmental organization (NGO) at the United Nations, dealing with the issue of ending the domestic and international sex trade that targets women and children. This step by the sisters to work with the antitrafficking movement represents an expansion into the global arena of their original vow to care for delinquent girls and women; they now care for women and girls at risk for a variety of reasons, including those suffering from HIV/AIDs, drug addiction, abusive relationships, and enslavement into prostitution. The lives of the sisters today are certainly not glamorous or easy. When I first met the Jamaica-Queens community of Good Shepherds at their house in 1995, their battered car had been stolen numerous times from the street in front of their modest home.

The Good Shepherds remain constant in their affirmation of women's rights and dignity, as is evidenced in their community sponsorship of programs for families and literacy, jobs, and rehabilitation. While their modes of living out their service to others may have changed to adopt less-judgmental and punitive attitudes toward "wayward" girls and women, the Christocentric focus of the Good Shepherd sisters remains the same. The congregation continues to care for the marginal and vulnerable and, more recently, to educate themselves about the structural causes of sex trafficking, child abuse, prostitution, and drug addiction even as their own numbers decline. For today's Good Shepherds, Sister Thorn is an artifact of their history, one that is not ignored but not highlighted unnecessarily. The fact that she is little known among younger members attests to the successful efforts of certain superiors from the 1940s onward to suppress discussion about her.

During her lifetime, although confined to her wheelchair or to bed in a cloistered setting, Margaret Reilly mediated a network of followers that reverberated across the nation and transnationally. The onset of her stigmata in a convent in 1921 pulled believers backward in shared cultural memory to their origins with Francis of Assisi, then drew them forward in time through the litany of Baroque mystics to the immense transnational literature on Passion mysticism, within which Sister Thorn's followers located her and themselves. In addition to her historical connection to the medieval origins of stigmatization and its Early Modern expressions, Sister Thorn's followers placed her in the lineage of recent European cults of stigmatisées in Austria, Belgium, France, Germany, Ireland, Italy, Portugal, and Spain. Her experiences gained power by attaching themselves to the revived cult of the Sacred Heart and its saintly promoters, who had inspired the founders of her religious order. In her life of supernatural and natural suffering, others found their own desires and histories mirrored. In her pain, many believers found something salvific and meaningful.

I have assumed throughout this exploration that the veracity of Margaret's stigmatization is not necessarily the key to understanding her significance. Believers and skeptics have had their say in the preceding pages. What mattered equally was the desire of an audience for it to be true, a wish that was already present in those who became devoted to her and who systematically worked to inscribe her within the hagiographic and mystical traditions of the Passion of Christ. These motives reflected psychological and sociological forces, allowing Sister Thorn to represent many different things to many subjects, a group that included her own relatives and friends, the Good Shepherd sisters, Benedictines, Discalced Carmelites, Dominicans, Franciscans, Holy Cross fathers, Jesuits, Passionists, numerous bishops, diocesan clergy, physicians, and scholars. As a sociologist has pointed out, "Saints are saints for other people but they are also made saints by other people."[31] In the psychological realm, the desire of Christians for victims, stigmatics, and visionaries reflects unconscious processes of identification with an oppressed figure who will eventually triumph, a fantasy that helped American Catholic clergy and laity to manage the transition from their immigrant or hyphenated identities to that of full-fledged patriots and flourishing citizens.

No matter what these individuals and cohorts imagined about Sister Thorn, certain pieces of evidence point to her as a fraudulent stigmatic: the classic conversion symptom of her paralysis on the very day she was being asked to leave the convent; the short duration of the bleeding wounds and the lack of witnesses to and physical evidence of their onset; the controversial crucifix image on her chest and wall that closely resembled a commercial stamp; the confusion in the written record regarding the timing, location, and appearance of her various physical markings; and the many poltergeist incidents at the convent that she could have performed.

Testimony supporting her genuineness, however, came from trustworthy eyewitnesses who beheld and nursed her wounds and from the affirmations of Sister Carmelita Quinn, Dr. McParlan and Cardinal James McIntyre. The latter, when he became archbishop of Los Angeles, continued to campaign on behalf of Sister Thorn. He gave the Good Shepherds in California his only photograph of her in order to convince them "that while the religious of her own Congregation did not all approve or believe in her saintliness, that there were OTHERS WHO DID."[32] He also gave a rosary to the superior, telling her: "DO NOT LET ANYONE DEPRIVE YOU OF THE PRIVILEGE OF HAVING A SAINT IN YOUR CONGREGATION."[33] Indeed, a female mystic could help the sisters to escape, if only briefly, the limits of their secondary status within the Catholic Church and to receive favorable attention for the divine favor showered on their religious community. As a candidate for sainthood, Sister Thorn would join the other "blood sisters" of the Catholic Church and enhance the status of the Good Shepherds as a special locus of Jesus's redemptive power.

Conclusion

In the history of Catholic spirituality in interwar America, Sister Thorn represents the dilemmas that faced the in-between generation. This liminal group has been closely identified with the women who brought into being the cult of Saint Jude during the 1930s; they were not immigrants themselves, but as daughters of immigrants, they experienced the unique stresses of being torn between Old and New World gender and religious norms.[1] Sister Thorn, too, is a transitional figure who lived the devotional Catholicism characteristic of immigrant life in America since the mid-1800s, which drew its strength and habits from European precedents. But some of Sister Thorn's followers were already engaging in the liturgical reforms that would soon produce a more active understanding of a public faith that characterized the European church in the 1930s and international Catholicism during the Cold War. In his analysis of the competing strands of American Catholic spirituality between 1900 and 1950, Joseph Chinnici has identified how the liturgical movement emerged to offer an alternative to an existing devotional (in his terms, Eucharistic) model. Ian Linden describes how this same process shifted the core of Christian action by repositioning the church away from its "sterile and abrasive dualism," namely, its perception that church and state were inherently opposed.[2] To take France as one example, the crusade to make the church more integral to society had varying results. It spawned movements on the political right, such as Action Française, which the church condemned in 1926. Yet it also saw the rise of progressive tendencies under the umbrella of "Catholic Action"—movements tailored toward various sectors of the population, from workers, farmers, and sailors to students and middle-class citizens who began to understand the church as having a mission to every dimension of society. Of course, the church did not always applaud these ventures. It usually opposed the militancy of worker-priests and, as it had done with psychoanalysis, rejected any tendency toward materialist thinking that might color Catholic social action.

As a consequence of the emergence of an activist understanding of faith, the American who prayed in private to Sister Thorn for intercessory aid in the 1940s was finding a spiritual landscape that now fused household and civic forms. This postimmigrant generation was likely to have joined in intimate family gatherings such as the veneration of the Blessed Sacrament or the enthronement of the Sacred Heart, but its attentions were also sought for public rituals such as the Block Rosary, the stadium rallies of the Eucharistic Congresses, and the street processions of the Holy Name Society. As anticommunism became a catalyst of much Catholic writing and practice during the postwar decades, Catholics began to perceive that prayer could be a vehicle for turning private spirituality to public purposes, an expansive notion that implied responsibility for the social sphere beyond a welter of purely personal devotions. This was still a distance from Vatican II and Pope John XXIII's assertion of the need for a faith "adapted to our own times," but the public presence of prayer signaled a change in Catholic belief and behavior. The tilt in mood and focus toward the public sphere and social justice was demonstrated in the life paths of several nuns who knew Sister Thorn, women who began their lives as cloistered subjects of a male-dominated institution but who went on to become forceful leaders in the new Leadership Conference of Women Religious and spokespersons for the reform of religious life following Vatican II.

Yet in the year that Margaret Reilly made her final vows, American attention was riveted by reports of the prolonged Catholic exorcism of a possessed woman in Earling, Iowa, which lasted a record twenty-three days over several months. The Earling exorcism became the best-known supernatural event of the decade and one of the last episodes of demonic possession in modern Catholic history. It reached large audiences through the pamphlet written in German by a witness that was translated into English at St. John's Abbey in Minnesota. (Forty years later, the case was said to have been a major inspiration for William Peter Blatty's novel *The Exorcist*.) The exorcist in the Earling case, Brother Theophilus Riesinger (1868–1941)—a Capuchin friar known as the "warrior knight"—claimed that he drove "billions and billions of devils" from the body of forty-year-old Emma Schmidt by addressing them in English, German, and Latin. The possessed woman had been diagnosed as "a pure hysterical case," but doctors had failed to help her. Brother Riesinger, by contrast, had already successfully treated nineteen cases of demonic possession.[3]

The Earling exorcism occasioned many comments from priests and physicians in the United States. As they drew connections between diabolical possession and stigmatics who were troubled by demons, notably the cases of Catherine Emmerich and Therese Neumann, they repeated the pattern seen at Peekskill of linking American encounters with the supernatural to European precedents. That this transnational flow became a reciprocal rather than a one-way process is seen in the fact that from Bavaria, Therese Neumann claimed to witness the events in Iowa in a trance state, seeing from afar the "frightful battle" under way between Saint Michael's angels and Lucifer's demons. Although Neumann's clairvoyance may have a natural explanation in the fact that Brother Riesinger also came from Bavaria and kept close ties to his three brothers there, the attempts to draw parallels between Catholic America and Europe are nevertheless instructive.[4]

By fluidly merging the past and present, the Earling exorcism became an event that propelled Catholics from homogeneous time into "messianic time," transforming the United States into a battleground where cosmic forces are always wrangling and shaping an environment that made Sister Thorn's stigmata less incredible. The message to American Catholics was clear: even though Christ's casting out of devils took place in ancient Palestine, today, in the cornfields of Iowa or on the Hudson Palisades of New York, Lucifer and Antichrist were still lurking to snatch the unwary. Just as Sister Thorn's followers worked to smooth her life into an acceptable narrative but found themselves shifting between routine and cosmic time, so did the narrative features of the Earling exorcism travel back and forth between the ordinary and extraordinary. The irruption of evil forces in America propelled those living in ordinary time to a heightened need to derive lessons from reminders such as Earling and Peekskill. For one surgeon from Milwaukee, the moral of the Iowa exorcism was that "Satan has seemed too unreal." He continued: "No more vivid picture has been presented to us of the losing battle which the great enemy of the human race has been waging against the 'camp of Christ.'"[5] For a second group of Catholics—priests—the message of Earling confirmed the singular powers of the ordained ministry to cast out demons.

A third function of the presence of the demonic in early twentieth-century America was to deflect anger at God onto hatred of the devil. Catholics suffering injustice in the United States could not blame the omnipotent God, so it is not surprising that as members of the "camp of Christ," they turned to messianic genres and militant rhetoric to express their emotions. The exorcist's naming of the actual devils who were expelled at Earling—Beelzebub, Jacob, Judas, Lucifer, and Mina—added a familiar note to these ghoulish stories that touched even Virgil Michel (1890–1938), a Benedictine who later became a prominent liturgical reformer in the Catholic Church. Associated with the reform movement pioneered at the same abbey in Minnesota that had translated the Earling materials, Michel, like Dorothy Day and Thomas Merton, became one of several influential Americans in the interwar era who attempted to put together the "fractured inheritance" of Catholic spirituality that had cordoned off spirituality from social reform.[6] During the Earling episode, however, a younger Michel fixated on the demonic. He recalled that "for a time it was fashionable to scoff at demoniacal possession as part and parcel of an outmoded superstition of bygone ages of ignorance—like the attitude of a lifetime ago in regard to the miracles of Lourdes." Now, he noted, "our age and civilization needs to learn anew a lesson that was vainly laughed to scorn in past generations."[7] Fortunately, he concluded, the Iowa exorcism had "brought many priests and bishops to a more serious consciousness of existing conditions."[8] In Earling, Michel displayed a traditionalist bent by responding as Lukas Etlin had to Sister Thorn: as a seeker hungering for personal contact with the supernatural.

At Earling and Peekskill, men used the bodies of women to foster that encounter and to affirm their own sacramental powers. Like Emma Schmidt, Margaret Reilly was another barometer of the omnipresence of Satan, his possessive schemes, and the fragility of the religious life against his designs. At Peekskill, among her many encounters with evil spirits, she once "beheld fifty demons walking around her bed when she received Holy Communion, with Beelzebub, the prince of devils, near. Sometimes they were under horrible forms, and usually stood on their hind legs."[9] Sister Thorn's diabolic torments predictably led one priest to a defense of sacerdotalism, a concern always lurking within clerical involvement in popular cults. "It is absolutely forbidden Catholics to frequent Spiritistic séances," Father Scanlan argued, "to consult fortune-tellers, to join in false worship, to participate in the membership of any society that maintains A SECRET AGAINST AND ABOVE the reach of the seal of confession. . . . It is Christian A-B-C's that NO DISEMBODIED HUMAN SOUL can have NATURAL contacts with the living. The haunting of houses and deranged mentalities, if real, is the WORK OF DEMONS who live when they lay claim to being either human or humane."[10] In this outburst, the priest affirms the church's condemnation of spiritualism as demonic and a false form of worship.

Popular and clerical responses to the reports of demonic possession and of stigmata in the 1920s did not indicate that the hierarchy believed these things to be an embarrassment to the Catholic Church. Instead, supernatural and diabolical events delivered warnings to Americans that they had become careless in defending Catholic tradition by combating its persecutors, whether they be the Ku Klux Klan, spirit mediums, or devils. Furthermore, a heightened supernaturalism among Catholics served them in the twentieth century as it had in thirteenth: as a form of cultural resistance to irreligion and as a way to empower religious orders. At least part of the debate over Sister Thorn, a female mystic, touched concerns about refashioning a masculine subject. The church worried about the crumbling of differences between the sexes in the Jazz Age, while at the same time, priests feared losing their power in the confessional to secular professionals. By insisting upon controlling convents and women like Sister Thorn, laymen and clergy reconfirmed their commitment to patriarchy. But increased attention to the supernatural also revealed anxieties about the cultural integration of American Catholics in general. Their obsession with the presence of demons in their midst suggests the unsettled state of second-generation Catholics and their ministers in America. The anxiety of priests to affirm their authority over natural and supernatural worlds showed itself in the details of these exorcisms and stigmatizations.

By rejecting Theosophy, Christian Science, Masonry, spiritualism, fortune-telling, palmistry, numerology, and astrology (each listed and condemned by Father Scanlan in the passage above), and also psychoanalysis (condemned by Monsignor Fulton Sheen), Catholics would show themselves to be genuine Christians and worthy Americans who were not slaves to emotions "and other varieties of dense spiritual coma." Their detachment from the lures of the world allowed them to "expect here below, nothing but labor and suffering," and to rejoice in that fact. Paradoxically, Catholics were urged to be joyful about the church's endorsement of constant suffering and sacrifice as weapons against "the stinkbugs of occultism."[11] Accordingly, Margaret Reilly took satisfaction from Jesus's promise that "we cannot change the world, taking out all its thorns, making its tasks easy and its burden light; modulating all its discord into harmonies, transforming its ugliness into beauty. But we can have our own heart renewed by the grace of God, and thus the world will be made over for us. A new heart makes all things new. A heart of love will find love everywhere. A soul of song will find sweet music everywhere."[12]

It is sometimes hard for contemporary persons to "find sweet music" in the outlook of Sister Thorn, who rejoiced in her intimate contact with Jesus during her sleepless nights by reckoning: "The more pain He gives me, the more I love Him, because suffering increases love."[13] The clergy, too, looked for "complete immolation for the happy victim," calling Margaret "one of those moths that will be drawn into the Sun."[14] The traditions within Christian mysticism that thrived on metaphors of engulfment, immolation, and annihilation helped express a cultural crisis from the 1920s to the 1940s, a period when assimilation was at once desirable and frightening to American Catholics. The contours of that older, devotional spirituality were already being challenged, however, by the movement for liturgical reform, which hoped to shift the locus of Catholics' attention from the tabernacle to the altar and to involve the laity in the Mass rather than consigning them to the role of spectators to clerical power and sacrificial rhetoric. The debates among Catholics about the supernatural also appear as part of the church's debates over the proper understanding of the Eucharist. To some historians, the Eucharist framed "the structures that dominated Catholic spiritual life in the twentieth century," and the "whole phenomenon was a symbol of the church, its self-perception and struggle for identity in American society."[15] If this is the case, then many of the priests who involved themselves with Sister Thorn allied themselves with the older, devotional model, as seen by their attempts to use the Mass, spiritual retreats, and discernment of mystics as occasions to preserve their own status as elevated and unique.[16]

Catholic strategies of severe penance are less appealing to twenty-first-century persons because of a vastly changed social, theological, and medical context in which a theology of vicarious atonement and constant physical pain makes little sense. Indeed, modern cancer treatments may have been able to eliminate Sister Thorn's pain altogether, and possibly even her disease. But during her lifetime, the veneration of spiritual victimhood and the certainty of the presence of demons were among several Catholic "off-modern" responses to modernization. First, the peripheral and secluded locales of Peekskill and Earling echoed events in the Catholic past in which God tested ordinary persons in ordinary places. Second, Sister Thorn contributed to the creation of a transnational Catholic identity in this era, when the American church was striving to subordinate immigrant identities to a Catholic one. As it tried to override ethnic particularisms, the church emphasized the need to reclaim Catholicism's universal character and mission, especially after the wartime destruction of 1914–18. The vitality of mystical phenomena, including stigmata, in the 1920s contributed to this process of cultural reconstruction by asserting the reality of supernature and by professing the church's unique relationship to divine power. Finally, Sister Thorn's case demonstrates an earlier stage in a process of transformation within American Catholic lived religion, namely, a moment prior to a shift from Passion mysticism to an energistic model of the meaning of spiritual suffering. Since Sister Thorn's lifetime, as seen in contemporary websites devoted to stigmatics, the energistic model has come to prevail. Pain and suffering are minimized in the manner of "human potential" movements, which instead "accentuate the positive." In their online settings, stigmatics serve as inspirational figures who are appropriated in highly personal ways, resembling "extreme athletes" who represent extraordinary energies that they use in the pursuit of the absolute limits of human capacities rather than as proofs of the infinite capacities of God. The remaking of the stigmatic self continues in the twenty-first century with suffering of a different sort.

Notes

Abbreviations

AANY   Archives of the Archdiocese of New York, Yonkers, N.Y.

ARGS   Archives of the Sisters of the Good Shepherd, Jamaica, N.Y.

AOSB/M   Archives of the Order of St. Benedict, Conception Abbey, Clyde, Missouri

AOSB/W   Archives of the Congregation of Benedictine Sisters of Perpetual Adoration, Clyde, Missouri, then held in St. Louis

CCLO-UNDA   Charles L. O'Donnell Manuscripts, Archives of the University of Notre Dame, Notre Dame, Ind., 3/12 Folder: Margaret Reilly

CCMM-UNDA   Collection of Miscellaneous Manuscripts, Archives of the University of Notre Dame, Notre Dame, Ind., 1/38

CJWC-UNDA   John W. Cavanaugh Papers, Archives of the University of Notre Dame, Notre Dame, Ind., 11/08-09

JA   Jesuit Archives, Farm Street, London

NYT   *New York Times*

SMCQ   Sister Mary Carmelita Quinn documents, Archives of the Sisters of the Good Shepherd, Jamaica, N.Y.

SMCQ-SMCT   Sister Mary Carmelita Quinn, "Sister Mary Crown of Thorns, R.G.S., a Religious of the Convent of the Good Shepherd, Peekskill, New York," Archives of the Sisters of the Good Shepherd, Jamaica, N.Y.

Introduction

1. William J. Ennis, SJ, June 27, 1922, to Archbishop Patrick Hayes, AANY microfilm, Hayes correspondence. "Non probatus" means "not passed."

2. Estimates of the worldwide death toll from the Spanish influenza range from 20 million to 100 million. In the United States, approximately 650,000 people died from the flu or the resulting pneumonia.

3. Obviously, every parish in the nation did not meet the bishops' time line of two years, and the parochial school plan was never fully realized.

4. This congregation, founded in 1588 by Pope Sixtus V, who created the congregational structure to administer the Vatican, was renamed in 1969 as the Congregation for the Causes of Saints.

5. The only alleged Irish stigmatic of the twentieth century is the Marian visionary Christina Gallagher, and her stigmata are far from being acknowledged.

6. Joe Nickell, *Looking for a Miracle: Weeping Icons, Relics, Stigmata, Visions, and Healing Cures* (New York: Prometheus Books, 1993), 219.

7. A list of Catholic stigmatics, compiled in a 1894 publication, is still cited as authoritative despite its errors. Antoine Imbert-Gourbeyre, *La stigmatisation: L'exstase divine et les miracles de Lourdes: Réponse aux Libres-Penseurs*, vol. 1 (Paris: Bellet, 1898).

8. Pierre Adnès, *Dictionnaire de Spiritualité*, vol. 16 (Paris: Editions Beauchesne, 1937–; fasc. 95 Coll. 1:211–43), 1229. Regarding inedia, Thurston reported that Lateau was never a large eater, but after her ecstasies and stigmata had begun in 1868, she ate less and less and never on Fridays. March 30, 1871, was recorded as the last day when she could eat and digest any solid food without acute suffering. Herbert Thurston, *The Physical Phenomena of Mysticism*, ed. J. H. Crehan (London: Burns, Oates, 1952), 349.

9. Rev. H. Austin, *The Stigmata: History of Various Cases* (London: Thomas Richardson and Son, 1883), 218–19. The account of Lateau quoted here is an English translation of the observations of Dr. Lefebvre. The very reference to the frequent appearance of the prayer figure with extended arms (the Orantes) in the art of the catacombs of Rome suggests the desire to link the modern stigmatic to an unbroken tradition in Christianity.

10. "The Ecstasy of Louise Lateau," *Young Crusader* 5, no. 2 (February 1873): 72. I thank Mary Oates, CSJ, for the citation. This children's magazine article excerpted the translated account of Dr. Lefebvre cited immediately above.

11. See two collections of essays on the Americas: Allan Greer and Jody Bilinkoff, eds., *Colonial Saints: Discovering the Holy in the Americas, 1500–1800* (New York: Routledge, 2003); and Margaret Cormack, ed., *Saints and Their Cults in the Atlantic World* (Columbia, S.C.: University of South Carolina Press, 2007).

12. John Adams to Abigail Adams, October 9, 1774, in *The Adams Family Correspondence*, ed. L. H. Butterfield (Cambridge, Mass.: Belknap Press of Harvard University Press, 1963), 1:166–67.

13. R. Bruce Mullin, *Miracles and the Modern Religious Imagination* (New Haven, Conn.: Yale University Press, 1996), 114.

14. Nancy Lusignan Schultz, *Mrs. Mattingly's Miracle* (New Haven, Conn.: Yale University Press, 2011). The case is discussed in more detail in chapter 3.

15. Ann Taves, *The Household of Faith: Roman Catholic Devotions in Mid-Nineteenth-Century America* (Notre Dame, Ind.: University of Notre Dame Press, 1986), 132.

16. Information on Sally Collins is from the Holy Family sisters archive in San Francisco, California, and reports in the *San Francisco Post* and *San Francisco Chronicle*, April 20, 1873. The Holy Family sisters were founded in 1872 as an apostolic institute to serve poor families. Collins had a difficult relationship with them.

17. Laurie Finke, cited in Elizabeth Petroff, *Body and Soul: Essays on Medieval Women and Mysticism* (New York: Oxford University Press, 1994), 215.

18. A new reader in the field illustrates the range of topics and approaches: James Fisher and Margaret McGuinness, eds., *A Catholic Studies Reader* (New York: Fordham University Press, 2011).

19. The point is well made by Arthur Kleinman in *The Illness Narratives: Suffering, Healing, and the Human Condition* (New York: Basic Books, 1989), 28.

20. Stephen Schloesser, *Jazz Age Catholicism: Mystic Modernism in Postwar Paris, 1919–1933* (Toronto: University of Toronto Press, 2005), prologue.

21. Robert A. Orsi, "Printed Presence: Twentieth-Century Catholic Print Culture for Youngsters in the United States," in *Education and the Culture of Print in Modern America*, ed. Adam R. Nelson and John L. Rudolph (Madison, Wisc.: University of Wisconsin Press), 83. Discussion of "in-between" generations is mostly from Robert A. Orsi, *Thank You, St. Jude: Women's Devotion to the Patron Saint of Hopeless Causes* (New Haven, Conn.: Yale University Press, 1996).

22. James T. Fisher, *On the Irish Waterfront: The Crusader, the Movie, and the Soul of the Port of New York* (Ithaca, N.Y.: Cornell University Press, 2009), 76.

23. Kathleen Sprows Cummings, *New Women of the Old Faith: Gender and American Catholicism in the Progressive Era* (Chapel Hill: University of North Carolina Press, 2010), 57.

24. Louis Althusser famously used the term "interpellation" to refer to how the individual is produced as a subject by social relations. Louis Althusser, *Essays on Ideology* (New York: Verso, 1970), 11.

25. Carol K. Coburn and Martha Smith, *Spirited Lives: How Nuns Shaped Catholic Culture and American Life, 1836–1920* (Chapel Hill: University of North Carolina Press, 1999), 80.

26. Apparently, Mother Raymond made four copies of her typescript: one for the RGS motherhouse in Angers, one for herself (which ended up in the hands of Sister Alexia), one for Archbishop Hayes, and the final copy perhaps for the convent chaplain, Father Brady.

27. The full title of Sister Carmelita Quinn's account is "Sister Mary Crown of Thorns, R.G.S., a Religious of the Convent of the Good Shepherd, Peekskill, New York" (undated).

28. Ibid., 20–26. Mergen's dates are 1879–1971.

29. Ibid., 83–116.

30. "Communications of Our Lord to 'Margaret,'" copied at Peekskill by Lukas Etlin, November 17–30, 1923, 98, ARGS.

31. "Communications of Our Lord to 'Margaret,'" copied at Peekskill by Lukas Etlin, Christmas 1922, ARGS.

32. Garrigou-Lagrange, who published *The Three Ages of the Interior Life* (1938), was perhaps the best-known Thomist of the twentieth century and was a teacher of Karol Wojtyla, who later became Pope John Paul II.

33. Rev. Thomas à Kempis Reilly, OP, "Spinations," ARGS.

34. Here the term "monastery" refers to cloistered nuns. Walter Gabriel Scanlan, OP (1881–1950), served at St. Dominic's parish in Detroit beginning in 1929.

35. Three-page letter to Sister Clare Nolan from Mrs. George McInerney Crandles of New Jersey, loaned to the author.

36. Schloesser, *Jazz Age Catholicism*, 14. Schloesser considers French postwar philosophers, writers, artists, and musicians (Jacques Maritain, Georges Bernanos, Georges Rouault, Charles Tournemire) "as various expressions of Catholic dialectical realism."

Chapter 1

1. In the various accounts of this episode, the priest is not named. It was likely Father Brady from the Reilly's parish, St. Francis de Sales.

2. "Communications of Our Lord to 'Margaret,'" copied at Peekskill by Lukas Etlin, November 17–30, 1923, ARGS.

3. "Clyde Chronicles," which consists of the data used by Sister Carmelita in compiling her life of Sister Thorn from Mother Raymond Cahill's narrative. ARGS.

4. SMCQ-SMCT, 9. It is unknown how and where Margaret acquired a hair shirt in Manhattan. Rev. Herbert Thurston surmised that Monsignor Taylor, her confessor, was responsible for asking Margaret to surrender her hair shirt to him and for promising her that the Lord would favor her with a cross as a substitute. Not long after this, in 1916, Margaret reported her first supernatural experience, and the crucifix appeared the following year.

5. Jane Howard Harrington, photocopied letter, ARGS. She was a friend of Margaret's cousin, Rita Connolly, and attended the Ursuline academy in Ohio where Margaret visited.

6. Sister Mary Carmelita Quinn, "Clyde Chronicles," 17, ARGS.

7. Sister Thorn did not have "visions" in the sense of beholding a saint with her own

eyes but instead received what are called "inner locutions" in Catholic mystical theology, wherein she alone heard the voices of Jesus, Mary, and various saints.

8. Copy of Raymond's manuscript, pp. 20–25, written for the RGS Mother General in Angers, France, inserted with SMCQ-SMCT, 20, 21.

9. Ibid., 21.

10. However, Margaret told Lukas Etlin that Jesus named her Thorn to be a thorn in the side of the sisters and help them return to rigorous adherence to convent rules.

11. "Words addressed to Margaret Reilly by Jesus in a vision of January 18, 1917," recorded by Lukas Etlin, OSB, during his visit to Peekskill, November 17–30, 1923, ARGS. In Christian tradition, lilies symbolize chastity and purity.

12. SMCQ-SMCT, 27.

13. Obituary for Mother Raymond, *Catholic News* (Newark, N.J.), April 1, 1939.

14. Margaret Reilly's niece (and namesake) also reported receiving a privileged bit of information while visiting her aunt at Peekskill. The transmission of "secret" knowledge by convented women to their younger female relatives seemed a way of assuring relatives that even though they were cloistered, nuns were not irrelevant to the world.

15. Information from seven-page biographical sketch of Mother Raymond by her niece and nephew, ARGS.

16. Raymond in SMCQ, 20–26. It was not uncommon for nuns and sisters to take the names of male saints, perhaps as a way to "reverse or minimize gender limitations." Jo Ann McNamara, *Sisters in Arms: Catholic Nuns through Two Millennia* (Cambridge, Mass.: Harvard University Press, 1996), 82. Raymond of Nonnatus, as his name suggests, was also patron saint of the unborn.

17. Sister Martha Marie Crowley, June 10, 1975, sent by Carol Quirk to author, 1995.

18. Raymond, "Assaults of the Evil Spirit," in SMCQ, 23.

19. Raymond in SMCQ, 28 (no date).

20. Raymond, "Assaults," 27.

21. SMCQ-SMCT, 81. This detail seems added by Carmelita in imitation of the life of Saint Catherine of Siena; it is not reported anywhere else.

22. Mary Connolly (1865–1971) was Margaret's first cousin. Mary's mother, Isabel McLoughlin, was the sister of Margaret's mother, also named Mary. Rita's father was Henry Connolly.

23. Charles L. O'Connell, CSC, to Archbishop Patrick Hayes, February 19, 1922, microfilm of Hayes correspondence, AANY.

24. The title of "Visitor" refers to the Good Shepherd sister, chosen by the superior general, who observed each of the congregations in the religious order on a nearly annual basis.

25. Raymond narrative (my emphasis).

26. Hickey to Etlin, December 10 or 18, 1924, OSB, Clyde archives, St. Louis.

27. Mother Raymond to Sister Sebastian, March 8, 1922, ARGS.

28. Letter from Sister Sebastian to Sister Inez, August 30, 1922, ARGS. The "lettering" may refer to the inscription "INRI" atop the crucifix for *Jesus Nazareni Rex Judaeorum* (Jesus of Nazareth, King of the Jews), using the Roman alphabet, which had no letter *J*.

29. Mother Raymond to Sister Sebastian.

30. Letter of Sister Sebastian, OP, New York City, to Sister Inez, OP, St. Mary of the Springs, Ohio, August 30, 1922, ARGS.

31. Unfortunately, there is no record of Sister Mary Carmelita Quinn viewing or touching Margaret's wounds. According to her, Margaret "told me when I sat beside her

in the 1920s that she had asked our Lord to remove the VISIBLE signs of the stigmata, which He did, but she continued to suffer the pains in the same areas, though the bleeding discontinued."

32. Typescript notes by SMCQ, p. 20, at ARGS.

33. Raymond in SMCQ-SMCT, 64.

34. *Golden Memories of the Sisters of the Good Shepherd, 1884–1934* (Troy, N.Y.: n.p., 1934), 39.

35. S. Tarcisius [Anderson], "Sisters of the Good Shepherd—Villa Loretto, Peekskill, N.Y." (1952).

36. Raymond in SMCQ, 29.

37. Ibid., 28, for January 18, 1922. The story is recounted on pages 28–30.

38. Benedict Bradley, OSB (1867–1945), may be the source of information on these events since Lukas Etlin did not give retreats at Peekskill until 1923. Bradley had been teaching at the Benedictine prep school in Newark, New Jersey, since 1920 and also served as confessor to the sisters at Convent Station, where he was impressed by a mystically inclined novice, Miriam Teresa Demjanovich (1901–27), whose reflections on spiritual perfection he edited and ultimately published. Her cause for sainthood, the first from New Jersey, is still proceeding.

39. Raymond in SMCQ-SMCT, 62.

40. McParlan to Carmelita, May 18, 1927, AOSB/M.

41. Sister Mary of the Good Shepherd Tellers was RGS provincial for the New York region between 1920 and 1929, which included the convents of Boston, Brooklyn, New York City, Peekskill, and Troy. She was a major figure in Sister Thorn's case.

42. Mother Raymond to Rita, February 15, 1922, RGS, Cahill, R., file.

43. SMCQ-SMCT, 28–29.

44. McParlan to Sister Paul, OSD, October 13, 1922, AOSB/M. He continued: "She is not allowed to have anything blessed, as it was creating too much talk and arousing too much curiosity." This comment refers to Margaret's custom of making and distributing images of the Sacred Heart of Jesus, which she claimed had been supernaturally blessed for her. The badges are discussed in chapter 5. In a letter to Father Etlin, McParlan declared: "Yesterday was the culmination of one of her Prophecies or letters dictated by Our Dear Lord. 'Thorn, you are not to go to the novitiate, the novitiate will come to you.'" McParlan to Etlin, December 12/9, 1925, AOSB/M.

45. Using federal census records from the convent, I was able to identify Sister Paschal as Bridget Costigan.

46. Sister Mary of St. Tarcisius to Sister Mary Carmelita Quinn, December 2, 1975, ARGS. However, since Mary Anderson's birth date is given as "about 1900," she was at least sixteen years younger than Margaret Reilly.

47. McGivney to Thurston, February 27, 1925, CJWC-UNDA (emphasis in original).

48. Margaret Hanway Armstrong (1878–1953), born in Brooklyn to a father who was an Irish editor and journalist, married Sir Harry Gloster Armstrong in 1912. Gloster, born in Ireland, converted to Catholicism in 1905 during his colorful life in the military, theater, commerce, and consulate.

49. The "Gallen letters" are discussed in chapter 4.

50. McGivney to Thurston, February 27, 1925, CJWC-UNDA.

51. McGivney to Thurston, n.d., CJWC-UNDA. McGivney refers to Margaret as "Kate," following the precedent in Thurston's article about her.

52. McParlan to Etlin, September 19, 1927, AOSB/M. Cited earlier in the chapter.

53. Rev. Francis Valitutti to Hayes, February 1, 1922, AANY, Hayes correspondence, "Petitions."

54. Rev. Winfrid Herbst, SDS, to Hayes, September 28, 1923, AANY, Hayes correspondence, "Petitions."

55. Thomas J. Rowland, "Irish-American Catholics and the Quest for Respectability in the Coming of the Great War, 1900–1917," *Journal of American Ethnic History* 15, no. 2 (Winter 1996): 3–31.

56. The term comes from Edward Muir, *Ritual in Early Modern Europe* (Cambridge, UK: Cambridge University Press, 1997), and refers to the nearly three centuries of the reshaping of Christian tradition by Protestants and Catholics.

57. James Fisher, *The Catholic Counterculture in America, 1933–1962* (Chapel Hill: University of North Carolina Press, 1989), 76.

58. William M. Halsey, *The Survival of American Innocence: Catholicism in an Era of Disillusionment, 1920–1940* (Notre Dame, Ind.: University of Notre Dame Press, 1980).

59. SMCQ, 16. The Presentation sisters, founded in Cork in 1776, arrived in Manhattan in 1874 when Mother Joseph Hickey brought a group of twelve sisters to teach at St. Michael's parish school and to care for destitute children. Because it was atypical for cloistered nuns to teach school, in 1907 the Presentation sisters added a paved rooftop for their own recreation to seclude them from the public. See, for example, Marjorie Phillips's painting, *Nuns on the Roof* (1922), Phillips Collection, Washington, D.C.

60. SMCQ, 1.

61. The Reilly children were Mary, John (d.), Helen, Thomas, Annabelle (d.), Catherine, and Margaret.

62. SMCQ-SMCT, 39.

63. Ibid., 1.

64. As reported to SMCQ, "Thorn," 1–2.

65. As recently as the 1970s, anthropologist Nancy Scheper-Hughes found that in Ireland, "there is a strong tendency among Irish mothers and fathers to repress, deny, and ignore babies' demands for physical gratification and stimulation (including sucking, rocking, and holding) to the extent that Irish toddlers are remarkably undemanding and frequently shy and withdrawn." Nancy Scheper-Hughes, *Saints, Scholars, and Schizophrenics: Mental Illness in Rural Ireland* (Berkeley: University of California Press, 1979), 133–34.

66. SMCQ, 4, 9. Guardian angels were a new emphasis in the popular Catholicism of that era. Gemma Galgani's *Diary* records her daily conversations with her angel, for instance, as did Padre Pio's.

67. SMCQ, 5. The sisters came from Emmitsburg, Maryland.

68. Ibid., 6.

69. Margaret inscribed this address in her sodality handbook, now in the possession of Susan Walter and loaned to the author. In 1891 at least one millionaire, Andrew Carnegie, had situated his mansion as far north as Prospect Hill, Fifth Avenue and 91st Street, causing it to be renamed Carnegie Hill.

70. Marion R. Carey, "'From the East Side to the Seaside': Irish Americans on the Move in New York City," in *The New York Irish*, ed. Ronald H. Bayor and Timothy J. Meagher (Baltimore: Johns Hopkins University Press, 1996), 408.

71. Ibid., 399.

72. Ibid., 401.

73. Information about St. Francis de Sales parish appears in *The Catholic Church in the United States: Undertaken to Celebrate the Golden Jubilee of His Holiness, Pope Pius X*, vol. 3

(N.p.: Catholic Editing Company, 1914), 326. In 1913 the church's first pastor, Reverend Hoey, died, succeeded by Msgr. James V. Lewis, formerly secretary to Cardinal Farley. From this point, the parish debt was reduced quite rapidly, securing an untroubled future for the community.

74. The letterhead of St. Francis parish stationery lists an address of 135 E. 96th Street; the *AIA Guide* to New York City lists the convent, at 15 E. 96th Street, as a private limestone townhouse repurposed as a convent in 1915.

75. After William Schickel died in 1907, the firm continued to practice under the direction of Isaac E. Ditmars. At the time, Ditmars became engaged in building the Cathedral of the Sacred Heart in Newark, New Jersey.

76. SMCQ-SMCT, binder with Quinn's memories of Sister Thorn, AOSB/W, inside File Quinn.8 "Crown of Thorns." Sister Carmelita called this the 76th Street church, although Blessed Sacrament is located at Broadway and 71st Street. Margaret attended confession there with Msgr. Taylor. It is a long walk from the Reilly home on the Upper East Side across Central Park to Blessed Sacrament Church, founded in 1887. In 1919 the congregation built a larger church at 152 West 71st Street following the razing of the original church in 1917. *Golden Jubilee, Church of the Blessed Sacrament* (1937), excerpted on the parish website at www.blessedsacramentnyc.com/history.htm.

77. SMCQ-SMCT, 2.

78. Ibid., 13.

79. The theme of patriarchal domesticity is explored in Nancy Christie, "Introduction," *Households of Faith* (Montreal: McGill University Press, 2002), 3–33.

80. Reported in Dr. James J. Walsh's typed "History" of Margaret Reilly. The explosion was also covered in the *New York Times* ("Explosion Uptown Kills and Wrecks," November 24, 1911). Apparently, the practice of "toasting" the dynamite to thaw it before use led to the explosion inside a construction shed, resulting in one death and numerous injuries and broken windows. Mr. Reilly and his son, the contractors, were charged with homicide by police.

81. SMCQ-SMCT, 15. Prior to this point, only Mrs. Reilly and their pastor had seen the crucifix.

82. Ibid., 1, 11.

83. The notion of a Catholic International is still being articulated. Here, I draw upon materials from "Religious Internationals in the Modern World," a conference at Oxford University in January 2009, which considered a religious international as "a cluster of voluntary transnational organizations and representations crystallizing around international issues, in which both 'ordinary' believers and religious specialists could serve as protagonists."

84. The story is well told in John T. McGreevy, *Catholicism and American Freedom: A History* (New York: Norton, 2003), 39–40, 115.

85. Because not all dioceses had the density of Catholic population and the income base of New York City, the construction of Catholic elementary and secondary schools progressed unevenly throughout the nation.

86. Margaret did not attend school at Blessed Sacrament since its parish school was not built until 1903, when it was staffed by the Sisters of Charity.

87. In 1952 the City University of New York purchased this Bronx campus and expanded onto the site. Manhattanville moved to Purchase, New York.

88. Patricia Byrne, CSJ, "The Society of the Sacred Heart in the United States, 1914–1990," unpublished manuscript, 4.

89. SMCQ-SMCT, 2.

90. Ibid., 81.

91. SMCQ, 4.

92. Ibid., 6. "Dolor" means sorrow in Latin. This attribution of Mary was usually paired with the crucified Christ representing the "Man of Sorrows."

93. The impact of devotional culture in Margaret Reilly's life is detailed in chapter 5.

94. SMCQ, 1.

95. Ibid., 5.

96. Emmet Larkin, "The Devotional Revolution in Ireland, 1850–1875," *American Historical Review* 77 (June 1972): 625–52.

97. The memory is from Sister Carmelita Quinn, "Requested sketch of life of: Sr. M. Carmelita Quinn," October 5, 1972, AOSB/W.

98. Etlin, "Communications of Our Lord to Margaret," 88.

99. Colleen McDannell, *The Christian Home in Victorian America, 1840–1900* (Bloomington: Indiana University Press, 1986), 67.

100. McDannell contends that the lack of a Catholic domestic ideology prior to 1880 resulted from Irish Americans' necessary preoccupation with poverty, jobs, and tenement life. Ibid., 52–53. She seeks to overturn the false assumption that American popular culture is Protestant while Catholic culture is somehow "European." Although a certain level of affluence allowed Catholic families to focus upon interior decoration, she claims, they were not necessarily European-centered in their culture. In the area of spirituality, I have found that even after 1900, the Irish continued to look to France and Germany as spiritual centers, importing advice books along with certain strands of theology to help increase the piety of the laity.

101. Mother Raymond in SMCQ-SMCT, 39.

102. Information in this paragraph is from SMCQ-SMCT, 6–9.

103. Herbert Luthy provides a succinct summary of the Catholic outlook: "The edifice of the Catholic Church rests on separating the functions of 'those who pray' from 'those who suffer.' In the hierarchy of values embodied in its own hierarchy, sanctity, meditation and charity are placed much higher than utilitarian work, which is necessary for the needs of the body, but not for the salvation of the soul." *Le Passe present* (Monaco: Editions de Rocher, 1965), 63.

104. SMCQ-SMCT, 11.

105. SMCQ, 30.

106. SMCQ-SMCT, 10.

107. Ibid., 42.

108. SMCQ-SMCT, 26, 27, 34.

109. McGinn three-page report, appended to McGivney report, CJWC-UNDA, 3.

110. McGivney letter to Thurston, marked "strictly confidential," n.d., JA.

111. SMCQ-SMCT, 82.

112. The information in this paragraph appears in ibid., 67.

113. Ibid., 68.

114. The RGS sponsored a fund drive led by Senator Martin G. McCue to improve the 150-acre tract at Throgs Neck and to build a home that could receive 1,000 girls. *NYT*, October 19, 1921.

115. Anecdote from interview with Carol Quirk.

116. SMCQ-SMCT, 58.

117. When the Reilly papers in the RGS archives became restricted, I was unable to successfully research this and other points of information.

118. Raymond even collected the opinions of five sisters of the Paraclete Point RGS house: one is satisfied, but "laments the difficulty[?]"; another laments the "[word indistinct]." The last page lists about forty-five initiates, including Sister Mary of the Crown of Thorns. The final nine women are identified only by their baptismal names, not having been invested yet with their new religious names.

119. The Ursulines of Brown County, who were legally incorporated under that title, arrived in Ohio in 1845 to establish an academy for young women. They were led by an Englishwoman, Julia Chatfield, who had converted to Catholicism under the influence of the Ursulines at the school she attended in southern France. The academy lasted until 1981, when running the boarding school became no longer feasible.

120. SMCQ-SMCT, 17. She may have undergone more surgery in March 1921.

121. SMCQ, 17. Ennis's first encounter with the Good Shepherd sisters dated probably from the 1880s during his third year of probation as a Jesuit in Angers, France, the location of the RGS Generalate.

122. SMCQ, 18.

123. Letter from Ennis to Hayes, June 27, 1922, in which he says that Margaret's eagerness to talk about herself is a strike against her. Hayes correspondence, AANY. Ennis may have received further information about Reilly from his sister, a Good Shepherd member.

124. SMCQ, 21.

125. SMCQ, 61.

126. SMCQ, 62.

127. Notebook of Mother Raymond, "Assaults of the Evil Spirit," in SMCQ, 44–63.

128. SMCQ, 44.

129. December 10, 1921, SMCQ, 44.

130. Ibid., 44–45.

131. Raymond, "Assaults," 62.

132. Ibid., December 13–14, 1921.

133. SMCQ, 61.

134. SMCQ, December 11, 1921, 45.

135. See John R. Dichtl, *Frontiers of Faith: Bringing Catholicism to the West in the Early Republic* (Lexington: University Press of Kentucky, 2008), 115–16.

136. Rev. John W. Cavanaugh, CSC, "Report of Trip to Peekskill," 7, CJWC-UNDA, 4/02, and CJWC 3. It is not clear whether Cavanaugh saw Margaret's deformed feet. This detail conjures up comparisons to photos taken of female hysterics with curled-back toes, as well as the images of hystero-epileptic attacks appearing in *Demoniacs in Art* (1887) by Charcot and Richer. Examples appear in Emily S. Apter, *Feminizing the Fetish: Psychoanalysis and Narrative Obsession in Turn-of-the-Century France* (Ithaca, N.Y.: Cornell University Press, 1991); and Pierre Janet, *From Anguish to Ecstasy* (Paris: Alcan, 1926), especially volume 1.

137. Raymond, "Assaults," January 3, 1922, 47. Raymond describes the cross that she was wearing at the time as a "pardon crucifix."

138. As mentioned by Herbert Thurston, "The Problem of Stigmatization," *Studies* 22 (June 1933): 225.

139. Raymond, "Assaults," 53, 57.

140. Ibid., February 21, 1922.

141. On "liminality" and the liminal, see Victor Turner, *The Ritual Process: Structure and Anti-Structure* (Ithaca, N.Y.: Cornell University Press, 1977; 1969).

142. José De Vinck, *Revelations of Women Mystics from the Middle Ages to Modern Times* (New York: Alba House, 1985), 83. More information on Josefa appears in chapter 6.

143. Ibid., 93.

144. Ibid., 82, 86.

145. Attacks on Margaret's purity are consistent with long-standing tradition of a "heroics of virginity" in female hagiography. See Jane Tibbetts Schulenberg, *Forgetful of Their Sex: Female Sanctity and Society, ca. 500–1100* (Chicago: University of Chicago Press, 1998), 414; Thomas J. Heffernan, *Sacred Biography: Saints and Their Biographers in the Middle Ages* (New York: Oxford University Press, 1988); and Anne Schutte's introduction to Cecelia Ferrazzi, *Autobiography of an Aspiring Saint*, ed. Anne Schutte (Chicago: University of Chicago Press, 1996), xxiv: "The act of sex was unavoidably tied to original sin. Virginity was a heroic virtue far greater than avoiding other sins. Monastic life honored and was dominated by renunciation of the flesh in all its forms." Here Catholics differ from Victorian constructions of womanhood that looked back to ancient Greco-Roman models of uterine weakness to explain women's propensity for illness and suffering.

146. For the meanings of demonic temptations in the life of Gemma Galgani, see the relevant entries in "A Saint's Alphabet" in Rudolf Bell and Cristina Mazzoni, *The Voices of Gemma Galgani: The Life and Afterlife of a Modern Saint* (Chicago: University of Chicago Press, 2003).

147. These bodily violations, which frequently appear in the biographies of other stigmatics, suggest the strong emphasis upon the virtue of female chastity in Catholicism and the need to attribute impurity to some overwhelming force (Satan) rather than to the woman herself.

148. Cavanaugh, "Report," 4.

149. Ibid., 5.

150. "Case of Sister Margaret (Reilly) Thorn, Sisters of the Good Shepherd, stigmatist: Narrative of a Father Bertrand, a Passionist," April 3, 1922, CCMM 1/38, UNDA.

151. April 3, 1922. Colette of Corbie was a 15th-century French anchoress. When she took up a public mission after having visions of Francis of Assisi, she was appointed by the schismatic Pope Benedict XIII as the superior of all Minoress convents. Canonized in 1807, she is known for her ecstasies, visions of the Passion, and persistent efforts to reform the Poor Clares in answer to a dream vision. One branch of the Poor Clares is still named the Colettines.

152. March 21, 1922.

153. Raymond, "Assaults," 54.

154. Ibid., July 17, 1922, 59.

155. Ibid., 47.

156. McParlan to Lukas Etlin, OSB, October 18, 1926, AOSB/M.

157. Letter from Father Brady to Cardinal Hayes, December 9, 1928, ARGS.

158. Herbert Thurston, *Surprising Mystics*, ed. J. H. Crehan (London: Burns and Oates, 1955), 167.

159. Piero Camporesi, *Juice of Life: The Symbolic and Magic Significance of Blood* (New York: Continuum, 1995), especially chapter 3.

Chapter 2

1. I thank Susan Guditus Walter, the poet's daughter, for supplying the poem.

2. Other historical accounts locate the tree in the field adjacent to Van Cortlandt Manor.

3. Letter from Sister Tarcisius, RGS, to Sister Carmelita, OSB, December 16, 1975, ARGS.

4. *NYT*, April 5, 1987.

5. Claude Langlois, *Le catholicisme au féminin* (Paris: Cerf, 1984), 67. The Laic Laws reduced Catholic control and presence in education in France and limited the conferring of degrees to the state but largely left the women's congregations alone, since they enjoyed popular support as teachers.

6. The full title of the RGS is "Sisters of Our Lady of Charity of the Good Shepherd of Angers."

7. In contrast to the Mercy sisters, who were invited to New York by Archbishop John Hughes, the RGS had to struggle against his opposition to be introduced there, since their work with fallen women was generally regarded as less important than Catholic charitable work for children. Catholic women's orders also received state funds for their care of children. Maureen Fitzgerald, "The Perils of 'Passion and Poverty': Women Religious and the Care of Single Women in New York City, 1845–1890," *U.S. Catholic Historian* 10, nos. 1 and 2 (1992): 45–58.

8. Information on the founding dates of RGS communities comes from Sister Mary of St. Teresita, RGS, *The Social Work of the Sisters of the Good Shepherd* (Cleveland: Cadillac Press, 1938), "Synopsis" at end of volume.

9. James C. G. Conniff, *The Good Shepherd Story* (Peekskill: Sisters of the Good Shepherd, 1957), 80.

10. Ibid., where he is named as D. H. Anderson.

11. Katherine Conway, *Fifty Years with Christ the Good Shepherd: The Story of the Fold in Newark, 1875–1925* (Norwood, Mass.: Plimpton Press, 1925), 73.

12. When the RGS sold its property at East End Avenue and 90th Street in 1928, it was valued at about $3 million. "Catholic Sisters in Big Realty Deal," *NYT*, November 20 and 28, 1928.

13. In 1924 the mansion was serving as the first Museum of the City of New York. When it was restored, it became a house museum in 1936.

14. Conway, *Fifty Years*, 37.

15. Martin J. Scott, SJ, *Convent Life* (New York: P. J. Kenedy, 1919), 227.

16. S. Tarcisius [Anderson], "Sisters of the Good Shepherd—Villa Loretto, Peekskill, N.Y." (1952). Other historians made similar judgments. James Conniff reported that Archbishop Hughes's "Irish heritage, after all, places a monumental premium on chastity. . . . [Y]ou are liable to encounter, even in a learned man of venerable years, a surprisingly rigid attitude toward anyone—particularly a woman—who has fallen from grace." Conniff, *Good Shepherd Story*, 78. For confirmation of the persistence of these unbending moral attitudes in Ireland through the 1970s, see Nancy Scheper-Hughes, *Saints, Scholars, and Schizophrenics: Mental Illness in Rural Ireland* (Berkeley: University of California Press, 1979), 249: "The continuity of a penitential version of Christianity—a tradition emphasizing sin, guilt, the innate weakness of human nature, the need for purification and rituals of self-mortification, a distrust of reason, a fear of sex, and a high regard for fasting and sexual abstinence."

17. Suellen Hoy, *Good Hearts: Catholic Sisters in Chicago's Past* (Urbana: University of Illinois Press, 2006), 51.

18. Fitzgerald, "The Perils of 'Passion and Poverty,'" 47–8, cites William Sanger, *The History of Prostitution* (New York, 1859), 456–60; and the *Second Annual Report of the Commissioners of Public Charities and Correction* (New York, 1860), 122–27.

19. These subcultures of New York City are wonderfully chronicled in Luc Sante, *Low Life* (New York: Vintage, 1991).

20. On the history of "third orders," see Michael Walsh, *Dictionary of Catholic Devotions* (San Francisco: HarperSanFrancisco, 1993).

21. Sister Tarcisius Anderson states that the 90th Street group later bought or rented part of Mount Saint Florence.

22. *Golden Memories of the Sisters of the Good Shepherd, 1884–1934* (N.p.: Troy, N.Y., 1934), 38. The account of Sister Tarcisius claims that Mother Magdalene intended the Peekskill land, in time, to be "utilized for a Provincial House."

23. After Mother Presentation's death in 1892, Mother Mary of Saint Veronica succeeded her and oversaw construction of a large building for the children who were wards of the Good Shepherds. In 1898 Mother Mary of Saint Loretto, provincial of Brooklyn, became the third superior. When she was stricken with paralysis in 1905, Mother Mary Immaculata O'Grady, the Troy foundress, became superior.

24. Source: 1911 tax report. S. Tarcisius, "Sisters of the Good Shepherd."

25. Teresita, *Social Work*, 77. Scott describes the fourth vow as "devotion to the uplift of fallen and unfortunate women." Scott, *Convent Life*, 226.

26. Jo Ann McNamara, *Sisters in Arms: Catholic Nuns through Two Millennia* (Cambridge, Mass.: Harvard University Press, 1996), 616.

27. Dorothy M. Brown and Elizabeth McKeown, *The Poor Belong to Us: Catholic Charities and American Welfare* (Cambridge, Mass.: Harvard University Press, 1997), 53–54.

28. Religious of the Good Shepherd, *Culled from the Cloister, Commemorating Their Silver Jubilee at Troy, New York: 1884–1909* (1909), 30.

29. A scandal involving the harsh punitive treatment of the Magdalens by the RGS in Cork, Ireland, in the 1960s became a motion picture in 2002 called *The Magdalen Sisters*. That convent was burned down by an arsonist in November 2012.

30. Religious of the Good Shepherd, *Culled from the Cloister*, 29.

31. S. M. o.t. R. Kellogg, "Delinquent Adolescent Girls in a Good Shepherd Training School," unpublished research, Catholic University of America, 1936, 39. The data came from St. Germaine Home at Peekskill.

32. Scott, *Convent Life*, 228.

33. See the examples from the Hartford house in Jennifer Cote, "'Habits of Vice': The House of the Good Shepherd and Competing Narratives of Female Delinquency in Early Twentieth-Century Hartford," *American Catholic Studies* 122 (2011): 33–34.

34. Brown and McKeown, *The Poor Belong to Us*, 116.

35. *Catholic News*, May 8, 1937.

36. John J. Dunn to Patrick J. Hayes, February 9, 1922, Hayes correspondence, AANY.

37. The large brick building that housed the sisters had been completed in 1909 thanks to the "constructive ability of M. M. Immaculata O'Grady," who was in charge of Peekskill at the time. Tarcisius, "Sisters of the Good Shepherd."

38. Ron Hansen, *Mariette in Ecstasy* (New York: Harper Perennial, 1992), 4.

39. Walter Gabriel Scanlan, OP, "Thorn: A Story of Divine Providence," ARGS, 168.

40. Hoy, *Good Hearts*, 70.

41. Rivka Eisikovits, "The Sisters of Our Lady of Charity of the Good Shepherd, 1835–1977: A Study in Cultural Adaptation" (Ph.D. diss., University of Minnesota, 1978), 91.

42. Ibid., 85.

43. Ibid., 86–91.

44. For example, "Brides of Christ," 1940s, by Isidore O'Brien, Franciscan preacher, at a Cenacle retreat given in New York.

45. Rebecca Sullivan, *Visual Habits: Nuns, Feminism, and American Postwar Popular Culture* (Toronto: University of Toronto Press, 2005), 124.

46. Conniff, *Good Shepherd Story*, 103.

47. Sullivan, *Visual Habits*, 155.

48. Scott, *Convent Life*, 141.

49. Jo Ann McNamara, however, observes that instead of encouraging women religious to identify with the plight of laywomen, the power of priests and bishops isolated nuns from laywomen and tied them to "the clerical force," where, unfortunately, they still had no power as women or as religious. She suggests that the "vow of obedience threatened to subsume other religious vows." McNamara, *Sisters in Arms*, 616.

50. Examples of women's ingenuity in making convent life more expressive are in *Building Sisterhood: A Feminist History of the Sisters, Servants of the Immaculate Heart of Mary* (Syracuse, N.Y.: Syracuse University Press, 1997).

51. McNamara, *Sisters in Arms*, 614.

52. *Building Sisterhood*, 10.

53. Carol K. Coburn and Martha Smith, *Spirited Lives: How Nuns Shaped Catholic Culture and American Life, 1836–1920* (Chapel Hill: University of North Carolina Press, 1999), 13.

54. Ibid., 14.

55. Elizabeth Alice Clement, *Love for Sale: Courting, Treating, and Prostitution in New York City, 1900–1945* (Chapel Hill: University of North Carolina Press, 2006), 49.

56. Ibid., 50.

57. Thomas Hine, *The Rise and Fall of the American Teenager* (New York: Harper-Perennial, 1999), 178.

58. Mary Douglas, "The Debate on Women Priests," in *Risk and Blame: Essays in Cultural History* (New York: Routledge, 1992), 289.

59. For more details of the ceremonies for women, see Scott, *Convent Life*, 107–21. So-called bride mysticism had been well developed in Germany for centuries.

60. Quoted in *Annals of the Good Shepherd: Philadelphia, 1850–1925, by a Member of the Order* (1925), 236.

61. The RGS added this date to their annual calendar when Mother Euphrasia was canonized on May 2, 1940.

62. There are pre–Vatican II feast dates. Many feast days were changed and consolidated after 1965. Now sisters may choose any date for their vows ceremony.

63. Monica Furlong, *Thérèse of Lisieux* (London: Virago, 1987), 95.

64. Bonnie Smith, *Ladies of the Leisure Class* (Princeton, N.J.: Princeton University Press, 1981), 175.

65. McNamara, *Sisters in Arms*, 616, 644.

66. *The Tablet* (Brooklyn), June 10, 1922.

67. On the history of distinctive monastic garb, see Elizabeth Kuhns, *The Habit: A History of the Clothing of Catholic Nuns* (New York: Doubleday, 2003).

68. Undated, unpaged typescript, ARGS.

69. McNamara details the results of this shift for professional training of nuns in the 1950s and 1960s. McNamara, *Sisters in Arms*, 628ff. Coburn and Smith point out that, although American sisters did lag behind public schoolteachers in training in the era after

World War I, many states had low requirements for its public teachers. Sisters often dedicated their entire lives to teaching and gained extensive on-the-job training over their lifetimes, which may have made them better prepared than has been recognized. Coburn and Smith, *Spirited Lives*, 151–53.

70. John T. McGreevy, *Catholicism and American Freedom: A History* (New York: Norton, 2003), 182.

71. Ibid., 187.

72. See Paul Blanshard, *Communism, Democracy, and Catholic Power* (Boston: Beacon Press, 1951).

73. Brown and McKeown, *The Poor Belong to Us*, 118. Since 1997, the discovery of abuse at the so-called Magdalene Laundries or Asylums in Ireland, which were run by Protestants and Catholics since the 1930s, led to a national scandal and the publication of several books and a film about the oppressive conditions there, compounded by the lack of any admission of guilt on the part of church officials. At Peekskill, the sisters directed a laundry but ultimately ended it.

74. "Communications of Our Lord to 'Margaret,'" copied at Peekskill by Lukas Etlin, November 17–30, 1923, ARGS.

75. Raymond/Lukas in SMCQ-SMCT, 89, no date in 1922 or 1923.

76. Teresita, *Social Work*, 77.

77. Ibid., 81.

78. "The Good Shepherd Sisters follow the rule of Saint Augustine, adapted by Saint Francis de Sales, modified for their special purpose by Saint John Eudes." (Philadelphia RGS convent brochure, Philadelphia Archdiocesan Historical Research Center.) They follow a modified form of enclosure, sing or chant the daily office in choir, but combine the active with the contemplative life in their work for women.

79. However, after her stigmata were reported, Margaret refused a Jesuit confessor and was convinced that a Manhattan Jesuit had been slandering her. Comment from a letter of Benedict Bradley, OSB, to Lukas Etlin, December 12, 1922, ARGS. Margaret probably refers to William Ennis, SJ, discussed in chapter 1.

80. Thomas McParlan, letter to Lukas Etlin, December 9, 1925, AOSB/M. Murillo's canvas was acquired by the Louvre Museum in 1852 for the largest price ever paid to date for a single painting. It became popular with Protestants, too, if not entirely for pious reasons, then for aesthetic reasons as proof of refinement. The use of Christian art as home decoration gained popularity in nineteenth-century America as mass-produced objects became more available and as Protestants had greater contact with Catholic immigrants and their European cultural roots. Colleen McDannell, *Material Christianity: Religion and Popular Culture in America* (New Haven: Yale University Press, 1995), 59.

81. Undated, unsigned typescript, 3, ARGS. Author attribution suggested by the phrase, "she is satisfied to leave everything to me as Archbishop."

82. The similar treatment of Nellie Orgen by the RGS is discussed in chapter 6.

83. As recorded in SMCQ, 113–14.

84. Anne Cawley Boardman, *Good Shepherd's Fold: A Biography of St. Mary Euphrasia Pelletier, R.G.S.* (New York: Harper and Bros., 1955), 238–45.

85. Miraculous healings were attributed to Pelletier within forty-five years of her death. One example occurred in 1913 at the Memphis convent where Mary Magdalen Hodges claimed to be cured of cancer through the intercession of Euphrasia. Sister Mary of St. John Eudes, RGS, *A Miracle in Memphis* (Memphis: Convent of the Good Shepherd, 1961).

In another case, a child living in a Good Shepherd house in Arras, France, was cured of a malignant facial ulcer after applying relics of Pelletier to her skin in 1925. Boardman, *Good Shepherd's Fold*, 279.

86. Abbé Louis Chasle, *Sister Mary of the Divine Heart, Born Droste zü Vischering—Sister of the Good Shepherd* (Paris: Beauchesne, 1925).

87. Conniff, *Good Shepherd Story*, 40–41. While James Conniff states that Villa Loretto took in women sixteen to twenty-one years old, Sister Tarcisius recalled that it accepted women aged 18 and older for its nearly 200,000 square feet of space. Ibid., 89. *Peekskill Evening Star*, January 30, 1985.

88. Conniff, *Good Shepherd Story*, 102.

89. January 30, 1985, clipping, ARGS.

90. *Golden Memories of the Sisters of the Good Shepherd*, 39.

91. 1907: ibid., 31.

92. Ibid., 9.

93. The Benedictine sisters had purchased their first printing machines in 1901. At Clyde, those nuns assigned to the printery set type for its magazines. The case of Juliana Bresson, who worked there for more than fifty years, was typical. Born in 1904, she joined the Benedictine Sisters of Perpetual Adoration in 1923. Because of her youth, she had to study in the boarding school before she was then assigned to the printing operation. Sister Juliana learned to use foundry type, which set one letter one metal piece at a time. About six years later, the sisters purchased a printing machine called an "Intertype," which was similar to the "Linotype" printers. She learned to use the Intertype machine typeset on it for eighteen years, along with oiling, cleaning, and repairing it. After a forty-seven-year run, the Intertype was exchanged in 1972 for the "IBM cold type" system, which Sister Juliana ran for nine years.

94. *Golden Memories of the Sisters of the Good Shepherd*, 40.

95. "Welcomes Inquiry at Home for Girls," *NYT*, August 9, 1929. The doctor was Thomas B. Joyce.

96. Ibid.

97. Many Americans are familiar with the fraudulent Maria Monk and Rebecca Reed narratives, written by a set of Protestant clergymen. The story of the infamous 1834 Charlestown convent burning is told in Nancy Schultz, *Fire and Roses: The Burning of the Charlestown Convent, 1834* (New York: Free Press, 2000).

98. "Catholic Institution Is Burned in Quebec," *NYT*, January 5, 1923.

99. Margaret Regensburg, "The Religious Sisters of the Good Shepherd and the Professionalization of Social Work" (Ph.D. diss., State University of New York, Stony Brook, 2007), 60.

100. "Sisters of the Good Shepherd" (1948). However, a brochure published in Philadelphia describes the Magdalens as wearing a brown habit like the Carmelites.

101. Religious of the Good Shepherd, *Culled from the Cloister*, 32.

102. Ibid., 37.

103. In Catholicism generally, a high percentage of stigmatics were members of tertiary orders.

104. Studied in Clement, *Love for Sale*, 17, 79–81.

105. Ibid., 79. See also Barbara Meil Hobson, *Uneasy Virtue: Prostitution and the American Reform Tradition* (Chicago: University of Chicago, 1990).

106. Conniff, *Good Shepherd Story*, 90.

107. This statistic is a marked contrast to the present, when the majority of persons served by Catholic charities in the United States are non-Catholic. Brown and McKeown, *The Poor Belong to Us*, 197.

108. Ibid., 130–32.

109. Ibid., 135.

110. Teresita, *Social Work*, 105–8.

111. Ibid., 107.

112. Ibid., 108.

113. Ibid.

114. "Three Drug Addicts Admit Shoplifting," *NYT*, June 3, 1923.

115. *NYT*, September 3, 1890, and December 27, 1919. Jennifer Cote provides similar examples of escaping inmates from the Hartford Good Shepherd house. Cote, "Habits of Vice," 42–44.

116. Teresita, *Social Work*, 93.

117. Ibid., 94.

118. Ibid., 119.

119. Ibid., 110–11.

120. Ibid., 90.

121. Brown and McKeown, *The Poor Belong to Us*, 53. The umbrella organization of 212 agencies called Catholic Charities of New York was established in 1920. The Strong Commission investigations involved accusing the state board of charities of poor oversight of charitable institutions and of possible complicity in ignoring violations.

122. Elizabeth Lunbeck, *The Psychiatric Persuasion* (Princeton, N.J.: Princeton University Press, 1997), 6.

123. Fitzgerald, "The Perils of 'Passion and Poverty,'" 48–49.

124. Teresita, *Social Work*, 109.

125. Lunbeck, *Psychiatric Persuasion*, 275.

126. Teresita, *Social Work*, 110.

127. Coburn and Smith, *Spirited Lives*, 7.

128. After crowning himself emperor in 1804, Napoleon became interested in establishing centralized control of the public school system in France to minimize Catholic control. Still, the church benefited from his Concordat with the pope in 1801 and his mandate that the Catholic faith must be taught in the *lycées*, which were intended to train future government officials. His nephew, Louis-Napoleon, was later elected president of the Second Republic, but after declaring himself emperor after a coup d'état, he found himself thrust out of power after the Revolution of 1848.

129. Undated, unsigned typescript, ARGS.

130. Similar conclusions were reached by Robert A. Orsi, *Thank You, St. Jude: Women's Devotion to the Patron Saint of Hopeless Causes* (New Haven, Conn.: Yale University Press, 1996), regarding the lives of the "in-between" generation of Catholics.

131. Leslie Tentler, *Catholics and Contraception: An American History* (Ithaca, N.Y.: Cornell University Press, 2005), chapter 3.

Chapter 3

1. The phrase is from James J. Walsh in a letter to Edward Anderson, SJ. Father Bertrand's document is cataloged as CCMM 1/38 in the Archives of the University of Notre Dame (UNDA). It consists of eighteen typed pages and appears to have been sent there by Dr. James J. Walsh. The following material is cited from this document. Attached to

it is a typed note from Sister Mary Carmelita Quinn stating, "Mother Raymond said Oct. 22, 1928: 'Father Bertrand's account is exaggerated. It is inexact and should not be circulated.'" Four other copies of Bertrand's report are in the ARGS. The Passionist archives also possess a copy.

2. Sr. Mary Albertina, OSD, gave her opinion of the several papers circulating about Margaret: "Fr. Bertrand's is inexact, and not reliable. No one can understand why he bungled it so. Don't quote him." Sr. M. Albertina to Rev. F. M. Walz, April 2, 1923, ARGS.

3. Bertrand letter, 37, Passionist archives, Newark.

4. The Passionists had a community in Dunkirk, New York, which was the likely source of his information.

5. See Brady's letter to Hayes about attending Margaret's perpetual vows ceremony, December 8, 1928. Brady and Etlin became good friends during Etlin's Peekskill visits between 1923 and 1927. Brady was also a past president of Dunwoodie Seminary and therefore would have known Joseph Nelson.

6. Information about Margaret Reilly's life from Mother Raymond's report appears in chapter 1.

7. At this time, Catholic theologians were engaged in debates on the authentic nature and types of mystical contemplation, and different orders generally tended to remain loyal to their own founders, such as John of the Cross or Teresa of Avila, as they interpreted them. The longtime chaplain of the RGS motherhouse in Angers was a diocesan priest, Auguste Saudreau (1859–1946). As the author of *The Degrees of the Spiritual Life* (1896), one such reflection on forms of contemplation, he was familiar reading to a Good Shepherd superior like Mother Raymond.

8. Savinien Louismet's books included *The Mystical Life* (1917); *Mystical Initiation* (1923); *Mysticism, True and False* (1924); and *The Mystical Knowledge of God* (1925).

9. *American Catholic Quarterly Review*, July and October 1915 and January 1916.

10. Savinien Louismet, preface, *The Mystical Life*, 2d ed. (1918), xi.

11. For a less-enthusiastic view, see Augustin Poulain (1836–1919), a Jesuit who was cautious about exaggerated forms of spirituality, such as the victim soul.

12. Louismet, *The Mystical Life*, xii.

13. C. J. T. Talar, "A Naturalistic Hagiography: J.-K. Huysmans' *Sainte Lydwine of Schiedam*," in *Sanctity and Secularity during the Modernist Period: Six Perspectives on Hagiography around 1900*, ed. L. Barmann and C. J. T. Talar (Brussels: Bollandist Society, 1999), 151–81.

14. McGivney letter to Thurston, n.d., JA.

15. T. Wegener, *Sr. Anne Catherine Emmerich* (Eng. trans., 1898), 336.

16. Ibid., 336, 337. The story came from a priest who reported it to Emmerich's scribe, Clemens Brentano.

17. Herbert Thurston, *The Physical Phenomena of Mysticism*, ed. J. H. Crehan (London: Burns, Oates, 1952), 335 (footnote 1).

18. Marina Warner, *From the Beast to the Blonde* (New York: Farrar, Straus and Giroux, 1994), 47.

19. See Maggie Kilgour, *From Communion to Cannibalism: An Anatomy of Metaphors of Incorporation* (Princeton, N.J.: Princeton University Press, 1990), especially the introduction and chapter 3. In the Eucharist, at least since the doctrine of transubstantiation was mandated at the Fourth Lateran Council (1215), "host and guest can come together without one subsuming the other, as both eat and are eaten." Kilgour, *From Communion to Cannibalism*, 79.

20. Raymond in SMCQ, 64.

21. Ibid., 68. There were also complaints of Thorn's meddling with "Dr. Joyce" (78), referring to the attending physician at Peekskill.

22. Benedict Anderson, *Imagined Communities* (London: Verso, 1998).

23. SMCQ, letter to Rev. Carroll Stuhlmueller, CP, January 24, 1983.

24. SMCQ, 27.

25. Saint Luke was not only the patron saint of doctors but also of artists because of a sixth-century legend identifying him as the painter of numerous icons of the Virgin. Together with the familiar ox, a painter's palette is one of Saint Luke's iconographic attributes.

26. On the Beuron style as embodying a revival of Byzantinism, see Michael Paul Driskel, *Representing Belief: Religion, Art, and Society in Nineteenth-Century France* (University Park: Pennsylvania State University Press, 1992), 248–9. The Clyde chapel's intricate and ornate scheme reflects its dedication to the Immaculate Conception. It became a minor basilica on its fiftieth anniversary in 1941.

27. When Etlin died in 1927, Carmelita was given the enormous responsibilities of directing the Caritas program and editing the magazine. She also used Etlin's sketches to complete the design and construction of the Mundelein Benedictine convent and chapel in Illinois, which was finished in 1949.

28. For discussion of these transformations across midcentury, see Margaret McGuinness, "Let Us Go to the Altar: Eucharistic Devotions, 1926–1976," in *Habits of Devotion: Catholic Religious Practice in Twentieth-Century America*, ed. James M. O'Toole (Ithaca, N.Y.: Cornell University Press, 2004).

29. Bishop Norbert Weber, "Father Lukas Etlin, OSB: A Short Biography" (Clyde, Mo., 1931), 47, 48, 50. Conception Abbey archives.

30. Edward E. Malone, OSB, "Father Lukas Etlin, OSB: Apostle of the Eucharist" (Clyde, Mo., 1961), 50.

31. Weber, "Father Lukas Etlin," 24.

32. Biographical information comes from ibid. Only one brief mention is made of Etlin's visits to the Good Shepherd nuns (55) in the month of his death and none of his relationship with Sister Thorn. The biographical pamphlet by Edward E. Malone, OSB, "Father Lukas Etlin, OSB: Apostle of the Eucharist," focuses on that dimension of his piety. Etlin's beatification process, begun in 1960, has made it impossible for me to gain access to most of his papers. After his death, numerous prayer cards were printed and circulated for private use.

33. Faulhaber's remark is cited in Guenter Lewy, *The Catholic Church and Nazi Germany* (New York: McGraw-Hill, 1965), 124.

34. Malone, "Father Lukas Etlin," 45.

35. Letter to Cardinal McIntyre, November 19, 1953, unsigned copy, "Bishops and Cardinals" file, AOSB/W.

36. Ibid., 39, 55.

37. See Paula Kane, "'She Offered Herself Up': The Victim Soul and Victim Spirituality in Catholicism," *Church History* 71, no. 1 (March 2002): 80–119.

38. "Chronicles" of OSB convent, Clyde, Mo., and photocopy at AOSB/W.

39. A torn copy of this clipping is archived at ARGS. The full clipping is available at AANY with the Margaret Reilly letters.

40. Raymond, "Assaults of the Evil Spirit," in SMCQ, 59.

41. Herbert Thurston, *Surprising Mystics*, ed. J. H. Crehan (London: Burns and Oates, 1955), 167.

42. McParlan to Etlin, September 19, 1927, AOSB/M.

43. SMCQ, "Clyde Chronicles," 29.

44. *Newark Evening News*, May 19, 1937, referring to the 1922 *New York World* article.

45. Healing miracles were reported at numerous American sites in this decade, including the Archdiocese of Boston, where visitors to the grave of an Irish priest in Malden began to report cures. Patrick J. Hayes, "Massachusetts Miracles: Controlling Cures in Catholic Boston, 1929–30," in *Saints and Their Cults in the Atlantic World*, ed. Margaret Cormack (Columbia, S.C.: University of South Carolina Press, 2006), 111–27.

46. Photo postcard in file sent by M. Francis Xavier to M. Dolorosa, February 1983, Quinn papers, "Crown of Thorns," AOSB/W.

47. See, for example, Jodi Bilinkoff, "Confessors, Penitents, and the Construction of Identities," in *Culture and Identity in Early Modern Europe (1500–1800): Essays in Honor of Natalie Zemon Davis*, ed. Barbara B. Diefendorf and Carla Hesse (Ann Arbor: University of Michigan Press, 1993), 83–100.

48. F. M. R. Walshe, "Comments and a Reply," *Catholic Medical Guardian* 16 (1938): 166.

49. Aug. [Augustin] Poulain, "Mystical Theology," *Catholic Encyclopedia* XIV, 621.

50. Thurston, *Surprising Mystics*, 168.

51. Thurston, *The Physical Phenomena of Mysticism*, 365. Saint Lidwine became a favorite of decadent author J.-K. Huysmans, who published her biography in 1901.

52. December 15, 1923, Lukas Etlin to Sister Margaret, uncataloged item at ARGS.

53. Lucetta Scaraffia and Gabriella Zarri, eds. *Women and Faith: Catholic Religious Life in Italy from Late Antiquity to the Present* (Cambridge, Mass.: Harvard University Press, 1999), 7.

54. A sociology of secrets was first taken up by Georg Simmel in an article published in 1906: "The Sociology of Secrecy and of Secret Societies," *American Journal of Sociology* 11, no. 4 (1906): 441–98.

55. Sister Sebastian to Sister Inez, August 30, 1922, ARGS.

56. Thurston, *The Physical Phenomena of Mysticism*, 232.

57. Lady Armstrong to Archbishop Hayes, May 4, 1922, Hayes correspondence, microfilm, AANY. According to the *New York Times*, however, Armstrong's mother grew up in Brooklyn, so it is unclear why she died in Ireland. "Lady Armstrong Dies at Age of 75," *NYT*, May 29, 1953.

58. Lady Armstrong to Archbishop Hayes, January 13, 1934, Hayes correspondence, microfilm, AANY.

59. "We are leaving for France on the 31st May. Thorn was able to tell me from our Lord why Mother General sent for us." Hickey, Newark Convent to Lukas Etlin, May 10 [1924?], AOSB/M.

60. "Provincial," [Charles O'Donnell, CSC] to Reverend Mother [Raymond Cahill], January 12, 1922, CCLO-UNDA, 3/12.

61. SMCQ-SMCT," 69.

62. [Father Walter G. Scanlan, OP,] "Thorn: A Story of Divine Providence," ARGS.

63. Benedict Bradley, OSB, to Lukas Etlin, OSB, December 8, 1922, ARGS.

64. "R. P. Benedict Bradley, OSB, Dec. 20, 1945," Archives of St. Mary's Abbey, N.J. My thanks to Benet Caffrey, OSB, archivist.

65. Bradley to Etlin, December 8, 1922. These five letters were retyped by Sister Carmelita Quinn from the handwritten originals.

66. He also spoke to them about Saints Teresa and Gertrude. Bradley to Etlin, December 1, 1922, ARGS.

67. Bradley to Etlin, December 27, 1922, ARGS.

68. Bradley to Etlin, December 1, 1922, ARGS.

69. Bradley to Etlin, December 8, 1922, ARGS.

70. Bradley to Etlin, December 12, 1922, ARGS. The badges are discussed in chapter 5.

71. Ibid.

72. There is no evidence that the two men ever met, but Freud became a corresponding member of the Society for Psychical Research that Thurston had joined in 1919 at age sixty-three.

73. See, for example, Michael P. Carroll, *Catholic Cults and Devotions: A Psychological Inquiry* (Montreal: McGill University Press, 1989).

74. Bernard Basset, *The English Jesuits: From Campion to Martindale* (New York: Herder & Herder, 1968), 391.

75. The Jesuits had founded the College of St. Omer in Artois, France, in 1593 and then relocated it twice, first to Bruges (1762) and then to Liège (1773) in Flanders after the Jesuits were suppressed; they fled the Continent during the French Revolution and reached the school's final location in the mansion and grounds donated by a grateful Jesuit student at Stonyhurst in Lancashire, England, in 1795.

76. A full listing of Thurston's publications appears in Joseph Crehan, *Father Thurston: A Memoir* (London: Sheed and Ward, 1952).

77. Herbert Thurston, ed., *Butler's Lives of the Saints* (12 vols., 1926–38). An English layman, Donald Attwater, published a second edition of Thurston in 1956.

78. Crehan, *Father Thurston*, 145.

79. The phrase comes from *Beauraing and Other Apparitions: An Account of Some Borderland Cases in the Psychology of Mysticism* (London, 1934).

80. Crehan, preface to Thurston, *Surprising Mystics*.

81. Crehan, *Father Thurston*, 164.

82. Walshe obituary cited in ibid., 111.

83. Even this fact is contradicted by Padre Pio's supporters during the shrill debates over Pio's canonization. Gemelli claimed to have examined Pio first in 1920, again in 1922, and on subsequent occasions, but Pio's fanatics claim that no such exams actually occurred. I have been unable to locate copies of Gemelli's report on Pio. An excellent study of Gemelli's career and significance appears in Daria Columbo, "Psychoanalysis and the Catholic Church in Italy: The Role of Father Agostino Gemelli, 1925–1953," *Journal of the History of the Behavioral Sciences* 39, no. 4 (Fall 2003): 333–48.

84. Loulie was Ruth Mary Louise Guiney Martin, born in 1912. Loulie's British father had died of influenza in 1913; her Irish American mother, also named Louise, died of grief in 1914. See Paula Kane, *Separatism and Subculture: Boston Catholicism, 1900–1920* (Chapel Hill: University of North Carolina Press, 1994), 235, 238.

85. Nesta of the Forest to Thurston, January 1, 1939, Thurston papers, 39.3.4.2.

86. Thurston papers, JA, 39.3.3.

87. Herbert Thurston, "The Holy Shroud and the Verdict of History," *The Month* 101 (1903): 17–29.

88. Herbert Thurston, "'Georges Marasco' and Some Others," *The Month* 145 (1925): 64.

89. "Edith Cavell," *Historical Encyclopedia of Nursing*, ed. Mary Ellen Snodgrass (Santa Barbara, Calif.: ABC-CLIO, 1999), 37.

90. Thurston, "'Georges Marasco' and Some Others," 57.

91. Thurston, *The Physical Phenomena of Mysticism*, 110.

92. See Thurston's chapter on "Hysteria and Dual Personality" in ibid. His comment on Mrazek appears in "'Georges Marasco' and Some Others," 56.

93. F. M. R. Walshe to Joseph Crehan, SJ, February 7, 1956, Thurston correspondence, JA.

94. Thurston, *Surprising Mystics*, 210.

95. Thurston papers, JA, 39.3.3, 1913/1905. The Nellie Brown file contains five or so handwritten school notebooks describing her conversion, written at the request of Reverend Thompson. It is unclear if these are in her own hand or are transcriptions by someone else. Brown claimed that Nellie's first wound appeared on May 5, 1916 [or January 1917?], following premonitions earlier in the year.

96. Thurston papers, JA.

97. Thurston, "Padre Pio," *The Month*, February 1920, 128–29, cited by Crehan in *Father Thurston: A Memoir*, 168. I could not locate this article, which Crehan indexed as July 1920, 64–8, p. 208.

98. Thurston, "'Georges Marasco' and Some Others." The portion on Margaret Reilly is the third of the four-part article.

99. The story was given to me by Dominica Rinaldi, then the RGS Archivist. She also suggested the name of Msgr. William Doheny, CSC, (1898–1982), although the Archives of the University of Notre Dame could not confirm that fact.

100. Thurston, "'Georges Marasco' and Some Others," part 3, 8.

101. Ibid., 9.

102. Ibid.

103. On Charles C. Martindale's life but with little information on his activities or impact, see Philip Caraman, *C. C. Martindale* (London: Longmans Green and Co., 1967). The prolific Martindale seems to have provided Catholic publishers Sheed and Ward with nearly its entire list from the 1920s until his death.

104. Carroll, *Catholic Cults and Devotions*, 133.

105. M. Roland Dalbiez, "Miracle and Logic," *Catholic Medical Guardian* 15, no. 3 (July 1937): 76.

106. A. C. Doyle, *The Roman Catholic Church: A Rejoinder* (London: Psychic Press, 1929), 5.

107. T. Slater, SJ, "Superstition," *American Catholic Quarterly Review* 47 (January 1922): 150–54.

108. Herbert Thurston, *Modern Spiritualism* (London: Sheed and Ward, 1928); Herbert Thurston, *The Church and Spiritualism* (Milwaukee: Bruce, 1933); Herbert Thurston, *Spiritualism* (London: Catholic Truth Society, 1934).

109. The papacy had condemned spiritualism in 1898 and again in 1917.

110. Thurston, *The Physical Phenomena of Mysticism*, 123.

111. Stephen Schloesser, *Jazz Age Catholicism: Mystic Modernism in Postwar Paris, 1919–1933* (Toronto: University of Toronto Press, 2005), 118.

112. Ibid., 14.

113. Geoff Dyer, *The Missing of the Somme* (London: Penguin, 1994), 122. Two frequently cited texts on the war are Paul Fussell's *The Great War and Modern Memory* (London: Oxford University Press, 1975), and Jay Winter, *Sites of Memory, Sites of Mourning: The Great War in European Cultural History* (New York: Cambridge University Press, 1995).

114. Dyer, *The Missing*, 19–25, 104.

115. Winter, *Sites of Memory, Sites of Mourning*, 26.

116. American deaths in battle were 53,513; other casualties totaled 63,195 dead and 204,002 wounded.

117. The Rainbow Division was 95 percent Irish Catholic, dating its origins to the former "Fighting Irish" 69th Regiment from the Civil War. As a tribute from the city of New York to Father Duffy's patriotism, a statue honoring him was erected in Duffy Square in 1937.

118. Francis P. Duffy, *Father Duffy's Story* (New York: George H. Doran, 1919), 38. The cardinal referred to was Hayes's predecessor, John Farley, who died in 1918.

119. Christopher Clark, "The New Catholicism and the European Culture Wars," in *Culture Wars: Secular-Catholic Conflict in Nineteenth-Century Europe*, ed. Christopher Clark and Wolfram Kaiser (Cambridge, UK: Cambridge University Press, 2003), 18.

120. As I finished writing this book, Nancy Lusignan Schultz's *A Capital Miracle* (New Haven: Yale University Press, 2011) on the Mattlingly miracles was published. I thank her for sharing information about her topic.

121. In neighboring Montreal, where French Catholics were closer to their royalist origins, a healing cult had emerged around the figure of Brother André (Alfred Bessette, 1845–1937), who, despite his humble occupation as a doorman for forty years at Notre Dame College, founded the oratory of St. Joseph, becoming himself an object of veneration for his purported cures. He was canonized in 2010 following the acceptance of his second miracle.

122. Ruth Harris, *Lourdes: Body and Spirit in a Secular Age* (New York: Viking Press, 1999).

123. Paolo Apolito, *The Internet and the Madonna: Religious Visionary Experience on the Web* (Chicago: University of Chicago Press, 2005), 9.

124. Jan Goldstein, *Console and Classify: The French Psychiatric Profession in the Nineteenth Century* (New York: Cambridge University Press, 1987); David Blackbourn, *Marpingen: Apparitions of the Virgin Mary in a Nineteenth-Century German Village* (New York: Vintage, 1995).

125. This thesis is illustrated in American literature by Tracy Fessenden in *Culture and Redemption: Religion, the Secular, and American Literature* (Princeton, N.J.: Princeton University Press, 2007).

126. Robert A. Orsi, *Thank You, St. Jude: Women's Devotion to the Patron Saint of Hopeless Causes* (New Haven, Conn.: Yale University Press, 1996), 14–18. On the emergence of a range of separatist Catholic institutions in the United States as part of a deliberate strategy, see Kane, *Separatism and Subculture*.

127. Father Brady came to Peekskill during the 1923–27 visits of Lukas Etlin and the two "became intimate friends." Quinn file, 16, SMCQ, AOSB/W. In the "Clyde Chronicles," Carmelita reported that the two priests discussed prayer and penance (29). Lukas showed Brady the wooden five-pointed, nail-studded heart that he wore over his heart as an instrument of penance. Brady ordered two of them, which Sister Carmelita packed for mailing to him. Brady said he would wear both when preaching—one to inflame his own heart and the other the heart of his listeners. One of these wooden hearts belonging to Lukas was worn by Sister Thorn during Lukas's trips to Peekskill. She later presented that heart to Sister Carmelita, who kept it as a treasured memento. She wore it to Rome in 1950 and 1952 when Benedictine prioresses made Holy Year visits in Rome (29). I saw the wooden heart at the AOSB/W.

128. Montague Summers, *The Physical Phenomena of Mysticism with Especial Reference to the Stigmata, Divine and Diabolic*, 2nd ed. (London: Rider & Co., 1950), 245. Summers is, however, an unreliable source on mysticism. This topic is taken up again in chapter 6.

129. Josefa Menendez, *The Way of Divine Love* (Rockford, Ill.: Tan Books, 1973), 43.

130. Letter signed "Sr. Mary of St. Margaret Mary Roche," dated May 22, 1944, ARGS.

131. Weber, "Father Lukas Etlin," 5.

132. Rev. Winfrid Herbst, SDS, St. Nazianz, Wisc., to Archbishop Hayes, September 28, 1923, Hayes correspondence, AANY microfilm.

133. In Brazil, Sister Amalia of Jesus Scourged provides an example of multiple devotions merged into one: in 1929, while serving as a missionary sister, she received the stigmata and had a vision of Jesus and Mary, who asked her to promote a new Rosary of the Tears of Mary to overthrow the devil and the reign of hell.

134. Oscar Wilde quoted in Richard Davenport-Hines, *Gothic: Four Hundred Years of Excess, Horror, Evil, and Ruin* (New York: North Point Press, 1999), 195.

135. On modern sainthood, see John Mecklin, *The Passing of the Saint: A Study of a Cultural Type* (Chicago: University of Chicago Press, 1941).

136. The second American-born saint was Mother Katharine Drexel (1858–1955) of Philadelphia, Pennsylvania, canonized in 2000, bringing the total of American saints to eight. No Irish Americans are represented. Despite their statistical predominance in U.S. sisterhoods, no Irish American sisters are in line at present to become "servants of God" at the local level or "venerables" recognized by the Vatican.

Chapter 4

1. These events included apparitions of the Virgin Mary. See David Blackbourn, *Marpingen: Apparitions of the Virgin Mary in a Nineteenth-Century German Village* (New York: Vintage, 1995); J. Bouflet and P. Boutry, *Apparitions of the Virgin* (Paris: Grasset, 1997); Zimdars-Swartz, *Encountering Mary: From La Salette to Medjugorje* (Princeton, N.J.: Princeton University Press, 1991).

2. A. Poulain, "Mystical Theology," *The Catholic Encyclopedia*, vol. 14 (New York: Robert Appleton Company, 1912), 621–22 (italics mine). Also see P. Adnès, "Stigmates," *Dictionnaire de Spiritualité*, vol. 16 (Paris: Editions Beauchesne, 1937–; fasc. 95 Coll. 1:211–43); "Stigmatization," *Dictionnaire de théologie catholique*, vol. 14, part 1, ed. A. Vacant and others (Paris: Librairie Letouzey et Ané, 1909–50), cols. 2617–19; Rev. E. Dublanchy, SM, "L'Ascetique," in *Dictionnaire de théologie catholique*, vol. 1/2 (Paris: Librairie Letouzey et Ané, 1923), 2037–55.

3. Some of these accounts were tinged with anti-Protestant and anti-Semitic views as well, as in Augustus Rohling's study, *Louise Lateau, Her Stigmas and Ecstasy: An Essay Addressed to Jews and Christians of Every Denomination* (N.p.: Hickey and Co., 1881).

4. Sources are unclear about the date of Margaret's second operation. In the last thirty years, ulcer surgery has rarely been necessary thanks to developments in medicine in 1982 that identified the *Helicobacter pylori* bacteria as the cause of ulcers. Endoscopy can diagnose and treat bleeding ulcers in the stomach or duodenum. Coincidentally, the specific characteristics of ulcers are referred to as stigmata.

5. The salt version of mercury chloride was taken internally to stimulate the liver and duodenum and to kill bacteria. It was also used to treat syphilis, although it was not the most useful of the mercury compounds for that purpose.

6. Letter at the JA. The same information appears in Walsh's letter to Father John W. Cavanaugh dated July 7, 1922, immediately after Walsh's Peekskill visit. CJWC-UNDA. Cavanaugh was accompanied by Father John McGinn, identified as "an expert on abnormal psychology" who was then a sociology professor at Notre Dame.

7. James A. McGivney, SJ, to Father Thurston, February 27, 1925, CJWC-UNDA. This is the first of two letters to Thurston, both labeled "Strictly Confidential." The second

letter is undated but was written after Thurston published his discussion of "Kate Ryan" in an article in *The Month* (February 1925), CJWC-UNDA.

8. *The Month* (February 1925), CJWC-UNDA. McGivney follows Thurston's change of Miss Murphy's name to Mahoney in his article.

9. McGivney to Thurston, undated letter on letterhead from Kohlmann Hall, 501 East Fordham Road, New York City, CJWC-UNDA.

10. The choice of the genre of the threatening anonymous letter is suggestive. Margaret, working as an office cleaner for Bernard Baruch, surely knew that in 1915 he had been the victim of a poison-pen campaign accusing him of profiteering during World War I. This campaign led to his investigation before a congressional committee. See James Grant, *Bernard M. Baruch* (New York: John Wiley and Sons, 1997), chapter 8. Dr. John B. Lynch, who examined Margaret's eyes, had also been a target of slanderous letters from a New York man claiming to be a French aristocrat. "Begging Letter Writer Says He's a Baron," *NYT*, March 10, 1901.

11. Anonymous to Rev. Mother Francis [McGenty], Feast of Pentecost, 1922, ARGS.

12. Ibid. (emphasis mine).

13. James A. McGivney to Patrick Hayes, October 27, 1923, ARGS.

14. Ibid.

15. Thomas Gallen appears in the 1920 U.S. census as living in New York City in a rented residence with his wife, the former Mary Mahoney. He is listed as fifty-four years old but possibly younger, and she is listed as thirty-nine. This would place his birth year between 1866 and 1870 and hers around 1881. Scores of Mary Mahoneys appear in the 1910 federal census, even in Ward 16, the Upper East Side where the Reillys and Dr. Gallen lived. The address on the anonymous letters puts the Gallen residence at 319 East 86th Street, a few blocks from Margaret's childhood home and the 90th Street Good Shepherd house.

16. In 1921 Hayes debated Margaret Sanger twice in the *New York Times* and had preached a sermon at St. Patrick's Cathedral and produced a pastoral letter in response to her appearance at Town Hall in November, which had resulted in her arrest due to his pressure on the police captain. Sanger had been a target of Catholic ire since 1913, when she had published several frank columns in the New York socialist paper *The Call*—columns that served as one of the first sex manuals for women written by a woman. In 1914 her pamphlet *Family Limitation* was being distributed by locals of the International Workers of the World, leading to her prosecution under the Comstock laws. These laws were supported by the Catholic Church, although the church had nothing to do with their passage by Protestants in the 1870s (Gene Burns, *The Moral Veto: Framing Contraception, Abortion, and Cultural Pluralism in the United States* [Cambridge, UK: Cambridge University Press, 2005], 130, 132). Forced to escape to London in 1915 to avoid a possible prison sentence, Sanger returned to New York after her pardon by President Woodrow Wilson that same year. In 1916 she opened the first birth control clinic for women in Brooklyn. Her monthly journal, *Birth Control Review* (1917–40), contains ample coverage of the American Birth Control League's debates with the Catholic Church.

17. On the lack of sources, see the discussion by Leslie Tentler, *Catholics and Contraception: An American History* (Ithaca, N.Y.: Cornell University Press, 2005). This topic returns in chapter 7.

18. "Church Control?," *Birth Control Review* 5 (December 1921): 1.

19. One rumor had it that the pope delayed Hayes's elevation for other reasons, namely, the hooliganism of Irish members of St. Patrick's Cathedral who stoned the nearby Union Club for flying a British flag on Thanksgiving Day 1920. *Time*, September 30, 1935.

20. McGivney to Hayes, November 3, 1923, ARGS.

21. Letter #1, ARGS. The envelope is postmarked May 25, 1917.

22. The phrase is from McGivney's letter to Thurston, February 27, 1925.

23. Letter no. 2, ARGS, May 12.

24. McGivney to Hayes, November 3, 1923, ARGS.

25. The term is from Elizabeth Petroff, *Body and Soul: Essays on Medieval Women and Mysticism* (New York: Oxford University Press, 1994).

26. James J. Walsh, "History," a typed, seven-page statement about Margaret Reilly dated September [?] 1922, ARGS.

27. Kathy Peiss, "'Charity Girls' and City Pleasures: Historical Notes on Working-Class Sexuality, 1880–1920," in *Passion and Power: Sexuality in History*, ed. by Kathy Peiss and Christina Simmons (Philadelphia: Temple University Press, 1989), 57–69.

28. Elizabeth Alice Clement, *Love for Sale: Courting, Treating, and Prostitution in New York City, 1900–1945* (Chapel Hill: University of North Carolina Press, 2006), 69.

29. Elizabeth Lunbeck, *The Psychiatric Persuasion* (Princeton, N.J.: Princeton University Press, 1997). Also see Paula Fass, *The Damned and the Beautiful: Youth Culture in the 1920s* (New York: Oxford University Press, 1979); and Regina Kunzel, *Fallen Women, Problem Girls: Unmarried Women and the Professionalization of Social Work* (New Haven: Yale University Press, 1993).

30. Thomas Hine, *The Rise and Fall of the American Teenager* (New York: HarperPerennial, 1999).

31. Virginia C. Young, "The Problem of the Delinquent Woman," *Birth Control Review* (February 1922). The author cites race as an additional factor in the plight of women in the cities.

32. "A Catholic Woman on Birth Control," *Birth Control Review* (January 1922): 17.

33. Introduction to *The New York Irish*, ed. Ronald H. Bayor and Timothy J. Meagher (Baltimore: Johns Hopkins University Press, 1996), 5.

34. *Time*, February 25, 1924. Electrotherapy was popular in the early 1900s to aid neurasthenia, nervous disorders, and chronic pain and was even considered promising as a cure for diabetes.

35. McParlan to Lukas Etlin, October 18, 1926, AOSB/M.

36. McParlan to Etlin, July 22, 1926, AOSB/M.

37. McParlan to Etlin, October 15, 1926, AOSB/M.

38. McParlan to Etlin, November 4, 1925, AOSB/M.

39. McParlan could represent an instance of the abject masculine, another possible psychic position. On the abject and abjection in Catholic gender notions, see Julia Kristeva, *Powers of Horror: An Essay on Abjection* (New York: Columbia University Press, 1982), and commentary on that text by Patricia Eliot, *From Mastery to Analysis: Theories of Gender in Psychoanalytic Feminism* (Ithaca, N.Y.: Cornell University Press, 1991).

40. Bradley to Etlin, December 8, 1922, ARGS.

41. McParlan to SMCQ, July 15, 1927, AOSB/M.

42. McParlan to Sister Carmelita, November 21, 1926, AOSB/M.

43. McParlan to Lukas Etlin, September 19, 1927, AOSB/M.

44. In the 1930s, Walsh coauthored a book on controlling fertility, *The Sterile Period in Family Life*, which hedged its bets on how to determine that exact time. Within a few years, even the "rhythm method" could not be discussed in the Catholic press. Tentler, *Catholics and Contraception*, 106, 118.

45. Kathleen Sprows Cummings, *New Women of the Old Faith: Gender and American*

Catholicism in the Progressive Era (Chapel Hill: University of North Carolina Press, 2010), 48. An excellent treatment of Walsh appears on pages 45–49, emphasizing his role as a Catholic apologist who reiterated the position that all forms of "modernism" were merely rediscoveries of Catholic medieval precedents. Having finished college in the year of Margaret's birth, Walsh had entered the Jesuits in 1885, but poor health forced him to resign from the order six years later. He remained close to his former Jesuit colleagues, however, spending time with the America House Jesuit community in Manhattan while a professor and acting dean at Fordham University's medical school. The *Campion House Diary* of 1926–46 lists him as a frequent visitor and dinner guest of the Jesuits. Raymond E. Schroth, *Fordham: A History and a Memoir* (Chicago: Loyola University Press, 2002), 125–28.

A stereotypical Irish bachelor, Walsh did not marry until 1915, when he was fifty. His first child, a son, was born when he was fifty-two, and a daughter followed two years later. Julia Huelat Freed, Walsh's wife, was a 1907 graduate of Barnard College and some twenty years his junior. *Campion House Diary*, 1926–46, Georgetown University Library Archives and Special Collections; "Blame Dissenters for Fordham Split," *NYT*, November 10, 1912.

46. When Walsh met him, Boissarie was director of the Lourdes Medical Bureau, the position he held from 1891 until 1917. Mark Micale, *Approaching Hysteria: Disease and Its Interpretations* (Princeton, N.J.: Princeton University Press, 1995), 269 (note 143), 270; and James J. Walsh, *Cures: The Story of the Cures That Fail* (New York: D. Appleton and Company, 1923).

47. *NYT*, November 9 and 10, 1912. Walsh had helped Fordham to achieve a Class-A rating in 1912, but the American Medical Association had warned that the school's rating would fall without certain changes, which Walsh and several colleagues believed they had been empowered by the university to pursue. The Jesuit president of Fordham, however, had other ideas. After being undermined by the president, who had no intention of implementing the necessary upgrades to the medical school's faculty and facilities, Walsh felt compelled to depart.

48. One of the earliest of many histories of hysteria to illustrate this point is Ilza Veith, *Hysteria: The History of a Disease* (Chicago: University of Chicago Press, 1965).

49. *NYT*, February 26, 1922, and March 16, 1922. See also the report in the *Journal of the American Society for Psychical Research* 16 (1922): 422–41.

50. Walsh to Father Cavanaugh, July 7, 1922, CJWC-UNDA. Walsh wrote to Cavanaugh at the suggestion of Archbishop Hayes that the two men discuss Margaret's case.

51. Walsh, "History." Handwritten notation on first page states: "Sent 1922 Dr. Walsh."

52. Walsh to Cavanaugh, July 7, 1922.

53. Ibid. Baruch had an Irish personal secretary, Miss Mary Boyle, and an Irish housemaid, either of whom may have hired Margaret Reilly.

54. I have not seen a reference to this event in any other source.

55. Walsh to Most Reverend Dear Archbishop, June 28, 1922, ARGS. Walsh was born in Archbald, Pennsylvania, a coal-mining town on the Lackawanna River about 100 miles from New York City, and he attended a parochial school in Wilkes-Barre.

56. Ibid.

57. John B. Lynch, M.D., to Walsh, August 13, 1922, CJWC-UNDA.

58. James J. Walsh, *Psychotherapy* (New York: D. Appleton, 1912), 590. His book, dedicated to the Jesuits, was developed from a series of lectures that he delivered at Fordham University beginning in 1907.

59. Charcot's favorite model, Augustine, experienced episodes of color blindness. Elaine Showalter, *Hystories: Hysterical Epidemics and Modern Culture* (New York: Columbia Uni-

versity Press, 1997), 36. Color blindness among hysteric patients was also observed by Virchow, in whose laboratory Walsh had trained in Vienna.

60. All quotations in this paragraph are from James J. Walsh, Letter to the Editor, *Fortnightly Review* (St. Louis), November 1, 1927, 436. As soon as Therese Neumann was described as "hysteric," defenders arose to denounce the doubters.

61. Walsh, "History."

62. Ibid.

63. Colleen McDannell, *Material Christianity: Religion and Popular Culture in America* (New Haven: Yale University Press, 1995), 170.

64. Beard coined the term in 1869. For a history of the generation of Americans who treated nervous disorders, see F. G. Gosling, *Before Freud: Neurasthenia and the American Medical Community, 1870–1910* (Urbana and Chicago: University of Illinois Press, 1987).

65. W. Norris Clarke, SJ, *Woodstock Letters* 80 (1951): 94.

66. Jose Brunner, *Freud and the Politics of Psychoanalysis* (Oxford: Blackwell, 1995), 93.

67. After World War I, Walsh presented a lecture at Fordham with the title "Psycho-Neuroses and the War," perhaps reflecting some psychoanalytic influence.

68. Walsh, *Psychotherapy*, 778.

69. Book review of Walsh, *Cures: The Story of the Cures That Fail*, *NYT*, August 19, 1923.

70. Robert Kugelmann, *Psychology and Catholicism: Contested Boundaries* (Cambridge, UK: Cambridge University Press, 2011), 162. This book appeared after my manuscript was completed, but it offers a lengthy interpretation of the contributions of James J. Walsh.

71. James J. Walsh to Reverend dear Father Parsons, October 8, 1925, *America* magazine archives, Georgetown University Library Archives and Special Collections. With the letter, Walsh enclosed Father Bertrand's account of his visit to Margaret Reilly for the *America* archives.

72. On liberal Protestant fascination with New Thought, see Leigh Schmidt, *Restless Souls: The Making of American Spirituality from Emerson to Oprah* (San Francisco: Harper, 2005).

73. Kugelmann, *Psychology and Catholicism*, 160–61.

74. C. Kevin Gillespie, *Psychology and American Catholicism: From Confession to Therapy?* (New York: Crossroad Publishers, 2001), 104. Jung's contradictory outlook can be seen in his essay "Why I am not a Catholic" and his simultaneous appreciation for the Jesuits' method of engaging all five senses in the Ignatian spiritual exercises.

75. *NYT*, September 12, 1912. Fordham did not establish a Psychology Department until 1934. Sir Henry Head, one of the leading experts on Parkinson's disease, died of that illness in 1940.

76. One of the few American clergymen to appreciate Freud was Thomas Verner Moore, a Carthusian monk whose impact was felt through his teaching of men and women at Catholic institutions. Gillespie, *Psychology and American Catholicism*, 44–45. In the 1960s, when new models of psychology emerged to challenge the earlier dominance of psychoanalysis and behaviorism, Catholics would again bypass Freud, throwing their support behind the humanistic approaches of Abraham Maslow and Carl Rogers, who were friendly to Catholic insistence on free will and conscious experience as cornerstones for human behavior. Ibid., 102–5.

77. M. Roland Dalbiez, "Miracle and Logic," *Catholic Medical Guardian* 15, no. 3 (July 1937): 76.

78. *NYT*, March 10, 1947. Sheen's statements angered many Catholic professionals and led eighteen men to form the National Guild of Catholic Psychiatrists, the first "faith-

based" society recognized by the American Psychiatric Association. For its history, see Abraham Nussbaum, "Profession and Faith: The National Guild of Catholic Psychiatrists, 1950–1968," *Catholic Historical Review* 93, no. 4 (2007): 845–65.

79. Walsh, "History."

80. Ibid.

81. James J. Walsh to Most dear Reverend Archbishop (Archbishop Hayes), February 19, 1923, ARGS.

82. Showalter, *Hystories*, 37.

83. Ibid., 37, 260.

84. Sigmund Freud and Josef Breuer, *Studies on Hysteria*, 1893–95, 290.

85. Elisabeth Bronfen, *The Knotted Subject: Hysteria and Its Discontents* (Princeton, N.J.: Princeton University Press, 1998), 256.

86. Margaret's behavior is consistent with Jacques Lacan's definition of hysterics—namely, that they are outside of sexual choice, preferring to avoid choosing between masculine and feminine poles. This position may describe Margaret's inconsistency and explain the variable opinions that others held about her, which found her at once seductive and saintly, insolent and submissive, calculating and fragile, gossipy and reticent, giddy and serious.

87. For example, someone praying for Saint Gertrude heard these words from Jesus: "She for whom thou prayest is My dove, who has no guile in her, for she rejects from her heart as gall all the guile and bitterness of sin. She is My chosen lily, which I love to bear in My hands, for it is My delight and My pleasure to repose in the purity and innocence of this chaste soul. She is My rose, whose odor is full of sweetness because of her patience in every adversity and the thanksgiving which she continually offers Me, which ascend before Me as the sweetest perfumes." *Life and Revelations of Saint Gertrude the Great* (Rockford, Ill: TAN Books, 2002).

88. Micale, *Approaching Hysteria*, 279, citing Mary James, "The Therapeutic Practices of Jean-Martin Charcot (1825–1893) in Their Historical and Social Context" (Ph.D. diss., University of Essex, 1989).

89. Micale, *Approaching Hysteria*, 280.

90. On photographs of Galgani and her peculiar choice of clothing, see Rudolf Bell and Cristina Mazzoni, *The Voices of Gemma Galgani: The Life and Afterlife of a Modern Saint* (Chicago: University of Chicago Press, 2003), 210.

91. Micale, *Approaching Hysteria*, 273.

92. Kenneth L. Woodward, *Making Saints: How the Catholic Church Determines Who Becomes a Saint, Who Doesn't, and Why* (New York: Simon and Schuster, 1990), 219.

93. Prospero Lambertini did not become pope until 1740. He was serving as archbishop of Bologna when he undertook "De servorum Dei beatificatione et beatorum canonizatione" (1734–38).

94. Jacalyn Duffin, *Medical Miracles: Doctors, Saints, and Healing in the Modern World* (Oxford University Press, 2009), 185.

95. This experiment evolved into an occasional series of "Days of Religious Psychology," which in 1948 became the International Congress of Religious Psychology.

96. The Second World War interrupted travel; thus the German scholars could not attend in 1938 and meetings were suspended between 1940 and 1945. In all, eight meetings were held between 1935 and 1958, sometimes at locations other than the convent at Avon-Fontainebleau.

97. Bruno de Jesus Marie (1892–1962) was the religious name of Jacques Froissart, who

converted to Catholicism in 1915 and joined the Order of Discalced Carmelites. He was a close friend of Jacques Maritain and revived the journal *Etudes Carmélitaines* in 1931. In the early issues, he wrote a series of articles on "Madeleine," the infamous patient of Pierre Janet.

98. J. Lhermitte, "The Medical Problem of Stigmatization," *Etudes Carmélitaines* 2 (October 1936): 71. This number of the *Etudes* contains the papers on stigmatization from the conference held on April 17–19, 1936, at the monastery of the Carmelites of Avon-Fontainebleau.

99. Unnamed Claretian priest and Vatican consultant quoted in Woodward, *Making Saints*, 176.

100. F. M. R. Walshe, "Stigmata—Comments and a Reply," *Catholic Medical Guardian* 16 (1938): 166. Walshe was a neurologist born in London of Irish parents. He served as editor of *Brain* from 1937 to 1953.

101. Ibid., 165.

102. Ibid., 166.

103. Walshe's theory seemingly anticipates a similar turn in literary studies from the author's "intention" to the audience's "reception" of a text.

104. Micale, *Approaching Hysteria*, 269.

105. In a volume devoted to the study of masochism, Charles Brenner's essay makes a useful distinction between primary masochism and moral masochism. Brenner, "The Masochistic Character: Genesis and Treatment," in *Essential Papers on Masochism*, ed. Margaret Hanly (New York: New York University Press, 1995), 360–82.

106. Sigmund Freud, "Three Essays on the Theory of Sexuality" (1905d) and "Instincts and their Vicissitudes" (1915); Freud, "The Economic Problem of Masochism" (1924c).

107. After Freud's work published between 1905 and 1924 (see previous note), some key post-Freudian texts on masochism include Fenichel (1925, 1945); Reich (1940); Reik (1940); Grunberger (1956); Berliner (1958); Shengold (1967, 1971, 1988), Lowenstein (1957); Brenner (1959); A. Miller (1979); and Chasseguet-Smirgel (1991). On women's rebelliousness, see Colette Soler, *What Lacan Said about Women: A Psychoanalytic Study* (New York: Other Press, 2006).

108. Showalter, quoted in Brunner, *Freud and the Politics of Psychoanalysis*, 98.

109. Father Bertrand, "Account of Margaret Riley," 7, Passionist Historical Archives, New Jersey. This typescript is nearly identical to the one at UNDA.

110. A similar situation for France is summed up by the many examples of suffering women provided by Richard Burton in *Holy Women, Holy Blood* (Ithaca, N.Y.: Cornell University Press, 2004), chapter 5.

111. Paula Kane, "'She Offered Herself Up': The Victim Soul and Victim Spirituality in Catholicism," *Church History* 71, no. 1 (March 2002): 80–119.

112. Ariel Glucklich, *Sacred Pain: Hurting the Body for the Sake of the Soul* (New York: Oxford University Press, 2001). Information in this paragraph comes from pages 80–89.

113. Antoine Vergote, *Guilt and Desire: Religious Attitudes and Their Pathological Derivatives* (New Haven, Conn.: Yale University Press, 1988), 154.

114. Nancy McWilliams, *Psychoanalytic Diagnosis* (New York: Guilford Press, 1994), 274, 275.

115. See Arthur Kleinman, *The Illness Narratives: Suffering, Healing, and the Human Condition* (New York: Basic Books, 1989), 28.

116. Glucklich, *Sacred Pain*, 202.

117. Ibid., 89.

118. Robert A. Orsi, "Mildred, Is It Fun to Be a Cripple?," chapter 1 of *Between Heaven and Earth: The Religious Worlds People Make and the Scholars Who Study Them* (Princeton, N.J.: Princeton University Press, 2005).

119. Jorge Cañizares-Esguerra, *Puritan Conquistadors: Iberianizing the Atlantic, 1550–1700* (Stanford, Calif.: Stanford University Press, 2006), 49–50.

120. Daria Columbo, "Psychoanalysis and the Catholic Church in Italy: The Role of Father Agostino Gemelli, 1925–1953," *Journal of the History of the Behavioral Sciences* 39, no. 4 (Fall 2003): 333.

121. Gillespie, *Psychology and American Catholicism*, 16–18.

122. David Shapiro's *Neurotic Styles* (New York: Basic Books, 1965) outlined the basic features of hysterical (histrionic) style as associated with repression as a defense mechanism, the forgetting of something by keeping it from consciousness by its cognitive style of diffuseness, impressionistic mode of expression, vagueness, and lack of factual content.

123. Gallen anecdote told by Father James McGivney in his letter to Herbert Thurston, February 27, 1925, JA.

124. Lunbeck, *Psychiatric Persuasion*, 213.

125. Robert Resch, "Jacques Lacan," in *Encyclopedia of Social Theory*, vol. 2, ed. George Ritzer (Thousand Oaks, Calif.: Sage Publications, 2005), 429.

126. Elizabeth Roudinesco, *Jacques Lacan and Co.* (London: Free Association Books, 1990), 261.

127. Vergote, *Guilt and Desire*, 114.

128. Ibid., 192.

129. Ibid., 146. But see his caveat that follows: hysteric symptoms are manifesting an occult memory that cannot be expressed knowingly by the subject, whereas stigmatics consciously embrace the meaning of the wounds that they experience as symbolic wounds.

130. Ibid., 193. The subject can be male as well, which would classify stigmatics like Padre Pio as hysterical.

131. Ibid., 206, in the description of Vergote's general procedure for studying the psychology of mysticism and psychopathological forms of religion.

132. Ibid., 197.

133. Amy Hollywood explores the fascination with mysticism among secular French intellectuals such as Bataille, Beauvoir, Lacan, and Irigaray in *Sensible Ecstasy: Mysticism, Sexual Difference, and the Demands of History* (Chicago: University of Chicago Press, 2002).

134. Phyllis Chesler, *Women and Madness* (Garden City, N.J.: Doubleday, 1972), 75.

135. Alice Jardine, *Gynesis: Configurations of Woman and Modernity* (Ithaca, N.Y.: Cornell University Press, 1985), 160.

136. See Diane Jonte-Pace, *Speaking the Unspeakable: Religion, Misogyny, and the Uncanny Mother in Freud's Cultural Texts* (Berkeley: University of California Press, 2001).

137. Ibid., 11.

138. Mary Ann Doane, "The Clinical Eye: Medical Discourses in the "Woman's Film" in the 1940s," in *The Female Body in Western Culture: Contemporary Perspectives*, ed. Susan Suleiman (Cambridge, Mass.: Harvard University Press, 1985), 152–72.

139. Susan Bordo, *Unbearable Weight: Feminism, Western Culture, and the Body* (Berkeley: University of California, 1993), 33.

140. See Tentler, *Catholics and Contraception*, chapter 2.

141. Ann Douglas, *Terrible Honesty: Mongrel Manhattan in the 1920s* (New York: Farrar, Straus, and Giroux, 1995), 123–24, 54. Douglas demonstrates how art, fiction, education, and theater sought to promote a "terrible honesty" through their craft, spurred on by the

novelty of psychoanalysis and a zealous desire to purge "all words like 'sacred,' 'sacrifice,' and 'soul'" from usage.

142. Ibid., 1.

Chapter 5

1. The sculptor was Joseph Sibbel (1850–1907) of Germany, who died in New York City; he was well-known for his ecclesiastical statues at Dunwoodie Seminary, New York; St. Ignatius, New York City; St. Paul's Cathedral, Pittsburgh; and the Cathedral of St. Joseph, Hartford.

2. Pius XI wrote: "But we must ever remember that the whole virtue of the expiation depends on the one bloody sacrifice of Christ, which without intermission of time is renewed on our altars in an unbloody manner, 'For the victim is one and the same, the same now offering by the ministry of priests, who then offered Himself on the cross, the manner alone of offering being different' (Council of Trent, Session XXIII, Chapter 2). Wherefore with this most august Eucharistic Sacrifice there ought to be joined an oblation both of the ministers and of all the faithful, so that they also may 'present themselves living sacrifices, holy, pleasing unto God' (Romans xii, 1)." "Miserentissimus Redemptor," May 8, 1928.

3. McGivney, SJ, to Archbishop Hayes, November 3, 1923, ARGS.

4. Margaret combined manufactured items with handmade work on other occasions, as in a gift for Sister Carmelita in 1928 in which she cut an image of the infant Jesus from a Clyde holy card and surrounded it with a hand-painted chalice, Host, and crown of thorns.

5. The *Woodstock Letters* reported in 1901 that the Sacred Heart altar outrivaled everything in the church except the new high altar and the baptistery, which were themselves paid for by anonymous donors who financed the costly marble for the altar and a Tiffany glass dome for the baptistery. *Woodstock Letters* 30, no. 2 (1901).

6. Patrick Dooley, *Fifty Years in Yorkville; or, Annals of the Parish of St. Ignatius of Loyola and St. Lawrence O'Toole* (New York: Parish House, 1917), 326.

7. Ibid., 330.

8. Robert A. Orsi, "Printed Presence: Twentieth-Century Catholic Print Culture for Youngsters in the United States," in *Education and the Culture of Print in Modern America*, ed. Adam R. Nelson and John L. Rudolph (Madison: University of Wisconsin Press, 2010), 82–83. Orsi speaks of an "incarnational modernity," meaning that against the materialism of the modern world, "Catholic modernity included the incarnated supernatural and experiences of real presences."

9. Stephen Schloesser, *Jazz Age Catholicism: Mystic Modernism in Postwar Paris, 1919–1933* (Toronto: University of Toronto Press, 2005), 14, describes how postwar Catholics "self-consciously considered themselves to be off-modern: anti-modernist in their adhesion to tradition and ultra-modernist in their embrace of time's forward motion."

10. Robert A. Orsi, *Between Heaven and Earth: The Religious Worlds People Make and the Scholars Who Study Them* (Princeton, N.J.: Princeton University Press, 2005), 55. Catholic devotional items, known as sacramentals, are examined in Colleen McDannell, *Material Christianity: Religion and Popular Culture in America* (New Haven: Yale University Press, 1995), chapter 2.

11. An interesting analysis of the devotion since the 17th century appears in the pamphlet by David Morgan titled *The Sacred Heart of Jesus: the Visual Evolution of a Devotion* (Amsterdam: Amsterdam University Press, 2008). On the success of the devotion in the United States since the late nineteenth century, see Ann Taves, *The Household of Faith* (Notre Dame, Ind.: University of Notre Dame Press, 1986), 34–35.

12. Armando Favazza, *Bodies under Siege: Self-Mutilation, Nonsuicidal Self-Injury, and Body Modification in Culture and Psychiatry*, 2d ed. (Baltimore: Johns Hopkins University Press, 1996), 15.

13. Raymond Jonas, *The Tragic Tale of Claire Ferchaud and the Great War* (Berkeley: University of California Press, 2005), 46, 170 (note 10). Jonas also reports that until the army halted the process, images of the Sacred Heart were superimposed on the French flag and distributed to French troops during World War I.

14. Ibid.; Michael P. Carroll, *Catholic Cults and Devotions: A Psychological Inquiry* (Montreal: McGill University Press, 1989), 146; pamphlet, ARGS. The RGS has commemorated Mother Divine Heart through posting a Power Point presentation on the Internet.

15. Taves, *Household of Faith*, 57.

16. Richard D. E. Burton, *Holy Tears, Holy Blood: Women, Catholicism, and the Culture of Suffering in France, 1840–1970* (Ithaca, N.Y.: Cornell University Press, 2004), xxiii.

17. McDannell, *Material Christianity*, chapter 5.

18. Carroll, *Catholic Cults and Devotions*, 147–48.

19. Lukas Etlin, sermon to sisters on the Feast of the Sacred Heart, in Bishop Norbert Weber, "Father Lukas Etlin, OSB: A Short Biography" (Clyde, Mo.: N.p., 1931), 38.

20. Paula Kane, "'She Offered Herself Up': The Victim Soul and Victim Spirituality in Catholicism," *Church History* 71, no. 1 (March 2002): 80–119.

21. This masculine role is analyzed by Tine van Osselaer, "'Heroes of the Heart': Ideal Men in the Sacred Heart Devotion," *Journal of Men, Masculinities, and Spirituality* 3, no. 1 (2009): 22–40.

22. Marion Morgan, "The Sacred Heart of Jesus in Roman Catholic Tradition," *One in Christ* 24 (1988): 238.

23. "Reparation, Theology of," *New Catholic Encyclopedia*, vol. 12 (New York: McGraw-Hill, 1967), 380.

24. Pope Benedict XVI has recently authorized the revival of indulgences—to the consternation of progressive Catholics. "Sin, and Its Indulgences," *NYT*, February 13, 2009. A traditional understanding of purgatory was professed by the Council of Trent at Session XXV:

> Whereas the Catholic Church, instructed by the Holy Ghost, has from the Sacred Scriptures and the ancient tradition of the Fathers taught in Councils and very recently in this Ecumenical synod (Sess. VI, cap. XXX; Sess. XXII cap. ii, iii) that there is a purgatory, and that the souls therein are helped by the suffrages of the faithful, but principally by the acceptable Sacrifice of the Altar; the Holy Synod enjoins on the Bishops that they diligently endeavor to have the sound doctrine of the Fathers in Councils regarding purgatory everywhere taught and preached, held and believed by the faithful (Denzinger, "Enchiridon," 983). Further than this, the definitions of the Church do not go, but the tradition of the Fathers and the Schoolmen must be consulted to explain the teachings of the councils, and to make clear the belief and the practices of the faithful.

Edward Hanna, "Purgatory," *The Catholic Encyclopedia*, vol. 12 (New York: Robert Appleton Company, 1911). Accessed online at http://www.newadvent.org/cathen/12575a .htm.

25. Jon Butler, "Catholicism as a Model for American Religious History," in *Belief in History*, ed. Thomas Kselman (Notre Dame, Ind.: University of Notre Dame Press, 1991), 296.

26. Thomas M. Schwertner, *The Eucharistic Renaissance* (New York: Macmillan, 1926), 292. The imprimatur for this 1926 book was from Cardinal Hayes of New York.

27. See Steven M. Avella and Jeffrey Zalar, "Sanctity in the Era of Catholic Action: The Case of St. Pius X," *U.S. Catholic Historian* 15, no. 4 (Fall 1997): 57–80; Margaret McGuinness, "Let Us Go to the Altar: American Catholics and the Eucharist, 1926–1976," in *Habits of Devotion: Catholic Religious Practice in Twentieth-Century America*, ed. James M. O'Toole (Ithaca, N.Y.: Cornell University Press, 2004).

28. Rebecca Lester, "Embodied Voices: Women's Food Asceticism and the Negotiation of Identity," *Ethos* (Society for Psychological Anthropology, Washington, D.C.) 23, no. 2 (1995): 214.

29. Ibid. Lester borrows here from medievalist Caroline Bynum.

30. Herbert Kramer, *Crucified with Christ* (New York: P. J. Kenedy, 1949), 208.

31. Hillary Kaell, "'Marie-Rose, Stigmatisée de Woonsocket': The Construction of a Franco-American Saint Cult, 1930–1955," *CCHA Historical Studies* 73 (2007): 7–26 (footnote 83, citing Boyer, *She Wears a Crown of Thorns: Marie Rose Ferron (1920–1936) Known as "Little Rose," the Stigmatized Ecstatic of Woonsocket, R.I.*, chapters 3–7).

32. SMCQ, 75.

33. Ibid., 7.

34. Ibid., 75. The descendants of Margaret's sister, Ellen, have her sewing kit, thimble, needles, and so on.

35. Notes from Sister Carmelita Quinn in answer to questionnaire from Claire Nolan, RGS, February, 1983, 23, AOSB/W.

36. Jeffrey Hamburger, *Nuns as Artists: The Visual Culture of a Medieval Convent* (Berkeley: University of California Press, 1997).

37. Letter from Sister Mary Carmelita Quinn to M. Dolorosa, August 22, 1967, SMCQ.

38. Diana George and Mariolina Rizzi Salvatori, "Holy Cards/Immaginette: The Extraordinary Literacy of Vernacular Religion," *College Composition and Communication* 60, no. 2 (December 2008): 250–84.

39. Karen-Edis Barzman, "Sacred Imagery and the Religious Lives of Women, 1650–1850," in *Women and Faith: Catholic Religious Life in Italy from Late Antiquity to the Present*, ed. Lucetta Scaraffia and Gabriella Zarri (Cambridge, Mass.: Harvard University Press, 1999), 247.

40. Ibid., 247.

41. *The Annals of the Good Shepherd Philadelphia, 1850-1926, by a Member of the Order* (Philadelphia: Convent of the Good Shepherd: 1925), 223–34.

42. Kramer, *Crucified with Christ*, 219.

43. Patricia Wittberg, *The Rise and Fall of Catholic Religious Orders* (Albany: SUNY Press, 1994), 19.

44. Patrick J. Hayes, "Massachusetts Miracles: Controlling Cures in Catholic Boston, 1929–30," in *Saints and Their Cults in the Atlantic World*, ed. Margaret Cormack (Columbia, S.C.: University of South Carolina Press, 2006), 111–27. All information about this case comes from Hayes's chapter.

45. Ibid., footnote 52; O'Sullivan to O'Connell, March 17, 1930, in Archdiocese of Boston Archives, Power, Rev. Patrick J., M-1587.

46. McParlan to Etlin, November 3, 1926, AOSB/M.

47. McParlan to Carmelita, August 8, 1927, AOSB/M.

48. "Art Show Planned to Aid Needy Girls," *NYT*, December 3, 1933.

49. McParlan to Lukas, July 15, 1927, AOSB/M.

50. McParlan to Carmelita, May 18, 1927, AOSB/M.

51. McParlan to Carmelita, January 13, 1928, AOSB/M.

52. Claire Farago treats a similar problem in a study of the mid-nineteenth-century Southwest in "Transforming Images: New Mexican Santos between Theory and History," in *The Visual Culture of American Religions*, ed. David Morgan and Sally M. Promey (Berkeley: University of California Press, 2001), 191–208.

53. SMCQ, Etlin portion, 98.

54. Clare Nolan, material compiled in three-ring binder, 26, ARGS.

55. SMCQ-SMCT, 72–74.

56. While Pope Pius XI had praised Alacoque and her Jesuit confessor, Claude de la Columbière, the succeeding pope, Pius XII, took pains to state that Alacoque did not initiate the devotion in the Visitation convent chapel at Paray-le-Monial, insisting instead that it had been part of an ongoing, living faith among Roman Catholics. Pius XII, "You Shall Draw Waters in Joy from the Fountains of the Savior" (1956).

57. Karl Rahner, *The Heart of the Savior*.

58. Herbert Thurston and Donald Attwater, eds., *Butler's Lives of the Saints*, vol. 10, (New York: Kenedy, 1962), 242.

59. Joseph Chinnici has spoken of the codes implicated in visual images of late nineteenth-century Catholicism in his examination of the successful devotion of Saint Thérèse of Lisieux to the Holy Face of Jesus. Chinnici, "Deciphering Religious Practice: Material Culture as Social Code in the Nineteenth Century," *U.S. Catholic Historian* 19, no. 3 (Summer 2001): 1–19.

60. See Raymond Jonas, *France and the Cult of the Sacred Heart: An Epic Tale for Modern Times* (Berkeley: University of California Press, 2000).

61. Michael Carroll has noted the peculiar absence of the Sacred Heart devotion in the scholarship of Herbert Thurston, whose Jesuit order was among its prime promoters. Carroll, "The Sacred Heart of Jesus," *Catholic Cults and Devotions*, 133.

62. Kay Turner, *Beautiful Necessity: The Art and Meaning of Women's Altars* (London: Thames and Hudson, 1999).

63. McDannell has described the home altar as "the symbolic bridge between heaven and earth" in *Material Christianity*, 38.

64. Herbert Thurston, *Surprising Mystics*, ed. J. H. Crehan (London: Burns and Oates, 1955), 42.

65. Mother Hickey, RGS, described her special cause, Nellie Organ of Cork, in diminutive and floral terms in a letter to Etlin: "Have you read the Life of our 'Little Nellie' or as she is sometimes called the 'Little Violet of the B. Sacrament'?" Floral images were also associated with Francis of Assisi, the most feminized of male saints, whose well-known writings are called "fioretti."

66. SMCQ, 93.

67. In Marcel Mauss's classic formulation of it in *The Gift* (1925), gift giving defines social order because it creates an obligation for repayment.

68. SMCQ, 71.

69. December 27, 1922, ARGS.

70. SMCQ, 35.

71. Benedict Bradley, OSB, to Lukas Etlin, December 27, 1922, ARGS.

72. Bradley to Etlin, December 8, 1922, ARGS.

73. Margaret Reilly did send gifts to her own family. To her niece, Margaret Lynn, for

example, she sent a nun doll dressed in the woolen habit of the Good Shepherd, which has remained in the family's possession. This same niece also received a sewing kit from her aunt.

74. Letter to Cardinal James McIntyre, November 19, 1953, copy, "Bishops and Cardinals" file, AOSB/W (probably written by Sister Dolorosa Mergen, Conception Abbey, Clyde, Missouri, who at that time had served as First Prioress General).

75. Benedict Bradley to Lukas Etlin, December 1, 1922, ARGS.

76. McParlan to S. Carmelita, August 8, 1927, AOSB/M.

77. Benedict Bradley to Lukas Etlin, December 12, 1922, ARGS.

78. Margaret Armstrong to Archbishop Hayes, December 19, [1926]. Although the year is omitted in the letter, it can be ascertained by her mention of the opening of the Broadway play *Autumn Fire*. Written by Irish-born T. C. Murray, the play ran from October 26, 1926, to December 1926.

79. Armstrong to Hayes, May 4, 1922, Hayes correspondence, AANY.

80. SMCQ, 78.

81. Max Weber, *Economy and Society: An Outline of Interpretive Sociology*, vol. 1 (New York: Bedminster Press, 1968), 241–44.

82. Taves, *Household of Faith*, 132.

Chapter 6

1. I use the term as discussed by Peter Brown in his second edition of *The Rise of Western Christendom: Triumph and Diversity, AD 200–1000* (Malden, Mass.: Blackwell, 2003).

2. I was unable to find any mention of Margaret Reilly in the McIntyre collection in the Archdiocese of Los Angeles Archival Center. On McIntyre's legacy in Los Angeles, see Mike Davis, *City of Quartz: Excavating the Future in Los Angeles* (New York: Verso, 1990).

3. For a discussion of localism in Catholic cults, see David Blackbourn, *Marpingen: Apparitions of the Virgin Mary in a Nineteenth-Century German Village* (New York: Vintage, 1995), chapters 2 and 5.

4. "Case of Sister Margaret (Reilly) Thorn, Sisters of the Good Shepherd, stigmatist: Narrative of a Father Bertrand, a Passionist," April 3, 1922, CCMM 1/38, UNDA.

5. Stephen Haliczer, *Between Exaltation and Infamy: Female Mystics in the Golden Age of Spain* (New York: Oxford University Press, 2002), 265.

6. Pierre DeLooz, "Toward a Sociological Study of Canonized Sainthood in the Catholic Church" (1962), in *Saints and Their Cults: Studies in Religious Sociology, Folklore, and History*, ed. Stephen Wilson (New York: Cambridge University Press, 1987), 194.

7. Michael Freze, *They Bore the Wounds of Christ: The Mystery of the Sacred Stigmata* (Huntington, Ind.: Our Sunday Visitor, 1989) 280. It is less clear, however, why Freze finds it significant that Neumann died on September 18, 1962, two days before the anniversary of Padre Pio's stigmatization on September 20, 1918.

8. The medieval representation of Christ as mother in mystical discourse regarded his side wound as a breast and hence equivalent to the provision of food to the faithful as the Eucharist.

9. SMCQ-SMCT, 27.

10. Ibid., 33.

11. See Paolo Apolito, *Apparitions of the Madonna at Oliveto Citra* (University Park, Pa.: Pennsylvania State University Press, 1998).

12. Ibid., 236.

13. See James T. Fisher, *Dr. America: The Lives of Thomas A. Dooley, 1927–1961* (Amherst,

Mass.: University of Massachusetts Press, 1997), 236. Dooley proved to be an unreliable candidate for sainthood, however, due to his secret homosexuality, his shadowy connections to the CIA in its Vietnamese operations, and even challenges to his heroic medical reputation as the "jungle doctor of Laos."

14. Kenneth L. Woodward, *Making Saints: How the Catholic Church Determines Who Becomes a Saint, Who Doesn't, and Why* (New York: Simon and Schuster, 1990), 224, 226, 225.

15. Ibid., 226.

16. Ibid., 15.

17. Robert A. Orsi, *Thank You, St. Jude: Women's Devotion to the Patron Saint of Hopeless Causes* (New Haven, Conn.: Yale University Press, 1996).

18. Kathleen Cummings has pointed to related uses of the saints in the early twentieth century as inspirations for an American Catholic Church, citing the case of Elizabeth Ann Seton, which was opened in 1911, and of Kateri Tekakwitha, who had to be posthumously made an American citizen in order to qualify. Cummings, *New Women of the Old Faith: Gender and American Catholicism in the Progressive Era* (Chapel Hill: University of North Carolina Press, 2010), 28–38.

19. From "Little Nellie," anonymous pamphlet provided by the RGS convent, Sunday's Well, Cork, Ireland, 14.

20. Hickey's visit to the Newark RGS community is corroborated in Katherine Conway, *Fifty Years with Christ the Good Shepherd: The Story of the Fold in Newark, 1875-1925* (Norwood, Mass.: Plimpton Press, 1925), 120–21.

21. Information on Hickey comes from the funeral sermon delivered by James J. Byrne, bishop of Boise, September 6, 1960. Her meeting with Reilly is discussed in chapter 1.

22. Thomas M. Schwertner, *The Eucharistic Renaissance* (New York: Macmillan, 1926), 26. In Schwertner's account, other children mentioned with Nellie included Louis Manoha (1904-14) and Livietto (1910-17), whose lives were quickly published as pamphlet literature distributed by the Apostleship of Prayer, an organization that promoted the Sacred Heart.

23. The tradition of venerating youthful victims for their "symphony of suffering" continues into the present day. A recent American example is the cult of Audrey Santo (1984-2007) of Worcester, Massachusetts, a spiritual descendant of Little Nellie who became known to her followers as "Little Audrey."

24. Pius X, "Quam singulari," August, 1910, accessed at Wikisource, "Catholic Church Encyclicals."

25. On the shift in Eucharistic teaching, see Margaret McGuinness, "Let Us Go to the Altar: American Catholics and the Eucharist, 1926-1976," in *Habits of Devotion: Catholic Religious Practice in Twentieth-Century America*, ed. James M. O'Toole (Ithaca, N.Y.: Cornell University Press, 2004).

26. Debra Campbell, "American Catholic Memoirs," in *The Catholic Studies Reader*, ed. James T. Fisher and Margaret McGuinness (New York: Fordham University Press, 2011), 25.

27. Orsi, *Thank You, St. Jude*, 155.

28. Ibid., 156.

29. Cristina Mazzoni, "Visions of the Mystic/Mystical Visions," *Annali d'Italianistica* 13 (1995): 371–86.

30. Cristina Mazzoni, *St. Hysteria: Neurosis, Mysticism, and Gender in European Culture* (Ithaca, N.Y.: Cornell University Press, 1996). One type of mystical discourse called *Brautmystik*, or bride mysticism, describes the mystical union of Christ with the soul as the

sexual encounter of bride and groom. The union can also be thought of as the dissolution of the self.

31. Dr. Thomas McParlan to Sister Paul, OSD, May 20, 1922, ARGS.

32. These Host miracles also made a subversive claim: Therese Neumann was said to be able to receive Communion without the assistance or presence of a priest—surely an irregularity that church officials would challenge.

33. American pilgrims to Konnersreuth in the twenties included Bishop Joseph Schrembs of Cleveland and Elizabeth Marable Brennan, who published favorable accounts of their visits for American readers. On World War I analogies, see Mme. Marthe Ponet (under pseudonym Jeanne Danemarie), *Le Mystère des Stigmatisés de Catherine Emmerich à Thérèse Neumann* (Paris: Bernard Grasset, 1933).

34. Professor Pabstmann quoted in Charles M. Carty, *The Two Stigmatists: Padre Pio and Teresa Neumann* (N.p.: Radio Replies Press Society, 1956), 109. Schrembs is also noted above.

35. Huber quoted in Carty, *Two Stigmatists*, 104.

36. Ibid., 111.

37. Ulrike Wiethaus, "Bloody Bodies: Gender, Religion and the State in Nazi Germany," *Studies in Spirituality* 12 (2002): 189–202.

38. On the limited success of this view, see Michael O'Sullivan, "West German Miracles: Catholic Mystics, Church Hierarchy, and Postwar Popular Culture," *Zeithistorische Forschungen/Studies in Contemporary History*, Online-Ausgabe, 6 (2009): H.1.

39. As a child in Montreal, Rose had been healed of a leg wound by the charismatic Brother André Bessette, founder of the St. Joseph Oratory.

40. Hillary Kaell concludes that, aside from Ferron, examples of victimhood do not appear in Franco-American culture. According to Kaell, Boyer modeled Ferron's cult on Thérèse of Lisieux, who had died in 1897 and was speedily canonized in 1925. Thérèse was from Normandy, birthplace of certain leading Quebecois clergy who promoted Thérèse in Canada for nationalistic as well as religious purposes. Kaell, "'Marie-Rose, Stigmatisée de Woonsocket': The Construction of a Franco-American Saint Cult, 1930–1955," *CCHA Historical Studies* 73 (2007): 7–26. Rose's other great promoter was Lionel Groulx of Quebec, who ultimately declined to present her to Rome as a Canadian saint.

41. In the appendix, for example, where Boyer printed twenty-two letters from eyewitnesses to Rose's miraculous healings, fourteen came from English-speaking Americans. Ibid., 19.

42. A contemporary mystic, Sister Miriam Teresa Demjanovich (1901–27) of New Jersey, also inspired a prayer league, albeit twenty years after her death. Her spiritual adviser was Benedict Bradley, the Benedictine who also intervened in Sister Thorn's life.

43. Kaell, "'Marie-Rose, Stigmatisée de Woonsocket.'"

44. José De Vinck, *Revelations of Women Mystics from the Middle Ages to Modern Times* (New York: Alba House, 1985), 82.

45. Ibid., 83.

46. All quotations in this paragraph appear in ibid., 83, 89, 90.

47. Mercier's vicar general, Cardinal Joseph-Ernest van Rooey, who conducted the observations, succeeded Mercier as archbishop of Mechelen from 1921 to 1961.

48. Due to the popularity of Pio's cult, his corpse was exhumed in 2008 in order to preserve it as a relic that will be displayed periodically for pilgrims.

49. D. Scott Rogo, *Miracles: A Parascientific Inquiry into Wondrous Phenomena* (New York: Dial Press, 1982), 70.

50. *NYT*, September 24, 1998.

51. Festa cited in Martino Conti, "Padre Gemelli filosofo della prima persecuzione contro padre Pio da Pietrelcina?," *Frate Francesco* 69, no. 1 (April 2003): 127–47.

52. Rev. John Schug, *Padre Pio* (Huntington, Ind.: Our Sunday Visitor, 1976), 61–62.

53. Pio, *Secrets of a Soul: Padre Pio's Letters to His Spiritual Director*, ed. Gianluigi Pasquale (Pauline Books and Media, 2003), no. 511.

54. Apolito, *Apparitions of the Madonna at Oliveto Citra*, 167; Schug, *Padre Pio*, 47.

55. Evidence is not clear-cut about who actually observed and studied Pio's wounds. Even Gemelli was apparently frustrated in his attempt to examine Pio during his 1920 visit to the monastery.

56. "Amico Bignami," from "Who Named It?," at http://www.whonamedit.com/doctor .cfm/2484.html. Pio was also seen by Luigi Romanelli of Barletta and several journalists who portrayed Gemelli to the public as someone predisposed to doubt Padre Pio. See Martino Conti, "Padre Gemelli, philosopher of the first persecution against Padre Pio da Pietrelcina?," *Frate Francesco: Revista di Cultura Francescana* 69, no. 1 (April 2003): 127–47.

57. Bernard Ruffin, *Padre Pio: The True Story* (Huntington, Ind.: Our Sunday Visitor), 150.

58. Ibid., 178. The best study of Gemelli is Daria Columbo, "Psychoanalysis and the Catholic Church in Italy: The Role of Father Agostino Gemelli, 1925–1953," *Journal of the History of the Behavioral Sciences* 39, no. 4 (Fall 2003): 333–48, which places Gemelli's career in the context of the Catholic-dominated political and intellectual culture of Italy during the fascist era.

59. Gemelli cited in Columbo, "Psychoanalysis and the Catholic Church in Italy."

60. The anecdote is cited in Woodward, *Making Saints*, 186. The same suggestion is also reported about Therese Neumann on websites dedicated to her.

61. A. Poulain, "Mystical Stigmata," *The Catholic Encyclopedia*, vol. 14 (New York: Robert Appleton Company, 1912). Accessed online March 10, 2010, http://www.newadvent.org/ cathen/14294b.htm.

62. Ian Wilson, *The Bleeding Mind: An Investigation into the Mysterious Phenomenon of Stigmata* (London: Weidenfeld and Nicolson, 1988), 95. Details of the case are on 94–99.

63. On Pio's military discharge, see Goffredo Bartocci and Roland Littlewood, "Modern Techniques of the Supernatural: A Syncretism between Miraculous Healing and Modern Media," *Social Theory and Health* 2, no. 1 (February 2004): 18–28. Pio is described as a military chaplain in World War I, though this point has not been verified. (*Irish Times*, December 1997). Also see Juliet Mitchell, *Mad Men and Medusas: Reclaiming Hysteria* (New York: Basic Books, 2000), 159–61. I am not attempting a full-scale analysis of the case of Padre Pio here, but for the first study of shell shock as a form of male hysteria, see Elaine Showalter, *The Female Malady: Women, Madness, and English Culture, 1830–1980* (New York: Pantheon, 1985), chapter 7. For male hysteria as part of a larger cultural failure to undertake collective understanding of the male self, see Mark S. Micale, *Hysterical Men: The Hidden History of Male Nervous Illness* (Cambridge, Mass.: Harvard University Press, 2008); and Jan Goldstein, "The Uses of Male Hysteria: Medical and Literary Discourse in Nineteenth-Century France," *Representations* 34 (Spring 1991): 134–65.

64. Mitchell, *Mad Men and Medusas*.

65. On the controversy surrounding Pio's cause for canonization, see Woodward, *Making Saints*, 184–90.

66. Ibid., 158.

67. Woodward's emphasis upon Pio's cause is somewhat different. Writing before Pio's canonization and convinced that Pio's cause would not be forwarded soon, Woodward

suggested that the Capuchins in the United States and Italy would delay matters because of internal divisions, and he also noted that many details of Pio's case were kept secret from general audiences.

68. The phrase is from Irish-born journalist Margaret Buchanan Sullivan, quoted in Cummings, *New Women of the Old Faith*, 29. Sullivan used the pseudonym "An American Woman" (17).

69. An example from the Internet is http://www.spirit-digest.com/MHB%20editorials/natuzza.htm. The report of her funeral is at http://www.zenit.org/en/articles/modern-mystic-mourned-in-italy.

70. Roland Littlewood and Goffredo Bartocci, "Religious Stigmata, Magnetic Fluids and Conversion Hysteria: One Survival of 'Vital Force' Theories in Scientific Medicine?," *Transcultural Psychiatry* 42, no. 4 (2005): 596–609.

71. Palma is profiled Antoine Imbert-Gourbeyre, *Les Stigmatisées*, vol. 2 (Paris: V. Palmé, 1873).

72. Palma also experienced Eucharistic miracles. It was said that she "would repeatedly vomit undigested hosts, even though she had not taken communion recently, and she often fell into trances during which a host would miraculously materialize in her open mouth." Rogo, *Miracles*, 64.

73. According to Gary Macey, "Laity retained direct access to the divine by means of widely diverse, locally grounded and largely unregulated popular devotions," whereas clergy maintained power by "tightly controlled universally undifferentiated liturgies." Macey, *Treasures from the Storeroom: Medieval Religion and the Eucharist* (Collegeville, Minn.: Liturgical Press, 1999), 183.

74. See the article by Michael Nanko at http://www.romancatholicimperialst.com/2009/11/natuzza-evolo-died-on-nov-1-at-85.html.

75. This paragraph borrows from Paolo Apolito, *The Internet and the Madonna: Religious Visionary Experience on the Web* (Chicago: University of Chicago, 2005), 117–18, 12–13.

76. Ibid., 116.

77. Ibid., 120.

78. Kevin M. Schultz, *Tri-Faith America: How Catholics and Jews Held Postwar America to Its Protestant Promise* (New York: Oxford University Press, 2011).

Chapter 7

1. Mother Hickey to Lukas Etlin, August 19, 1926, ARGS.

2. Thomas McParlan to Lukas Etlin, April 15, 1927, AOSB/M.

3. August 7, 1927. Chronic pain and illness were certainly no barriers to the achievements of religious women. In the Good Shepherd congregation, Mother Hickey took her vows in 1881 after certain requirements had been waived because her health was so poor. She was taken to Lourdes, where she returned four more times, convinced that the Virgin Mary had preserved her health. From these delicate beginnings, Hickey went on to become a leader in the RGS, a promoter of liturgical reform for a more interactive Mass, and an advocate of women's education in nontraditional fields such as chemistry.

4. Mother Hickey to Lukas Etlin, December 23, 1925, ARGS.

5. Margaret Armstrong to Herbert Thurston, June 13, 1937, Thurston papers, JA.

6. Father Bertrand, "Account of Margaret Reilly," Passionist Historical Archives, New Jersey, 24.

7. Leslie Tentler, *Catholics and Contraception: An American History* (Ithaca, N.Y.: Cornell University Press, 2005), chapter 3; James Fisher, *On the Irish Waterfront*; Robert Orsi, *Thank*

You, St. Jude: Women's Devotion to the Patron Saint of Hopeless Causes (New Haven, Conn.: Yale University Press, 1996), 159.

8. Archbishop Hayes, "Christmas Pastoral Letter," December 14, 1921.

9. See Elizabeth McKeown, *War and Welfare: American Catholics and World War I* (New York: Garland, 1988). For a study of Catholic social reform to 1925, see Deirdre M. Moloney, *American Catholic Lay Groups and Transatlantic Social Reform in the Progressive Era* (Chapel Hill: University of North Carolina Press, 2002). On the relationship between Catholic charities and the state, see Dorothy M. Brown and Elizabeth McKeown, *The Poor Belong to Us: Catholic Charities and American Welfare* (Cambridge, Mass.: Harvard University Press, 1997). On New York sisterhoods and health care, see Bernadette McCauley, *Who Shall Take Care of Our Sick?: Roman Catholic Sisters and the Development of Catholic Hospitals in New York City* (Baltimore: Johns Hopkins University Press, 2005).

10. Jay Winter, *Sites of Memory, Sites of Mourning: The Great War in European Cultural History* (Cambridge, UK: Cambridge University Press, 1996), 55.

11. Ibid., 56.

12. Ibid., 55. On women in spiritualism, see Molly McGarry, *Ghosts of Futures Past* (Berkeley: University of California Press, 2008); and Alex Owen, *The Darkened Room* (Philadelphia: University of Pennsylvania Press, 1990).

13. Thomas McParlan to Lukas Etlin, November 4, 1925, AOSB/M.

14. Letter from Mother Raymond Cahill to Sr. Dolorosa Mergen, August 7, 1937, Quinn.8, "Crown of Thorns" file, AOSB/W (italics mine).

15. According to Web-MD (http://www.webmd.com), the first symptoms of pancreatic cancer are typically pain (sometimes severe pain in the upper abdomen that can penetrate to the back), sudden weight loss, and jaundice. Pancreatic cancer can also cause other cancer-related symptoms, such as fatigue and depression. The pain of pancreatic cancer may be constant or intermittent and can be caused by the spread of tumors to the network of nerves surrounding the pancreas. Dr. Walsh's prescription of calomel (a mercury compound) may have worsened Margaret's health, however, since mercury can lead to permanent damage of the central nervous system.

16. On the death of Mother Raymond by S. M. Mary, OSB, to Carmelita Quinn (Peekskill), May 30, 1939, ARGS.

17. Lady Armstrong to Herbert Thurston, June 13, 1937, Thurston letters, 39.3.3., JA.

18. Lady Armstrong to Archbishop Hayes, May 19, 1924, Hayes correspondence, AANY. On the culture of the "happy invalid" in twentieth-century Catholicism, see Robert Orsi, "Mildred, Is It Fun to Be a Cripple?," chapter 1 of *Between Heaven and Earth: The Religious Worlds People Make and the Scholars Who Study Them* (Princeton, N.J.: Princeton University Press, 2005.

19. Broaca was in fact a gifted athlete who excelled in baseball, basketball, football, and track in high school. The joke about his hitting came from some interviews reporting that Broaca taught himself from an article in *Boy's Life*.

20. On Saint Jude, who filled the role of an all-purpose nonethnic saint, see Orsi, *Thank You, St. Jude*.

21. McParlan to Sister Paul, OSD, October 13, 1922, ARGS.

22. *Newark Evening News*, May 19, 1937.

23. Ibid.

24. Bertrand, "Account of Margaret Riley," 29.

25. "Narrative of Father Bertrand, a Passionist," CCMM-UNDA, 1/38, 1922, 18.

26. For more about the life (1887–1978) of the private man who led seven championship

teams, see Alan H. Levy, *Joe McCarthy: Architect of the Yankee Dynasty* (Jefferson, N.C.: McFarland, 2005).

27. Before entering the priesthood, McIntyre at age sixteen had held a job with a Wall Street brokerage firm.

28. Tracy Fessenden, *Culture and Redemption: Religion, the Secular, and American Literature* (Princeton, N.J.: Princeton University Press, 2007), 186.

29. American sociologists have reported for at least twenty years on the diminishing numbers of women in religious life. See, for instance, Helen Rose Ebaugh, *Women in the Vanishing Cloister* (New Brunswick, N.J.: Rutgers University Press, 1993); and Patricia Wittberg, *The Rise and Fall of Catholic Religious Orders* (Albany: SUNY Press, 1994).

30. The total number of RGS members includes apostolic and contemplative sisters, the latter numbering several hundred.

31. DeLooz, "Towards a Sociological Study of Canonized Sainthood in the Catholic Church," in *Saints and their Cults*, ed. Cormack, 199. The passage continues: "The opinion of others is not sufficient in itself to create a saint. Opinion must be strong enough to provoke a public cult."

32. Letter to Cardinal James McIntyre, November 19, 1953, unsigned copy, "Bishops & Cardinals" file, AOSB/M.

33. Sister Carmelita Quinn, notes in response to questionnaire from Clare Nolan, RGS, October 10, 1978, answered by Quinn during February 1983, AOSB/M (capitals in original).

Conclusion

1. Robert A. Orsi, *Thank You, St. Jude: Women's Devotion to the Patron Saint of Hopeless Causes* (New Haven, Conn.: Yale University Press, 1996), especially 40–42.

2. Joseph P. Chinnici, *Living Stones: The History and Structure of Catholic Spiritual Life in the United States* (New York: Macmillan, 1989); Ian Linden, *Global Catholicism* (New York: Columbia University Press, 2009), 24.

3. "Exorcist and Energumen," *Time*, February 17, 1936. In the United States, Riesinger had a career on the fringes of Margaret Reilly's life, having served at several parishes of the Archdiocese of New York and as the spiritual director of a stigmatic nun in the Midwest.

4. *Begone Satan! A Soul-Stirring Account of Diabolical Possession; Woman Cursed by Her Own Father, Possessed from 14th Year till 40th Year*, 6th printing (Collegeville, Minn.: St. John's Abbey, 1935), 47, 44. Before serving in Milwaukee and Dubuque as a missionary priest, Riesinger had served three parishes in New York between 1900 and 1912.

5. Dr. John Dundon to Rev. Celestine Kapsner, OSB, *Begone Satan!*, back cover of pamphlet. The sequel to *Begone Satan!* was another stirring apocalyptic pamphlet about exorcism called *Mary Crushes the Serpent*.

6. See Chinnici, *Living Stones*, 175.

7. Virgil Michel, foreword, *Begone Satan!*

8. *Begone Satan!*, 48.

9. SMCQ-SMCT, 62.

10. Walter Gabriel Scanlan, OP, "Thorn: A Story of Divine Providence," ARGS.

11. Ibid.

12. Message of Jesus to Margaret as recorded by Mother Raymond and Lukas Etlin, SMCT, 89. This passage also serves as an epigraph for chapter 7.

13. Ibid., 79.

14. Charles O'Donnell, CSC, to Monsignor John F. Brady, September 23, 1923, CCLO-UNDA, 3/12.

15. Chinnici, *Living Stones*, 148. Chinnici calls the Eucharistic movement central to Catholic experience until the end of World War II, although it lingered on for some years until it was replaced by the liturgical movement's vastly different emphasis on active participation of the laity in the Mass and in the church. Ibid., 156.

16. The clergy's response to social and spiritual crises through the discernment of spirits in prior centuries has been explored by Nancy Caciola, *Discerning Spirits: Divine and Demonic Possession in the Middle Ages* (Ithaca, N.Y.: Cornell University Press, 2003); and Dyan Elliott, *Proving Woman: Female Spirituality and Inquisitional Culture in the Late Middle Ages* (Princeton, N.J.: Princeton University Press, 2004).

Index

The abbreviation "MR" refers to Margaret Reilly/Sister Thorn; "RGS" refers to the Sisters of the Good Shepherd. Page numbers in *italic* type refer to illustrations.